T0049585

THE ROUGH GUIDE TO
TEXAS
& THE SOUTHWEST

This book includes extractions from *The Rough Guide to the USA* written
by Stephen Keeling, Maria Edwards, Todd Obolsky, Annelise Sorensen,
Georgia Stephens and Greg Ward, updated by Stephen Keeling and
published in 2023 by Apa Publications Ltd. A big thank you to all the
contributing authors of *The Rough Guide to the USA*.

ROUGH
GUIDES

Contents

Introduction to
Texas & the Southwest

Few areas of the United States offer as many unforgettable travel experiences as Texas and the Southwest (the states of Arizona, Nevada, New Mexico and Utah). The region's red deserts, canyons and wide, open plains present a remarkable panorama of sweeping, colourful vistas, jagged peaks of sandstone, and cactus-strewn ranches that stretch as far as the eye can see. Here are miles of trackless wilderness, a bounty of outdoor recreation and a surprisingly cosmopolitan urban scene. Cities such as Austin, Santa Fe, Las Vegas and San Antonio offer lively escapes from the great outdoors. Whether you're in seek of wild nights of country, blues or rock music, historic architecture, schmoozing with high-rollers in casinos or chowing down at the hottest barbecue and Tex-Mex spots. But it's the stunningly diverse and achingly beautiful landscape of Texas and the Southwest that will you draw you back here again and again, in seek of your next adventure.

Here you have the mighty Grand Canyon and spectacular Carlsbad Caverns, the otherworldly landscapes of White Sands National Park and Monument Valley, the endless, rolling grasslands of Texas, the bike trails of Moab, and the old cowboy towns of Arizona. You can soak up the mesmerizing vistas in the Zion, Bryce Canyon and Capitol Reef national parks in Utah, stand in awe at the top of Canyon de Chelly, hike the Davis Mountains in Texas, windsurf in the Gulf of Mexico, float down the San Juan River, and drive long desert segments of Route 66. Or you could easily plan a trip that focuses on the out-of-the-way hamlets, remote prairies, eerie ghost towns and forgotten byways that are every bit as iconic as the showpiece parks and monuments.

VALLEY OF FIRE STATE PARK, NEVADA

Native American culture is especially strong in the Southwest. The Hopi, Navajo and Tohono O'odham among many others manage several world-class national monuments and parks, while galleries and museums throughout the region recognize their huge contribution to American art, crafts and culture. The remains of great Ancestral Puebloan cities at Bandelier National Monument, Canyon de Chelly and Chaco Canyon emphasize the long history of Native Americans in the region, while the incredible Taos Pueblo has been continually inhabited for at least 1,000 years.

Beginning with Spanish conquistadors and missionaries in the 16th century, prospectors in search of gold and silver, cattle barons, cowboys and ranchers, copper kings, and immigrant settlers all made their way to the "Wild West". You can still visit Spanish missions in Arizona like San Xavier del Bac; legendary sites like the Alamo in San Antonio, where James Bowie and Davy Crockett made their fateful last stand against the Mexican army; follow the exploits of Billy the Kid in New Mexico or Wyatt Earp in Tombstone, Arizona; learn about the Mormons in Salt Lake City; admire the work of artist Georgia O'Keeffe in Santa Fe and architect Frank Lloyd Wright at Taliesin West; look for signs of UFOs in Roswell; visit the Sixth Floor Museum at Dealey Plaza in Dallas, scene of JFK's assassination in 1963; contemplate the legacy of Kennedy's successor Lyndon B. Johnson in Austin; and tour the Space Center in Texas where the legendary words "Houston, we have a problem" were beamed around the world in 1970.

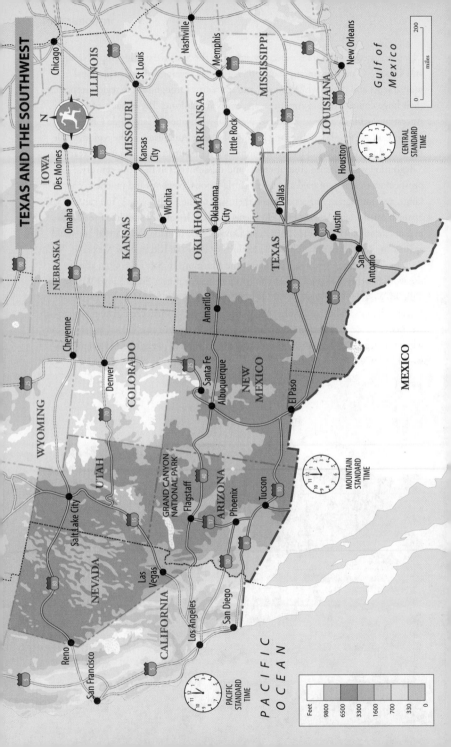

There are also the thrills of rodeo, ballooning over snowcapped mountains, and of whitewater rafting down a frothing river. You can ride mountain bikes over rocky passes, ski, hike, go rock climbing, kayaking and backpacking – the point is to get outdoors, to enjoy the wilderness, the scenery, the crisp air and the blue skies. And while there is no such thing as a typical Southwestern experience, there can be few places where strangers can feel so confident of a warm reception.

Where to go

Texas really is huge, bigger than most European nations, with a booming oil-industry, legendary barbecue and Tex-Mex joints and plenty of Stetson- and cowboy boot-wearing men (and women), though its cities are diverse and cosmopolitan with a large and influential Mexican and Latino community. Sweltering Houston is vast, with a spate of excellent restaurants and art centres, not least the Menil Collection and the Rothko Chapel. The nearby Space Center is the legendary NASA command hub, open for tours. The mostly swampy Gulf Coast of Texas does boast some wonderful beaches and historic towns such as Galveston and Corpus Christi, while Padre Island is a water sports and windsurfing magnet. Austin, the liberal-leaning capital of Texas, is best known for its dynamic music scene and annual South by Southwest festival, as well as the elegant State Capitol building and the LBJ Library and Museum, dedicated to the 36th president of the USA and proud Texas native. Between here and San Antonio lies the Texas Hill Country, full of pleasant towns and some of the best barbecue spots in the USA. San Antonio itself is a laid-back, likeable city, anchored by the cafés and shops of River Walk and the Alamo, one of America's most venerated historic sites. Dallas is another vast suburban city, best known for its museums associated with the assassination of JFK in 1963, but also a burgeoning culinary scene. Neighboring Fort Worth is a real surprise, with a spate of fascinating attractions that include cattle drives at the Stockyards, and the delightful Kimbell Art Museum. To really appreciate the size of Texas you need to explore its seemingly endless northern and western plains. The Panhandle contains Lubbock, with its memorials to rock 'n' roll icon Buddy Holly, and Amarillo, home to the quirky Cadillac Ranch and a memorable stretch of Route 66. In the west, the Davis Mountains, artsy Marfa and tranquil Big Bend National Park see far less tourists, while El Paso serves as a gateway to Mexico and New Mexico in the Southwest.

Santa Fe is New Mexico's capital and one of the oldest cities in the USA, an enticing blend of Spanish colonial architecture, historic churches, art galleries and absorbing museums, not least the wonderful Georgia O'Keeffe Museum, dedicated to the seminal painter of the Southwest. From here, the scenic High Road runs across the Sangre de Cristo Mountains to Taos, another historic, artsy enclave known for its galleries and still active Native American Pueblo. You can also visit long abandoned refuges of the Ancestral Puebloans at Bandelier National Monument and Chaco Canyon. Albuquerque is anchored by another Spanish colonial old town, while southern New

THE MORMONS

Arizona, Texas, Nevada and especially Utah are home to huge Mormon communities today. Led by Brigham Young, the Mormons – or Latter Day Saints (LDS) – were Utah's earliest white settlers, arriving in the Salt Lake area, which then lay outside the USA, in 1847. At first they provoked great suspicion and hostility back East. Relations eased when the Mormon Church dropped polygamy in 1890 and statehood followed in 1896; to this day, over sixty percent of Utah's three-million-strong population are Mormons. World-wide, the Church of Jesus Christ of Latter-Day Saints today claims around 16 million members. Notable Mormons include Utah senator Mitt Romney, singers Donny and Marie Osmond and Gladys Knight, and Stephenie Meyer (author of the Twilight series). The religion is characterized by its emphasis on total obedience to church authority, the practice of tithing (giving up one tenth of your income, usually to the church itself), the sanctity of the family unit, and a strict code of behaviour that forbids the consumption of alcohol, tobacco and even caffeine. Young church members are also expected to take on a missionary posting for at least one year. The church's two authoritative texts are the Bible and the Book of Mormon. The most controversial practice remains that of polygamy. Although the church formally forbid polygamy over a century ago, it is still known to be practised in Utah and in neighbouring states.

THE BOOK OF MORMON

The Mormon church was founded in 1830 by Joseph Smith, a farmhand from Vermont. Smith claimed to have been visited by an angel five years earlier while he was living in Palmyra, New York; the angel, named Moroni, led Smith to a set of inscribed golden plates, which Smith translated into what would become the Book of Mormon. The story they told was of an Israelite family that fled Jerusalem in 600 BC for a new "Promised Land." The patriarch, Lehi, had three sons, Nephi, Laman and Lemuel; Nephi kept faith with God, while Laman and Lemuel threw in their lot with the heathen "Lamanites" – supposed ancestors of Native Americans. A classic good-versus-evil war waged for a thousand years between the Nephites and the Lamanites, until the Nephites were exterminated. The last survivor among them – Moroni, "son of Mormon" – buried the plates to ensure that their story would one day be told.

Mexico contains the remarkable Carlsbad Caverns, Billy the Kid memorials and museums around Fort Sumner, UFO kitsch in Roswell, and the gleaming White Sands National Park.

Over in Arizona you can trace more Spanish history in Tucson and at colonial missions such as San Xavier del Bec, while cacti-rich Saguaro National Park preserves a slice of iconic Southwestern desert. The Old West is celebrated in Tombstone (home of the OK Corral), while the sprawling city of Phoenix is a major cultural hub and location of Frank Lloyd Wright's Taliesin West. Arizona is best known, however, for its mesmerizing natural attractions. The resort town of Flagstaff is the gateway to Grand Canyon National Park, one of the world's most awe-inspiring sights, while the Petrified Forest, Monument Valley and Hopi Mesa are studded with iconic landscapes. Native American culture past and present is on display at Canyon de Chelly and the Havasupai and Hualapai reservations, while Sedona has become the nation's foremost New Age town.

Utah is home to some of America's greatest national parks; Arches, Bryce Canyon, Canyonlands, Capitol Reef, and Zion alone could occupy weeks of your time with their trails, slot canyons, peaks and vistas. Moab is an adventure sports hub, especially good for mountain biking, while the San Juan River offers float trips and kayaking. Salt Lake City is the state's pristine capital, the hub of the Mormon church and gateway to the ski resorts of the Wasatch Range, as well as the ever-shrinking Great Salt Lake and the shimmering salt flats beyond. Much of Nevada is empty, desert wilderness, but Las Vegas in its southern corner has become of the world's biggest resorts, a strip of fantastical hotels, restaurants and casinos, flashy nightclubs and celebrity chef restaurants.

In the northwest, Reno is a smaller, cheaper version of Las Vegas, with the old mining town of Carson City the state capital closer to beautiful Lake Tahoe on the California border. To experience Nevada's sun-baked hinterland, visit the Great Basin National Park, on the border with Utah, or isolated Elko, with its reminders of its Basque community.

When to go

Texas and the Southwest are subject to dramatically shifting weather patterns, most notably produced by westerly winds sweeping across the continent from the Pacific. Temperatures in the any of the mountain ranges connected to the **Rockies** correlate closely with altitude, so nights can be cold even in high summer in Arizona and New Mexico. Beyond the mountains in the extensive arid deserts of the **Southwest** the mercury regularly soars above 100°F (38°C), though the atmosphere is not usually humid enough to be as enervating as that might sound and air conditioning is ubiquitous. To the east, the plains of Texas are alternately exposed to seasonal icy winds and humid tropical airflows from the Gulf of Mexico – it can freeze or even snow in winter as far south as Dallas.

AVERAGE TEMPERATURE (°F) AND RAINFALL

To convert °F to °C, subtract 32 and multiply by 5/9

	Jan	Feb	Mar	Apr	May	Jun	Jul	Aug	Sep	Oct	Nov	Dec
DALLAS												
Max/min	57/39	62/43	69/50	77/58	84/66	91/73	95/77	95/76	88/69	78/59	67/49	58/41
Days of rain	5	6	7	9	11	9	6	6	7	8	6	6
FLAGSTAFF, AZ												
Max/min	43/20	46/22	52/26	59/31	68/37	78/45	80/53	77/52	72/44	62/34	51/26	43/20
Days of rain	5	5	5	3	2	2	10	11	6	4	3	4
HOUSTON												
Max/min	64/47	68/50	74/56	79/63	86/70	91/75	94/77	94/77	90/73	82/65	73/56	66/49
Days of rain	8	7	7	7	10	11	10	11	10	8	8	8
LAS VEGAS												
Max/min	60/29	67/34	72/39	81/45	89/52	99/61	103/68	102/66	95/57	84/47	71/36	61/30
Days of rain	2	2	2	1	1	1	2	2	1	1	1	2
SALT LAKE CITY												
Max/min	37/23	44/28	54/36	63/42	72/50	84/59	92/66	90/65	79/55	65/43	50/33	38/25
Days of rain	6	6	7	8	7	4	3	4	5	5	6	6
SANTA FE, NM												
Max/min	41/19	47/23	55/28	63/34	72/42	81/51	82/55	80/54	74/47	63/37	50/26	41/19
Days of rain	2	2	3	3	4	5	10	10	6	4	3	3
TUSCON, AZ												
Max/min	66/42	70/45	76/49	83/55	92/63	100/72	100/77	97/75	94/70	85/60	74/49	66/43
Days of rain	4	3	3	2	1	2	11	12	5	3	3	4

The best overall times to visit the Southwest are winter and spring (Dec–May), when temperatures are mild in the mountains and warm in the deserts. In Utah, it's better to visit later (April–June, or Sept–Oct), when the national parks are more accessible. Texas is also best in the spring or autumn, when you'll avoid the sweltering summer heat and the rainiest periods.

Tornadoes (or "twisters") are a frequent local phenomenon in Texas (an average of 132 touchdown annually), tending to cut a narrow swath of destruction in the wake of violent spring or summer thunderstorms (primarily April–June). The Red River Valley in north Texas is especially prone to tornadoes. Tornadoes are fairly rare in Arizona, New Mexico, Nevada and Utah. Tropical storms and hurricanes can also impact Texas, especially along the Gulf Coast; the most devastating in recent years were Hurricane Hanna (2020), Hurricane Harvey (2017), and Hurricane Ike (2008). Take hurricane warnings very seriously – flooding in the wake of storms is often more dangerous than the initial high-speed winds.

Author picks

Our hard-travelling author has visited every corner of this vast, magnificent region and has picked out their personal highlights.

Most scenic highways The High Road blazes a mesmerizing path across the Sangre de Cristo Mountains between Santa Fe and Taos, while the Scenic Drive through Zion National Park is one of the most memorable (see page 98).It's possible to follow the legendary Route 66 across several states: Amarillo and the Panhandle in Texas (see page 87); Santa Fe, Gallup and Albuquerque in New Mexico; and Flagstaff, Arizona (see page 113).

Best microbreweries Since the 1990s America has been experiencing a craft beer revolution, led by the likes of *Beaver Street Brewery* in Flagstaff (see page 129); *Marble Brewery* in Albuquerque (see page 115); and *Blue Star* in San Antonio (see page 77).

Classic diners Few American icons are so beloved as the roadside diner, where burgers, apple pie and strong coffee are often served 24/7. *Buns N' Roses* outside Marfa in Texas occupies a no-frills metal Quonset hut that serves filling breakfast all (see page 90). As the name suggests, the 66 Diner in Albuquerque is a 1950s-style throwback, while Frontier (see page 115) is a University of New Mexico favourite. In Sedona, Arizona, the Coffee Pot (see page 130) is famed for offering 101 types of omelette. The Moab Diner (see page 154) in Utah dates back to the 1960s.

Top wildlife spots Texas and especially the Southwest is incredibly rich in wildlife, with national parks such as Grand Canyon (see page 131) especially good at preserving deer, rodents and desert birdlife. Big Thicket National Preserve in Texas (see page 60) is also home to deer, but also alligators, armadillos, possums, hogs and panthers, as well as hundreds of bird species. In isolated Big Bend National Park (see page 90) in West Texas you might spy mountain lions, black bears, roadrunners and javelinas (a bit like wild hogs). Padre Island National Seashore (see page 63) on the Gulf Coast is prime bird-watching territory (pelicans, terns and kestrels among them).

Our author recommendations don't end here. We've flagged up our favourite places – a perfectly sited hotel, an atmospheric café, a special restaurant – throughout the Guide, highlighted with the ★ symbol.

ROUTE 66 DINER, ALBUQUERQUE

PELICANS AT PADRE ISLAND

20

things not to miss

It's obviously not possible to see everything that Texas and the Southwest have to offer in one trip. What follows is a selective and subjective taste of the region's highlights: stunning national parks, spectacular drives, spirited cities and stunning natural phenomena. All highlights are colour-coded by chapter and have a page reference to take you straight into the Guide, where you can find out more.

1 SAN ANTONIO'S RIVER WALK, TX
See page 73
This delightful riverside promenade enlivens Downtown San Antonio with open-air cafes, boutiques and boat rides.

2 SPACE CENTER HOUSTON, TX
See page 59
NASA's most famous space command hub is open for enlightening guided tours, just outside Houston.

3 FORT WORTH, TX
See page 82
Often overshadowed by its wealthy neighbour, Dallas, Fort Worth has its own superb art museums, barbecue joints, and the spectacle of the Stockyards.

4 MARFA, TX
See page 89
It's worth making the long journey across the plains of West Texas to this charming, artsy town, taking in the arts and crafts and the mysterious "Marfa Lights".

5 BIG BEND NATIONAL PARK, TX
See page 90
One of America's least visited national parks is often blissfully uncrowded, with gorgeous vistas across the Rio Grande canyons.

6 SANTA FE, NM

See page 103

This enticing Spanish colonial city has a history that precedes the founding of the USA by almost 200 years.

7 SCENIC HWY-12, UT

See page 98

Utah is smothered with gorgeous scenery, but this winding route takes in some of the best of Bryce Canyon National Park and Grand Staircase–Escalante.

8 SAGUARO NATIONAL PARK, AZ

See page 122

Few Southwestern scenes are as iconic as a cacti-strewn desert, with this park outside Tucson preserving great swathes of giant saguaro cactus.

9 ARCHES NATIONAL PARK, UT

See page 152

Sprinkled with over 2,000 delicate stone arches, plus multi-coloured rocks, desert trails and buttes, this is one of Utah's must-see parks.

10 LAS VEGAS, NV

See page 159

From the Strip's clubs and pool parties, Eiffel Tower and Egyptian pyramid to its many casinos, Las Vegas will blow your mind as well as your wallet.

11 ANCESTRAL PUEBLOAN SITES, NM

See page 108

Scattered through desert landscapes such as New Mexico's magnificent Bandelier National Monument and Arizona's Canyon de Chelly, the dwellings of the Ancestral Puebloans afford glimpses of an ancient and mysterious world.

12 GRAND CANYON, AZ

See page 131

Explore the innermost secrets of this wondrous spot on many of its superb hiking trails at the heart of one of America's best-loved parks.

13 SOUTH BY SOUTHWEST, TX

See page 68

This thriving ten-day festival in Austin is one of the nation's best music festivals and plays host to bands from around the world – and Texas, too.

14 BARBECUE, HILL COUNTRY, TX

See page 31

Perhaps no other cuisine is as essentially American as barbecue – smoked ribs, pulled pork and brisket – with Hill Country in Texas boasting the nation's top pitmasters.

15 MONUMENT VALLEY, AZ

See page 138

Massive sandstone monoliths stand sentinel in this iconic Southwestern landscape.

13

14

15

16 TOMBSTONE, AZ
See page 124
Relive the gunfight at the OK Corral in one of the most iconic "Wild West" cowboy towns.

17 ZION NATIONAL PARK, UT
See page 142
This mesmerizing canyon gets ever narrower until the road ends and you hike up a shallow riverbed that's cut a slot in the moss-draped rocks.

18 TALIESIN WEST, AZ
See page 126
Seminal American architect Frank Lloyd Wright built his Western home and base just outside Phoenix, now open for illuminating tours.

19 SEDONA, AZ
See page 129
America's "New Age" capital makes for a tranquil few days hiking, art and craft shopping or just soaking up the good vibes.

20 SIXTH FLOOR MUSEUM AT DEALEY PLAZA, TX
See page 78
See where John F Kennedy was gunned down in 1963, taking in the poignant memorials to the 35th US president nearby in downtown Dallas.

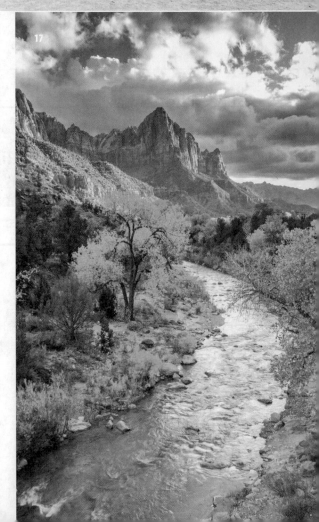

The Photographers & The Evidence

Itineraries

The following itineraries span the entire length of this incredibly diverse region, from some of the oldest towns in the USA to the most glamorous cities and the jaw-dropping Grand Canyon. Given the vast distances involved, you may not be able to cover everything, but even picking a few highlights will give you a deeper insight into the Southwest's natural and historic wonders.

CLASSIC TEXAS AND THE SOUTHWEST

This three-week tour gives a taster of the USA's iconic landscapes and cities from Texas to Nevada, incorporating sections of historic Route 66.

❶ Houston, TX The largest city in Texas is home to the Menil Collection, the Rothko Chapel, NASA, the Astros (baseball), the Texans (American football) and Beyonce. See page 54

❷ Dallas/Fort Worth, TX This vast, dual metropolitan area has a bit of everything, from barbecue joints to gourmet restaurants, the Dallas Museum of Art to the site of JFK's assassination, and from real cowboys at the Fort Worth Stockyards to the Dallas Cowboys NFL team. See page 77

❸ Amarillo and the Panhandle, TX Start following legendary Route 66 across the Texas Panhandle, taking in 1950s diners and the whimsical Cadillac Ranch. See page 87

❹ Santa Fe, NM As you continue west on I-40 across New Mexico, detour to the state capital, a glorious ensemble of Spanish adobe and baroque. See page 103

❺ Bandelier National Monument, NM Make time to see these impressive ruins built by the Ancestral Puebloans thousands of years ago. See page 107

❻ Monument Valley, AZ Cut across northern New Mexico and through the Navajo Nation into Arizona, where one of the most iconic Western landscapes awaits. See page 138

❼ Bryce Canyon National Park, UT The craggy spires of rock known as "hoodoos" are the focus of this park, which contains the largest concentration of them on the planet. See page 148

❽ Grand Canyon, AZ Head south to Flagstaff, gateway to one of the grandest, most mind-blowing natural wonders in the world. See page 131

❾ Hualapai Indian Reservation, AZ Extend your exploration of the Grand Canyon with a visit to this Native American enclave and the jaw-dropping Skywalk. See page 136

Create your own itinerary with Rough Guides. Whether you're after adventure or a family-friendly holiday, we have a trip for you, with all the activities you enjoy doing and the sights you want to see. All our trips are devised by local experts who get the most out of the destination. Visit **www.roughguides.com/trips** to chat with one of our travel agents.

⑩ Las Vegas, NV Around four hours' drive west of the Grand Canyon lies America's playground, a confection of mega-casinos, swanky restaurants and pool parties in the middle of the desert. See page 159

THE BEST OF TEXAS

Texas is rich in history, stunning scenery and invariably empty roads the further away you get from the big cities. This two- to three-week tour is best experienced by car, making a loop from Houston (you could also start in Dallas/Fort Worth).

❶ Houston Tour the galleries of the Museum District and Hermann Park, take in an Astros baseball game, or visit NASA's Space Center. See page 54

❷ Austin The capital of Texas is a likeable, progressive city, with a justly earned reputation for live music, excellent food and the fascinating LBJ Library and Museum. See page 64

❸ Dallas/Fort Worth This sprawling metro area is loaded with a diverse array of attractions, including the Sixth Floor Museum at Dealey Plaza, the Fort Worth Stockyards and Kimbell Art Museum. See page 77

❹ Marfa & the Davis Mountains Drive out to West Texas to hike the leafy trails of the Davis Mountains, before visiting the artsy community of Marfa and the mysterious "Marfa Lights". See page 89

❺ Big Bend National Park Explore this beautiful, normally empty park, which preserves the desert and scrub wilderness, mountains and canyons of the Rio Grande valley. See page 90

❻ Hill Country Take a break in Hill Country before you get to San Antonio, perusing the boutiques, tearooms and barbecue joints in Fredericksburg and Luckenbach. See page 71

❼ San Antonio This predominantly Hispanic city is best known for the Alamo, the tranquil River Walk, below street level, and of course, excellent Mexican food. See page 72

❽ Corpus Christi & Padre Island Head to the Gulf of Mexico and watersports hub Padre Island, after making a pilgrimage to the Selena Museum in Corpus Christi. See pages 62 and 63

❾ Galveston End your journey with a drive along the Gulf Coast's Bluewater Highway to Galveston, with its attractive historic district, boisterous bars and beaches. See page 60

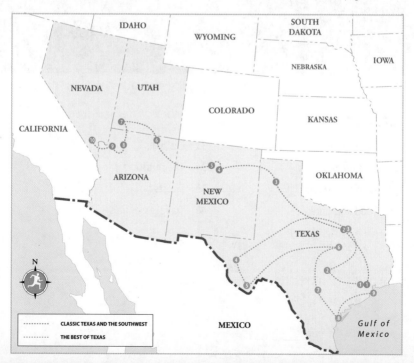

BLUE SWALLOW MOTEL, ROUTE 66

Basics

Getting there

Anyone travelling to Texas and the Southwest from abroad should start by deciding which area to explore first; the region is so vast that it makes a huge difference which airport you fly into. Once you've chosen whether to hit the plains of Texas, the national parks of Utah, the casinos of Vegas or the splendour of the Southwest deserts, you can then buy a flight to the nearest hub city.

In general, ticket prices are highest from July to September, and around Easter, Thanksgiving and Christmas. Fares drop during the shoulder seasons – April to June, and October – and even more so in low season, from November to March (excluding Easter, Christmas and New Year). Prices depend more on when Americans want to head overseas than on the demand from foreign visitors. Flying at weekends usually costs significantly more; prices quoted below assume midweek travel and include taxes.

Flights from the UK and Ireland

More than twenty US cities are accessible by nonstop flights from the UK, including Austin–Bergstrom International Airport, Dallas Fort Worth International Airport and Houston's George Bush Intercontinental Airport in Texas, and Harry Reid International Airport (Las Vegas), Salt Lake City International Airport and Phoenix Sky Harbor International Airport in the Southwest. At these gateway cities, you can connect with onward domestic flights to smaller regional airports: Albuquerque International Sunport, Flagstaff Pulliam Airport, Reno–Tahoe International Airport, San Antonio International Airport, Santa Fe Regional Airport, Tucson International Airport and many others. Direct services (which may land once or twice on the way, but are called direct if they keep the same flight number throughout their journey) fly from Britain to nearly every other major US city.

Nonstop flights to Dallas and Houston from London take around 10 hours 30 minutes; the London to Las Vegas flight takes around 10 hours 45 minutes; and flying time to Salt Lake City is 10 hours 25 minutes or so. Following winds ensure that return flights take an hour or two less. One-stop direct flights via the US East Coast add time to the journey but can work out cheaper than nonstop flights.

The only nonstop scheduled services to the Texas and the Southwest from Ireland at the time of writing was the American Airlines service to Dallas from Dublin, but with numerous non-stop flights to other regional hubs in the US, it's relatively straightforward to fly into the region via one change.

As for fares, Britain remains one of the best places in Europe to obtain flight bargains, though prices vary widely and remain historically high in the post-Covid-19 era. Presuming you book ahead, in low or shoulder season you should be able to find a return flight to destinations such as Dallas, Houston or Las Vegas for £600–700, or to Salt Lake City for around £800, while high-season rates can more than double. These days the fares available on the airlines' own websites are often just as good as those you'll find on more general travel websites.

With an open-jaw ticket, you can fly into one city and out of another, though if you're renting a car remember that there's usually a high drop-off fee for returning a rental car in a different state than where you picked it up. An air pass can be a good idea if you want to see a lot of the country. These are available only to non-US residents, and must be bought before reaching the USA (see page 27).

Flights from Australia, New Zealand and South Africa

For passengers travelling from Australasia to Texas and the Southwest, the most expensive time to fly has traditionally been during the northern summer (mid-May to end Aug) and over the Christmas period (Dec to mid-Jan), with shoulder seasons covering March to mid-May and September, and the rest of the year counting as low season. Fares no longer vary as much across the year as they used to, however.

Instead, fares on the regular Air New Zealand, Qantas and United flights from eastern Australian

---

A BETTER KIND OF TRAVEL

At Rough Guides we are passionately committed to travel. We believe it helps us understand the world we live in and the people we share it with – and of course tourism is vital to many developing economies. But the scale of modern tourism has also damaged some places irreparably, and climate change is accelerated by most forms of transport, especially flying. We encourage all our authors to consider the carbon footprint of the journeys they make in the course of researching our guides.

PACKAGES AND TOURS

Although independent travel is usually cheaper, countless flight and accommodation packages allow you to bypass all the organizational hassles. A typical package from the UK might be a return flight plus mid-range hotel accommodation for three nights in Las Vegas/ Dallas/Salt Lake City, starting at around £1000 per person in low season and more like £2000 at peak periods.

Fly-drive deals, which give cut-rate car rental when a traveller buys a transatlantic ticket from an airline or tour operator, are always cheaper than renting on the spot, and give great value if you intend to do a lot of driving. They're readily available through general online booking agents such as Expedia and Travelocity, as well as through specific airlines. Several of the operators listed here also book accommodation for self-drive tours.

cities to Los Angeles, the main US gateway airport, tend to start at around Aus$1400 in low season, or more like Aus$2000 in summer. Flying from Western Australia can add around Aus$300–400. Qantas flies non-stop from Sydney to Dallas (from Aus$1800 in low season), while United flies non-stop Sydney to Houston for about the same.

From New Zealand, the cost of flying from Auckland or Christchurch to LA ranges from roughly NZ$1400– 1800 across the year, or more like NZ$1800–2300 to Las Vegas via LA. American Airlines flies non-stop Auckland to Dallas for around NZ$1900–2500.

From South Africa, non-stop flights from Cape Town or Johannesburg cost around ZAR13,000–17,000 to New York and ZAR17,000–20,000 to Houston or Dallas, depending on the time of year.

Various add-on fares and air passes valid in the continental US are available with your main ticket, allowing you to fly to destinations across Texas and the Southwest. These must be bought before you go.

AIRLINES

Aer Lingus ⓦ aerlingus.com
Air Canada ⓦ aircanada.com
Air India ⓦ airindia.com
Air New Zealand ⓦ airnewzealand.com
Alaska Airlines ⓦ alaskaair.com
American Airlines ⓦ aa.com
British Airways ⓦ ba.com
Delta Air Lines ⓦ delta.com
Emirates ⓦ emirates.com
Frontier Airlines ⓦ flyfrontier.com
Hawaiian Airlines ⓦ hawaiianair.com
JAL (Japan Airlines) ⓦ jal.com
JetBlue ⓦ jetblue.com
KLM ⓦ klm.com
Qantas Airways ⓦ qantas.com.au
Singapore Airlines ⓦ singaporeair.com
South African Airways ⓦ flysaa.com
Southwest ⓦ southwest.com

United Airlines ⓦ united.com
Virgin Atlantic ⓦ virgin-atlantic.com
WestJet ⓦ westjet.com

AGENTS AND OPERATORS

Adventure World Australia ⓦ adventureworld.com.au, New Zealand ⓦ adventureworld.co.nz
American Holidays Ireland ⓦ americanholidays.com
Wotif Australia ⓦ wotif.com

Getting around

Distances in Texas and the Southwest are so great that it's essential to plan in advance how you'll get from place to place. Amtrak provides a skeletal but often scenic rail service, and there are usually good bus links between the major cities. Even in rural areas, with advance planning, you can usually reach the main points of interest without too much trouble by using local buses and charter services.

That said, travel is almost always easier if you have a car. Many worthwhile and memorable Southwestern destinations are far from the cities: even if a bus or train can take you to the general vicinity of one of the great national parks, for example, it would be of little use when it comes to enjoying the great outdoors.

By rail

Travelling on the national Amtrak network (☎800 872 7245, ⓦ amtrak.com) is rarely the fastest way to get around, though if you have the time it can be a pleasant and relaxing experience. The Amtrak system isn't comprehensive in Texas and the Southwest. There are four main routes: the California Zephyr from Chicago to Denver which cuts across central Utah via Salt Lake City; the Southwest Chief from Chicago

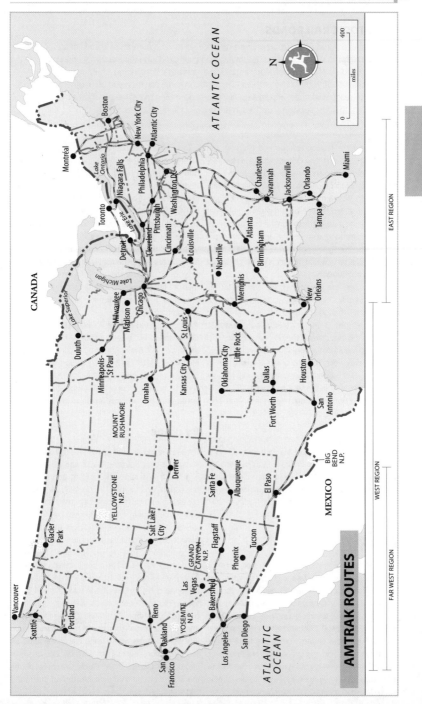

AMTRAK ROUTES

HISTORIC RAILROADS

While Amtrak has a monopoly on long-distance rail travel, a number of historic or scenic railways, some steam-powered or running along narrow-gauge mining tracks, bring back the glory days of train travel. Many are purely tourist attractions, doing a full circuit through beautiful countryside in two or three hours, though some can drop you off in otherwise hard-to-reach wilderness areas. Fares vary widely according to the length of your trip. We've covered the most appealing options in the relevant Guide chapters.

to Los Angeles via Albuquerque and Flagstaff; the Sunset Limited from New Orleans to LA via Houston, San Antonio, El Paso and Tucson; and the Texas Eagle from Chicago to LA via Dallas, Austin, San Antonio and Tucson. What's more, these cross-country routes tend to be served by one or at most two trains per day, so in large areas of the region the only train of the day passes through at three or four in the morning. Amtrak also runs the coordinated, but still limited, Thruway bus service that connects some cities that their trains don't reach.

For any one specific journey, the train is usually more expensive than taking a Greyhound bus, or even a plane, though special deals, especially in the off-peak seasons (Sept–May, excluding Christmas), can bring the cost down – the off-peak rail fare from Chicago to Albuquerque, for example, starts at around $125 one-way when booking online at least a month in advance (for a coach seat, not a sleeper). Money-saving passes are also available (see page 27).

Even with a pass, you should always reserve as far in advance as possible; all passengers must have seats, and some trains are booked solid. Sleeping compartments start at around $600 per night, including three full meals, in addition to your seat fare, for one or two people. However, even standard Amtrak quarters are surprisingly spacious compared to aeroplane seats, and there are additional dining cars and lounge cars (with full bars and sometimes glass-domed 360° viewing compartments).

By bus

If you're travelling on your own and plan on making a lot of stops, buses are by far the cheapest way to get around. The main long-distance operator, Greyhound (☎800 231 2222, ⓦgreyhound.com, international customers without toll-free access can also call ☎214 849 8100 open 24/7), links all major cities and many towns. Out in the country, buses are fairly scarce, sometimes appearing only once a day, if at all. However, along the main highways, buses run around the clock to a full timetable, stopping only for meal breaks (almost always fast-food chains) and driver changeovers.

To avoid possible hassle, travellers should take care to sit as near to the driver as possible, and to arrive during daylight hours – many bus stations are in dodgy areas, at least in large cities. In many smaller places, the post office or a gas station doubles as the bus stop and ticket office. Reservations can be made in person at the station, online or on the toll-free number. Oddly they do not guarantee a seat, so it's wise to join the queue early – if a bus is full, you may have to wait for the next one, although Greyhound claims it will lay on an extra bus if more than ten people are left behind. For long hauls there are plenty of savings available – check the website's discounts page.

Other operators include Trailways (☎877 908 9330, ⓦtrailways.com), whose regional divisions cover some parts of the country more comprehensively; Megabus (☎877 462 6342; ⓦus.megabus.com), whose low-cost service covers Austin, Dallas, Houston and San Antonio in Texas; and Flixbus (ⓦflixbus.com), which offers routes across Texas and the Southwest.

By plane

Despite the presence of good-value discount airlines – most notably Southwest and JetBlue – air travel is a much less appealing way of getting around the country than it used to be. With air fuel costs escalating even faster than gas costs, and airlines cutting routes, demanding customers pay for routine services and jacking up prices across the board, the days of using jet travel as a spur to vacation adventuring are long gone. To get any kind of break on price, you'll have to reserve well ahead of time (at least three weeks), preferably not embark in the high season, and be firm enough in your plans to buy a "non-refundable" fare – which if changed can incur costs of $100 or more. Nonetheless, flying can still cost less than the train – though still more than the bus. In those examples where flying can make sense for short local hops, we mention such options wherever appropriate throughout this Guide. Otherwise, phone the airlines or visit their websites to find out routes and schedules.

PRE-TRIP PLANNING FOR OVERSEAS TRAVELLERS

AMTRAK PASSES

The USA Rail Pass (30-day/10 segments/$499) covers the entire Amtrak network for the designated period, though you are restricted to a set number of individual journeys. Passes can be bought from the Amtrak website (ⓦamtrak.com).

AIR PASSES

The main American airlines offer air passes for visitors who plan to fly a lot within the USA. These must be bought in advance and are often sold with the proviso that you cross the Atlantic with the same airline or group of airlines (such as Star Alliance). Each deal will involve the purchase of a certain number of flights, air miles or coupons. Other plans entitle foreign travellers to discounts on regular US domestic fares, again with the proviso that you buy the ticket before you leave home. Check with the individual airlines to see what they offer and the overall range of prices.

By car

For many, the concept of cruising down the highway, preferably in a convertible with the radio blasting and the wind in your hair, is one of the main reasons to set out on a tour of Texas and the Southwest. The romantic images of countless road movies are not far from the truth, though you don't have to embark on a wild spree of drinking, drugs and sex to enjoy driving across America. Apart from anything else, a car makes it possible to choose your own itinerary and to explore the astonishing wide-open landscapes that may well provide your most enduring memories of the country.

Driving in the cities, on the other hand, is not exactly fun, and can be hair-raising. Yet in larger places a car is by far the most convenient way to make your way around, especially as public transport tends to be spotty outside the major cities. Many urban areas, especially in the West, have grown up since cars were invented. As such, they sprawl for so many miles in all directions – Phoenix, Dallas and Houston are classic examples – that your hotel may be fifteen or twenty miles from the sights you came to see, or perhaps simply on the other side of a freeway that can't be crossed on foot.

Renting a car

To rent a car, you must have held your licence for at least one year. Drivers under 25 may encounter problems and must pay higher than normal insurance premiums. Rental companies expect customers to have a credit card; if you don't, they may let you leave a cash deposit (at least $500), but don't count on it. All the major rental companies have outlets at the main airports, but it can often be cheaper to rent from a city branch. Reservations are handled centrally, so the best way to shop around is either online, or by calling their national toll-free numbers. Potential variations are endless; certain cities and states are consistently cheaper than others, while individual travellers may be eligible for corporate, frequent-flier or AAA discounts. In low season you may find a tiny car (a "subcompact") for as little as $200 per week, but a typical budget rate would be more like $35–40 per day or around $245 per week including taxes. You can get some good deals from strictly local operators, though it can be risky as well. Make reading up on such inexpensive vendors part of your pre-trip planning.

Even between the major operators – who tend to charge $50–100 per week more than the local competition – there can be a big difference in the

GREEN TORTOISE

One alternative to long-distance bus torture is the fun, countercultural Green Tortoise, whose buses, complete with foam cushions, bunks, fridges and rock music, mostly ply the West and the Northwest of the country, but can go as far as New Orleans, Washington DC and New York. There are numerous seductive options (though many have been on "hiatus" since the COVID-19 epidemic), each allowing plenty of stops for hiking, river-rafting, bathing in hot springs and the like.

Green Tortoise's main office is in San Francisco (ⓦgreentortoise.com).

DRIVING FOR FOREIGNERS

Foreign nationals from English-speaking countries can drive in the USA using their full domestic driving licences (International Driving Permits are not always regarded as sufficient). Fly-drive deals are good value if you want to rent a car (see page 27), though you can save up to fifty percent simply by booking in advance with a major firm. If you choose not to pay until you arrive, be sure you take a written confirmation of the price with you. Remember that it's safer not to drive right after a long transatlantic flight – and that most standard rental cars have automatic transmissions.

quality of cars. Industry leaders like Alamo, Hertz and Avis tend to have newer, lower-mileage cars and more reliable breakdown services. Always be sure to get unlimited mileage and remember that leaving the car in a different city from the one where you rented it can incur a drop-off charge of $200 or more.

Small print and insurance

When you rent a car, read the small print carefully for details on Collision Damage Waiver (CDW), sometimes called Liability Damage Waiver (LDW). This form of insurance specifically covers the car that you are driving yourself – you are in any case insured for damage to other vehicles. At $12–25 a day, it can add substantially to the total cost, but without it you're liable for every scratch to the car – even those that aren't your fault. Increasing numbers of states are requiring that this insurance be included in the weekly rental rate and are regulating the amounts charged to cut down on rental-car company profiteering. Some credit card companies offer automatic CDW coverage to customers using their card; contact your issuing company for details. Alternatively, European residents can cover themselves against such costs with a reasonably priced annual policy from companies like Insurance4CarHire (ⓦ insurance-4carhire.com).

The American Automobile Association, or AAA (ⓣ 800 222 4357, ⓦ aaa.com), provides free maps and assistance to its members and to members of affiliated associations overseas, such as the British AA and RAC. If you break down in a rented car, call one of these services if you have towing coverage, or the emergency number pinned to the dashboard.

CAR RENTAL AGENCIES

Alamo USA ⓣ 800 462 5266, ⓦ alamo.com
Avis USA ⓣ 800 230 4898, ⓦ avis.com
Budget USA ⓣ 800 527 0700, ⓦ budget.com
Dollar USA ⓣ 800 800 3665, ⓦ dollar.com
Enterprise USA ⓣ 800 261 7331, ⓦ enterprise.com
Hertz USA ⓣ 800 654 3131, ⓦ hertz.com
Holiday Autos USA ⓣ 866 392 9288, ⓦ holidayautos.com
National USA ⓣ 800 227 7368, ⓦ nationalcar.com
Thrifty USA & Canada ⓣ 800 847 4389, ⓦ thrifty.com

Cycling

Cycling is another realistic mode of transport. An increasing number of big cities have cycle lanes and local buses equipped to carry bikes (strapped to the outside), while in country areas, roads have wide shoulders and fewer passing motorists. Unless you plan to cycle a lot and take your own bike, however, it's not especially cheap. Bikes can be rented for $20–50 per day, or at discounted weekly rates, from outlets that are usually found close to beaches, university campuses, Utah ski resorts in summer and good cycling areas. Local visitor centres have details.

The national non-profit Adventure Cycling Association, based in Missoula Montana (ⓦ adventure cycling.org), publishes maps of several lengthy routes, detailing campgrounds, motels, restaurants, bike shops and places of interest. Many individual states

HITCHHIKING

Hitchhiking in the United States is generally a bad idea, especially for women, making you a potential victim both inside (you never know who you're travelling with) and outside the car, as the odd fatality may occur from hitchers getting a little too close to the highway lanes. At a minimum, in the many states where the practice is illegal (Nevada and Utah in the Southwest), you can expect a steep fine from the police and, on occasion, an overnight stay in the local jail. The practice is still fairly common, however, in more remote rural areas (especially in Texas), with little or no public transport.

issue their own cycling guides; contact the state tourist offices (see page 47). Before setting out on a long-distance cycling trip, you'll need a good-quality, multispeed bike, panniers, tools and spares, maps, padded shorts and a helmet (legally required in many states and localities). Plan a route that avoids interstate highways (on which cycling is unpleasant and usually illegal) and sticks to well-maintained, paved rural roads. Of problems you'll encounter, the main one is traffic: RVs, huge eighteen-wheelers and logging trucks can create intense backdraughts capable of pulling you out into the middle of the road.

Backroads Bicycle Tours (W backroads.com), and the HI-AYH hostelling group (see page 30) arrange multi-day cycle tours, with camping or stays in country inns; where appropriate we've also mentioned local firms that offer this.

Greyhound, Amtrak and major airlines will carry passengers' bikes – dismantled and packed into a box – for a small fee.

Accommodation

The cost of accommodation is significant for any traveller exploring Texas and the Southwest, especially in the resorts and cities, but wherever you travel, you're almost certain to find a good-quality, reasonably priced motel or hotel. If you're prepared to pay a little extra, wonderful historic hotels and lodges can offer truly memorable experiences.

The four price codes we give in the Guide (see box above) are based on a standard double room for one night, including breakfast, in peak season, though substantial discounts are available at slack times. Unsurprisingly, the sky's the limit for luxury hotels, where exclusive suites can easily run into four figures. Many hotels will set up a third single bed for around $15–25 extra, reducing costs for three people sharing. For lone travellers, on the other hand, a "single room" is usually a double at a slightly reduced rate at best. A dorm bed in a hostel usually costs $20–45 per night, but standards of cleanliness and security can be low, and for groups of two or more the saving compared to a motel is often minimal. In certain parts of Texas and the Southwest, camping makes a cheap – and exhilarating – alternative. Alternative methods of finding a room online are through wairbnb.com and the free hosting site W couchsurfing.org.

Wherever you stay, you'll be expected to pay in advance, at least for the first night and perhaps for further nights, too. Most hotels ask for a credit card imprint when you arrive, but many still accept cash for the actual payment. Reservations – essential in busy areas in summer – are held only until 6pm, unless you've said you'll be arriving late. Note that some cities and resorts – probably the ones you most want to visit – tack on a hotel tax that can raise the total tax for accommodation to as much as fifteen percent.

Note that as well as the local numbers we give in the Guide, many hotels have freephone numbers (found on their websites), which you can use within the USA.

Hotels and motels

The term "hotels" refers to most accommodation in the Guide. Motels, or "motor hotels", tend to be found beside the main roads away from city centres, and are thus much more accessible to drivers. Budget hotels or motels can be pretty basic, but in general standards of comfort are uniform – each room comes with a double bed (often two), a TV, phone and usually a portable coffeemaker, plus an attached bathroom. Above $100 or so, the room and its fittings simply get bigger and include more amenities, and there may be a swimming pool and added amenities such as irons and ironing boards, or premium cable TV (HBO, Showtime, etc). Almost all hotels and motels now offer wi-fi, albeit sometimes in the lobby only.

The least expensive properties tend to be family-run, independent "mom 'n' pop" motels, but these are rarer nowadays, in the big urban areas at least. When you're driving along the main interstates there's a lot to be said for paying a few dollars more to stay in motels belonging to the national chains. These range from the ever-reliable and cheap Super 8 and Motel 6 through to the mid-range Days Inn and La Quinta up to the more commodious Holiday Inn Express and Hampton Inn.

During off-peak periods, many motels and hotels struggle to fill their rooms, so it's worth bargaining to get a few dollars off the asking price, especially at independent establishments. Staying in the same place for more than one night may bring further reductions. Also, look for discount coupons, especially in the free magazines distributed by local visitor centres and welcome centres near the borders between states. These can offer amazing value – but read the small print first. Online rates are also usually cheaper, sometimes considerably so.

Few budget hotels or motels bother to compete with the ubiquitous diners by offering full breakfasts, although most will provide free self-service coffee, pastries and if you are lucky, fruit or cereal, collectively referred to as "continental breakfast".

ACCOMMODATION PRICE CODES

Throughout this section accommodation is categorized according to a price code, which roughly corresponds to the following price ranges. Price categories reflect the cost of the **cheapest available double room with breakfast** in the most expensive, mid-summer, period. All prices should be taken as a rule of thumb, however, and are best used as points of comparison – hotel rates hop up and down depending on occupancy, the economy, special events and online deals. You may be able to get cheaper rooms if you book at the last minute, or conversely if you reserve well in advance.

$	under $100
$$	$100–199
$$$	$200–300
$$$$	Over $300

B&Bs

Staying in a B&B is a popular, often luxurious, alternative to conventional hotels in Texas and the Southwest. Some B&Bs consist of no more than a couple of furnished rooms in someone's home, and even the larger establishments tend to have fewer than ten rooms, sometimes without TV or phone, but often laden with potpourri, chintzy cushions and an assertively precious Victorian atmosphere. If this cosy, twee setting appeals to you, there's a range of choices throughout the region, but keep a few things in mind. For one, you may not be an anonymous guest, as you would in a chain hotel, but may be expected to chat with the host and other guests, especially during breakfast. Also, some B&Bs enforce curfews, and take a dim view of guests stumbling in after midnight after an evening's partying. The only way to know the policy for certain is to check each B&B's policy online – there's often a lengthy list of do's and don'ts.

The price you pay for a B&B always includes breakfast (sometimes a buffet on a sideboard, but more often a full-blown cooked meal). The crucial determining factor is whether each room has an en-suite bathroom; most B&Bs provide private bath facilities, although that can damage the authenticity of a fine old house. At the top end of the spectrum, the distinction between a "boutique hotel" and a "bed-and-breakfast inn" may amount to no more than that the B&B is owned by a private individual rather than a chain. In many areas, B&Bs have united to form central booking agencies, making it much easier to find a room at short notice; we've given contact information for these where appropriate.

Historic hotels and lodges

Throughout the region, many towns still hold historic hotels, whether dating from the arrival of the railroads or from the heyday of Route 66 in the 1940s and 1950s. So long as you accept that not all will have up-to-date facilities to match their period charm, these can make wonderfully ambient places to spend a night or two. Those that are exceptionally well preserved or restored may charge $200 or more per room, but a more typical rate for a not overly luxurious but atmospheric, antique-furnished room would be more like $120–150.

In addition, several national parks feature long-established and architecturally distinguished hotels, traditionally known as lodges, that can be real bargains thanks to their federally controlled rates. The only drawback is that all rooms tend to be reserved far in advance. Among the best are El Tovar and Grand Canyon Lodge on the South and North rims, respectively, of the Grand Canyon; and the Lodge at Bryce Canyon and Zion National Park Lodge in Utah.

Hostels

Hostel-type accommodation is not as plentiful in the USA as it is in Europe, but provision for backpackers and low-budget travellers does exist. Unless you're travelling alone, most hostels cost about the same as motels; stay in them only if you prefer their youthful ambience, energy and sociability. Many are not accessible on public transport, or convenient for sightseeing in the towns and cities, let alone in rural areas.

These days, most hostels are independent, with no affiliation to the HI-AYH (Hostelling-International-American Youth Hostels; ⓦ http://hiusa.org) network. Many are no more than converted motels, where the "dorms" consist of a couple of sets of bunk beds in a musty room, which is also let out as a private unit on demand. Most expect guests to bring sheets or sleeping bags. Rates range from $25 to about $45 for a dorm bed, and from $50–80 for a double room, with prices in the major cities at the higher end. Those few hostels that do belong to HI-AYH tend to impose curfews and limit daytime access hours, and segregate dormitories by sex.

Food and drink

The USA is not all fast food. Every state offers its own specialities, and regional cuisines are distinctive and delicious. In addition, international food turns up regularly – not only in the big cities, but also in more unexpected places. Many farming and ranching regions – Nevada in particular – have a number of Basque restaurants; Southwestern cuisine and Tex-Mex food have become their own genres; and bison, elk and other wild game-based dishes can be found in towns all over the region.

In the big cities, you can pretty much eat whatever you want, whenever you want, thanks to the ubiquity of restaurants, 24-hour diners, and bars and street carts selling food well into the night. Also, along all the highways and on virtually every town's main street, restaurants, fast-food joints and cafés try to outdo one another with bargains and special offers. Whatever you eat and wherever you eat it, service is usually prompt, friendly and attentive – thanks in large part to the institution of tipping. Waiters depend on tips for the bulk of their earnings; fifteen to twenty percent is the standard rate, with anything less sure to be seen as an insult.

Regional cuisine

Many US regions have developed their own cuisines, combining available ingredients with dishes and techniques of local ethnic groups. Broadly, steaks and other cuts of beef are prominent in Texas, while Mexican food (with its prolific use of use of chili peppers) is popular throughout Texas and the Southwest. Local trout and salmon are ubiquitous throughout the mountains of Utah, while the Gulf of Mexico provides Texas with fresh fish, oysters and shrimp. In the Southwest, indigenous Native American communities continue to cook their traditional food; you will see Navajo frybread everywhere, a kind of fried taco dished up with minced beef. Wild game, including bison (buffalo), is also popular (often served as burgers).

There are some local differences. In Texas, barbecue is serious business, especially prevalent in the Hill Country near Austin, and tends to be cooked closed pit style with a smokier flavour than other regions of the USA. Steak in general is very big in Texas, as is chicken-fried steak. Tex-Mex is probably the most famous Southwestern style food, based on but not entirely the same as northern Mexican cuisine. Tex-Mex dishes like chili con carne, fajitas, tacos, enchiladas and tostadas come with heavy dollops of shredded cheese, a chili and cheese sauce known simply as "*queso*" (Spanish for "cheese"), red beans, chicken, beef, pork and chili peppers. Caldwell is the "*kolache* capital of Texas", where the traditional Czech dessert (sweet fruit pastries) has become a local delicacy, though pecan pie is the official "state pie" of Texas. Vietnamese food is also popular and delicious in Texas, thanks to a large émigré population.

New Mexican cuisine (also popular in Nevada and Utah) uses a lot of New Mexico chiles (green and red), piñon nuts and Mexican-style breakfast burritos and *sopapillas* (fried pastries). Texas claims to have invented "frito pie" (corn chips topped with red chili sauce, beans, ground beef and cheese) but Santa Fe is a worthy rival. You'll also find a lot of blue corn dishes – pancakes, enchiladas and tortillas – in New Mexico.

Arizona is known for its Native American fry bread, with the Fry Bread House in Phoenix especially good. *Chimichanga* (deep-fried burrito served with sour cream and guacamole) is a Mexican-inspired dish that's popular (especially at El Charro in Tucson), along with the Cheese Crisp (open-faced cheese-drenched quesadilla) and Sonoran hot dogs (smothered with bacon, pinto beans, jalapeños, onions, tomatoes and mayonnaise).

Nevada well known for its juicy steaks (served at legendary spots like the Golden Steer in Las Vegas), though the ubiquitous (and gigantic) "casino buffet" in Las Vegas has become almost as iconic. Basque restaurants are common throughout Northern Nevada (many Basque shepherds emigrated here a century ago), with lamb shank a popular dish, washed down with "Picon punch", a cocktail made with Amer Picon – a French spirit flavoured with bitter orange.

EATING PRICE CODES

Throughout the guide, eating out listings are categorized according to a price code, which roughly corresponds to the following price ranges. Price categories reflect the cost of **a two-course meal for one with a drink**.

$	under $25
$$	$25–49
$$$	$50–75
$$$$	Over $75

VEGETARIAN AND VEGAN EATING

In the big US cities at least, being a vegetarian – or even a vegan – presents few problems. However, don't be too surprised in rural areas if you find yourself restricted to a diet of eggs, grilled-cheese sandwiches and limp salads. Note however, that baked beans nationwide, and the nutritious-sounding red beans and rice dished up Texas and the Southwest, usually contain bits of diced pork.

Cornish miners even introduced Cornish pasties to the state, still available at BJ Bull Bakery in Elko.

Utah is known for its own bevvy of specialties, including pickle pie, raspberry shakes from Bear Lake, Navajo tacos, "funeral potatoes" (deep fried, cornflake-crusted potato chunks), and fry sauce.

Finally, there are also regional variations on American staples. You can get plain old burgers and hot dogs anywhere, but for a truly American experi-ence, grab a "Awful-Awful" burger and fries combo in northern Nevada, green chile cheeseburgers at the Owl Bar in New Mexico, a sweet "Western Sundae" at Luv-It Frozen Custard in Las Vegas, or the region's signature Sonoran hot dogs (see page 31) in Arizona. Almost every state has at least one spot claiming to have invented the hamburger (Texas has a claim that goes back to the 1880s), and regardless of where you go, you can find a good range of authentic diners where the buns are fresh, the patties are large, handcrafted and tasty, and the dressings and condi-ments are inspired.

Other cuisines

In the cities, in particular, where centuries of settle-ment have created distinctive local neighbourhoods, each community offers its own take on the cuisine of its homeland. Houston has excellent Vietnamese restaurants, Nevada its Basque diners, and Houston and Las Vegas have their Chinatowns. Mexican food is so common throughout Texas and the Southwest it might as well be an indigenous cuisine. The food is different from that found south of the border, focusing more on frying and on a standard set of staples. The essentials, however, are the same: lots of rice and black or pinto beans, often served refried (boiled, mashed and fried), with variations on the tortilla, a thin corn or flour pancake that can be wrapped around fillings and eaten by hand (a burrito);

folded and filled (a taco); rolled, filled and baked in sauce (an enchilada); or fried flat and topped with a stack of filling (a tostada).

Italian food is widely available, too; the top-shelf restaurants in cities tend to focus on the northern end of the boot, while the tomato-heavy, gut-busting portions associated with southern Italian cooking are usually confined to lower-end, chequered-table-cloth diners with pictures of Frank and Dino on the walls. Pizza restaurants occupy a similar range from high-end gourmet places to cheap and tasty dives.

When it comes to Asian food, Indian cuisine is usually better in the cities, though there are increasing exceptions as the resident population grows. When found in the Chinatown neighbourhoods of major cities Chinese cooking can be top-notch, and often inexpensive – beware, though, of the dismal-tasting "chop suey" and "chow mein" joints in the suburbs and small towns. Japanese, once the preserve of the coasts and sophisticated cities, has become widely popular in the region, with sushi restaurants in all price ranges and chain teriyaki joints out on the freeways. Thai and Vietnamese restaurants, meanwhile, provide some of the best and cheapest food available, sometimes in diners mixing the two, and occasionally in the form of "fusion" cooking with other Asian cuisines (or "pan-Asian", as it's widely known).

Drink

Austin, Dallas, Santa Fe and Las Vegas are the consummate boozing towns – filled with tales of famous, plastered authors indulging in famously bad behaviour – but almost anywhere you shouldn't have to search very hard for a comfortable place to drink. You need to be 21 years old to buy and consume alcohol in the USA, and it's likely you'll be asked for ID if you look under 30.

"Blue laws" – archaic statutes that restrict when, where and under what conditions alcohol can be purchased – are held by many states, and prohibit the sale of alcohol on Sundays. Utah (which, being predominantly Mormon, has the most byzantine rules) restricts the alcohol content in beer to just 5 percent ABV at grocery stores and supermarkets, but the usual range is available at bars and clubs (though only till 1am), and at state-controlled liquor stores. In contrast, Arizona, New Mexico and especially Nevada maintain liberal drinking rules. Texas also maintains relatively open drinking laws though there are five (rural) "dry" counties and liquor sales are banned on Sundays.

Note that if a bar is advertising a happy hour on "rail drinks" or "well drinks", these are cocktails made from the liquors and mixers the bar has to hand (as opposed to top-shelf, higher-quality brands).

Beer

The most popular American beers may be the fizzy, insipid lagers from national brands, but there is no lack of alternatives. The craze for microbreweries started in northern California several decades ago, and today even the smaller towns in Texas and the Southwest have their own share of decent handcrafted beers. Texas brand Lone Star has its dedicated followers, but there are now numerous competitors (over 100 microbreweries), from Rahr & Sons Brewing Company in Fort Worth and Peticolas Brewing Company in Dallas, to Saint Arnold Brewing Company in Houston and Ranger Creek in San Antonio. New Mexico is another craft beer hotspot, with the likes of La Cumbre Brewing leading a growing list of small-batch producers.

Indeed, microbreweries have undergone an explosion in most parts of the country in recent years and brewpubs can now be found in virtually every sizeable US city and college town. Almost all serve a wide range of good-value, hearty food to help soak up the drink. For more on craft beers, see ⓦ craftbeer.com.

Wine

Wine isn't as big here as in California, say, but there are local producers, typically of varying quality, and always a few standouts in each state that may merit a taste while you're on your journey. Arizona has a relatively developed wine industry with over 120 wineries and tasting rooms across the state. Willcox and Sonoita are the primary Arizona wine regions, in the southern half of the state (Sauvignon Blanc, Cabernet Sauvignon, Malbec and Merlot). You'll also find a smattering of vineyards in the central and northern parts of the state, in places like Old Town Cottonwood and Sedona in the Verde Valley region. New Mexico has its own wineries, with over 60 vineyards and tasting rooms, and even Texas has seen a burgeoning wine industry in recent decades, primarily in the North-Central Region and Trans-Pecos Regions.

Festivals

In addition to the main US public holidays – on July 4, Independence Day, the entire country takes time out to picnic, drink, salute the flag, and watch or participate in fireworks displays, marches, beauty pageants, eating contests and more, to commemorate the signing of the Declaration of Independence in 1776 – there is a diverse multitude of engaging local events in Texas and the Southwest: arts-and-crafts shows, county fairs, ethnic celebrations, music festivals, rodeos, sandcastle-building competitions, chilli cookoffs and countless others.

Certain festivities, such as Burning Man in Nevada, are well worth planning your holiday around but obviously other people will have the same idea, so visiting during these times requires an extra amount of advance effort, not to mention money. Halloween (Oct 31) is also immensely popular. No longer just the domain of masked kids running around the streets banging on doors and demanding "trick or treat", in some bigger cities Halloween has evolved into a massive celebration. Thanksgiving Day, on the fourth Thursday in November, is more sedate. Relatives return to the nest to share a meal (traditionally, roast turkey and stuffing, cranberry sauce, and all manner of delicious pies) and give thanks for family and friends. Ostensibly, the holiday recalls the first harvest of the Pilgrims in Massachusetts, though Thanksgiving was a national holiday before anyone thought to make that connection.

Annual festivals and events

For further details of the festivals and events listed below, including more precise dates, see the relevant page of the Guide (where covered) or access their websites. The state tourist boards (see page 47) can provide more complete calendars for each specific area.

JANUARY

National Cowboy Poetry Gathering Elko, NV ⓦ westernfolklife. org. See page 169.
Sundance Film Festival Park City, UT ⓦ sundance.org.

FEBRUARY

La Fiesta de los Vaqueros (the "Tucson Rodeo") Tucson, AZ ⓦ tucsonrodeo.com.

MARCH

South by Southwest Music Festival Austin, TX ⓦ sxsw.com. See page 68.

APRIL

Arizona International Film Festival Tucson, AZ ⓦ filmfestivalarizona.com.
Country Thunder Florence, AZ countrythunder.com.
Fiesta San Antonio San Antonio, TX ⓦ fiestasanantonio.org. See page 77.

Gathering of Nations Pow Wow Albuquerque, NM
ⓦ gatheringofnations.com.
Texas SandFest Port Aransas, TX. ⓦ texassandfest.org.

MAY

Electric Daisy Carnival Las Vegas, NV ⓦ lasvegas.
electricdaisycarnival.com.
Folk Festival Kerrville, TX (into June) ⓦ kerrvillefolkfestival.org.
Living Traditions Festival Salt Lake City, UT ⓦ saltlakearts.org/
livingtraditionspresents
Tejano Conjunto Festival San Antonio, TX
ⓦ guadalupeculturalarts.org.
UTOPiAfest Burnet, TX. ⓦ utopiafest.com.

JUNE

Nevada State Fair Carson City, NV ⓦ nevadastatefair.org.
Utah Arts Festival Salt Lake City, UT ⓦ uaf.org.
Utah Shakespeare Festival Cedar City, UT (into early Oct)
ⓦ bard.org.

JULY

National Basque Festival Elko, NV ⓦ elkobasqueclub.com. See
page 169.
UFO Festival Roswell, NM ⓦ ufofestival.com.

AUGUST

Billy the Kid Pageant and Old Lincoln Days Lincoln, NM.
ⓦ discoverruidoso.com.
Burning Man Black Rock City, NV (into Sept) ⓦ burningman.com.
See page 168.
Great American Duck Race Deming, NM ⓦ demingduckrace.
com.
Hopi Native Arts & Cultural Festival Flagstaff, AZ
ⓦ hopifestival.com.
Indian Market Santa Fe, NM ⓦ swaia.org. See page 103.
Inter-Tribal Ceremonial Gallup, NM
ⓦ gallupintertribalceremonial.com. See page 116.

SEPTEMBER

Arizona State Fair Phoenix, AZ (into Oct). ⓦ azstatefair.com.
Fiestas de Santa Fe Santa Fe, NM ⓦ santafefiesta.org. See page
103.
Fort Worth Oktoberfest Fort Worth, TX ⓦ fortworthoktoberfest.
com.
Great Reno Balloon Race Reno, NV ⓦ renoballoon.com.
Life is Beautiful Music & Art Festival Las Vegas, NV
ⓦ lifeisbeautiful.com.
Moab Music Festival Moab, UT ⓦ moabmusicfest.org.
New Mexico State Fair Albuquerque, NM ⓦ statefair.exponm.
com.
Panhandle South Plains Fair Lubbock, TX ⓦ southplainsfair.
com.
State Fair of Texas Dallas, TX (into Oct) ⓦ bigtex.com.
Utah State Fair Salt Lake City, UT ⓦ utahstatefair.com.

OCTOBER

Austin City Limits Music Festival Austin, TX ⓦ aclfestival.com.
Heber Valley Music & Cowboy Poetry Gathering Heber Valley,
UT ⓦ hebervalleycowboypoetry.com.
Helldorado Days Tombstone, AZ ⓦ tombstonehelldorado.com.
See page 124.
International Balloon Fiesta Albuquerque, NM ⓦ balloonfiesta.
com.
PRIDE Festival Las Vegas, NV ⓦ lasvegaspride.org/pride-festival.

NOVEMBER

Texas Book Festival Austin, TX ⓦ texasbookfestival.org.

DECEMBER

Phoenix Festival of the Arts Phoenix, AZ
ⓦ phoenixfestivalofthearts.org.

The outdoors

**Coated by red-rock deserts, cut by deep
canyons and capped by great mountains,
Texas and the Southwest is blessed with
fabulous backcountry and wilderness
areas. Here you can experience the
full breathtaking sweep of America's
wide-open stretches. For beaches and
sub-tropical heat, make for the Gulf of
Mexico coast in Texas.**

National parks and monuments

The National Park Service administers both national
parks and national monuments. Its rangers do a
superb job of providing information and advice to
visitors, maintaining trails and organizing such activities as free guided hikes and campfire talks.

In principle, a national park preserves an area of
outstanding natural beauty, encompassing a wide
range of terrain and prime examples of particular
landforms and wildlife. Thus Saguaro has pristine
desert and forests of the nation's largest cacti, while
Grand Canyon offers towering granite walls and
spectacular mile-high views. A national monument
is usually much smaller, focusing perhaps on just
one archeological site or geological phenomenon,
such as Bandelier in New Mexico. Altogether, the
national park system in the USA comprises around
four hundred units, including national seashores,
lakeshores, battlefields and other historic sites.

While national parks tend to be perfect places
to hike – almost all have extensive trail networks –
all are far too large to tour entirely on foot (Grand
Canyon, for example, is bigger than the state of

MAIN ATTRACTIONS IN NATIONAL PARKS

The Park Service website, ⓦnps.gov, details the main attractions of the national parks, plus opening hours, the best times to visit, admission fees, hiking trails and visitor facilities.

Rhode Island). Even in those rare cases where you can use public transport to reach a park, you'll almost certainly need some sort of vehicle to explore it once you're there.

Most parks and monuments charge admission fees, ranging from $5 to $35, which usually cover a vehicle and all its occupants for up to a week. For anyone on a touring vacation, it may well make more sense to buy the Inter-agency Annual Pass, also known as the "America the Beautiful Pass". Sold for $80 at all federal parks and monuments, or online at ⓦstore. usgs.gov, this grants unrestricted access for a year to the bearer, and any accompanying passengers in the same vehicle, to all national parks and monuments, as well as sites managed by such agencies as the US Fish and Wildlife Service, the Forest Service and the BLM (Bureau of Land Management). It does not, however, cover or reduce additional fees like charges for camping in official park campgrounds, or permits for backcountry hiking or rafting.

Two further passes, obtainable at any park or online, grant free access for life to all national parks and monuments, again to the holder and any accompanying passengers, and also provide a fifty-percent discount on camping fees. The Senior Pass is available to any US citizen or permanent resident aged 62 or older for a one-time fee of $80, while the Access Pass is issued free to blind or permanently disabled US citizens or permanent residents. While hotel-style lodges are found only in major parks, every park or monument tends to have at least one well-organized campground. Often, a cluster of motels can be found not far outside the park boundaries. With appropriate permits – subject to restrictions in popular parks – backpackers can also usually camp in the backcountry (a general term for areas inaccessible by road).

Other public lands

National parks and monuments are often surrounded by tracts of national forest – also federally administered but much less protected. These too usually hold appealing rural campgrounds but, in the words of the slogan, each is a "Land Of Many Uses", and usually allows logging and other land-based industry (thankfully, more often ski resorts than strip mines).

Other government departments administer wildlife refuges, national scenic rivers, recreation areas and the like. The Bureau of Land Management (BLM) has the largest holdings of all, most of it open rangeland, such as in Nevada and Utah, but also including some enticingly out-of-the-way reaches. Environmentalist groups engage in endless running battles with developers, ranchers and the extracting industries over uses – or alleged misuses – of federal lands.

While state parks and state monuments, administered by individual states, preserve sites of more limited, local significance, many are explicitly intended for recreational use, and thus hold better campgrounds than their federal equivalents.

Camping and backpacking

The ideal way to see the great outdoors – especially if you're on a low budget – is to tour by car and camp in state and federal campgrounds. Typical public campgrounds range in price from free (usually when there's no water available, which may be seasonal) to around $40 per night. Fees at the generally less scenic commercial campgrounds – abundant near major towns, and often resembling open-air hotels, complete with shops and restaurants – are more like $25–50. If you're camping in high season, either reserve in advance or avoid the most popular areas.

Backcountry camping in the national parks is usually free, by permit only. Before you set off on anything more than a half-day hike, and whenever you're headed for anywhere at all isolated, be sure to inform a ranger of your plans, and ask about weather conditions and specific local tips. Carry sufficient food and drink to cover emergencies, as well as all the necessary equipment and maps. Check whether fires are permitted; even if they are, try to use a camp stove in preference to local materials. In wilderness areas, try to camp on previously used sites. Where there are no toilets, bury human waste at least six inches into the ground and 100ft from the nearest water supply and campground.

Health issues

Backpackers should never drink from rivers and streams; you never know what acts people – or animals – have performed further upstream. Giardia – a water-borne bacteria that causes an intestinal disease characterized by chronic diarrhoea, abdominal cramps, fatigue and weight loss – is a serious problem. Water that doesn't come from a tap

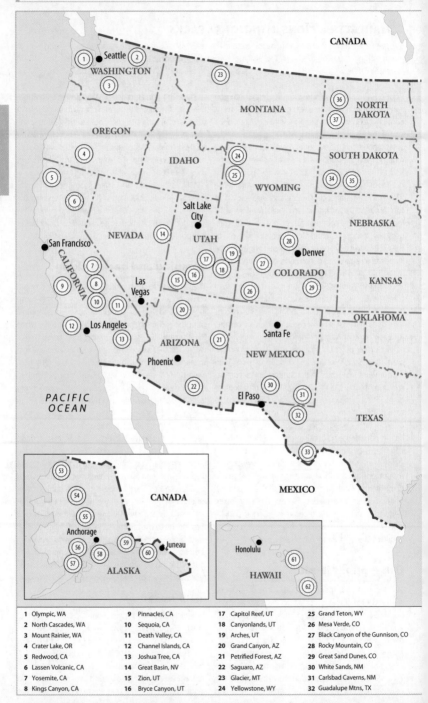

1 Olympic, WA	**9** Pinnacles, CA	**17** Capitol Reef, UT	**25** Grand Teton, WY
2 North Cascades, WA	**10** Sequoia, CA	**18** Canyonlands, UT	**26** Mesa Verde, CO
3 Mount Rainier, WA	**11** Death Valley, CA	**19** Arches, UT	**27** Black Canyon of the Gunnison, CO
4 Crater Lake, OR	**12** Channel Islands, CA	**20** Grand Canyon, AZ	**28** Rocky Mountain, CO
5 Redwood, CA	**13** Joshua Tree, CA	**21** Petrified Forest, AZ	**29** Great Sand Dunes, CO
6 Lassen Volcanic, CA	**14** Great Basin, NV	**22** Saguaro, AZ	**30** White Sands, NM
7 Yosemite, CA	**15** Zion, UT	**23** Glacier, MT	**31** Carlsbad Caverns, NM
8 Kings Canyon, CA	**16** Bryce Canyon, UT	**24** Yellowstone, WY	**32** Guadalupe Mtns, TX

US NATIONAL PARKS

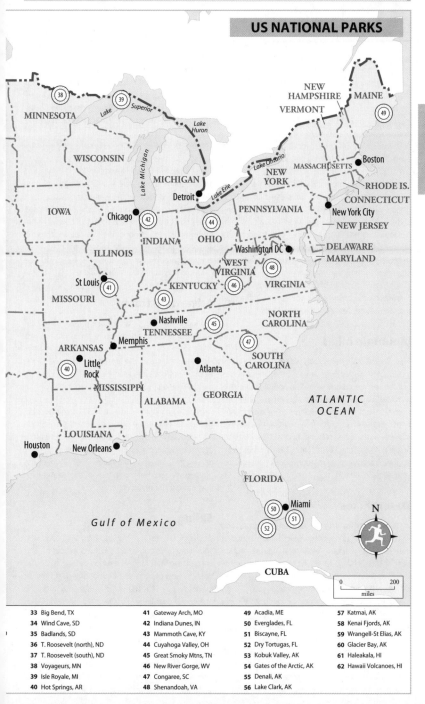

33 Big Bend, TX	41 Gateway Arch, MO	49 Acadia, ME	57 Katmai, AK
34 Wind Cave, SD	42 Indiana Dunes, IN	50 Everglades, FL	58 Kenai Fjords, AK
35 Badlands, SD	43 Mammoth Cave, KY	51 Biscayne, FL	59 Wrangell-St Elias, AK
36 T. Roosevelt (north), ND	44 Cuyahoga Valley, OH	52 Dry Tortugas, FL	60 Glacier Bay, AK
37 T. Roosevelt (south), ND	45 Great Smoky Mtns, TN	53 Kobuk Valley, AK	61 Haleakala, HI
38 Voyageurs, MN	46 New River Gorge, WV	54 Gates of the Arctic, AK	62 Hawaii Volcanoes, HI
39 Isle Royale, MI	47 Congaree, SC	55 Denali, AK	
40 Hot Springs, AR	48 Shenandoah, VA	56 Lake Clark, AK	

should be boiled for at least five minutes or cleansed with an iodine-based purifier or a giardia-rated filter.

Hiking at lower elevations should present few problems, though near water mosquitoes can drive you crazy; Avon Skin-so-Soft or anything containing DEET are fairly reliable repellents. Ticks – tiny beetles that plunge their heads into your skin and swell up – are another hazard. They sometimes leave their heads inside, causing blood clots or infections, so get advice from a ranger if you've been bitten. One species of tick causes Lyme Disease, a serious condition that can even affect the brain. Nightly inspections of your skin are strongly recommended.

Beware, too, of poison oak, which grows throughout the west, usually among oak trees. Its leaves come in groups of three (the middle one on a short stem) and are distinguished by prominent veins and shiny surfaces. If you come into contact with it, wash your skin (with soap and cold water) and clothes as soon as possible – and don't scratch. In serious cases, hospital emergency rooms can give antihistamine or adrenaline shots. A comparable curse is poison ivy, found throughout the country. For both plants, remember the sage advice, "Leaves of three, let it be".

Mountain hikes

Take special care hiking at higher elevations, for instance in the 12,000ft peaks of the Utah Rockies. Late snows are common, and in spring avalanches are a real danger, while meltwaters make otherwise simple stream crossings hazardous. Weather conditions can also change abruptly. Altitude sickness can affect even the fittest of athletes: take it easy for your first few days above 7000ft. Drink lots of water, avoid alcohol, eat plenty of carbohydrates and protect yourself from the sun.

Desert hikes

If you intend to hike in the desert, carry extra food and water, and never go anywhere without a map. Cover most of your ground in early morning: the midday heat is too debilitating. If you get lost, find some shade and wait. So long as you've registered, the rangers will eventually come looking for you.

At any time of year, you'll stay cooler during the day if you wear full-length sleeves and trousers, while a wide-brimmed hat and good sunglasses will spare you the blinding headaches that can result from the desert light. You may also have to contend with flash floods, which can appear from nowhere. Never camp in a dry wash, and don't attempt to cross flooded areas until the water has receded.

It's essential to carry – and drink – large quantities of water in the desert. In particular, hiking in typical summer temperatures requires drinking a phenomenal amount. Loss of the desire to eat or drink is an early symptom of heat exhaustion, so it's possible to become seriously dehydrated without feeling thirsty. Watch out for signs of dizziness or nausea; if you feel weak and stop sweating, it's time to get to the doctor. Check whether water is available on your trail; ask a ranger, and carry plenty with you even if it is.

When driving in the desert, carry ample water in the car, take along an emergency pack with flares, a first-aid kit and snakebite kit, matches and a compass. A shovel, tyre pump and extra gas are always a good idea. If the engine overheats, don't turn it off; instead, try to cool it quickly by turning the front end of the car towards the wind. Carefully pour some water on the front of the radiator, and turn the air conditioning off and the heat up full blast. In an emergency, never panic and leave the car: you'll be harder to find wandering around alone.

Adventure travel

The opportunities for adventure travel in the USA are all but endless, whether your tastes run towards whitewater rafting down the Colorado River, mountain biking in the deserts of Utah, kayaking around Lake Powell, horseback riding in Big Bend on the Rio Grande in Texas or Big Wall rock climbing in Grand Canyon.

While an exhaustive listing of all the possibilities could fill a huge volume, certain places have an especially high concentration of adventure opportunities, such as Moab, Utah (see page 154) or Flagstaff, Arizona (see page 128). Throughout the text we recommend guides, outfitters and local adventure-tour operators.

Skiing

Downhill ski resorts can be found all over the Southwest. Notably Park City, Snowbasin and Sundance in Utah, Mount Lemmon in Arizona, Taos Ski Valley in New Mexico, and Diamond Peak in Nevada. Expect to pay $45–100 per day (depending on the quality and popularity of the resort) for lift tickets, plus another $30 or more per day to rent equipment.

A cheaper alternative is cross-country skiing, or ski touring. Backcountry ski lodges dot mountainous areas across the region, such as the Enchanted Forest Cross Country Ski Area in New Mexico. They offer a range of rustic accommodation, equipment rental and lessons, from as little as $80 a day for skis, boots and poles, up to about $200 for an all-inclusive weekend tour.

Wildlife

Watch out for bears, deer, moose, mountain lions and rattlesnakes in the backcountry, and always consider the effect your presence can have on their environment.

Other than in a national park, you're highly unlikely to encounter a bear. Even there, it's rare to stumble across one in the wilderness. If you do, don't run, just back away slowly. Most fundamentally, it will be after your food, which should be stored in airtight containers when camping. Ideally, hang both food and garbage from a high but slender branch some distance from your camp. Never attempt to feed bears, and never get between a mother and her young. Young animals are cute; their irate mothers are not.

Snakes and creepy-crawlies

Though the deserts in particular are home to a wide assortment of poisonous creatures, these are rarely aggressive towards humans. To avoid trouble, observe obvious precautions. Don't attempt to handle wildlife; keep your eyes open as you walk, and watch where you put your hands when scrambling over obstacles; shake out shoes, clothing and bedding before use; and back off if you do spot a creature, giving it room to escape.

If you are bitten or stung, current medical thinking rejects the concept of cutting yourself open and attempting to suck out the venom. Whether snake, scorpion or spider is responsible, apply a cold compress to the wound, constrict the area with a tourniquet to prevent the spread of venom, drink lots of water and bring your temperature down by resting in a shady area. Stay as calm as possible and seek medical help immediately.

Sports

As well as being good fun, catching a baseball game at Houston's Minute Maid Park on a summer afternoon or joining the screaming throngs at a Cowboys football game in Dallas can give visitors an unforgettable insight into the region and its people. Professional teams almost always put on the most spectacular shows, but big games between college rivals, Minor League baseball games and even
Friday night high-school football games provide an easy and enjoyable way to get on intimate terms with a place and its people.

Specific details for the most important teams in all the sports are given in the various city accounts in this Guide. They can also be found through the Major League websites: Ⓦ mlb.com (baseball); Ⓦ nba. com (basketball); Ⓦ nfl.com (football); Ⓦ nhl.com (ice hockey); and Ⓦ mlssoccer.com (soccer).

Major spectator sports

Baseball, because the Major League teams play so many games (162 in the regular season, usually at least five a week from April to September, plus the October playoffs), is probably the easiest sport to catch when travelling. The ballparks – such as Houston's high-tech Minute Maid Park, the Arizona Diamondbacks's Chase Field in Phoenix, or Globe Life Field in Dallas – are great places to spend time. It's also among the cheapest sports to watch (from around $15–25 a seat for the bleachers), and tickets are usually easy to come by.

Pro football, the American variety, is quite the opposite. Tickets are exorbitantly expensive and almost impossible to obtain (if the team is any good), and most games are played in huge, fortress-like stadiums far out in the suburbs; you'll do better in a bar to watch it on TV. There are four pro teams in the region: the Houston Texans and Dallas Cowboys in Texas, the Arizona Cardinals in Phoenix, and the Las Vegas Raiders in Nevada.

College football is a whole lot better and more exciting, with chanting crowds, gymnastic cheer-leaders and cheaper tickets, which can be hard to obtain in football-crazed college towns in parts Texas and the Southwest. Top teams include the TCU Horned Frogs in Fort Worth, Texas; the Texas Longhorns in Austin, Texas; the UTSA Roadrunners in San Antonio, Texas; Arizona Wildcats in Tucson; Arizona State Sun Devils in Tempe, Arizona; and the Utah Utes in Salt Lake City.

Basketball also brings out intense emotions. The protracted pro playoffs run well into June. The five pro teams in the region are the Dallas Mavericks, Houston Rockets, Phoenix Suns, San Antonio Spurs and Utah Jazz (Salt Lake City). The men's month-long college playoff tournament, called "March Madness", is acclaimed by many as the nation's most exciting sports extravaganza, taking place at venues spread across the country in many small to mid-sized towns. The Arizona Wildcats (University of Arizona in Tucson), Houston Cougars (University of Houston), the TCU

Horned Frogs (Fort Worth, Texas) and Texas Tech Red Raiders (Lubbock, Texas) have all done well in recent years.

Ice hockey, usually referred to simply as hockey, was long the preserve of Canada and cities in the far north of the USA, but now penetrates the rest of the country. The Arizona Coyotes (Tempe, AZ), Dallas Stars in Texas and the Vegas Golden Knights (Paradise, Nevada) are the region's three pro NHL teams. Tickets tend to be hard to get and not cheap.

Other sports

Soccer remains much more popular as a participant sport, especially for kids, than a spectator one, and those Americans who are interested in it usually follow foreign matches like England's Premier League, rather than their home-grown talent. Major League Soccer (MLS) teams in the region include Austin FC, FC Dallas and Houston Dynamo FC in Texas, and Real Salt Lake in Utah.

The good news for international travellers is that any decent-sized city will have one or two pubs where you can catch games from England, various European countries or Latin America; check out Ⓦlivesoccertv.com for a list of such establishments and match schedules.

Golf, once the province of moneyed businessmen, has attracted a wider following in recent decades due to the rise of celebrity golfers such as Tiger Woods and the construction of numerous municipal and public courses. You'll have your best access at these, where a round of golf may cost from $15 for a beaten-down set of links to around $100 for a chintzier course. Private golf courses have varying standards for allowing non-members to play (check their websites) and steeper fees – well over $100 a person for the more elite courses.

Travel essentials

Accessible travel

By international standards, the USA is exceptionally accommodating for travellers with mobility concerns or other physical disabilities. By law, all public buildings, including hotels and restaurants, must be wheelchair accessible and provide suitable toilet facilities. Most street corners have dropped curbs (less so in rural areas), and most public transport systems include subway stations with elevators and buses that "kneel" to let passengers in wheelchairs board.

Costs

When it comes to average costs for travelling expenses, much depends on where you've chosen to go. A road trip around the backroads of Texas won't cost you much in accommodation, dining or souvenir-buying, although the amount spent on gas will add up – this varies from state to state, but at the time of writing the average price was between $2.90 (Texas) and around $4 per gallon (in Nevada). By contrast, getting around a city such as Salt Lake City, Dallas or Austin will be relatively cheap, but you'll pay much more for your hotel, meals, sightseeing and shopping. Most items you buy will be subject to some form of state – not federal – sales tax, from 5.125 percent (in New Mexico) to 6.85 percent (in Nevada). In addition, varying from state to state, counties and cities may add on another point or two to that rate; in Texas and the Southwest this means you'll be paying more like 7–8.5 percent in combined sales tax throughout the region.

Unless you're camping or staying in a hostel, accommodation will be your greatest expense while in Texas and the Southwest. A detailed breakdown is given in the Accommodation section, but you can reckon on at least $50–80 per day, based on sharing, more or less double that if travelling solo. Unlike accommodation, prices for good food don't automatically take a bite out of your wallet, and you can indulge anywhere from the lowliest (but still scrumptious) burger shack to the choicest restaurant helmed by a celebrity chef. You can get by on as little as $25 a day, but realistically you should aim for more like $50.

Where it exists, and where it is useful (which tends to be only in the larger cities), public transport is usually affordable, with many cities offering good-value travel passes. Renting a car, at $175–250 per week, is a far more efficient way to explore the broader part of the region, and, for a group of two or more, it could well work out a lot cheaper. Drivers staying in larger hotels in the cities should factor in the increasing trend towards charging even for self-parking; this daily fee may well be just a few dollars less than that for valet parking.

For attractions in the Guide, prices are quoted for adults, with children's rates listed if they are significantly lower or when the attraction is aimed primarily at youngsters; at some spots, kids get in for half-price, or for free if they're under six.

Tipping

In the USA, waiters earn most of their income from tips, and not leaving a fair amount is seen as an insult. Waiting staff expect tips of at least fifteen percent, and up to twenty percent for very good service. When sitting at a bar, you should leave at least a dollar per round for the barkeeper; more if the round is more than two drinks. Hotel porters and bellhops should receive at least $2 per piece of luggage, more if it has been lugged up several flights of stairs. About fifteen percent should be added to taxi fares, rounded up to the nearest 50¢ or dollar.

Crime and personal safety

No one could pretend that America is crime-free, although away from the urban centres crime is often remarkably low. All the major tourist areas and the main nightlife zones in cities are invariably brightly lit and well policed. By planning carefully and taking good care of your possessions, you should, generally speaking, have few problems.

Car crime

Crimes committed against tourists driving rented cars aren't as common as they once were, but it still pays to be cautious. In major urban areas, any car you rent should have nothing on it – such as a particular licence plate – that makes it easy to spot as a rental car. When driving, under no circumstances should you stop in any unlit or seemingly deserted urban area – and especially not if someone is waving you down and suggesting that there is something wrong with your car. Similarly, if you are accidentally rammed by the driver behind you, do not stop immediately, but proceed on to the nearest well-lit, busy area and call ☎911 for assistance. Hide any valuables out of sight, preferably locked in the trunk or in the glove compartment.

Electricity

Electricity runs on 110V AC. All plugs are two-pronged and rather insubstantial. Some travel plug adapters don't fit American sockets.

Entry requirements

For the latest information on Covid-19 restrictions, consult ⓦ https://travel.state.gov/content/ travel/en/international-travel.html.

Temporary restrictions aside, citizens of 35 countries – including the UK, Ireland, Australia, New Zealand and most Western European countries – can enter under the Visa Waiver Program if visiting the United States for a period of less than ninety days. To obtain authorization, you must apply online for ESTA (Electronic System for Travel Authorization) approval before setting off. This is a straightforward process – simply go to the ESTA website (ⓦ esta.cbp.dhs.gov), fill in your info and wait a very short while (sometimes just minutes, but it's best to leave at least 72hr before travelling to make sure) for them to provide you with an authorization number. You will not generally be asked to produce that number at your port of entry, but it is as well to keep a copy just in case, especially in times of high-security alerts – you will be denied entry if you don't have one. This ESTA authorization is valid for up to two years (or until your passport expires, whichever comes first) and costs $21, payable by credit card when applying. When you arrive at your port of entry you will be asked to confirm that your trip has an end date, that you have an onward ticket and that you have adequate funds to cover your stay. The customs official may also ask you for your address while in the USA; the hotel you are staying at on your first night will suffice. Each traveller must also undergo the US-VISIT process at immigration, where both index fingers are digitally scanned and a digital head shot is also taken for file.

Prospective visitors from parts of the world not mentioned above require a valid passport and a non-immigrant visitor's visa for a maximum ninety-day stay. How you'll obtain a visa depends on what country you're in and your status when you apply;

MARIJUANA AND OTHER DRUGS

Over recent years, the legalization of marijuana for recreational purposes has been introduced in a number of US states. Marijuana/cannabis is now fully legal in Arizona, Nevada and New Mexico. Pot, as it is commonly referred to in America, is now on sale at licensed shops in these states, though there are no Amsterdam-style coffeeshops anywhere as of yet. Rules as to whether only local residents can buy it and how much vary from state to state; smoking in public is usually still illegal and you must be over 21 to buy marijuana.

Paradoxically, the substance is still illegal at the federal level but this has not been creating problems in the above states. Several other states – like Utah – allow the usage of medical marijuana but only with a licence. Note that in states where pot is still illegal – like Texas – you can be prosecuted even if you have bought it legally elsewhere, so it's wise not to take it across state lines in such cases. Also note that all other recreational drugs remain illegal at both state and federal level, so even simple possession can get you into serious trouble.

check wtravel.state.gov. Whatever your nationality, visas are not issued to convicted felons and anybody who owns up to being a communist, fascist, drug dealer or guilty of genocide (fair enough, perhaps). On arrival, the date stamped on your passport is the latest you're legally allowed to stay. The Department of Homeland Security (DHS) has toughened its stance on anyone violating this rule, so even overstaying by a few days can result in a protracted interrogation from officials. Overstaying may also cause you to be turned away next time you try to enter the USA. To get an extension before your time is up, apply at the nearest Department of Homeland Security office, whose address will be under the Federal Government Offices listings at the front of the phone book. INS officials will assume that you're working in the USA illegally, and it's up to you to convince them otherwise by providing evidence of ample finances. If you can, bring along an upstanding American citizen to vouch for you. You'll also have to explain why you didn't plan for the extra time initially.

FOREIGN EMBASSIES IN THE USA

Australia 1601 Massachusetts Ave NW, Washington DC 20036, ☎ 202 797 3000, ⓦ usa.embassy.gov.au
Canada 501 Pennsylvania Ave NW, Washington DC 20001, ☎ 202 682 1740, ⓦ international.gc.ca
Ireland 2234 Massachusetts Ave NW, Washington DC 20008, ☎ 202 462 3939, ⓦ dfa.ie/irish-embassy/usa
New Zealand 37 Observatory Circle NW, Washington DC 20008, ☎ 202 328 4800, ⓦ mfat.govt.nz
South Africa 3051 Massachusetts Ave NW, Washington DC 20008, ☎ 202 232 4400, ⓦ saembassy.org
UK 3100 Massachusetts Ave NW, Washington DC 20008, ☎ 202 588 6500, ⓦ gov.uk/world/usa

Health

If you have a serious accident while in the USA, emergency medical services will get to you quickly and charge you later. For emergencies or ambulances, dial ☎ 911, the nationwide emergency number.

Should you need to see a doctor, look online or ask you hotel to recommend one. The basic consultation fee is $150–200, payable in advance. Tests, X-rays etc. are much more. Medications aren't cheap either – keep all your receipts for later claims on your insurance policy.

Foreign visitors should bear in mind that many pills available over the counter at home – most codeine-based painkillers, for example – require a prescription in the USA. Local brand names can be confusing; ask for advice at the pharmacy in any drugstore.

In general, inoculations aren't required for entry to the USA, though check the latest Covid-19 regulations before you travel. Visitors should also check what health precautions are necessary at both federal and state level, in particular with regards to mask-wearing and social distancing.

MEDICAL RESOURCES FOR TRAVELLERS

CDC ⓦ cdc.gov/travel. Official US government travel health site.
International Society for Travel Medicine ⓦ istm.org. Full listing of travel health clinics.

Insurance

In view of the high cost of medical care in the USA, all travellers visiting from overseas should be sure to buy some form of travel insurance. American and Canadian citizens should check whether they are already covered – some homeowners' or renters' policies are valid on holiday, and credit cards such as American Express often include some medical or other insurance, while most Canadians are covered for medical mishaps overseas by their provincial health plans. If you only need trip cancellation/interruption coverage (to supplement your existing plan), this is generally available at a cost of about six percent of the trip value.

ROUGH GUIDES TRAVEL INSURANCE

Rough Guides has teamed up with WorldNomads.com to offer great travel insurance deals. Policies are available to residents of over 150 countries, with cover for a wide range of adventure sports, 24hr emergency assistance, high levels of medical and evacuation cover and a stream of travel safety information. Roughguides.com users can take advantage of their policies online 24/7, from anywhere in the world – even if you're already travelling. And since plans often change when you're on the road, you can extend your policy and even claim online. Roughguides.com users who buy travel insurance with WorldNomads.com can also leave a positive footprint and donate to a community development project. For more information go to ⓦ roughguides.com/travel-insurance.

Internet

Almost all hotels and many coffeeshops and restaurants offer free wi-fi for guests, though some upmarket hotels charge for access. As a result, cybercafés, where you can use a terminal in the establishment for an hourly charge, are increasingly rare. Nearly all public libraries provide free internet access, but often there's a wait and machine time is limited.

LGBTQ+ travellers

The LGBTQ+ scene in America is huge, albeit heavily concentrated in the major cities. San Francisco, where between a quarter and a third of the voting population is reckoned to be gay or lesbian, is arguably the world's premier LGBTQ+ city. New York runs a close second, and up and down both coasts gay men and women in particular enjoy the kind of visibility and influence those in other places can only dream about. LGBTQ+ public officials and police officers are no longer a novelty. Resources, facilities and organizations are endless. Virtually every major city has a predominantly LGBTQ+ area and we've tried to give an overview of local resources, bars and clubs in each large urban area.

In Texas, Dallas boasts one of the biggest LGBTQ+ populations, with Oak Lawn one of the most dynamic "gayborhoods" in the USA (Dallas Pride takes place every September). Houston's LGBTQ+ community is similarly large, with Montrose its traditional heart, and the Pride Parade taking place in June. Austin also has a prominent LGBTQ+ scene, as does San Antonio. Elsewhere, Phoenix in Arizona (especially the Melrose District on Seventh Avenue), Santa Fe in New Mexico, Las Vegas in Nevada, and even Salt Lake City in generally conservative Utah are LGBTQ+-friendly with lively scenes.

In the rural heartland of Texas and the Southwest, however, life can look more like the Fifties – homosexuals are still oppressed and commonly reviled.

National publications are available from any good bookstore. Bob Damron in San Francisco (ⓦ damron.com) produces the best and sells them at a discount online. These include the Men's Travel Guide, a pocket-sized yearbook listing hotels, bars, clubs and resources for gay men; the Women's Traveller, which provides similar listings for lesbians; the Damron City Guide, which details lodging and entertainment in major cities; and Damron Accommodations, with 1000 accommodation listings for LGBTQ+ travellers worldwide.

Gayellow Pages in New York (ⓦ gayellowpages.com) publishes a useful directory of businesses in the USA and Canada, plus regional directories for New England, New York and the South. The Advocate, based in Los Angeles (ⓦ advocate.com) is a bimonthly national LGBTQ news magazine, with features, general info and classified ads. Finally, the International Gay & Lesbian Travel Association in Fort Lauderdale, FL (ⓦ iglta.org), is a comprehensive, invaluable source for LGBTQ+ travellers.

Mail

Post offices are usually open Monday to Friday from 8.30am to 5.30pm, and Saturday from 9am to 12.30pm, and there are blue mailboxes on many street corners. At time of publication, first-class mail within the USA costs 60¢ for a letter weighing up to 28 grams (an ounce), $1.40 for the rest of the world, though these costs are expected to rise annually. Airmail between the USA and Europe may take a week.

In the USA, the last line of the address includes the city or town and an abbreviation denoting the state ("CA" for California; "TX" for Texas, for example). The last line also includes a five-digit number – the zip code – denoting the local post office. It is very important to include this, though the additional four digits that you will sometimes see appended are not essential. You can check zip codes on the US Postal Service website, at ⓦ usps.com.

Rules on sending parcels are very rigid: packages must be in special containers bought from post offices and sealed according to their instructions. To send anything out of the country, you'll need to obtain green customs declaration form, available from a post office.

Maps

The free road maps distributed by each state through its tourist offices and welcome centres are usually fine for general driving and route planning.

Though most travellers now use GPS (SatNav) – which is available on smartphones and at all car rental offices – Rand McNally still produces maps for each state, bound together in the Rand McNally Road Atlas, and you're apt to find even cheaper state and regional maps at practically any gas station along the major highways. Britain's best source for maps is Stanfords, at 7 Mercer Walk in London (ⓦ stanfords.co.uk), and 29 Corn St in Bristol; it also has a mail-order service.

The American Automobile Association, or AAA ("Triple A"; ☎ 800 222 4357, ⓦ aaa.com) provides free maps and assistance to its members, as well as to British members of the AA and RAC. Call the main number to get the location of a branch near you;

OPENING HOURS AND PUBLIC HOLIDAYS

The traditional summer holiday period runs between the weekends of Memorial Day, the last Monday in May, and Labor Day, the first Monday in September. Many parks, attractions and visitor centres operate longer hours or only open during this period and we denote such cases as "summer" throughout the Guide. Otherwise, specific months of opening are given.

Government offices (including post offices) and banks will be closed on the following national public holidays:

Jan 1 New Year's Day
Third Mon in Jan Martin Luther King, Jr's Birthday
Third Mon in Feb Presidents' Day
Last Mon in May Memorial Day
July 4 Independence Day
First Mon in Sept Labor Day
Second Mon in Oct Columbus Day
Nov 11 Veterans' Day
Fourth Thurs in Nov Thanksgiving Day
Dec 25 Christmas Day

bring your membership card or at least a copy of your membership number.

If you're after really detailed maps that go far beyond the usual fold-out, try Thomas Guides (Ⓦmapbooks 4u.com). Highly detailed park, wilderness and topographical maps are available through the Bureau of Land Management for the West (Ⓦblm.gov) and for the entire country through the Forest Service (Ⓦfs.fed.us/maps). The best supplier of detailed, large-format map books for travel through the American backcountry is Benchmark Maps (Ⓦbenchmarkmaps.com), whose elegantly designed depictions are easy to follow and make even the most remote dirt roads look appealing.

Money

The US dollar comes in $1, $2, $5, $10, $20, $50 and $100 denominations. One dollar comprises one hundred cents, made up of combinations of one-cent pennies, five-cent nickels, ten-cent dimes and 25-cent quarters. You can check current exchange rates at Ⓦx-rates.com.

Bank hours generally run from 9am to 5pm Monday to Thursday, and until 6pm on Friday; the big bank names are Capital One, Chase, Bank of America, Citibank, Wells Fargo, and US Bank. With an ATM card, you'll be able to withdraw cash just about anywhere, though you'll be charged $2–5 per transaction for using a different bank's network. Foreign cash-dispensing cards linked to international networks, such as Plus or Cirrus, are also widely accepted – ask your home bank or credit card company which branches you can use. To find the location of the nearest ATM,

check with AmEx (Ⓦnetwork.americanexpress.com); Mastercard (Ⓦwww.mastercard.us); Accel (Ⓦwww.accelnetwork.com); or Plus (Ⓦusa.visa.com).

Credit and debit cards are the most widely accepted form of payment at major hotels, restaurants and retailers, even though a few smaller merchants still do not accept them. You'll be asked to show some plastic when renting a car, bike or other such item, or to start a "tab" at hotels for incidental charges; in any case, you can always pay the bill in cash when you return the item or check out of your room.

Phones

The USA currently has well over one hundred area codes – three-digit numbers that must precede the seven-figure number if you're calling from abroad (following the 001 international access code) or from a different area code, in which case you prefix the ten digits with a 1. It can get confusing, especially as certain cities have several different area codes within their boundaries; for clarity, in this Guide, we've included the local area codes in all telephone numbers. Note that some cities require you to dial all ten digits, even when calling within the same code. Numbers that start with the digits 800 – or increasingly commonly 888, 877 and 866 – are toll-free, but these can only be called from within the USA itself; most hotels and many companies have a toll-free number that can easily be found on their websites.

Unless you can organize to do all your calling online via Skype (Ⓦskype.com), the cheapest way to make long-distance and international calls is to buy a prepaid phonecard, commonly found in newsagents

CALLING HOME FROM THE USA

For country codes not listed below, dial 0 for the operator, consult any phone directory or log onto Ⓦ countrycallingcodes.com.

Australia 011 + 61 + area code minus its initial zero.

New Zealand 011 + 64 + area code minus its initial zero.

Republic of Ireland 011 + 353 + area code minus its initial zero.

South Africa 011 + 27 + area code.

UK 011 + 44 + area code minus its initial zero.

or grocery stores, especially in urban areas. These are cheaper than the similar cards issued by the big phone companies, such as AT&T, that are usually on sale in pharmacy outlets and chain stores, and will charge only a few cents per minute to call from the USA to most European and other western countries. Such cards can be used from any touchpad phone but there is usually a surcharge for using them from a payphone (which, in any case, are increasingly rare). You can also usually arrange with your local telecom provider to have a chargecard account with free phone access in the USA, so that any calls you make are billed to your home. This may be convenient, but it's more expensive than using prepaid cards.

If you are planning to take your mobile phone (more often called a cell phone in America) from outside the USA, you'll need to check with your service provider whether it will work in the country: you will need a tri-band or quad-band phone that is enabled for international calls. Using your phone from home will probably incur hefty roaming charges for making calls and charge you extra for incoming calls, as the people calling you will be paying the usual rate. Depending on the length of your stay, it might make sense to rent a phone or buy a compatible prepaid SIM card from a US provider; check Ⓦ triptel.com or Ⓦ telestial.com. Alternatively, you could pick up an inexpensive pay-as-you-go phone from one of the major electrical shops.

Senior travellers

Anyone aged over 62 (with appropriate ID) can enjoy a vast range of discounts in the USA. Both Amtrak and Greyhound offer (smallish) percentage reductions on fares to older passengers, and any US citizen or permanent resident aged 62 or over is entitled to free admission for life to all national parks, monuments and historic sites using a Senior Pass (issued for a one-time fee of $80 at any such site). This free admission applies to all accompanying travellers in the same vehicle and also gives a fifty-percent reduction on park user fees, such as camping charges.

For discounts on accommodation, group tours and vehicle rental, US residents aged 50 or over should consider joining the AARP (American Association of Retired Persons; Ⓦ aarp.org) for an annual $16 fee, or a multi-year deal; the website also offers lots of good travel tips, information and features. Road Scholar (Ⓦ roadscholar.org) runs an extensive network of educational and activity programmes for people over 60 throughout the USA, at prices in line with those of commercial tours.

Shopping

Texas and the Southwest offers plenty of shopping opportunities in the world – from the malls and boutiques of Dallas and Houston to the arts and crafts stalls of small towns across the plains, deserts and mountains. When buying clothing and accessories, international visitors will need to convert their sizes into American equivalents (see box, page 46). For almost all purchases, state taxes will be applied (see page 40).

Time

The continental US covers four time zones, and there's one each for Alaska and Hawaii as well. Most of Texas falls within the Central Time Zone (CT), one hour behind the East Coast (10am in New York is 9am in Dallas). However, the two westernmost counties in Texas (essentially El Paso) observe Mountain Time (MT), two hours behind the East Coast; the Mountain Time zone also includes Arizona, New Mexico and Utah.

Nevada falls in the Pacific Time Zone (PT), three hours behind the East Coast. The Eastern zone is a further five hours behind Greenwich Mean Time (GMT), so 3pm London time is 7am in Las Vegas, Nevada. The USA puts its clocks forward one hour to daylight saving time on the second Sunday in March and turns them back on the first Sunday in November. To make things even more confusing, most of Arizona does not observe daylight savings, meaning that it is

CLOTHING AND SHOE SIZES

WOMEN'S CLOTHING

American	4	6	8	10	12	14	16	18
British	6	8	10	12	14	16	18	20
Continental	34	36	38	40	42	44	46	48

WOMEN'S SHOES

American	5	6	7	8	9	10	11
British	3	4	5	6	7	8	9
Continental	36	37	38	39	40	41	42

MEN'S SHIRTS

American	14	15	15.5	16	16.5	17	17.5	18
British	14	15	15.5	16	16.5	17	17.5	18
Continental	36	38	39	41	42	43	44	45

MEN'S SHOES

American	7	7.5	8	8.5	9	9.5	10	10.5	11	11.5
British	6	7	7.5	8	8.5	9	9.5	10	11	12
Continental	39	40	41	42	42.5	43	44	44	45	46

MEN'S SUITS

American	34	36	38	40	42	44	46	48
British	34	36	38	40	42	44	46	48
Continental	44	46	48	50	52	54	56	58

on the same time as Pacific Time in the summer (the Navajo Nation does observe daylight savings).

Tourist information

Each state has its own tourist office (see box). These offer prospective visitors a colossal range of free maps, leaflets and brochures on attractions from overlooked wonders to the usual tourist traps. You can either contact the offices before you set off, or, as you travel around the country, look for the state-run "welcome centres", usually along main highways close to the state borders. In heavily visited states like Utah and Arizona, these often have piles of discount coupons for cut-price accommodation and food. In addition, visitor centres in most towns and cities – often known as the "Convention and Visitors Bureau", or CVB, and listed throughout this Guide – provide details on the area, as do local Chambers of Commerce in almost any town of any size.

Travelling with children

Children under 2 years old go free on domestic flights (assuming they sit on your lap; seats are charged full price) and for ten percent of the adult fare on international flights – though that also doesn't mean they get a seat, let alone frequent-flier miles. Most airlines now charge kids aged between 2 and 14 full-price tickets, though some country-specific discounts may apply for international flights. Discounts for Amtrak trains are better: children under 2 years go free (sharing a seat with an adult), but kids aged 2–12 also get 50 percent off. Bus travel is broadly similar to air travel – children (over 2) and adults pay the same full fare. Car-rental companies usually provide kids' car seats – which are required by law for children under the age of 4 – for a daily charge. You would, however, be advised to check, or bring your own; they are not always available. Recreational vehicles (RVs) are a particularly good option for families. Even the cheapest motel will offer inexpensive two-double bedrooms as a matter of course, which is a relief for non-US travellers used to paying a premium for a "family room", or having to pay for two rooms.

Virtually all tourist attractions offer reduced rates for kids. Most large cities in Texas and the Southwest have natural history museums or aquariums, and quite a few also have hands-on children's museums; in addition most state and national parks organize

STATE TOURISM INFORMATION

Arizona ☎866 275 5816, ⓦvisitarizona.com
Nevada ☎800 638 2328, ⓦtravelnevada.com
New Mexico ☎800 545 2070,
ⓦnewmexico.org
Texas ☎800 452 9292, ⓦtraveltexas.com
Utah ☎800 200 1160, ⓦvisitutah.com

children's activities. All the national restaurant chains provide highchairs and special kids' menus; and the trend for more upmarket family-friendly restaurants to provide crayons with which to draw on paper table-cloths is still going strong.

For a database of kids' attractions, events and activities all over Texas and the Southwest, check the useful site ⓦnickelodeonparents.com.

Getting around

The Americans with Disabilities Act (1990) obliges all air carriers to make the majority of their services accessible to travellers with disabilities, and airlines will usually let attendants of more severely disabled people accompany them at no extra charge.

Almost every Amtrak train includes one or more coaches with accommodation for handicapped passengers. Guide dogs travel free and may accompany blind, deaf or disabled passengers. Be sure to give 24 hours' notice. Hearing-impaired passengers can get information on ☎800 523 6590 (TTY/TDD).

Greyhound, however, has its challenges. Buses are not equipped with lifts for wheelchairs, though staff will assist with boarding (intercity carriers are required by law to do this), and the "Helping Hand" policy offers two-for-the-price-of-one tickets to passengers unable to travel alone (carry a doctor's certificate). The American Public Transportation Association, in Washington DC (ⓦapta.com), provides information about the accessibility of public transport in cities.

The American Automobile Association (contact ⓦhttp://aaa.com for phone number access for each state) produces the Handicapped Driver's Mobility Guide, while the larger car-rental companies provide cars with hand controls at no extra charge, though only on their full-sized (ie most expensive) models; reserve well in advance.

Resources

Most state tourism offices provide information for disabled travellers (see page 47). In addition, SATH, the Society for Accessible Travel and Hospitality, in New York (ⓦsath.org), is a not-for-profit travel-industry group of travel agents, tour operators, hotel and airline management, and people with disabilities. They pass on any enquiry to the appropriate member, though you should allow plenty of time for a response. Mobility International USA, in Eugene, OR (ⓦmiusa.org), offers travel tips and operates exchange programmes for disabled people; it also serves as a national information centre on disability.

The "America the Beautiful Access Pass", issued without charge to permanently disabled or blind US citizens, gives free lifetime admission to all national parks. It can only be obtained in person at a federal area where an entrance fee is charged; you'll have to show proof of permanent disability, or that you are eligible for receiving benefits under federal law.

Women travellers

A woman travelling alone in Texas and the Southwest is not usually made to feel conspicuous, or liable to attract unwelcome attention. Cities can feel a lot safer than you might expect from recurrent media images of demented urban jungles, though particular care must be taken at night: walking through unlit, empty streets is never a good idea, and, if there's no bus service, take a taxi.

In the major urban centres, if you stick to the better parts of town, going into bars and clubs alone should pose few problems: there's generally a pretty healthy attitude toward women who do so, and your privacy will be respected.

However, small towns may lack the same liberal or indifferent attitude toward lone women travellers. People seem to jump immediately to the conclusion that your car has broken down, or that you've suffered some strange misfortune. If your vehicle does break down on heavily travelled roads, wait in the car for a police or highway patrol car to arrive. If you don't already have one, you should also rent a mobile phone with your car, for a small charge.

Nobody should hitchhike anywhere in the USA. Similarly, you should never pick up anyone who's trying to hitchhike. If someone is waving you down on the road, ostensibly to get help with a broken-down vehicle, just drive on by or call the highway patrol to help them.

Avoid travelling at night by public transport – deserted bus stations, if not actually threatening, will do little to make you feel secure. Where possible, team up with a fellow traveller. On Greyhound buses, sit near the driver.

Should disaster strike, all major towns have some kind of rape counselling service; if not, the local sheriff's office will arrange for you to get help and counselling, and, if necessary, get you home. The

National Organization for Women (T 202 628 8669, W now.org) has branches listed in local phone directories and on its website, and can provide information on rape crisis centres, counselling services and feminist bookstores.

RESOURCES AND SPECIALISTS

Gutsy Women Travel Anaheim, CA W gutsywomentravel.com. International agency that provides practical support and organizes trips for lone female travellers.

The Women's Travel Group Bloomfield, NJ W thewomenstravelgroup.com. Arranges luxury and unusual vacations, itineraries, room-sharing and various activities for women.

Working in Texas and the Southwest

Permission to work in Texas and the Southwest can only be granted by the federal Immigration and Naturalization Service in the USA itself. Contact your local embassy or consulate for advice on current regulations, but be warned that unless you have relatives or a prospective employer in the USA to sponsor you, your chances are at best slim. Students have the best chance of prolonging their stay, while a number of volunteer and work programmes allow you to experience the country less like a tourist and more like a resident.

STUDY, VOLUNTEER AND WORK PROGRAMMES

American Field Service Intercultural Programs W afs.org, W afs.org.au, W afs.org.nz, W afs.org.za. Global UN-recognized organization running summer student exchange programmes to foster international understanding.

American Institute for Foreign Study W aifs.com. Language study and cultural immersion, as well as au pair and Camp America programmes.

BUNAC (British Universities North America Club) W bunac.org. Working holidays in the USA for international students and young people.

Camp America W campamerica.co.uk. Well-known company that places young people as counsellors or support staff in US summer camps, for a minimum of nine weeks.

Council on International Educational Exchange (CIEE) W ciee.org. Leading NGO offering study programmes and volunteer projects around the world.

Earthwatch Institute W earthwatch.org. Long-established international charity with environmental and archeological research projects worldwide.

Go Overseas W gooverseas.com. Specializes in gap year programmes and internships around the world, including a good number of opportunities in the USA.

Texas

CATTLE DRIVE SHOW, FORT WORTH STOCKYARDS

1 Texas

Still cherishing its heritage as an independent nation – which it was from 1836 to 1845 – Texas stands proudly apart from the rest of the USA. While the sheer size of the state – 700 miles from east to west and more than 800 from top to bottom – gives it great geographical diversity, its 28.7 million residents are firmly bound together by a shared history and culture. Though the fervent state pride on show just about everywhere might seem a touch extreme to outsiders, Texas undeniably has a lot going for it.

The coastline of Texas curves southward more than 350 miles from Port Arthur on the Louisiana border (a petrochemical town and birthplace of Janis Joplin) to the delta of the Rio Grande, which snakes northwest to form a 900-mile natural border with Mexico. Encompassed in this eastern section of the state is an interesting mix of big-city life and rural, backwoods culture.

The swampy, forested **east** is more like Louisiana than the pretty **Hill Country** or the agricultural plains of the northern **Panhandle**, while the tropical **Gulf Coast** has little in common with the mountainous **deserts** of the west. Changes in **climate** are dramatic: snow is common in the Panhandle, whereas the humidity in Houston is often unbearably thick.

There are 35 cities with a population of 100,000 or more, and each of the major tourist destinations is unique. Hispanic **San Antonio**, for example, with its Mexican population and rich history, has a laidback feel absent from commerce-driven **Houston** or **Dallas**, while trendy **Austin** revels in a lively music scene and an underground DIY ethos. One thing shared by the whole of Texas is **state pride**: Texas is a special place and its friendly residents know it.

Brief history

Early inhabitants of Texas included the Caddo in the east and nomadic Coahuiltecans further south. The **Comanche**, who arrived from the Rockies in the 1600s, soon found themselves at war when the **Spanish** ventured in looking for gold. In the 1700s, the Spanish began to build **missions** and **forts**, although these had minimal impact on the Indigenous population's nomadic way of life. When Mexico won its independence from Spain in 1821, it took Texas as part of the deal. At first, the Mexicans were keen to open up their land and offered generous incentives to settlers. Stephen F. Austin established Anglo-American colonies in the Brazos and Colorado River valleys. However, the Mexican leader, Santa Anna, soon became alarmed by Anglo aspirations to autonomy, and his increasing restrictions led to the eight-month **Texas Revolution** of 1835–36.

The short-lived **Republic of Texas**, which included territory now in Oklahoma, Kansas, New Mexico, Colorado and Wyoming, served to define the state's identity. In 1845, Texas joined the Union on the understanding that it could secede whenever it wished; this antiquated provision has resurfaced in modern-day Texas politics. The influence, especially in the north and east, of settlers from the Southern states and their attendant slave-centred cotton economy resulted in Texas joining the **Confederacy** during the Civil War (1860–65). During Reconstruction, settlers from both the North and the South began to pour in, and the phrase "Gone to Texas" was applied to anyone fleeing the law, bad debts or unhappy love affairs. This was also the period of the great **cattle drives**, when the longhorns roaming free in the south and west of Texas were rounded up and taken to the railroads in Kansas. The Texan – and national – fascination with the romantic myth of the **cowboy** has its roots in this. Today,

Highlights

❶ The Rio Grande Valley Tiny, historic border towns dot one of the least-visited regions of the state. See page 64

❷ Catching a concert in Austin The live music capital of the US and a hotbed for Americana, outlaw country and the blues, with enough music venues to keep any visitor busy for weeks. See page 70

❸ San Antonio's River Walk Spend a few hours strolling along this scenic cobblestone path lined by many of the city's best restaurants and bars. See page 73

❹ Fort Worth From cattle drives in the rootin'-tootin' Stockyards, to world-class galleries in the Cultural District, Fort Worth is Texas' best-kept secret. See page 82

❺ Marfa An improbable minimalist arts community in the middle of the West Texas desert. See page 89

❻ Hiking in Big Bend National Park The Rio Grande rushes through astonishing canyons in this remote wilderness, crisscrossed by some of the best hiking trails that you can find in the USA. See page 90

HIGHLIGHTS ARE MARKED ON THE MAP ON PAGE 54

1

the unofficial cowboy uniform – Stetson, boots and bandana – is virtually a state institution.

The twentieth century onwards

Along with ranching and agriculture, **oil** has been crucial. After the first big gusher in 1901, at Spindletop on the Gulf Coast, the focus of the Texas economy shifted almost overnight from agriculture toward rapid industrialization. Boom towns popped up as wildcatters chased the wells and millions of dollars were made as ranchers, who had previously thought their land only fit for cattle, sold out at vast profit. Today, Texas produces one-fifth of all the domestic oil in the United States, and the sight of nodding pump jacks is one of the state's most potent images. But the state's commitment to renewable energy is becoming a part of the landscape, too, as gleaming white **wind turbines** sprout up like mushrooms in the Panhandle-Plains region.

Houston

The fourth largest city in the United States, **HOUSTON** is an ungainly beast of a place, choked with successive rings of highways and high humidity. Despite this, its sheer

HIGHLIGHTS
1 The Rio Grande Valley
2 Catching a concert in Austin
3 San Antonio's River Walk
4 Fort Worth
5 Marfa
6 Hiking in Big Bend National Park

TEXAS

energy, its relentless Texas pride and, above all, its refusal to take itself totally seriously, lends it no small appeal. For visitors, its well-endowed museums, highly regarded performing arts scene and decent nightlife mean there is always something to do.

If you have just a short time, concentrate on the superb galleries of the **Museum District** and **Hermann Park**, which are linked to **downtown**, some five miles northeast, by light rail. The unique personal culture of the city is most evident in the **Montrose** area, which lies west of downtown and overlaps with the Museum District.

Uptown, also called the **Galleria** district after its massive upscale mall, is three miles west. Just outside the Loop, the Galleria's three hundred or so shops and restaurants spread north along Post Oak Boulevard; and there is little to do around here except shop and eat.

Brief history

The city's very existence has always depended on wild speculation and boom-and-bust excess. Founded on a muddy mire in 1837 by two real estate-booster brothers from New York – their dream was to establish it as the capital of the new Republic of Texas – Houston was soon superseded by the more promising site of Austin, even while somehow developing itself as a commercial centre.

Oil, discovered in 1901, became the foundation, along with cotton and real estate, of vast private fortunes, and over the next century wildly wealthy philanthropists poured cash into swanky galleries and showpiece skyscrapers. That colossal self-confidence helped Houston weather devastating oil crises in the 1980s, and later on it endured the **Enron** corporate scandal. Houston has also developed a growing workforce eager to bring **alternative energy** to scale. Solar and wind projects offer the most promise in Texas; more than 25 percent of Houston's energy load, for instance, comes from wind.

Several **megachurches** headquartered downtown – with smooth-talking celebrity pastors like Joel Osteen – have become powerful social, cultural and political forces, drawing as many as fifty thousand people to their Sunday services, which are open to the public.

Downtown Houston

Houston's skyline remains a dramatic monument to capitalism, ambition and glitz and nowhere is this more evident than **downtown**. Note that the observation deck in the IM Pei-designed **JP Morgan Chase Tower**, 600 Travis St, the state's highest building, is no longer open. Also notable is the nearby Philip Johnson-designed **Penzoil Place**, 711 Louisiana St, while the lobby of the historic **JP Morgan Chase Building**, 712 Main St, is an Art Deco masterpiece completed in 1929.

Sam Houston Park

Daily dawn–dusk • **Museum** Tues–Sat 10am–4pm • Charge; house tours at 10am, 11.30am, 1pm & 2.30pm, charge • ⓦ heritagesociety.org

Nestled below the skyscrapers, **Sam Houston Park** is an appealing green space dotted with restored historic structures from all walks of nineteenth-century life, including a compact **museum** run by the Heritage Society. House tours leave from 1100 Bagby St.

The Museum District and Montrose

Five miles southwest of downtown, the quiet oak-lined streets of the **Museum District** are enjoyable to explore on foot – a rarity for Houston. There are two main concentrations of exhibition spaces, with one entire complex dominated by the collections of oil millionaires **John and Dominique de Menil**. The Menil galleries and the Houston Center for Photography are in the **Montrose** district, which spreads west of downtown.

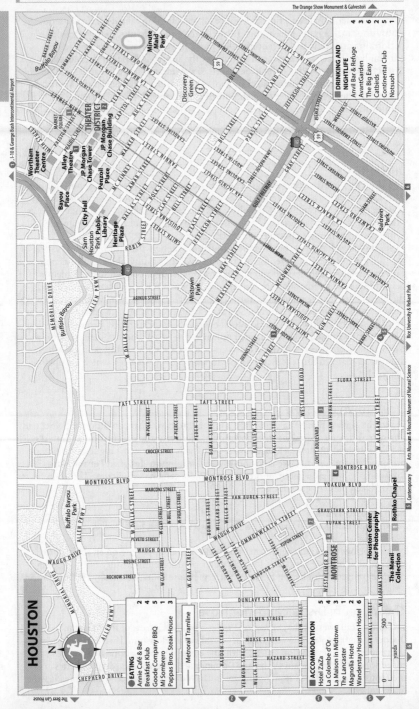

HOUSTON

EATING
Annie Café & Bar 2
Breakfast Klub 4
Goode Company BBQ 5
Mi Sombrero 1
Pappas Bros. Steak House 3

ACCOMMODATION
Hotel ZaZa 5
La Colombe d'Or 4
La Maison in Midtown 3
The Lancaster 1
Magnolia Hotel 2
Wanderstay Houston Hostel 6

DRINKING AND NIGHTLIFE
Anvil Bar & Refuge 4
AvantGarden 3
The Big Easy 6
Catbirds 2
Continental Club 5
Notsuoh 1

Metrorail Tramline

Montrose is one of Houston's hippest neighbourhoods and **Westheimer**, the district's main drag, has enough tattoo parlours, vintage clothes stores, experimental art galleries and junk shops to feel refreshingly bohemian. Montrose has also long been the base of a very visible **LGBTQ community**, and a solid assortment of gay bars and clubs remain.

The district also extends south to pleasant **Hermann Park** and the appealing **Rice University** area, both accessible by the light-rail system. Just beyond **Mecom Fountain**, the park has a Japanese meditation garden and is a nice place to grab an ice cream and go for a stroll.

The Menil Collection

1533 Sul Ross St • Wed–Sun 11am–7pm • Free • Ⓦ menil.org

A magnificent purpose-built gallery, designed by Renzo Piano, houses the private **Menil Collection**. Displayed in spacious, naturally lit white-walled rooms, the superb works range from Paleolithic carvings to Surrealist paintings. Artists with rooms to themselves include Picasso, Max Ernst and René Magritte. There's also a fine array of Alaskan Tlingit masks and an excellent bookstore, too.

Rothko Chapel

3900 Yupon St • Mon–Sat 10am–6pm, Sun 10am–11am • Free • Ⓦ rothkochapel.org

The minimalist ecumenical **Rothko Chapel** contains fourteen sombre paintings commissioned by the de Menils from Mark Rothko shortly before his death. The artist, who worked with architect Philip Johnson in designing the chapel, considered these to be his most important works and their power in this tranquil space is undeniable. The broken obelisk in the small park outside is dedicated to Dr Martin Luther King, Jr. Check the website for talks and events hosted at the chapel, from Sufi dancing to meditations.

Houston Center for Photography

1441 W Alabama St • Wed & Thurs 11am–7pm, Fri 11am–5pm, Sat & Sun 11am–7pm • Free • Ⓦ hcponline.org

The **Houston Center for Photography** features work from emerging American photographers. Although it doesn't have its own collection, the small space exhibits some of the most striking visual art produced in the Southwest. The centre also offers numerous excellent courses and workshops throughout the year.

Museum of Fine Arts

1001 Bissonnet St & 5601 Main St • Wed 11am–5pm, Thurs 11am–9pm, Fri & Sat 11am–6pm, Sun 12.30–6pm • Charge; free Thurs • Ⓦ mfah.org

At the intersection of Bissonet and Main streets, the expansive **Museum of Fine Arts** features an eclectic collection spanning a panoply of eras, filling its impressive buildings with everything from Renaissance art to rare African gold, with a couple of wings entirely devoted to decorative arts. Crane your neck upward from the Matisses and Rodins in the pine-shaded **Cullen Sculpture Garden** outside for a view of the downtown skyline.

Houston Museum of Natural Science

5555 Hermann Park Drive • Daily 9am–5pm • Charge; free Thurs 2–5pm • Ⓦ hmns.org

At Hermann Park's **Houston Museum of Natural Science**, most exhibitions are geared toward kids. But at the museum's **Wiess Energy Hall**, you can pour crude oil over a cluster of clear marbles to learn, for example, that Middle Eastern light crude is similar in viscosity to West Texas intermediate crude. You can also decide for yourself which technologies – such as solar, wind and geothermal – are most likely to ease the world's energy crunch. The museum's **Cockrell Butterfly Center** (daily 9am–5pm; extra charge) is a giant three-storey greenhouse where you can walk among exotic butterflies.

ARRIVAL AND DEPARTURE

By car Downtown Houston lies at the intersection of I-10 (San Antonio–New Orleans) and I-45 (Dallas–Galveston), but the city is a sprawling one, so sights are widely dispersed.

By plane George Bush Intercontinental Airport (@fly2 houston.com), 23 miles north, is a main hub for several airlines, while the smaller, domestic William P. Hobby Airport (@fly2houston.com), 7 miles southeast of downtown, is a major hub for Southwest. Taxis downtown cost about $60 from Intercontinental, $40 from Hobby.

METROBus (@ridemetro.org) also offers routes into downtown from both airports.

By bus The Greyhound terminal is centrally located at 2121 Main St.

Destinations Austin (4 daily; 3hr); Dallas (10 daily; 4hr 10min); El Paso (4 daily; 18hr 15min): Fort Worth (10 daily; 7hr); San Antonio (7 daily; 3hr 15min).

By train Amtrak arrives at 902 Washington Ave, on the western fringe of downtown. There's a daily service to San Antonio (5hr 10min).

GETTING AROUND AND INFORMATION

By car You'll need to rent a car to see the best of Houston, particularly since taxis are expensive; all the major companies are represented at the airports.

By light rail or bus Houston's public transport system is largely inadequate for a city of its size, but the downtown METRO-Rail light-rail service runs primarily north–south covering about 8 miles, mostly along Main and Fanin streets, between the University of Houston (UH) and Reliant Park; the Museum District stop is in the middle. Fares are based on zones; the downtown and surrounding area are in

Zone 1. METRO also operates dozens of bus routes, including the free and environmentally friendly GreenLink bus service (as Route 412; Mon–Fri 6.30am–6.30pm), which has eighteen stops downtown.

By bike Bikes can be placed on the front of city buses and are not a bad option. There are Houston BCycle (@houston bcycle.com) ridesharing stations all over the city.

Visitor centre 1001 Avenida de las Americas (Tues–Fri 8am–5pm, Sat & Sun 10am–5pm; ☎800 446 8786, @visit houstontexas.com).

ACCOMMODATION

SEE MAP PAGE 56

Inexpensive **hotels** are concentrated in three areas: near Reliant Stadium (southwest of downtown), and outside the Loop along either I-45 or I-10. Upmarket, business-oriented chains abound downtown and near the Galleria. **B&Bs** offer a welcome alternative in a city as potentially alienating as Houston, and there are a few **budget** options.

Hotel ZaZa 5701 Main St @hotelzaza.com/#houston. Trendy decor, with themed suites like the "Casablanca" wrapped around a sleek pool. There's a full range of amenities and the hotel boasts a fine position near Hermann Park and museums. $$$$

La Colombe d'Or 3410 Montrose Blvd @lacolombedor. com. With a dozen-plus suites and an ideal setting near the museums, this quaint but luxurious property is the smartest hotel in town. If you can't afford a room, sip a cocktail at the small, elegant bar. $$$$

★ **La Maison in Midtown** 2800 Brazos St @lamaison midtown.com. Central and exceedingly comfortable B&B with several handsome rooms and amenities including jacuzzis. $$

The Lancaster 701 Texas Ave @thelancaster.com. Lady Bird Johnson's Houston hotel of choice, in the heart of the Theater District. It's a sophisticated, old-world option with a variety of rooms and suites, an included buffet breakfast and a restaurant serving upscale meals. $$$$

Magnolia Hotel 1100 Texas Ave @magnoliahotel houston.com. A modern boutique hotel in an excellent downtown location. Most of the rooms are surprisingly spacious and all come with a wide range of amenities. There's a good-sized pool on the roof, but it's worth going up there for the views alone, which are spectacular, especially at night. $$$

★ **Wanderstay Houston Hostel** 4018 Chartres St @wanderstayhotels.com. Easily the best hostel in Houston, with co-ed and female-only dorms, as well as compact but cheap private rooms, some en suite. Amenities include a shared kitchen, 24hr tea and coffee, bike rentals, free fast wi-fi, free street parking and free luggage storage. Dorms $, doubles $

EATING

SEE MAP PAGE 56

Annie Café & Bar 1800 Post Oak Blvd @theannie houston.com. Innovative Southwestern cuisine from celebrated chef Robert del Grande. Dishes on the dinner menu are more extravagant; try the pheasant with bacon and sage. From the cheaper "Bar Bites" menu, try the chicken flautas or pigs in a blanket. $$$

Breakfast Klub 3711 Travis St @thebreakfastklub.

com. Obama campaign staffers favoured this popular breakfast spot when their office was located across the street. Serves unique dishes like wings and grits, as well as more traditional morning fare. $

Goode Company BBQ 5109 Kirby Rd @goodecompany barbeque.com. Good, reasonably priced barbecue joint, with big portions of beef brisket, revered pecan pie and

1

outdoor seating. This is the original location; there are several other branches as Goode Company Hamburgers & Taqueria and Goode Company Seafood that have other specialties. $\overline{\$\$}$

★ **Mi Sombrero** 3401 N Shepard Drive ⓦmisombrero. com. An authentic mom-and-pop Tex-Mex joint a few miles north of downtown that's been around since 1978.

It's excellent value, with cheap dinner plates such as three chicken tacos. $\overline{\$\$}$

Pappas Bros. Steak House 5839 Westheimer Rd ⓦpappasbros.com. Leather booths, marble columns, mahogany panelling and brass trim set the stage for you to devour an in-house, dry-aged slab of beef. $\overline{\$\$\$\$}$

DRINKING AND NIGHTLIFE

SEE MAP PAGE 56

There's no shortage of things to do in the evening in Houston. While downtown has a few good **bars**, you'll find more lively offerings in **Montrose**, particularly along Westheimer Road.

★ **Anvil Bar & Refuge** 1424 Westheimer Rd ⓦanvil houston.com. Smartly designed cocktail bar in an old tyre shop serving an assortment of expertly crafted drinks, plus a large selection of draughts. Though it's one of Houston's hipper establishments, it's rarely too packed.

AvantGarden 411 Westheimer Rd ⓦavantgarden houston.com. Eclectic bar with a commitment to local live music; acts perform on a few stages in the three-storey house. Listen to local bands blow the roof off the joint or relax with a drink outside by the fountain constructed out of recycled Petron tequila bottles.

The Big Easy 5731 Kirby Drive ⓦthebigeasyblues.com. Live zydeco on Sundays and blues available most other times is the double hit that draws a fun-loving crowd to this

Rice Village neighbourhood staple. The most you'll pay to get in is $5, so you can spend the rest of your money on beer.

★ **Catbirds** 1336 Westheimer Rd ⓦcatbirds.com. Laidback creative types swill cheap bottles of Lone Star Beer at this convivial dive bar with a pleasant patio and nightly specials.

Continental Club 3700 Main St ⓦcontinentalclub. com/houston. Cousin to the celeb-rated original in Austin (see page 70), this is a classic live-music venue on the light-rail line. Not for the claustrophobic (although there is an open patio out back), but it's worth it for acts that rarely disappoint. The standard bar drinks come at reasonable prices.

Notsuoh 314 Main St ⓦnotsuoh.com. Young artists and hipsters congregate at this engaging downtown bar featuring live music, poetry readings and wi-fi. Look for the old neon sign outside that reads "The Home of EASY CREDIT".

ENTERTAINMENT

Downtown's much-trumpeted **Theater District** (ⓦvisit houstontexas.com/theater), a seventeen-block area west of Milam Street between Congress and Capitol streets, holds most of the city's **performing arts**. For current listings, check the free *Houston Press* (ⓦhoustonpress.com).

Alley Theatre 615 Texas Ave ⓦalleytheatre.org. An

independent theatre with a variety of shows on two stages.

Wortham Theater Center 501 Texas Ave ⓦvisit houstontexas.com/theater/venues/wortham-center. An elaborate home to Houston's opera and ballet companies, as well as hosting a steady stream of popular plays.

Around Houston

Navigating the sprawl around Houston is not an inviting prospect, but there are a few sights that make it worth bearing. Chief among these is **Space Center Houston**, north of the city and long the focal point of the nation's space programme, and the **San Jacinto Battleground**, an important site in Texas' fight for independence from Mexico. At the outer edge of day-trip possibilities from Houston is the **Big Thicket National Preserve**, with forty miles of hiking trails through varied habitats.

Space Center Houston

1601 NASA Pkwy, 25 miles south of Houston off I-45 • Hours vary, but commonly Mon–Fri 10am–5pm, Sat & Sun 10am–6pm • Charge, plus parking • ⓦspacecenter.org

NASA has been controlling space flight from the **Johnson Space Center** at **Space Center Houston** here since the launch of *Gemini 4* in 1965 – locals love to point out that the first word spoken on the moon was "Houston". A working facility, the nerve centre of the International Space Station, it offers insight into modern space exploration, with

1

tram (trolley) tours giving behind-the-scenes glimpses into various NASA compounds. The crowds can be overwhelming, however, and with all the kids running around, it feels a bit like Disney World.

San Jacinto Battleground

3523 Independence Pkwy S, 22 miles east of Houston off the La Porte Freeway • Wed–Sun 9am–6pm • Charge • Ⓦ sanjacinto-museum.org

San Jacinto Battleground was the site of an eighteen-minute battle in 1836, when the Texans all but wiped out the superbly trained Mexican army. The fight is commemorated by a small museum and the world's tallest stone-column **monument** (570ft, topped by a 34ft-tall Lone Star). An elevator takes you to the observation floor, which provides views of the battlefield. Also normally installed a short distance away on Buffalo Bayou is the Battleship *Texas* (Ⓦ battleshiptexas.org), though tours will be on hold until sometime in 2024 while the ship undergoes restoration in Galveston.

Big Thicket National Preserve

6102 Farm to Market Rd 420, 97 miles from Houston on US-69/287, Kountze, Texas • **Visitor centre** Daily 9am–5pm • Free • Ⓦ nps.gov/bith

The **Big Thicket National Preserve** is a remarkable composite of natural elements from the Southwestern desert, central plains and Appalachian Mountains, with swamps and bayous to boot. The area once offered refuge for outlaws, runaway enslaved people and gamblers; now it just hides a huge variety of **plant** and **animal life**, including deer, alligators, armadillos, possums, hogs and panthers, and nearly two hundred species of birds.

Before entering the site, check in at the **visitor centre**, which has a wealth of information and brochures on the preserve's hiking, canoeing and backcountry camping possibilities. For an easy introduction to the varied habitats, drive 2.5 miles east of the visitor centre to the trailhead for the **Kirby Nature Trail**, a pleasant two-mile loop along the Village Creek.

The Gulf Coast

Look at the number of condo developments along the **Gulf Coast** and you will understand that this is a major getaway destination. The climate ranges from balmy at **Galveston** to subtropical at the Mexican border. Devastating hurricanes in 1900 and again in 2008 all but levelled Galveston; the old, salty city still offers history, shopping and low-key relief from Houston. **Corpus Christi** makes the best base to explore the relatively unspoiled northern beaches of **Padre Island National Seashore**.

Galveston

In 1890, **GALVESTON** – on the northern tip of Galveston Island, the southern terminus of I-45 – was a thriving port, far larger than Houston fifty miles northwest; many newly arrived European immigrants chose to stay here in the so-called "Queen of the Gulf". However, the construction of Houston's Ship Canal, combined with the hurricane of 1900 that killed more than six thousand people (as recounted in Erik Larson's excellent book *Isaac's Storm*), left the coastal town to fade away. But thanks to its pretty historic district and its popularity with Houston residents seeking a summer escape, Galveston experienced a revitalization. Today, its pastel shotgun houses echo New Orleans, while its boozy bars and edgy beach bums bring to mind Jimmy Buffett songs about sailors and smugglers.

1

Downtown Galveston

Downtown, the historic **Strand** district has been fitted with gaslights, upmarket shops, restaurants and galleries. There are museums, too: the Galveston Historic Seaport (Tues–Sun 10am–5pm; charge; ⓦgalvestonhistory.org), for instance, in a complex of shops and restaurants on Pier 21, just off Water Street, focuses on the port's role in trade and immigration during the nineteenth century; admission includes boarding the *Elissa*, an 1877 three-masted tall ship.

Between the Strand and the beaches to the south, Galveston boasts a profusion of historic homes open for guided tours. A standout is the ostentatious stone masterpiece **Bishop's Palace**, 1402 Broadway St (Daily 10am–5pm; charge; ⓦgalvestonhistory.org), with its stained glass, mosaics and marble.

The beaches

The downtown **beaches** of Seawall Boulevard are a bit rocky. They are hemmed in by a ten-mile-long seawall, which was constructed more than a century ago to protect Galveston from hurricanes. Slowly pedalling a **beach cruiser bike** along the seawall at sunset is a classic Galveston experience; contact Island Bicycle Company, 1808 Seawall Blvd, for rental options (ⓦislandbicyclecompany.com). **Stewart Beach**, on the eastern edge of town, offers a wide range of services and plenty of space for families to soak up the sun. Fifteen miles west from downtown, **Jamaica Beach** is comparatively quiet and a locals' favourite.

Galveston Island State Park

14901 FM 3005 • Daily 24hr • Charge • ⓦ tpwd.texas.gov

Six miles west of downtown, **Galveston Island State Park** preserves two thousand acres of marshland that are a haven for several bird species, particularly during spring and fall migrations. The park holds numerous easy trails that provide access to both the gulf and bay sides of the island. To really get a feel for the unique barrier island habitat, head out on a **kayak** along one of the generally calm water trails that surround the park; Artist Boat (ⓦartistboat.org), a group focused on coastal appreciation and preservation, sponsors kayak outings.

Moody Gardens

I-45 off the 61st St exit • Check website for hours • Day pass charge, entry for individual attractions available • ⓦ moodygardens.com

Brash and unabashedly touristy, **Moody Gardens** is Galveston's biggest attraction – for families, at least. The complex, on the west side of town, centres on three giant glass pyramids, and has an IMAX theatre, rainforest and an aquarium. Inclement weather makes a visit here much more appealing; otherwise it's hard to justify the costs and the hassle from the inevitable crowds.

ARRIVAL AND INFORMATION   GALVESTON

By car Driving from Houston to Galveston is straightforward: once it crosses over to the island, I-45 becomes Broadway, the town's main drag.

By bus Greyhound arrives at 714 25th St (a short taxi ride from downtown). There is no Amtrak service.

Visitor centre 2228 Mechanic St (Mon–Fri 8.30am–5pm, Sat 10am–5pm, Sun noon–5pm; ☏409 797 5144, ⓦ galveston.com).

ACCOMMODATION

Gaido's Seaside Inn 3700 Seawall Blvd ⓦgaidos-seaside-inn.com. A clean, friendly, no-frills choice, with a good-sized outdoor pool, hot tub, a pool bar overlooking the water and a free hot breakfast. $̅

Galveston Island State Park Campground 14901 FM 3005 ⓦtexasstateparks.reserveamerica.com. The state park has a range of pleasant campgrounds with fire pits and picnic tables; the beach-side sites have services, while the bay-side ones have water but no electricity. Bay-side pitches $̅, beach-side $̅

Grand Galvez 2024 Seawall Blvd ⓦgrandgalvez.com. Far and away the most exclusive spot to stay on the island, this regal hotel, built in 1911, has a beautiful pool, a grand lobby, restaurant (see page 62) and lobby bar. $̅$̅$̅

1

EATING, DRINKING AND ENTERTAINMENT

Brews Brothers 2404 Strand ☎417 763 2739. Huge selection of craft beers and a few of its own, as well as a bar that seems to go on forever. The staff are friendly and knowledgeable, there's a perennially smoke-filled cigar lounge out back and the whole place has an edgier feel than your typical brewpub.

Galvez Bar and Grill Grand Galvez, 2024 Seawall Blvd ⓦgrandgalvez.com. This hotel's elegant and recently renovated restaurant serves well-executed dishes with a focus on surf and turf, such as a blackened shrimp and crab fondue. Its Sunday brunch is one of the hottest tickets in the state. $$$

MOD Coffeehouse 2126 Post Office St ⓦmodcoffee house.com. Friendly hipster downtown coffeeshop featuring Fairtrade and organic blends. There's free wi-fi and the menu is full of healthy eats such as hummus with pita. $

Mosquito Cafe 628 14th St ⓦmosquitocafe.com. A local favourite, this breezy breakfast and lunch joint serves tasty salads and iced teas. The Thai chicken salad is a good bet, and the grilled shrimp tacos do not disappoint. $$

★ **Old Quarter Acoustic Café** 413 20th St ⓦold quarteracousticcafe.com. A great venue for folk, alt-country and blues; the late Texas singer-song-writer Townes Van Zandt wrote *Rex's Blues* about the café's owner, musician Rex Bell. Cash only. Most shows start around 8pm.

The Spot 3204 Seawall Blvd ⓦislandfamous.com/the spot. Lively bar and a nice family restaurant with a devoted following who come as much for the amazing Gulf views as for the four bars and three dozen TVs. The food is better than you might expect; go for the shrimp kisses (stuffed with pepper jack cheese and wrapped in bacon). $$

Corpus Christi

Laidback **CORPUS CHRISTI** is reached along the coast on the two-lane Hwy-35 from Houston or Galveston, or on I-37 from San Antonio. Originally a rambunctious trading post, it too was hit by a fierce hurricane, in 1919, but recovered, transforming itself into a centre for naval air training, petroleum and shipping. The city is an outdoor destination – fishing, sailing, birding and watersports (mostly located across the channel on Padre Island) are all hugely popular here – but there are a few worthy cultural diversions. Corpus Christi's streets aren't all that compelling to wander, though the tranquil **Heritage Park** (daily 6am–10pm, exteriors only; free; ☎361 826 3411), at 1581 N Chaparral, is an impressive collection of twelve Victorian homes and gardens.

Art Museum of South Texas

1902 N Shoreline Blvd • Tues–Sat 10am–5pm, Sun 1–5pm • Charge • ⓦartmuseumofsouthtexas.org

The impressive collection of the **Art Museum of South Texas** focuses on fine arts and crafts of the Americas. The bleach-white, Philip Johnson-designed building is stunning, with bright windows that give close-up views of freighters navigating Corpus Christi Bay; look for dolphins riding the bow wake. The museum also has an excellent small lunch spot, *Hester's*.

The Selena Museum

5410 Leopard St • Mon–Fri 10am–4pm • Charge • ⓦq-productions.com

Much of Corpus Christi's population is Hispanic, and the community was devastated in 1995 when 23-year-old singer **Selena** was shot dead in a downtown *Days Inn* parking lot by the former president of her fan club. Selena was on the verge of becoming the first major crossover star of **Tejano** music, and fifty thousand fans attended her funeral. The **Selena Museum** is stuffed with memorabilia, from her extravagant gowns to her red Porsche.

ARRIVAL, GETTING AROUND AND INFORMATION   CORPUS CHRISTI

By plane Corpus Christi International Airport (ⓦcorpus christiairport.com) is about 10 miles west of the city's centre; a taxi into town is around $30.

By bus The Greyhound bus station is downtown at 702 N Chaparral St.

Local buses The CCRTA (ⓦccrta.org) operates public transport in and around the city, including a good metro bus system. The website has detailed maps of the many routes.

Ferry From March to late Sept a pedestrian ferry operates from Peoples St to North Beach.

Visitor centre 309 N Water St (daily 9am–5pm; 10am–6pm in summer; ☎800 766 2322, ⓦvisitcorpuschristi.com).

ACCOMMODATION, EATING AND DRINKING

House of Rock 511 Starr St ⊚ texashouseofrock.com. A packed calendar of consistently stellar live music makes this the best spot to catch a rock band, even if it's not always easy to stake out a comfortable spot. The bar side has a bit more room, a huge selection of beers and no cover charge. $\overline{\underline{S}}$

Residence Inn Corpus Christi Downtown 309 S Shoreline Blvd ⊚ marriott.com. With a prime location and more style than any other option around, this Marriott property is the best accommodation choice in town. Amenities include an outdoor pool, free parking and free full American breakfast buffet. $\overline{\underline{SSS}}$

Water Street Oyster Bar 309 N Water St ⊚ waterst marketcc.com/oyster-bar-cc. Long-established raw bar/ sushi bar that serves decent burgers, too; the shrimp and crawfish po-boy is a steal. Part of a group that includes the Executive Surf Club, around the back at 306 N Chaparral Street – the nightly specials tend to draw crowds, though the local bands that play here are reason enough to drop in. $\overline{\underline{SS}}$

The Yardarm 4310 Ocean Drive ⊚ yardarmrestaurant corpuschristi.com. A nautical-themed bayfront restaurant in a cute yellow house, with excellent seafood plates at reasonable prices, including lobster thermidor, and the bouillabaisse, a rich seafood stew. $\overline{\underline{SS}}$

Padre Island National Seashore

The entrance is at 20420 Park Rd 22 and is open 24hr • Charge • ⊚ nps.gov/pais

Operated by the National Park Service, **Padre Island National Seashore** is not as unspoiled as its name suggests, with ranks of condos advancing steadily up the coast and a surprising amount of vehicular traffic on the beach itself. But it remains an excellent destination for **birdwatching** and waterborne activities, particularly **windsurfing** and **kayaking**. Any plans to head out on the water should include a stop in at **Worldwinds** (⊚ worldwinds.net), on Bird Basin Road 4.5 miles northwest of the visitor centre, which can provide suggestions on where and when to go as well as rent kayaks and boards.

Aside from water activities, simply walking along the **miles of beaches** is the most popular island pastime. If you visit from fall to spring, you'll stand a very good chance of spotting several **bird species** that migrate here by the thousands, including pelicans, terns and kestrels.

INFORMATION   PADRE ISLAND NATIONAL SEASHORE

Visitor centre At the park entrance (hours vary; ⊚ nps. gov/pais). The park officers here can provide information on the release of sea turtle hatchlings (in season).

Port Isabel and South Padre Island

The graceful Queen Isabella Causeway, northeast of Brownsville, connects **PORT ISABEL**, home to one of the biggest commercial fishing fleets in Texas, to **SOUTH PADRE ISLAND**, one of the rowdiest Spring Break destinations in the USA. As you might expect, most of the visitors' favourite activities don't extend beyond getting in the water, soaking up the sun's rays or drinking a **beer** or three. Though this is enough for most, Port Isabel itself holds a few engaging museums befitting a town proud of its nautical heritage. The best is the **Treasures of the Gulf Museum**, 317 E Railroad Ave (Wed–Sat 10am–4pm; charge; ⊚ portisabelhistory.com), which tells the story of three sixteenth-century Spanish galleons that sank not far offshore. In the same building, the **Port Isabel Historical Museum** (same hours and fee) showcases numerous artefacts from the US-Mexican War. Nearby at 421 E Queen Isabella Blvd, the Point Isabel Lighthouse (daily 9am–5pm; charge; ⊚ portisabellighthouse.com/lighthouse) offers stunning views from its upper deck.

ACCOMMODATION   PORT ISABEL AND SOUTH PADRE ISLAND

Palms Resort 3616 Gulf Blvd, South Padre Island ⊚ palmsresortcafe.com. This retro 1970s boutique lies just off the beach, with a heated pool and beachfront suites with kitchenettes. Premium chair and umbrella service for guests. $\overline{\underline{SS}}$

Upper Deck Hotel & Bar 120 E Atol St, South Padre Island ⊚ upperdeckhotel.com. A friendly, basic inn with retro motel rooms, outdoor pool and café, live music and

great staff, a few minute stroll from the beach. $\overline{5}\overline{5}$
Wanna Wanna 5100 Gulf Blvd, Beach Access 19, South Padre Island ⓦ wannawanna.com. Beachfront place with fifteen mostly themed rooms that are clean, if dated; those on the second floor have ocean views. The friendly onsite beach bar is a popular local hangout and serves basic fried platters and pub fare. $\overline{5}\overline{5}$

EATING AND DRINKING

Burger Shack & Beer Garden 413 E Maxan St, Port Isabel ☏ 956 433 5370. Old-school burger joint tucked away behind the lighthouse with a menu that holds no surprises. Still, if you're craving red meat on a bun, you can't hope to find better; expect freshly grilled patties oozing juice and flavour in a variety of iterations. The cosy beer garden out back occasionally hosts local bands. $\overline{5}$

Joe's Oyster Bar 207 E Maxan St, Port Isabel ⓦ gulf seafoodmarket.com. No frills seafood spot draws crowds with monumental portions of fried or boiled shrimp, oysters, stuffed crabs, and various iterations of fresh snapper, flounder and other Gulf fish. $\overline{5}$

Lobo Del Mar Café 204 W Palm St, South Padre Island ⓦ lobodelmarcafe.com. Linger over a dramatic sunset at this secluded restaurant with west-facing views of the Laguna Madre. Stalwarts on the menu include the *loboviche* (ceviche and shrimp cocktail) and the burgers. Live music every night 6–9pm. $\overline{5}\overline{5}$

Laredo and the Rio Grande Valley

LAREDO, population 250,000, is situated at the southern terminus of I-35 (the northern terminus is 1600 miles to the north in Duluth, MN). A busy bridge connects the USA to Mexico at the bottom of Convent Avenue, where a major Border Patrol presence exists. As battles between Mexican **drug cartels** have escalated in recent years, Laredo and its sister city across the border (Nuevo Laredo) have earned a violent reputation – most of the real risk is in Mexico though.

The focus of Laredo's main square is the pretty **St Augustin Cathedral**, a couple of blocks north of the Rio Grande at 200 St Augustin Ave, containing a modernist mural of the Crucifixion; there's a pleasant stone grotto outside. Otherwise, there's not much to do other than eat, drink and take in the atmosphere: this city, perhaps more than any other in Texas, reflects a strong **Latino influence**, evident in everything from the food to blaring hip-hop music.

The Rio Grande Valley

Heading southeast from Laredo down US-83 (called the **Zapata Hwy**) you pass through the **Rio Grande Valley**, a subtropical slice of South Texas decidedly well removed from the typical state itinerary. Actually a delta prone to flooding, the 180-mile-long valley contains few immediately identifiable sights, though a string of atmospheric farming communities, with tiny downtowns that have barely been touched in two hundred years, may warrant a trip this far south.

ACCOMMODATION AND EATING	LAREDO AND THE RIO GRANDE VALLEY

El Meson de San Agustin 908 Grant St, Laredo ⓦ elmesonsagustin.com. Beloved, hard-to-find spot across the street from the cathedral that serves some of the best Mexican food in the state, with a daily menu and meals such as chicken *flautas* with avocado cream, fish fillets, and rice and beans. $\overline{5}$

★ **La Posada Hotel** 1000 Zaragoza St, Laredo ⓦ la posada.com. On the main square, this historic and handsome place has spacious, well-appointed rooms, a lobby bar favoured by martini-drinking businessmen and two courtyard pools. The musician Ryan Bingham references the hotel in his song *Bread and Water*. $\overline{5}\overline{5}$

Austin

AUSTIN was a tiny community on the verdant banks of the (Texas) Colorado River when Mirabeau B. Lamar, president of the Republic of Texas, suggested in 1839

that it would make a better capital than swampy and disease-ridden Houston. Early
building had to be done under armed guard, while angry Comanche watched from the
surrounding hills. Despite this perilous location, Austin thrived.

Today the city wears its state capital status lightly. Since the 1960s, the laidback and
progressive city – an anomaly in Texas – has been a haven for artists, musicians and
writers, and many visitors come specifically for the **music**. And while complacency has
crept in – its "alternative" edge being packaged as just another marketing tool – artists
hungry for recognition are still attracted to this creative hotbed.

Due to a tech-fuelled population leap, brand-new towering condo complexes have
shot up to threaten Austin's small-town vibe. Still, it remains the best city in the state
for **cycling**, and the presence of the vast and pretty University of Texas campus adds to
the pleasant atmosphere. Within the city limits a great park system offers numerous
hiking and biking trails, plus a wonderful spring-fed swimming pool. In addition,
Austin makes a fine base for exploring the green **Hill Country** that rolls away to the west.

Downtown Austin

Downtown Austin is a supremely pleasant place to take a stroll; pick up a free self-
guided walking tours leaflet from the visitor centre (see page 68). Most of the city's
most popular sights are distributed around the prominent **Texas State Capitol** (Mon–Fri
7am–10pm, Sat & Sun 9am–8pm; free guided tours also available, call ☎512 305
8400 for schedule), which serves as a good visual reference. It's more than 300ft high,
taller than the Capitol in Washington, with a dusty-red granite dome that accents the
downtown skyline, especially when illuminated in the evening. The chandeliers, carpets
and even the door hinges of this colossal building are emblazoned with Lone Stars and
other Texas motifs. The dammed Colorado River – called Lady Bird Lake (formerly
Town Lake) – borders downtown to the south.

Congress Avenue

Congress Avenue, an attractive, walkable stretch of shops and office buildings that
slopes south from the Capitol down to Lady Bird Lake, is the heart of downtown. At
no. 700 is **The Contemporary Austin** (Wed noon–9pm; Thurs–Sun noon–6pm; charge,
free on Thurs; ⓦthecontemporaryaustin.org), an attractive space to explore trends in
modern art. It mostly showcases emerging artists, and the standard is generally pretty
high. Visit the Contemporary's **Laguna Gloria campus** at 3809 West 35th St for its cool
sculpture garden (Wed & Fri–Sun 9am–3pm, Thurs 9am–9pm; charge, free Thurs).

At no. 419, the **Mexic-Arte Museum** (Mon–Thurs 10am–6pm, Fri & Sat 10am–5pm,
Sun noon–5pm; charge; ⓦmexic-artemuseum.org) has a collection of traditional and
contemporary Latin American art. What it lacks in space it makes up for with its
strong selection – most of which is of Mexican origin – and studied arrangement.

Sixth Street and around

The party-oriented **Sixth Street** crosses Congress and at night it is crowded with
bar-hopping party people. If you're touring downtown during the day, visit the tiny
O. Henry Museum at 409 E 5th St (Wed–Sun noon–5pm; free; ⓦaustintexas.gov/
department/o-henry-museum), a period home dedicated to one of the literary lions of
Texas, William Sydney Porter (note the rosewood piano with mother-of-pearl inlay), or
cool off anytime in the elegant lobby of the *Driskill Hotel*, at Sixth and Brazos (see page
69), On Saturday morning, it's worth perusing the city's excellent **farmers' market**
(Sat 9am–1pm), at Republic Square Park, W Fifth and Guadalupe streets.

West of downtown but within walking distance at the intersection of N Lamar
Boulevard and Sixth Street, are **Waterloo Records** (600 N Lamar Blvd) and **Book People**
(603 N Lamar Blvd), the best music store and bookstore, respectively, in town. The
flagship **Whole Foods** (525 N Lamar Blvd) grocery store is also here (see map page 67).

1

THE CONGRESS AVENUE BRIDGE BATS

If you're visiting between March and November, take a walk at dusk down to where Congress Avenue crosses Lady Bird Lake to watch 1.5 million **Mexican free-tailed bats** – the world's largest urban bat colony – emerge in an amorphous black cloud from their hangout under the bridge. (Note: bat sightings are not guaranteed!) While the views from the bridge are great, you do have to contend with traffic, crowds and the smell of guano (or bat poop); other options include viewing the mass exodus from below on a Capital Cruise tour boat (𝕎 capitalcruises.com/bat-watching) or from the *Austin American-Statesman's* Bat Observation Center on the bridge's southeast side.

South Congress

Across the bridge from downtown, **South Congress** – or SoCo, as it's known – is a friendly strip of hip stores, bars and restaurants. With so many places that invite lingering, it's easy to whittle away an afternoon or evening here. Be sure to visit Uncommon Objects for unusual antiques and Allen's Boots for top-end Western wear. Several of this city's famous **food carts and trailers** parked streetside sell home-made snacks including cupcakes, tacos and barbecue sandwiches to keep you fuelled; check out 𝕎 austinfoodcarts.com for who's around.

Zilker Park and the Umlauf Sculpture Garden

2100 Barton Springs Rd · **Barton Springs Pool** Late April to late Feb Mon–Wed & Fri–Sun 5am–10pm, Thurs 5–9am & 7–10pm · Charge, cash only · 𝕎 austintexas.gov/department/barton-springs-pool · **Umlauf Sculpture Garden** Tues–Fri 10am–4pm, Sat & Sun 11am–4pm · Charge · 𝕎 umlaufsculpture.org

Austin is blessed with many fine green spaces, perhaps none more appealing than the 350-acre **Zilker Park**, a perfect retreat on sultry Austin afternoons. One of its main attractions is the spring-fed, deliciously cool and expansive **Barton Springs Pool**; even if you choose not to take a dip, it's still a great spot to see the full spectrum of Austin's denizens. Another appealing outdoor space, south of the pool on Robert E. Lee Road, is the **Umlauf Sculpture Garden**, a tranquil, grassy enclave dotted with more than one hundred works in bronze, terracotta, wood and marble.

The University of Texas

The campus is north of downtown and largely bounded by MLK Jr Blvd, Guadalupe St, Dean Keeton St and Red River St · 𝕎 utexas.edu

The **University of Texas** – and its fiercely supported Longhorn football team (𝕎 texassports.com), which plays on fall Saturdays at the 100,000-fan capacity Darrell K. Royal-Texas Memorial Stadium – has a tangible, almost defining, presence in Austin. You'll find most student activity in the inexpensive restaurants, vintage clothing shops and bookstores on the "Drag", the stretch of **Guadalupe Street** that runs along campus north from Martin Luther King Boulevard to 24th.

The campus

Oil has made "UT" one of the world's richest universities – its endowment is the second largest in the country – and its purchasing power is almost unmatched when it comes to rare and valuable books. The university's collection of manuscripts is available to scholars amid tight security in the **Harry Ransom Center**, in the southwest corner of campus, which houses a gallery (Tues–Fri 10am–5pm, Sat & Sun noon–5pm; free; 𝕎 hrc.utexas.edu) whose permanent collection includes a **Gutenberg Bible** and the **world's first photograph**. The quiet and beautiful **Battle Hall** houses UT's architecture library; note the stencilled open-truss ceiling. The best views in Austin are at sunset

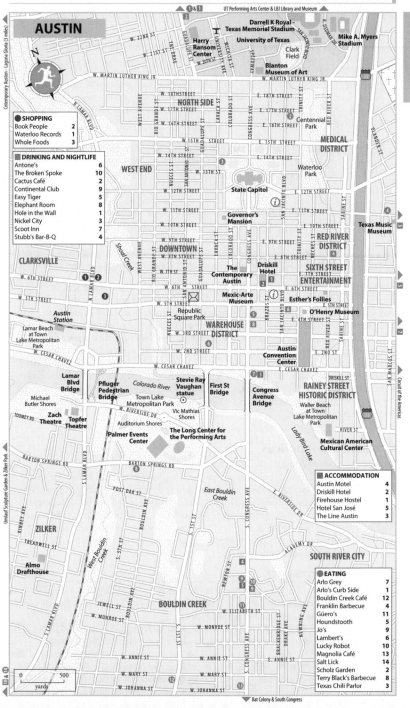

AUSTIN

Contemporary Austin – Laguna Gloria (3 miles)

UT Performing Arts Center & LBJ Library and Museum

Darrell K Royal –
Texas Memorial Stadium

University of Texas

Mike A. Myers
Stadium

Harry
Ransom
Center

Clark
Field

Blanton
Museum of Art

W. MARTIN LUTHER KING JR.

W. MARTIN LUTHER KING JR.

NORTH SIDE

Centennial
Park

**MEDICAL
DISTRICT**

● SHOPPING	
Book People	2
Waterloo Records	1
Whole Foods	3

■ DRINKING AND NIGHTLIFE	
Antone's	6
The Broken Spoke	10
Cactus Café	2
Continental Club	9
Easy Tiger	5
Elephant Room	8
Hole in the Wall	1
Nickel City	3
Scoot Inn	7
Stubb's Bar-B-Q	4

WEST END

Waterloo
Park

State Capitol

Governor's
Mansion

**RED RIVER
DISTRICT**

Texas Music
Museum

CLARKSVILLE

DOWNTOWN

The
Contemporary
Austin

Driskill
Hotel

**SIXTH STREET
ENTERTAINMENT**

Mexic-Arte
Museum

Esther's Follies

O'Henry Museum

Republic
Square Park

**WAREHOUSE
DISTRICT**

Austin
Station

Austin
Convention
Center

**RAINEY STREET
HISTORIC DISTRICT**

Lamar
Blvd
Bridge

Pfluger
Pedestrian
Bridge

Colorado River

Stevie Ray
Vaughan
statue

First St
Bridge

Congress
Avenue
Bridge

Waller Beach
at Town
Lake Metropolitan
Park

Michael
Butler Shores

Town Lake
Metropolitan Park

Lamar Beach
at Town
Lake Metropolitan
Park

Zach
Theatre

Topfer
Theatre

Vic Mathias
Shores

Auditorium Shores

Palmer Events
Center

The Long Center for
the Performing Arts

Mexican American
Cultural Center

ZILKER

East Bouldin
Creek

SOUTH RIVER CITY

Almo
Drafthouse

● ACCOMMODATION	
Austin Motel	4
Driskill Hotel	2
Firehouse Hostel	1
Hotel San José	5
The Line Austin	3

BOULDIN CREEK

● EATING	
Arlo Grey	7
Arlo's Curb Side	1
Bouldin Creek Café	12
Franklin Barbecue	4
Güero's	11
Houndstooth	5
Jo's	9
Lambert's	6
Lucky Robot	10
Magnolia Café	13
Salt Lick	14
Scholz Garden	2
Terry Black's Barbecue	8
Texas Chili Parlor	3

Umlauf Sculpture Garden & Zilker Park

Bat Colony & South Congress

0   500
yards

1

SXSW

Austin's ten-day **SXSW festival** (South by Southwest; ⓦ sxsw.com), held in mid-March, has become the pre-eminent music and film conference in the nation – and quite a bit more besides. In recent years it's also morphed into one of the nation's foremost stages for tech companies to display their latest creations, reflecting Austin's surging stock in the industry. However, it's not cheap: passes for all film, music and interactive events cost over $1600 in advance, increasing to over $1800 for a walk-up rate; you can also buy separate music-, film- and interactive-only passes as well at a reduced cost.

Even if you can't afford to attend, the city is an exciting place to be during SXSW and there are literally hundreds of **unofficial gigs and events** open to all. To most locals, in fact, what's going on inside the conference is of secondary importance to the opportunity to catch some of the best acts on the planet in their favourite haunts.

from the top of the **Texas Tower**, near the corner of 24th and Guadalupe (check website for schedule; charge; ⓦ tower.utexas.edu; reservations required).

LBJ Library and Museum

2313 Red River St • Daily 9am–5pm • Charge • ⓦ lbjlibrary.org

The **LBJ Library and Museum**, on the eastern edge of the UT campus, traces the career of the brash and egotistical Lyndon Baines Johnson from his origins in the Hill Country to the House of Representatives, the Senate and the White House. Forty-five million documents are housed here and it's worth a visit. JFK is said to have made Johnson his vice president to avoid his establishing a rival power base; but in the aftermath of Kennedy's assassination, Johnson's administration (1963–69) was able to push through a radical social programme; indeed, Barack Obama's 2010 healthcare bill was hailed as the most meaningful domestic legislation since the civil rights advancements of the LBJ era. The military thorn in Johnson's side, Vietnam, is presented here as an awful mess left by Kennedy for him to clear up, at the cost of great personal anguish.

Circuit of the Americas

9201 Circuit of the Americas Blvd • Event prices vary • ⓦ circuitoftheamericas.com

Purpose-built in 2012 to bring European Formula 1 racing to the US, this 3.4-mile undulating track about ten miles from downtown is dynamic even when empty. When not hosting the annual United States Grand Prix, it serves as the site for other racing contests, concerts and other entertainments (sometimes in its outdoor amphitheatre Austin360), and auto or architecture fans can tour the space and oversee the entire 1500-acre property from its 250ft tower (tours are given periodically, typically on weekends; check website for details).

ARRIVAL AND INFORMATION   AUSTIN

By plane Flights arrive at the Austin-Bergstrom International Airport (ⓦ austintexas.gov/airport), 8 miles southeast of town. It's around 20min to downtown Austin by taxi (Yellow Cab; ☎ 512 452 9999), while bus #100 runs pretty regularly every 20min (except late at night and early in the morning).

By bus The Greyhound bus station (☎ 512 458 4463) is around 5 miles north of downtown Austin situated on 916 E Koenig Lane.

Destinations Dallas (10 daily; 3hr 45min); Fort Worth (daily; 4hr); Houston (daily; 3hr); San Antonio (10 daily; 1hr 40min).

By train The Amtrak station (☎ 512 476 5684) is at the western edge of downtown at 250 N Lamar Blvd.

Destinations Dallas (1 daily; 5hr 50min); Houston (1 daily; 3hr 25min); San Antonio (1 daily; 3hr 25min).

Visitor centre 602 E 4th St (Mon–Fri 9am–5pm, Sat & Sun 10am–5pm; ☎ 866 GO AUSTIN, ⓦ austintexas.org).

GETTING AROUND

By bus The Capital METRO (w capmetro.org) runs buses downtown, crosstown and through the campus.

By MetroRail The commuter MetroRail route runs north 32 miles from downtown to the city of Leander.

On foot and by bike Austin is perfectly manageable on foot, as most of what you'll likely want to see is relatively close together. It also has one of the best networks of bike paths in the USA. Rent from Trek Bicycle Lamar, 517 S Lamar Blvd, just south of Barton Springs (w trekbikes. com). A downloadable city bike map is available from w austintexas.gov; the visitor centre and local bike shops have hard copies of it as well as of the excellent Town Lake Hike and Bike Trail.

ACCOMMODATION · SEE MAP PAGE 67

★ **Austin Motel** 1220 S Congress Ave w austinmotel. com. Stylish retro rooms in a trendy old motel in hip SoCo. A favourite with visiting musicians, it's across from the venerable *Continental Club*. $$$

The Driskill 604 Brazos St w driskillhotel.com. This handsome and historic downtown hotel is Austin's swankiest choice, with an opulent marble lobby and classily decorated rooms. If you can't afford to stay, drop by the lobby bar for a mid-afternoon whiskey sour. $$$$

Firehouse Hostel 605 Brazos St w firehousehostel. com. Bargain rates right in the heart of downtown, with cosy dorms and rooms (some en-suite) in a converted 19th-century fire station. Most of the guests head out to 6th St at night or hang in the on-site Firehouse Lounge. Dorms $, doubles $$

Hotel San José 1316 S Congress Ave w sanjosehotel. com. Chic boutique hotel in the SoCo district. Restored from an old motel, it has a variety of minimalist rooms, some with shared bath, along with lovely gardens and a tiny pool and is adjacent to *Jo's* coffeeshop (see below), which provides room service. The courtyard happy hour attracts a local crowd for Micheladas, a spicy beer cocktail on the rocks. $$$$

The Line Austin 111 E Cesar Chavez St w thelinehotel. com/austin. The rooms, kitted out with sleek grey carpet, local art and wood-block accents, are eminently comfortable. The hotel sports two notable all-day restaurants, the rooftop P6 cocktail bar, a pool and fitness room, and it's conveniently located for downtown sight-seeing at the head of the Congress St Bridge. $$$$

EATING · SEE MAP PAGE 67

CAFÉS

Houndstooth 401 N Congress Ave w houndstooth coffee.com. A modern spot for ultra-serious coffee drinkers; the staff and baristas are as friendly as they are knowledgeable. Locally owned and operated, with three other Austin locations. $

Jo's 1300 S Congress Ave w joscoffee.com. The original *Jo's* and still much beloved, this eclectic coffee spot serves drinks made from local roasts as well as a nice selection of breakfast tacos and filling sandwiches, as well as baked goods. The downtown location is at 242 W 2nd St. $

RESTAURANTS

Arlo's Curb Side 2908 Fruth St w arloscurbside.com. This insider favourite is a food truck outside *The Ballroom @ Spiderhouse* live venue, specializing in plant-based (i.e. vegan) comfort food, with sensational burgers and tacos (featuring ingredients like house-made seitan "bac'n" and patties, frito pie and *pico de gallo*). $

Arlo Grey 111 E Cesar Chavez St w thelinehotel.com. Elegant contemporary restaurant inside The Line hotel helmed by winner of hit US TV show "Top Chef" Kristen Kish, with Central Texas produce blended with French and Italian influenced dishes. $$$

Bouldin Creek Café 1900 S 1st St w bouldincreekcafe. com. Breakfast made from scratch is served all day at this buzzing vegetarian-only spot not far from SoCo. It has reasonable prices (try the free-range, three-egg omelette with two sides) and friendly staff. $$

★ **Franklin Barbecue** 900 E 11th St w franklinbbq. com. Long queues form well before this place opens – and it's easy to see why. Plates like brisket (priced per pound) and pulled pork exude more flavour than seems possible from mere meat, and desserts like banana bourbon pie are a decadent end to a lunch that is every bit worth the wait. $$

Güero's 1412 S Congress Ave w gueros.com. *Tacos al pastor* and fajitas are specialities at this busy, sprawling restaurant across the bridge, south of downtown. Vegan and gluten-free options, too. $

Lambert's 401 W 2nd St w lambertsaustin.com. Exercise your taste buds at this self-described "fancy barbeque" restaurant that puts a modern twist on the old Texas staple. Produce and meats are sourced from local farms and ranches. The oak-smoked pork ribs are excellent, as is the grilled gulf fish with low country rice. $$$

Lucky Robot 1303 S Congress Ave w luckyrobotatx. com Seek out this SoCo spot for the inventive sushi roll combinations, with specials like Voltron or Transformer and bowls, and the playfully artsy decor. (That mini R2D2 on your table? He dispenses soy sauce.) $$

Magnolia Café 1920 S Congress Ave w magnolia cafeaustin.com. A 24hr joint that's a local favourite for

1

Tex-Mex and cornmeal or gingerbread pancake breakfasts. A great place to refuel after a night living it up in SoCo. $\overline{\$\$}$

★ **Salt Lick** 18300 FM 1826, Driftwood Ⓦ saltlickbbq. com. A regular 30min pilgrimage for Austin's meat-lovers. This is the original location and the queues are every bit as long as they've always been; the brisket plates are still the main reason why. The atmosphere is exceedingly friendly and the conversation between strangers flows freely. Cash only and BYOB. $\overline{\$\$}$

Scholz Garten 1607 San Jacinto Blvd Ⓦ scholzgarten. com. This venerable German restaurant dates back to the bar opened by German immigrant August Scholz in 1866. It's since become a beloved local institution, and a popular spot to watch University of Texas football games. All the

classics are served: wienerschnitzel, beef tips and spätzle, bratwurst, currywurst and more. $\overline{\$\$}$

Terry Black's Barbecue 1003 Barton Springs Rd Ⓦ terryblacksbbq.com. An Austin institution, this no frills barbecue shack is part of a mini Texan (Lockhart) chain knocking out mouthwatering sliced brisket, jalapeno cheese sausage, pork ribs, turkey and a range of sides – you can also get the cheaper sandwiches. $\overline{\$\$}$

Texas Chili Parlor 1409 Lavaca St ☏ 512 472 2828. Rub shoulders with politicians and their staffers at this venerable lunch spot downtown near the State Capitol. The chilli comes in bowls of several varieties; the XXX version is hot enough to melt Formica. $\overline{\$}$

DRINKING AND NIGHTLIFE SEE MAP PAGE 67

Austin's **live music scene** is legendary – and rightly so. Though the clubs and bars of Sixth Street are touristy and jammed with drunken 20-somethings, there are plenty of good places elsewhere downtown, and it's easy enough to hop in a cab to some of the further-flung classic joints. Many of the **bars** double as music venues. Two newspapers carry listings: the daily *Austin American-Statesman* (Ⓦ statesman.com/austin360) and the alt-weekly *Austin Chronicle* (Ⓦ austinchronicle.com), as do the websites Ⓦ austintexas.org and Ⓦ do512.com.

BARS

★ **Easy Tiger** 1501 E 7th St Ⓦ easytigerusa.com. Always-packed beer garden close to downtown that also sports a bakery (grab a sensational chocolate chip cookie if you're feeling peckish). The stylish interior has exposed brick walls and arcade games, while outside there are ping pong tables, a container bar and dog-friendly park. Thirty draught beers as well as an impressive whiskey list and pub food including home-made sausages in pretzel buns.

Hole in the Wall 2538 Guadalupe St Ⓦ holeinthe wallaustin.com. Long-running dive near the UT campus with pool tables, live Americana music and dirt-cheap drinks.

Nickel City 1133 E 11th St Ⓦ nickelcitybar.com. Not too far from Franklin Barbecue (see page 69), this non-snooty local watering hole offers quality mixed drinks in a dive-ish setting, and has amassed resident fans on the way to being voted by several bar associations as one of the best in the US. Cheap enjoyable munchies provided by the Delray Café food truck installed at the end of the patio.

Scoot Inn 1308 E 4th St Ⓦ scootinnaustin.com. Owned by

the same folks who ran the sadly departed *Long Branch Inn*, this place attracts a similar but slightly younger crowd and has a nice outdoor beer garden and an eclectic live music calendar showcasing local talent.

LIVE MUSIC VENUES

★ **Antone's** 305 E 5th St Ⓦ antonesnightclub.com This historic Austin joint thankfully remains the best blues club in the city, a hot and sweaty haunt showcasing national and local acts.

The Broken Spoke 3201 S Lamar Blvd Ⓦ brokenspoke austintx.net. Neighbourhood restaurant (good chicken-fried steak) and foot-stomping honky-tonk dance hall in South Austin. The barn-like dance floor attracts great country acts; it's a lot of fun.

Cactus Café 2247 Guadalupe St Ⓦ cactuscafe.org. A bar and folk-oriented live music venue in the UT student union building that's an excellent spot to catch acoustic acts.

★ **Continental Club** 1315 S Congress Ave Ⓦ continentalclub.com. This long-standing classic is the city's premier place to hear hard-edged country or bluesy folk sung the Austin way.

Elephant Room 315 Congress Ave Ⓦ elephantroom. com. Austin's best spot for live jazz, this understated underground bar is dark and cramped, but consistently showcases stellar acts.

Stubb's Bar-B-Q 801 Red River St Ⓦ stubbsaustin.com. Indoor and outdoor stages feature eclectic bands of national repute – including a Sunday gospel brunch – which you can watch while chomping on great Texas-style brisket, sausage and ribs.

ENTERTAINMENT

★ **Alamo Drafthouse (South Lamar)** 1120 S Lamar Blvd Ⓦ drafthouse.com. The Alamo Drafthouse, with several locations, offers one of the best cinematic experiences in the USA. The theatres feature everything from pre-movie, title-specific montages to award-winning

documentaries – and pints of local beer and made-to-order food are served right at your comfy seat.

Esther's Follies 525 E 6th St Ⓦ esthersfollies.com. Austin's coolest cabaret spot combines spoofs of local and national politicians with Texas-style singing and dancing.

THE AUSTIN SOUND

Although Austin's folk revival in the 1960s attracted enough attention to propel Janis Joplin on her way from Port Arthur, Texas, to stardom in California, the city first achieved prominence in its own right as the centre of **outlaw country** music in the 1970s. **Willie Nelson** and **Waylon Jennings**, disillusioned with Nashville, spearheaded a movement that reworked country with an incisive injection of rock'n'roll. Venues like the now-closed *Armadillo World Headquarters*, far removed from the more conservative honky-tonks of the Plains, provided an environment that encouraged and rewarded risk-taking, experimentation and lots of sonic cross-breeding. These days the predominant **Austin sound** is a melange of country, folk and the blues, with strong psychedelic and alternative influences – but the scene is entirely eclectic. The tradition of black Texas bluesmen like Blind Lemon Jefferson and Blind Willie Johnson, as well as the rocking bar blues of Stevie Ray Vaughan, lives on through a top-notch **blues** club in the form of *Antone's*. And whatever the genre, the tradition of live music endures in the Austin City Limits series (ⓦacltv.com); concert performances in an intimate space downtown have been taped and broadcast on public television for more than forty years.

UT Performing Arts Center 23rd St and Robert Dedman Drive ⓦtexasperformingarts.org. The university's Performing Arts Center boasts a calendar filled with world-class events, from international dance troupes to plays and live-music acts. As you might expect, the busiest times of the year coincide with term-time.

The Hill Country

The rolling hills, lakes and valleys of the **HILL COUNTRY**, north and west of Austin and San Antonio, were inhabited mostly by Apache and Comanche until after statehood in 1845, when German and Scandinavian settlers arrived. Many of the log-cabin farming communities they established are still here, such as **New Braunfels** (famous for its sausages and pastries, and, more recently, its watersports), **Fredericksburg** and **Luckenbach**. You may still hear German spoken, and the German influence is also felt in local food and music; *conjunto*, for example, is a blend of Tex-Mex and accordion music. The whole region is a popular retreat and resort area, with some wonderful hill views and lake swimming, and some good places to camp.

New Braunfels

NEW BRAUNFELS, thirty miles north of San Antonio on I-35, was founded by German immigrants – mostly artisans and artists – in 1845 and quickly became a trade centre. Nowadays, the community, along with its equally historic satellite, **Gruene**, just northeast, makes its living from tourism. The town's two rivers – the Comal and the Guadalupe – are ideal for easy **rafting** and **tubing**, making this a popular weekend destination. If outdoor activities don't appeal, head downtown; the historic district has enough antique stores, galleries and restored buildings to fill a couple of hours.

INFORMATION AND ACTIVITIES   NEW BRAUNFELS

Visitor centre Exit 187 off I-35, 390 S Seguin Ave (Mon–Thurs 8am–5pm, Fri 8am–4pm; ☎800 572 2626, ⓦnewbraunfels.com); provides a list of accommodation, as well as information on renting rafts and tubes.

Rafting and tubing The long-running Rockin' R, 1405 Gruene Rd (ⓦrockinr.com), is one of the best outfits in town, offering raft and tube rentals and group tours of the Guadalupe River.

ACCOMMODATION, EATING, DRINKING AND ENTERTAINMENT

Gruene Hall 1281 Gruene Rd ⓦgruenehall.com. Top country stars have been performing for decades at the atmospheric clapboard *Gruene Hall*, and it's usually packed out. Drinks are cash only.

1

Heidelberg Lodges 1020 N Houston St ⓦheidelberg lodges.com. The various rooms, suites and two-bedroom cottages on offer here are rustic, though their river-front location on the Comal makes them a good deal. Motel rooms $\overline{\$\$}$, efficiencies/two bedrooms $\overline{\$\$\$}$

Huisache Grill 303 W San Antonio St ⓦhuisachegrill. com. The *Huisache Grill* serves sophisticated, reasonably priced contemporary cuisine such as grilled portobello sandwich for lunch and pecan-crusted pork tenderloin for dinner. $\overline{\$\$}$

Pat's Place 202 S Union Ave ⓦpatsplacenbtx.com. Popular with locals for its casual setting and rock-bottom prices, *Pat's* doles out basic pub food crowd-pleasers, with pretty much everything great value. $\overline{\$}$

Fredericksburg

On weekends in **FREDERICKSBURG**, crowds of well-heeled day-trippers from San Antonio and Austin throng Main Street's cutesy speciality stores and fancy tearooms. Several original structures make up the **Pioneer Museum** at 325 W Main St, including a church and a store (Mon–Sat 10am–5pm; charge; ⓦpioneermuseum.org). A little more incongruous here, the **National Museum of the Pacific War**, 340 E Main St (Mon & Wed–Sun 9am–5pm; charge; ⓦpacificwarmuseum.org), features a Japanese garden of peace and lays out a historical trail past aircraft, tanks and heavy artillery. That a World War II museum commemorating ocean battles is located in landlocked Fredericksburg is due to the town's being the birthplace of Admiral Charles W. Nimitz, who commanded the US Navy's Pacific fleet.

ACCOMMODATION FREDERICKSBURG

Full Moon Inn 3234 Luckenbach Rd ⓦfullmooninn. com. Attractive lodgings in rural cottages and cabins in the sleepy musical hamlet of Luckenbach, 10 miles southeast of Fredericksburg, immortalized in song by both Willie Nelson and Waylon Jennings. There are opportunities for swimming and fishing on the property's twelve acres, and breakfast is included. $\overline{\$\$}$

Lady Bird Johnson RV Park Campground 432 Lady Bird Drive ⓦreserveamerica.com. Field camping in the lovely surrounds of Lady Bird Johnson Municipal Park, 3 miles to the southwest off Hwy-16. $\overline{\$}$

Sunday House 501 E Main St ⓦsundayhouseinn.com. Of the numerous budget hotels along E Main St, this stately place is one of the more luxurious. Amenities include an outdoor pool and flatscreen TVs. $\overline{\$\$}$

EATING AND DRINKING

Becker Vineyards 464 Becker Farms Rd, Stonewall ⓦbeckervineyards.com. The Hill Country is a booming wine region, and the best of the bunch is Becker Vineyards, in an atmospheric stone barn 11 miles east of Fredericksburg, off Hwy-290. A bottle of Becker's tempranillo reserve is a great buy.

Friedhelm's Bavarian Inn 905 W Main St ☎830 997 6300. You can eat substantially and well at this German-inspired old-school restaurant, which specializes in heaped plates of hearty Bavarian fare. A sure bet: order from their 'Schnitzel Bank'. Should reopen in 2023 after a major renovation. $\overline{\$\$}$

Opa's Smoked Meat 410 S Washington St ⓦopas smokedmeats.com. If you're looking to stock up for a Hill Country picnic or day-trip, be sure to stop by *Opa's* first. There's a bewildering number of smoked meat varieties, including bratwurst and jalapeño beef sausage with cheddar as well as dense deli sandwiches and German side dishes and baked goods. Be sure to grab a pack of Opa's Sweet Fire Pickles to round everything off. $\overline{\$}$

San Antonio

With neither the modern skyline of an oil metropolis, nor the tumbleweed-strewn landscape of the Wild West, attractive and festive **SAN ANTONIO** looks nothing like the stereotypical image of Texas – despite being pivotal in the state's history. Standing at a geographical crossroads, it encapsulates the complex social and ethnic mixes of all of Texas. Although the Germans, among others, have made a strong cultural contribution, today's San Antonio is predominantly **Hispanic**. Now the seventh largest city in the USA, it retains an unhurried, organic feel and is one of the most pleasant places in Texas to spend a few days.

San Antonio is a delight to walk around, as its main attractions, including the pretty **River Walk**, the **Alamo**, **Market Square** and **HemisFair Park**, are all within strolling distance of each other. Slightly further out, but still accessible on foot, is the **King William Historic District** and the neighbouring **Blue Star Contemporary Arts Center**.

Brief history

Founded in 1691 by Spanish missionaries, San Antonio became a military garrison in 1718, and was settled by the Anglos in the 1720s and 1730s under Austin's colonization programme. It is most famous for the legendary **Battle of the Alamo**, in 1836, when General Santa Anna wiped out a band of ragtag Texas volunteers seeking independence from Mexico. After the Civil War, it became a hard-drinking, hard-fighting "sin city", at the heart of the Texas **cattle and oil empires**. Drastic floods in the 1920s wiped out much of the downtown area, but the sensitive **WPA programme** that revitalized two of the city's prettiest sites, **La Villita** and the **River Walk**, laid the foundations for its future as a major tourist destination. In recent years several massive hotels (think Vegas) have been constructed to accommodate the booming tourism and convention industries. The **military** has a major presence in San Antonio, too, with four bases in the metropolitan area.

The River Walk

Since mission times, the **San Antonio River** has been vital to the city's fortunes. Destructive floods in the 1920s and subsequent oil drilling reduced its flow, leading to plans to pave the river over. Instead, a careful landscaping scheme, started in 1939 by the WPA, created the Paseo del Rio, or **River Walk** (W thesanantonioriverwalk.com) now the aesthetic and commercial focus of San Antonio. The walk, located below street level, is reached by steps from various spots along the main roads and crossed by humpbacked stone bridges. Cobbled paths, shaded by pine, cypress, oak and willow trees, wind for 2.5 miles beside the jade-green water, with many of the city's dining and entertainment options strewn along the way.

La Villita

La Villita ("Little Town"; W lavillitasanantonio.com), on the River Walk opposite HemisFair Park, was San Antonio's original settlement, occupied in the mid- to late eighteenth century by Mexican "squatters" with no titles to the land. Only when its elevation enabled it to survive fierce floods in 1819 did this rude collection of stone and adobe buildings become suddenly respectable. It is now a National Historic District, turned over to a dubious "arts community" consisting mostly of overpriced craft shops.

The Alamo

300 Alamo Plaza • Daily 9am–5.30pm, summer 9am–7pm • Free • W thealamo.org

San Antonio's most distinctive landmark, the **Alamo**, lies smack in the centre of downtown. Inextricably associated with the battle that took place here in 1836, a defining moment in the Texas struggle for independence against Mexico, the Alamo has been immortalized in movies and songs, and exists now as a rallying cry for Texas spirit.

Its fame, however, has little to do with its original purpose. It was built in the eighteenth century by the Spanish, the first in a trail of **Catholic missions** established along remote stretches of the San Antonio River. The missions flourished from 1745 to 1775, but couldn't survive the ravages of disease and attack from the Apache and Comanche, and fell into disuse early in the nineteenth century.

The infamous **Battle of the Alamo** occurred on March 6, 1836, when five thousand Mexican troops assaulted the mission, which was defended by just under two hundred

1

volunteers dreaming of Texas autonomy. Driven by the battle cry of "Victory or Death!" the besieged band – a few native Hispanic-Texans, adventurers like Davy Crockett and Jim Bowie, and aspiring colonists from other states – held out for thirteen days against the Mexicans before their demise.

The site

Considering its fame, the Alamo is surprisingly small. All that is left of the original complex is its **chapel**, fronted by a large arched sandstone facade, and the **Long Barracks**. A stream of bus tours makes visits crowded and hectic; however, as it showcases the state's unique brand of pride and stubbornness, the Alamo is unmissable. No response but absolute reverence is permitted – a sign even insists visitors remove their hats. The grounds, with four acres of lush blooms, palms and cacti, are a haven from the commotion outside the grounds.

Buckhorn Saloon and Museum

318 E Houston St • Daily: summer 10am–8pm; rest of year 10am–5pm • Saloon free; upstairs museum charge • ⓦ buckhornmuseum.com

For a jaw-dropping slice of kitsch Americana, the **Buckhorn Saloon and Museum** can't be beat. During San Antonio's heyday as a cowtown, cowboys, trappers and traders

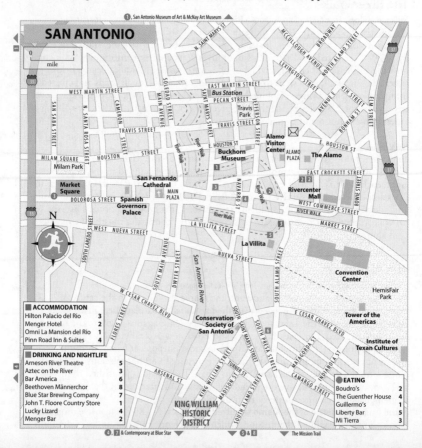

would bring their cattle horns to the original *Buckhorn Saloon* in exchange for a drink. The entire bar, a vast and lively Old West-themed space, has since been transplanted to this downtown location, where you can enjoy a mug of beer and a steak in the presence of hundreds of mounted horns and antlers. It is well worth exploring the extra floor, which displays a staggering collection of wildlife trophies and includes an informative and entertaining museum of Texas history.

San Fernando Cathedral and Market Square

San Antonio's Hispanic heart beats strongly west of the river. Nowhere is this more visible than at the **San Fernando Cathedral**, 115 W Main Plaza, established in 1731 and one of the oldest cathedrals in the USA. Mariachi Mass is held every Saturday at 5pm, when crowds overflow onto the plaza.

Market Square, a couple of blocks further northwest, dates from 1840. Its festive outdoor restaurants and stalls make it an appealing destination, especially during fiestas like Cinco de Mayo and the Day of the Dead. Fruit and vegetables are on sale early in the morning, while the shops are a compelling mix of colour and kitsch. **El Mercado**, an indoor complex, sells tourist-oriented gifts, jewellery and oddities.

HemisFair Park

200 S Alamo St • Daily 5am–midnight • Ⓦ hemisfair.org

It's a long walk on a hot day through the enormous **HemisFair Park** – a sprawling campus of administrative buildings with scant lawns – to the **Institute of Texan Cultures**, 801 E Durango Blvd (Thurs–Sun 10am–4pm; donation; Ⓦ texancultures.utsa. edu), but it's worth the trip. Mapping the social histories of 26 diverse Texas cultures, this lively museum has especially pertinent African American and Native American sections. Also in the park, the touristy 750ft **Tower of the Americas** (Mon–Thurs & Sun 10am–10pm, Fri & Sat 10am–11pm; Ⓦ toweroftheamericas.com) offers big views from its observation deck (charge).

King William Historic District

The 25-block **King William Historic District**, between the river and S Alamo Street, offers a different flavour to the city's sleeker pockets, its shady streets lined with the elegant late nineteenth-century homes of German merchants. It remains a fashionable residential area and has some stylish B&Bs; pick up **self-guided walking tours** outside the headquarters of the Conservation Society of San Antonio, 107 King William St (Ⓦ saconservation.org).

The grassroots **Contemporary at Blue Star** at 116 Blue Star (Wed noon–5pm, Thurs & Fri noon–8pm, Sat & Sun 10am–6pn; free; Ⓦ contemporarysa.org) makes an appealingly rakish contrast to the rest of the neighbourhood, with its brewpub, workshops, galleries and crafts stores.

McNay Art Museum

6000 N New Braunfels Ave, at Austin Hwy • Wed & Fri 10am–6pm, Thurs 10am–9pm, Sat 10am–5pm, Sun noon–5pm • Charge • Ⓦ mcnayart.org

Art lovers flock to the **McNay Art Museum**, easily one of the city's most beloved, as much for its exquisite exhibitions as for its striking architecture and the otherworldly escape it provides. This Moorish-style villa, complete with tranquil garden, was built in the 1950s to house the art collection of millionaire folk artist Marion Koogler McNay, and includes works from major players like Hopper and O'Keeffe. There's also a good roster of temporary exhibition, check online for details.

1

ARRIVAL AND DEPARTURE

By plane San Antonio International Airport (⊚flysan antonio.com) is just north of the I-410 loop that encircles most of the sights. VIA bus no.5 runs into downtown in around 30 minutes. A taxi ride to downtown costs about $28 (Yellow Cab; ☎210 222 2222). All the major car-rental agencies have counters in Terminal A.

By bus Greyhound operates from 500 N St Mary's St (☎210 270 5815).

Destinations Austin (10 daily; 1hr 30min); Dallas (10 daily; 5hr); Fort Worth (6 daily; 7hr); Houston (7 daily; 3hr 30min).

By train Amtrak arrives centrally at 350 Hoefgen St.

Destinations Austin (1 daily; 3hr 25min); Dallas (1 daily; 8hr 20min); Fort Worth (1 daily; 7hr); Houston (1 daily; 4hr 45min).

GETTING AROUND AND INFORMATION

By bus or streetcar In addition to a relatively good bus network, three downtown streetcar routes from Alamo Plaza (and route 5 downtown from the airport) serve the major attractions (every 10min). A one-day pass available from the VIA Downtown Information Center, 211 W Commerce St (Mon–Fri 7am–6pm, Sat 9am–2pm; ⊚viai nfo.net) can be used on all buses and streetcars.

By bike Bikes can be rented from the Blue Star Bike Shop 1414 S Alamo St (⊚bluestarbikeshop) and are an excellent option for exploring neighbourhoods beyond the River Walk.

By car Driving in Texas' second largest city can be stressful and parking is expensive – thankfully, most of the main attractions are within walking distance of each other.

By boat Go Rio Cruises offers river tours that make a 35min circuit of the River Walk, departing from several locations (⊚goriocruises.com) as well as a boat taxi service.

Visitor centre 317 Alamo Plaza (daily 9am–5pm; ☎210 244 2000, ⊚visitsanantonio.com).

ACCOMMODATION

SEE MAP PAGE 74

The pleasure of a moonlit amble along the River Walk back to your hotel is one of the joys of visiting San Antonio, so it's worth paying more to **stay in the centre**. Motels are clustered near Market Square on the west side of downtown; just north of Brackenridge Park on Austin Hwy; or on I-35 north toward Austin.

Hilton Palacio del Rio 200 S Alamo St ⊚hilton.com. Modularly constructed for the 1968 World's Fair in just nine months, this hotel features spacious rooms with balconies overlooking the River Walk. Pricey in peak season, but offers a prime location. §§§§

Menger Hotel 204 Alamo Plaza ⊚mengerhotel.com. Bang by the Alamo, this atmospheric, historic hotel was a famous destination on the great cattle drives; Teddy

Roosevelt recruited his "Rough Riders" here in 1898 for the Spanish-American War. The rooms don't quite live up to the glamour of the lobby, bar and communal areas. §§

★ **Omni La Mansion del Rio** 112 College St ⊚omni hotels.com. Rooms at the nicest hotel property on the River Walk come with a full range of amenities and Spanish Colonial decor, and some have courtyard access to the heated pool. §§§

Pinn Road Inn & Suites 2327 Pinn Rd ⊚pinnroadinn. com. Not the most central option, but a great deal for the rate (particularly the suites) and it's just a 10min drive to downtown. Rooms have charmingly dated decor, but all are clean and nicely furnished, with flatscreen TVs; the suites are larger and have kitchenettes. §

EATING

SEE MAP PAGE 74

★ **Boudro's** 421 E Commerce St ⊚boudros.com. This stylish River Walk Tex-Mex bistro serves creative New American/Southwestern mains including mesquite-grilled quail, plus a wonderful guacamole made at your table, and some killer prickly-pear margaritas. §§§

The Guenther House 205 E Guenther St ⊚guenther house.com. An hour or two savouring the cookies and cakes in this airy flour-mill-cum-museum in the King William Historic District makes for a decadent outing, but for a real treat come early for scrumptious Southern-style breakfasts including biscuits and gravy and a buttermilk pancake platter. §

Guillermo's 618 McCullough Ave ⊚guillermos downtown.com. Close to the River Walk, this cosy restaurant serves heaps of lovingly prepared Italian-American comfort food, including pizzas and spinach and

mushroom lasagne. §§

Liberty Bar 1111 S Alamo St ⊚liberty-bar.com. Popular, inexpensive restaurant and bar in a historic building dating back to the nineteenth century. Most items are good value; rotating menus feature specials such as duck breast salad or wild boar sausage with potatoes. It's also hard to choose between the desserts here but just be sure you choose something (good places to start are with the Fresh Lime Chess Pie or Minerva Hobart's Coconut Cake with pineapple). §§

★ **Mi Tierra** 218 Produce Row ⊚mitierracafe.com. With its bedazzlement of *piñatas*, fairy lights and fiesta flowers, this festive 24hr institution (also home to mariachi band performances) is the highlight of Market Square, serving good, inexpensive Tex-Mex staples and delicious sugary cakes at its *panadería*. Great bar, too. §

Downtown, the River Walk offers rowdy **bars and clubs**. Somewhat less touristy, **Houston Street** is fast becoming a party strip with a crop of slick yuppie bars, while **South Alamo Street** has a smattering of great dives and live music joints. The year's biggest event is April's ten-day **Fiesta San Antonio** (ⓦfiestasanantonio.org), marking Texas's victory in the Battle of San Jacinto with parades, cook-outs and Latin music.

BARS

★ **Bar America** 723 S Alamo St ☎ 210 223 1285. Three pool tables, two rows of booths with well-worn orange vinyl seating and the best jukebox in town make this 30-year-old family-run dive a favourite for a cross-section of locals. Between drafts and bottles, nearly four dozen beer options. **Beethoven Männerchor** 422 Pereida St ⓦsouthtown beethoven.com. Just off S Alamo St in the King William District, this private club (regularly open to the public) and beer garden is devoted to the preservation of German music and language. On the first Friday of each month from 5pm to midnight, stop by for cheap beer and huge dollops of delicious potato salad.
Blue Star Brewing Company 1414 S Alamo St ⓦ bluestar brewing.com. Home brews (the cask-conditioned ale is an especially good bet), food and live music – from Texas swing to Latin – in an airy arts complex in the King William District.
Lucky Lizard 302 E Commerce St ⓦ luckylizardsportsbar. com. At street level just a few steps up from the River Walk,

this rowdy and youthful sports bar is frequented by locals who flock here for the cheap drink deals, late night bites and live games on TV.
Menger Bar 204 Alamo Plaza ⓦmengerhotel.com. Cigar-smoking, top-shelf whiskey drinkers will feel right at home in this *Menger Hotel* bar, built in 1887 as a copy of the House of Lords pub in London.

LIVE MUSIC AND DANCE VENUES

San Antonio's live music scene isn't terribly diverse, but there are plenty of places to catch an act. Just a short drive away in the Hill Country you'll find some great old rural dance halls, including *Gruene Hall* in New Braunfels (see page 71). For listings, check the free weekly *Current* (ⓦ sacurrent.com).
Arneson River Theatre ⓦlavillitasanantonio.com. At this outdoor venue on the River Walk opposite La Villita, you can watch Mexican folk music and dance on a stage separated from the audience by the river.
Aztec on the River 104 N St Marys St ⓦ livenation.com. An opulent, immaculate Art Deco theatre currently hosting short-run productions and musical acts ranging from Charlie Puth and George Clinton to Queen tribute bands.
John T. Floore Country Store 14492 Old Bandera Rd, Helotes ⓦliveatfloores.com. Old country dance hall 20 miles northwest of San Antonio, with renowned tamales (starchy, corn-based dough cooked in a leaf wrapper) and outdoor dancing at the weekend. The best bands in Texas play here regularly.

Dallas

Contrary to popular belief, there's no oil in status-conscious **DALLAS**. Since its founding in 1841 as a prairie trading post, by Tennessee lawyer John Neely Bryan and his Arkansas friend Joe Dallas, successive generations of **entrepreneurs** have amassed wealth here through trade and finance, first using cattle and later oil reserves as collateral. The power of **money** in Dallas was demonstrated in the late 1950s, when its financiers threw their weight behind integration – potentially racist restaurant owners and bus drivers were pressured not to resist the new policies and Dallas was spared major upheavals. The city's image, however, was forever changed by the **assassination** of President Kennedy in 1963, and it took the building of the Dallas/Fort Worth International Airport in the 1960s, and the twin successes of the *Dallas* TV show and the Cowboys football team in the 1970s (and early 1990s), to bring back some sense of confidence.

These days, the city's occasional stuffiness is tempered by a typically Texas delight in self-parody – this is, after all, the city that calls itself "Big D".

Downtown

Downtown Dallas is a paean to commerce. Studding the elegant modern skyline, many of its skyscrapers are landmarks themselves. The most noteworthy is **Fountain Place Tower**, 1445 Ross Ave, designed by I.M. Pei, its sharp edges reminiscent of a blue crystal. At night, two miles of green argon tubing delineate the 72-storey **Bank of**

1

America Plaza at 901 Main St (tallest building in the city at 921ft), while the **Reunion Tower (561ft)**, 300 Reunion Blvd, on the west side of downtown next to the Amtrak station, looks like a giant 1970s microphone. For big views of the Big D, head to the observation deck (ⓦreuniontower.com), where there's also a restaurant.

One refuge from the downtown hubbub is the incongruous Philip Johnson-designed **Thanks-Giving Square**, at the intersection of Akard, Ervay and Bryan streets and Pacific Avenue. The serene setting is marked by fountains, a pleasant garden and modern spiralling chapel with a stunning series of stained-glass ceiling panels.

The Arts District

On the northern edge of downtown, the surprisingly walkable **Arts District** is Dallas' high-culture headquarters. Its focal point, the **Dallas Museum of Art**, 1717 N Harwood St (Tues–Thurs 11am–5pm, Fri 11am–9pm, Sat & Sun 11am–5pm; free, charge for special exhibitions; ⓦdma.org), has an impressive pre-Columbian collection in the Gallery of the Americas, along with artefacts from Africa, Asia and the Pacific, plus works by European artists.

Across North Harwood Street, the **Nasher Sculpture Center** (Wed–Sun 11am–5pm; charge; ⓦnashersculpturecenter.org) has a few galleries inside, but saves the best of its collection for the garden. Don't miss Scott Burton's meditative installation *Schist Furniture Group (Settee with Two Chairs)*. Cross Flora Street to get to the smaller **Crow Museum of Asian Art** at no. 2010 (Tues–Sun 11am–5pm; free; ⓦcrowcollection.org), which fills its very peaceful space with delicately hewn works from China, Cambodia and India.

West End, Dealey Plaza and around

The restored red-brick warehouses of the **West End Historic District**, the site of the original 1841 settlement on Lamar and Munger streets, are filled with speciality stores and theme restaurants; it's a touristy place, thronged at weekends. A few blocks south and west lies **Dealey Plaza**, forever associated with the **Kennedy assassination**. A small green space beside Houston Street's triple underpass, it has become one of the most recognizable urban streetscapes in the world. Whenever you come, you will find tourists snapping pictures. One block east of Dealey Plaza, in the John F. Kennedy Memorial Plaza on Main and Market streets, is the striking **John F. Kennedy Memorial**, designed by Philip Johnson and opened in 1970. Walk inside the minimalist, open-air concrete structure and you will feel removed from the city.

The Sixth Floor Museum at Dealey Plaza
411 Elm St • Wed–Sun 10am–6pm • Charge • ⓦ jfk.org

The **Texas Schoolbook Depository** itself is now the Dallas County Administration Building, the penultimate floor of which houses **the Sixth Floor Museum at Dealey Plaza**. Displays build up a suspenseful narrative, culminating in the infamous juddering 8mm footage of Kennedy crumpling into Jackie's arms; the images remain deeply affecting. The "gunman's nest" has been re-created and, whatever you believe about Lee Harvey Oswald's guilt, it's chilling to look down at the streets below and imagine the mayhem the shooter must have seen that day.

City Hall and Pioneer Plaza

The city's main administrative district, on the south side of downtown, is focused around **City Hall**, a cantilevered upside-down pyramid designed in 1972 by I.M. Pei. The **library** is located near here, while **Pioneer Plaza**, at Young and Griffin streets, holds the world's largest bronze sculpture, a monument to the mighty cattle drives of the West by Texas artist Robert Summers. It depicts forty life-size longhorn steers marching down a natural landscape under the guidance of three cowboys. It is a peaceful space, with an adjacent old cemetery.

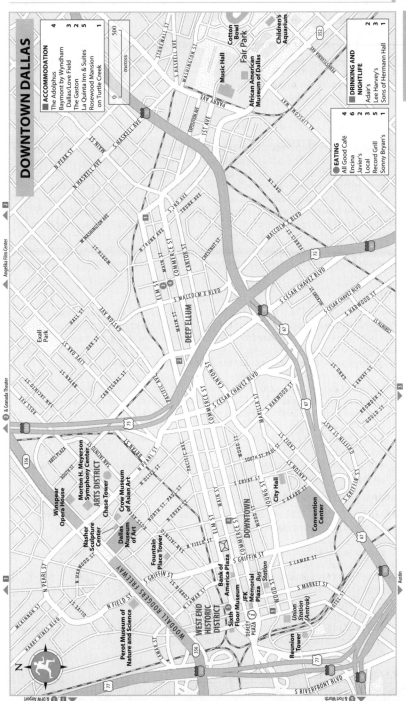

DOWNTOWN DALLAS

■ ACCOMMODATION

The Adolphus	4
Baymont by Wyndham Dallas/Love Field	3
The Gaston	2
La Quinta Inn & Suites	5
Rosewood Mansion on Turtle Creek	1

● EATING

All Good Café	4
Encina	6
Javier's	2
Local	3
Record Grill	5
Sonny Bryan's	1

■ DRINKING AND NIGHTLIFE

Adair's	2
Lee Harvey's	3
Sons of Hermann Hall	1

1

Dallas Heritage Village

1515 S Harwood St • Thurs–Sun 10am–4pm, to 9pm Thurs • Free • ⓦ oldcityparkdallas.org

Dallas's first park, **Old City Park**, is now both a recreational area and home to the **Dallas Heritage Village**, a living museum that charts the history of north Texas from 1840 to 1910. More than thirty buildings have been relocated to this bucolic spot south of I-30 from towns across the region, among them a farmhouse, a bank, a train station, a store, a church and a schoolhouse.

Deep Ellum

Deep Ellum – five blocks east of downtown between the railroad tracks and I-30 at Elm and Main streets – is the city's beguiling **alternative district** (ⓦ deepellumtexas.com). Famous in the 1920s for its jazz and blues clubs (and supposedly named by Blind Lemon Jefferson, though it's more likely to stem from the Southern pronunciation of "elm"), the old warehouse district has fallen on tough times in recent years. Locals say it earned an undeserved violent reputation (partly because of misinformation peddled by the mayor) and people stayed away. These days its bars, music clubs, galleries and restaurants – including some of the best in the city – are once again luring the crowds back. It's walkable and best visited in the late afternoon or early evening, when a gallery tour can be combined with a night out.

Fair Park

Not far southeast of Deep Ellum, **Fair Park**, a gargantuan Art Deco plaza bedecked with endless Lone Stars, was built to house the Texas Centennial Exposition in 1936, and now hosts the annual **State Fair of Texas** (ⓦ bigtex.com) for three weeks in October, the biggest event of its kind in the USA, with almost 2.25 million revellers on average. Its plethora of fine museums include the **African American Museum** (3536 Grand Ave; Tues–Fri 11am–5pm, Sat 10am–5pm; charge; ⓦ aamdallas.org), with a superb collection of folk art. The centrepiece of the park is the magnificent **Hall of State Building**, an Art Deco treasure of bronze statues, blue tiles, mosaics and murals, with rooms decorated to celebrate the different regions of Texas (3939 Grand Ave; Tues–Sat 10am–5pm, Sun 1–5pm; free).

In the Victory Park neighbourhood west of here, the **Perot Museum of Nature and Science** (2201 N Field St; Mon & Wed–Sat 10am–5pm, Sun 11am–5pm; charge; ⓦ perotmuseum.org) boasts exhibits on everything from fossils to dental hygiene. There are also plenty of child-friendly exhibits to keep the little ones entertained.

ARRIVAL AND DEPARTURE

DALLAS

By car Dallas proper is circled by Inner Loop 12 (or Northwest Hwy) and Outer Loop I-635 (which becomes LBJ Freeway).

By plane Dallas is served by two major airports. Dallas/Fort Worth (ⓦ dfwairport.com) is around 17 miles west. Dallas Area Rapid Transit (DART) light rail serves downtown Dallas, while the TEXRail station at Terminal B serves Fort Worth (ⓦ ridetrinitymetro.org/texrail-schedule). Taxis cost around $45 (Yellow Cab; ☎ 214 426 6262). The other airport, Love Field (ⓦ dallas-lovefield.com), used mostly by Southwest Airlines, lies about 9 miles northwest of Dallas. Taxis to downtown cost around $20.

By bus Greyhound is downtown at 205 S Lamar St.

Destinations Amarillo (3 daily; 6hr 50min); Austin (11 daily; 3hr 45min); El Paso (4 daily; 12hr 35min); Fort Worth (9 daily; 40min); Houston (10 daily; 4hr 10min); San Antonio (10 daily; 5hr).

By train Amtrak's 1916 Union Station is at 400 S Houston St. The Trinity Railway Express (ⓦ trinityrailwayexpress.org) service runs regular commuter trains between Dallas and Fort Worth.

Destinations Austin (1 daily; 5hr 50min); San Antonio (1 daily; 10hr 10min).

GETTING AROUND AND INFORMATION

By light rail or bus DART, the Dallas Area Rapid Transit system (ⓦ dart.org), is a light rail network that operates downtown and travels further afield to places including Mockingbird Station. Day passes are also good for the city's buses.

By tram (trolley) The free M-Line Trolley (Ⓦmata.org) runs north from the downtown Dallas Museum of Art up McKinney Ave to the West Village, a complex of restaurants and bars (every 15min Mon–Thur 7am–10pm, Fri 7am–midnight, Sat 10am–midnight, Sun 10am–10pm).

Visitor centre Downtown in the "Old Red" Courthouse, 100 S Houston St (daily 9am–5pm; ☎214 749 7730, Ⓦvisitdallas.com).

ACCOMMODATION   SEE MAP PAGE 79

★**The Adolphus** 1321 Commerce St Ⓦadolphus. com. Stunning historic downtown hotel, decorated with antiques. Said to be the most beautiful building west of Venice, Italy, when it was built in 1912, it's a glamorous place to stay. $\overline{\underline{$}}\overline{\underline{$}}\overline{\underline{$}}\overline{\underline{$}}$

Baymont by Wyndham Dallas/Love Field 2370 W Northwest Hwy Ⓦwyndhamhotels.com. Its location is anything but scenic, but the *Baymont* makes up for it with easy access to downtown and the airport, and comfortable accommodation at more than reasonable rates. Amenities include an indoor pool, gym and breakfast. $\overline{\underline{$}}$

★**The Gaston** 4802 Gaston Ave Ⓦthegaston.com. Fabulous B&B in Old East Dallas, just over two miles from

Downtown, with five luxurious rooms in a 1912 home – it's far more stylish and contemporary than the usual chintzy "Victorian" guesthouse. $\overline{\underline{$}}\overline{\underline{$}}$

La Quinta Inn & Suites 302 S Houston St Ⓦwyndham hotels.com. Good-value chain hotel with small, comfortable rooms and a decent continental breakfast. $\overline{\underline{$}}\overline{\underline{$}}$

Rosewood Mansion on Turtle Creek 2821 Turtle Creek Blvd Ⓦrosewoodhotels.com. Situated in a leafy Dallas neighbourhood, this is the city's most exclusive and expensive hotel; all its rooms and suites are exceedingly well appointed and stylish, with top-notch amenities including plush linens and large plasma TVs. It also features fine restaurants and a bar with terrace seating. $\overline{\underline{$}}\overline{\underline{$}}\overline{\underline{$}}\overline{\underline{$}}$

EATING   SEE MAP PAGE 79

Dallas's restaurant scene is largely defined by its **neighbourhoods**. Downtown, the **West End Historic District** is lively, if touristy, with rowdy chains; in hipper **Deep Ellum** you can chow down on anything from sushi to Mexican. Uptown, chic **West Village**, accessible on the McKinney Trolley, is a squeaky-clean cluster of bars and restaurants catering to youthful loft-dwellers. Northeast of downtown, parallel to I-75, **Lower Greenville Avenue** has a more eclectic feel.

★**All Good Café** 2934 Main St Ⓦallgoodcafe.com. Fresh home-style cooking at this cheery Deep Ellum haunt, which is more evocative of Austin than Dallas and transforms into a live Texas music venue in the evenings. Breakfast specials include the Hat Trick – *huevos rancheros* with peppered bacon and pancakes – while for dinner the short ribs are unfussy, carnivorous bliss. $\overline{\underline{$}}\overline{\underline{$}}$

Encina 614 W Davis St Ⓦencinadallas.com. Located in the (for Dallas) bohemian neighbourhood of Oak Cliff, this restaurant from chef Matt Balke focuses on fresh, local ingredients and attracts a young, professional crowd. Much of the menu is seasonal, with regular dishes such as tasty beer-battered catfish, goat guisada tacos and brisket and smoked gouda croquettes. $\overline{\underline{$}}\overline{\underline{$}}\overline{\underline{$}}$

Javier's 4912 Cole Ave Ⓦjaviers.net. At this handsome, long-running restaurant count on refreshingly traditional takes on Mexican food. It's not cheap, but the dishes are a revelation and include choices such as broiled shrimp in a diablo sauce (made from coffee, orange juice, tomato sauces and spices) and beef tenderloin stuffed with Chihuahua cheese and herbed butter. $\overline{\underline{$}}\overline{\underline{$}}\overline{\underline{$}}$

Local 2936 Elm St Ⓦlocaldallas.com. Upscale but unpretentious modern restaurant in a historic Deep Ellum building. Mains include a panko/cornflake-crusted sea bass; for dessert, the lavender lemon pound cake with meyer lemon ice cream and whipped lemon curd is divine. $\overline{\underline{$}}\overline{\underline{$}}\overline{\underline{$}}$

Record Grill 605 Elm St ☎214 742 1353. A small downtown greasy spoon with nothing in the way of atmosphere, but there's almost five decades of history here, and a good value double-meat bacon cheeseburger. Not far from the Sixth Floor Museum. $\overline{\underline{$}}$

Sonny Bryan's 2202 Inwood Rd Ⓦsonnybryans.com. The original location – it still looks like a shack – of this favourite local barbecue chain lies uptown. Get there in good time as the deliciously tender, smoky meat can be all snapped up by early afternoon. $\overline{\underline{$}}\overline{\underline{$}}$

DRINKING AND NIGHTLIFE   SEE MAP PAGE 79

The best **nightlife** destinations in Dallas are Deep Ellum and Lower Greenville, and there is a small cluster of good **bars** on Perry Avenue near Fair Park. Full listings can be found in Thursday's free *Dallas Observer* (Ⓦdallasobserver. com) or in the *Dallas Morning News* (Ⓦdallasnews.com). Deep Ellum has no shortage of hip live music venues.

Adair's 2624 Commerce St Ⓦadairssaloon.com. This Deep Ellum hole-in-the-wall attracts both old-timers and students with its hard-edged live honky-tonk music, and shuffleboard and pool tables. Happy hour 2–8pm Sun through Fri means drink prices are always manageable.

★**Lee Harvey's** 1807 Gould St Ⓦleeharveys.com.

1

PBR beer flows like water at this dive situated between downtown and Deep Ellum with rows of picnic tables on its patio and live music at weekends. A local institution with little attitude and a low-key crowd.

Sons of Hermann Hall 3414 Elm St ⓦ sonsofhermann hall.com. Delightfully old-school country venue, just beyond Deep Ellum, where the Texas masters come to play, and respectful young outfits pay tribute. Plus swing lessons, open-mic nights and acoustic jams.

ENTERTAINMENT

Angelika Film Center 5321 E Mockingbird Lane ⓦ angelikafilmcenter.com. Indie gem that shows art-house movies and has a sister screen in New York City.

AT&T Performing Arts Center 2403 Flora St ⓦ attpac. org. This modern complex with indoor and outdoor spaces for theatre performances and concerts is within walking distance of the Arts District museums and includes the Meyerson Center and the Winspear Opera House.

Granada Theater 3524 Greenville Ave ⓦ granada theater.com. Lovely old movie theatre with a full slate of regional bands across all genres and big-name acts, as well as Sunday-night TV-watching parties.

Morton H. Meyerson Symphony Center 2301 Flora St ⓦ dallassymphony.org. The Dallas Symphony Orchestra performs in this showpiece concert hall that also hosts regular performances by local symphonies and choral groups.

Winspear Opera House 2403 Flora St ⓦ dallasopera. org. The bright-red, state-of-the-art Winspear in the Arts District hosts performances by the Dallas Opera.

Fort Worth

Often dismissed as some kind of poor relation to Dallas, friendly **FORT WORTH** in fact has a buzz largely missing from its neighbour 35 miles to the east. Distinctly Western in character and history, in the 1870s it was a stop on the great cattle drive to Kansas, the **Chisholm Trail**, and when the railroads arrived it became a livestock market in its own right. Cowboys and outlaws populated the city in its early years and much of that character remains. But while the cattle trade is still a major industry and the **Stockyards** provide a stimulating, atmospheric slice of Old West life, Fort Worth also prides itself on excellent **museums** – the best in the state – and a compact, bustling and walker-friendly **downtown**.

Looking toward the future, the city has embarked on the massive **Trinity River Master Plan**, which when completed (scheduled for 2032) will include one of the largest urban parks in the US, plus trails and greenways along the Trinity River stretching all the way up to Dallas.

Downtown

The chief focus of **downtown** Fort Worth is **Sundance Square**, a leafy, red-brick-paved fourteen-block area of shops, restaurants and bars between First and Sixth streets. The square is ringed by glittering skyscrapers and pervaded with a genuine enthusiasm for the town's rich history.

Bass Performance Hall and around

525 Commerce St • ⓦ basshall.com

Filling the block bounded by Commerce, Calhoun, Fourth and Fifth streets, **Bass Performance Hall** is downtown's most arresting visual treat. A breathtaking building that recalls the great opera houses of Europe, it's fronted by angels blowing golden trumpets. Elsewhere, notice the **trompe-l'oeil murals** – especially the Chisholm Trail mural on Third Street between Main and Houston.

Sid Richardson Museum

309 Main St • Mon–Thurs 10am–5pm, Fri 10am–8pm, Sat 10am–5pm, Sun noon–5pm • Free • ⓦ sidrichardsonmuseum.org

Fans of cowboy art should head for the **Sid Richardson Museum**, which has an excellent collection of late works by Frederic Remington, including some of his best black-and-

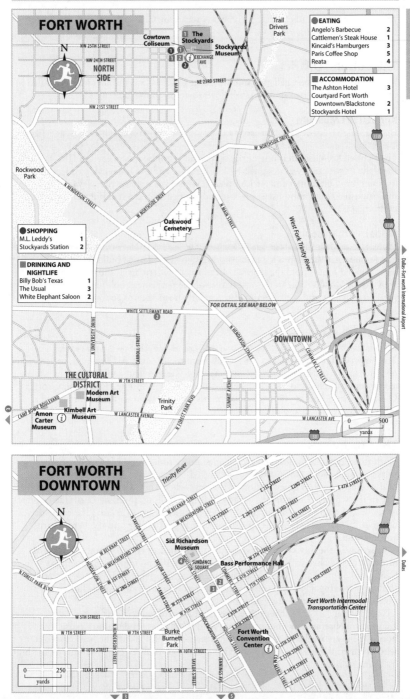

FORT WORTH

N
NORTH SIDE

NW 25TH STREET
NW 24TH STREET
NW 21ST STREET

Cowtown Coliseum
The Stockyards
Stockyards Museum
EXCHANGE AVE
NE 23RD STREET

Trail Drivers Park

Rockwood Park

N HENDERSON STREET
W NORTHSIDE DRIVE
Oakwood Cemetery
N MAIN STREET

W NORTHSIDE DRIVE

West Fork Trinity River

Dallas–Fort Worth International Airport

FOR DETAIL SEE MAP BELOW

WHITE SETTLEMENT ROAD

N UNIVERSITY DRIVE
CARROLL STREET

DOWNTOWN

N HENDERSON STREET
COMMERCE STREET

THE CULTURAL DISTRICT
W 7TH STREET
Modern Art Museum
CAMP BOWIE BOULEVARD
Amon Carter Museum
Kimbell Art Museum
Trinity Park
W LANCASTER AVENUE
N FOREST PARK BLVD
SUMMIT AVENUE
W LANCASTER AVE

0   500
yards

● EATING	
Angelo's Barbecue	2
Cattlemen's Steak House	1
Kincaid's Hamburgers	3
Paris Coffee Shop	5
Reata	4

■ ACCOMMODATION	
The Ashton Hotel	3
Courtyard Fort Worth Downtown/Blackstone	2
Stockyards Hotel	1

● SHOPPING	
M.L. Leddy's	1
Stockyards Station	2

■ DRINKING AND NIGHTLIFE	
Billy Bob's Texas	1
The Usual	3
White Elephant Saloon	2

FORT WORTH DOWNTOWN

N

Trinity River

W BELKNAP STREET
W WEATHERFORD STREET
W 1ST STREET
W 2ND STREET
N FOREST PARK BLVD
N HENDERSON STREET
TAYLOR STREET
LAMAR STREET
HOUSTON STREET

E 1ST STREET
E 2ND STREET
E 3RD STREET
E 4TH STREET

Sid Richardson Museum
SUNDANCE SQUARE
Bass Performance Hall
COMMERCE STREET
E 5TH STREET
E 7TH STREET

W 5TH STREET
W 7TH STREET
W 9TH STREET
W 10TH STREET

Burke Burnett Park

THROCKMORTON STREET
HOUSTON STREET
JENNINGS AVE

Fort Worth Convention Center

Fort Worth Intermodal Transportation Center

Dallas

E 5TH STREET
E 8TH STREET
E 12TH STREET
E 13TH STREET
E 14TH STREET
E 15TH STREET

TEXAS STREET
TEXAS STREET

0   250
yards

1

white illustrations, and early elegiac cowboy scenes by Charles Russell; it also hosts temporary exhibitions.

The Cultural District

Fort Worth has the best galleries and museums in Texas, most of them concentrated in the **Cultural District**, two miles west of downtown on the #2 bus.

Kimbell Art Museum

3333 Camp Bowie Blvd • Tues–Thurs & Sat 10am–5pm, Fri noon–8pm, Sun noon–5pm • Free; special exhibits charge (free Fri 5–8pm) • Ⓦ kimbellart.org

The **Kimbell Art Museum** is one of the best small art museums in the US. The vaulted, naturally lit structure was designed by Louis Kahn, and the impeccable collection includes pre-Columbian and African pieces, with some noteworthy Maya funerary urns, unusual Asian antiquities, pre-Columbian figures and a handful of Renaissance masterpieces.

Modern Art Museum

3200 Darnell St • Tues–Thurs, Sat & Sun 10am–5pm, Fri 10am–8pm • Charge, half price Sun & free every Fri • Ⓦ themodern.org

The **Modern Art Museum** is a Tadao Ando-designed modernist building whose light-flooded rooms hold the largest collection of modern art in the nation after New York's MoMA. Due to the vast nature of the permanent holdings, the exhibits rotate frequently, and the museum also regularly hosts theatre performances and film screenings.

Amon Carter Museum

3501 Camp Bowie Blvd • Tues, Wed, Fri & Sat 10am–5pm, Thurs 10am–8pm, Sun noon–5pm • Free • Ⓦ cartermuseum.org

The **Amon Carter Museum**, just up the hill from the Modern Art Museum, concentrates on American art, with stunning photographs of Western landscapes, as well as a fine assortment of Remingtons and Russells, and works by Winslow Homer and Georgia O'Keeffe. The adjoining **library** complements the collection with a wide range of related subject matter and offers free wi-fi.

The Stockyards

With its wooden sidewalks, old storefronts, dusty rodeos and beer-soaked honky-tonks, the ten-block **Stockyards** area – centred on Exchange Avenue, two miles north of downtown – offers an evocation of the days when Fort Worth was "the richest little city in the world". There are daily **cattle drives**, a huffing, shuffling cavalcade of fifteen or so Texas Longhorns, that occur, weather permitting, at 11.30am. The cattle drives begin at the corrals behind the Livestock Exchange Building and the herd returns around 4pm.

Museums in the Stockyards have an appealing small-town feel. Try the **Stockyards Museum** (131 E Exchange Ave; Mon & Thurs–Sat 10am–5pm, in summer also Sun noon–5pm; charge; Ⓦ stockyardsmuseum.org), in the huge Livestock Exchange Building, offering a lovingly compiled jumble of local memorabilia including steer skulls, pre-Columbian pottery and rodeo posters.

Next door at 121 E Exchange Ave, the **Cowtown Coliseum** (ticket prices vary; Ⓦ cowtowncoliseum.com) holds rodeos, Wild West shows and country music hoedowns every weekend. It's fronted by a statue of Bill Pickett, the black rodeo star who invented the unsavoury but effective practice of "bulldogging" – stunning the bull by biting its lip.

ARRIVAL AND DEPARTURE

FORT WORTH

By car I-30 between Fort Worth and Dallas runs east–west through the city, while I-35W runs north–south. Loop 820 encircles all the major sights.

By plane Dallas/Fort Worth (⍟dfwairport.com) is 17 miles northeast of town; the TEXRail service links it with downtown (⍟ridetrinitymetro.org/texrail-schedule).

By train or bus The Amtrak (☎817 332 2931) and Greyhound (☎817 429 3089) stations are both located southeast of downtown at 1001 Jones St.

Destinations (bus) Amarillo (3 daily; 6hr); Austin (10 daily; 4hr 25min); El Paso (6 daily; 11hr 30min); Houston (10 daily; 7hr); San Antonio (9 daily; 6hr 25min).

Destinations (train) Austin (1 daily; 4hr 12min); Dallas (1 daily 1hr); El Paso (1 daily; 24hr); San Antonio (1 daily; 7hr 45min).

GETTING AROUND AND INFORMATION

On foot The downtown Sundance Square and Stockyard areas are well patrolled and safe to walk around after dark.

By bus or shuttle Fort Worth's public transport system, Trinity Metro (⍟ridetrinitymetro.org), operates useful buses and shuttles.

By train The Trinity Railway Express (⍟trinityrailway express.org) runs a commuter service to Dallas.

By taxi Yellow Cab (☎817 426 6262)

Visitor centre Information booths can be found inside the Fort Worth Convention Center (1201 Houston St) in the Houston Street Lobby (see ⍟fortworth.com).

ACCOMMODATION

SEE MAP PAGE 83

The Ashton Hotel 610 Main St ⍟theashtonhotel. com. Small luxury hotel in a great location, featuring 39 individualized rooms appointed with custom furniture. The service is top-notch. $$$

Courtyard Fort Worth Downtown/Blackstone 601 Main St ⍟marriott.com. Friendly hotel in a downtown Art Deco building with more than 200 rooms and suites. Those on the upper floor have great views, and there's a pool. $$$

Stockyards Hotel 109 E Exchange St ⍟stockyardshotel. com. Good value on the edge of the Stockyards; you can stumble from the rowdy beer hall to your bed. The wood-accented homey rooms are comfortable, if unspectacular. $$

EATING

SEE MAP PAGE 83

Angelo's Barbecue 2533 White Settlement Rd ⍟angelosbbq.com. Venerable westside barbecue joint, north of the Cultural District. Locals declare the brisket here to be the best in the city. There's also great sides and desserts to complete the meal. $$

Cattlemen's Steak House 2458 N Main St ⍟cattlemenssteakhouse.com. Dim lighting and wall-sized portraits of prize steers set the scene at this Stockyards institution, beloved for its juicy steaks – from 16oz T-bones to 24oz Porterhouse – and icy margaritas. $$$

Kincaid's Hamburgers 4901 Camp Bowie Blvd ⍟kincaidshamburgers.com. This place used to be a grocery store, but since 1966 it's served the best unfussy 8oz hamburgers in Texas. $

Paris Coffee Shop 704 W Magnolia Ave ⍟pariscoffee shopfw.com. Busy breakfast and lunch spot that serves delicious, fresh grub. There are the classics – count on biscuits and gravy, steak sandwiches and the like – plus some more boujie options (think whole grain pancakes, brioche French toast and power grain bowls). The prices can't be beat. $

Reata 310 Houston St ⍟reata.net. One of the nicest places to eat in downtown's Sundance Square, with a tempting Southwestern menu that ranges from upscale cuisine, such as pepper-crusted tenderloin with port sauce, to home-style comfort food like chicken fried steak or chicken chile *relleños*. Top off the meal with the chocolate bread pudding *tamale* for dessert. Named after the ranch in *Giant*, James Dean's last movie. $$

DRINKING AND NIGHTLIFE

SEE MAP PAGE 83

You'd be hard pressed not to find something to your taste in after-dark Fort Worth, a city where roustabouts happily down beers next to modern jazz fans and bikers. **Bar crawling** is fun, and there's a great mix of **live music venues**. Check the *Fort Worth Weekly* (⍟fwweekly.com) or the *Fort Worth Star-Telegram* (⍟star-telegram.com) for **listings**. If you're after a rambunctious Wild West night out, head for the Stockyards.

Billy Bob's Texas 2520 Rodeo Plaza ⍟billybobstexas. com. The jewel in Cowtown's crown, this is the largest honky-tonk in the world, down in the Stockyards, with pro bull-riding, pool tables, bars, restaurants, stores, weekly swing and country dance lessons and big-name concerts.

★ **The Usual** 1408 W Magnolia Ave ⍟theusual.bar. Sleek cocktail lounge exuding cool – and pleasantly devoid of pretension – serving well-conceived house creations as well as all of the classics. Has more of a mixed crowd than you might expect and a steady line-up of quality DJs.

1

White Elephant Saloon 106 E Exchange Ave ⓦ whiteelephantsaloon.com. Notoriously wild and authentic old Stockyards saloon with a cowboy hat hall of fame and live acts nightly.

SHOPPING

SEE MAP PAGE 83

M.L. Leddy's 2455 N Main St ⓦ leddys.com. To stock up on top-of-the-line rhinestone Western wear, boots, saddles, exquisite handmade buckles or cowboy hats, head to Leddy's Ranch, which dresses some of the biggest acts in country music.

Stockyards Station 130 E Exchange Ave ⓦ fortworth tockyards.com. Large, open-air mall in the heart of the Stockyards. It's undeniably touristy, but it houses a general store, one that sells leather goods, another that offers a multitude of hot sauce options, and the Chief Record Shop (ⓦ chiefrecordsonline.com), which sells country music CDs.

The Panhandle

Inhabitants of the **Panhandle**, the northernmost part of the state, call it "the real Texas". On a map, it appears as a rectangular appendix bordering Oklahoma and New Mexico. A starkly romantic agricultural **landscape** strewn with tumbleweeds and mesquite trees, it fulfils the fantasy of what Texas should look like. When Coronado's expedition passed this way in the sixteenth century, the gold-seekers drove stakes into the ground across the vast and unchanging vista, despairing of otherwise finding their way home – hence the name **Llano Estacado**, or staked plains, which persists today (the Panhandle is the southernmost portion of the Great Plains).

Once the buffalo – and the natives – had been driven away from what was seen as uninhabitable frontier country, the Panhandle in the 1870s began to yield great **natural resources**. Helium, especially in Amarillo, as well as oil and agriculture, have brought wealth to the region, which is also home to large **ranches**.

The Panhandle holds few actual tourist attractions – its real appeal is its barren, rural beauty. But **music** has deep roots in the area, too. Songwriters such as Bob Wills, Buddy Holly, Roy Orbison, Waylon Jennings, Terry Allen, Joe Ely, Jimmie Dale Gilmore and Natalie Maines of the Dixie Chicks all grew up here.

Lubbock

With its faceless block buildings and simple homes, **LUBBOCK**, the largest city in the Panhandle, is at first glance unremarkable. Dig a little deeper, though, and you will find a complex city, one that accommodates Southern Baptism, the high-scoring Texas Tech university's Red Raiders football team and a songwriting history unmatched in the state, led by Buddy Holly (see box, page 87).

You can get an interesting overview of local history at the university's National Ranching Heritage Center (3121 4th St; Mon–Sat 10am–5pm, Sun 1–5pm; free; ⓦ ranchingheritage.org), northwest of downtown, where 38 original buildings illustrate the evolution of ranch life. Highlights include a one-room schoolhouse, a limestone and sandstone house built to protect a pioneer family from attacks by Native Americans and a blacksmith's shop complete with period trade equipment.

ARRIVAL, GETTING AROUND AND INFORMATION
LUBBOCK

By car I-27 bisects the centre of Lubbock, while Loop 289 encircles the city and defines its outer limits.

By air Lubbock's Preston Smith Airport (ⓦ ci.lubbock.tx.us/departments/airport) is a few minutes north of the city on I-27; taxis to downtown cost around $20 (West Texas Cab Company; ☎ 806 559 9900).

Local buses Citibus (ⓦ citibus.com) runs commuter routes within the Loop, stopping at around 7.45pm (Mon–Sat).

Visitor centre Sixth floor, 1500 Broadway (Mon–Fri 8am–5pm; ☎ 806 747 5232, ⓦ visitlubbock.org).

ACCOMMODATION

Baymont by Wyndham Lubbock West 6015 45th St ⓦ wyndhamhotels.com. Well-located motel (part of the

BUDDY HOLLY

Lubbock's claim to world fame is as the birthplace of **Buddy Holly**. Inspired by the blues and country music of his childhood – and a seminal encounter with the young Elvis Presley, gigging in Lubbock at the *Cotton Club* – Buddy Holly was one of rock'n'roll's first singer-songwriters. The Holly sound, characterized by steady strumming guitar, rapid drumming and his trademark hiccupping vocals, was made famous by hits such as *Peggy Sue*, *Not Fade Away* and *That'll Be the Day*. Buddy was killed at 22 in the Iowa plane crash of February 3, 1959 ("The Day the Music Died") that also claimed the Big Bopper and Ritchie Valens. Don't leave town without visiting the **Buddy Holly Center**, 1801 Crickets Ave (Tues–Sat 10am–5pm, Sun 1–5pm; charge; ⓦ ci.lubbock.tx.us/departments/buddy-holly-center), an impressive space that holds a collection of Holly memorabilia, including the black glasses he wore on the day he died.

Across the street from the center is the **Buddy Holly Statue**, an 8ft bronze figure that's the focal point of the Buddy and Maria Elena Holly Plaza. **Buddy's grave** is in Lubbock's cemetery at the end of 34th Street; take the right fork inside the gate, and the grave, decorated with flowers and guitar picks, is on the left.

Wyndham chain) with no-frills rooms, a restaurant and a pool with waterfalls. Breakfast is included. $\overline{\$\$}$
Woodrow House B&B 2629 19th St ⓦ woodrowhouse. com. Ten rooms, each with a different theme – there's even

one in a restored train carriage – in a mansion-style modern house opposite Texas Tech. There's a pool and the included breakfast is nicely prepared. $\overline{\$\$}$

EATING AND DRINKING

Cagle Steaks 8732 4th St ⓦ caglesteaks.com. Classic Texas Plains steak restaurant where the vegetable options don't extend much beyond a baked potato or fries. A 16oz rib eye with all the trimmings is decent value. $\overline{\$\$}$
Lone Star Oyster 5116 58th St Slide ☎ 806 797 3773. Beloved, well-worn dive bar that has been around for ages. As the name suggests, they serve oysters and assorted seafood dishes, but the real draws are the rock-bottom drink prices and the lively atmosphere. $\overline{\$\$}$
Tom and Bingo's BBQ 3006 34th St ⓦ tomandbingos.

com. This tiny family-run institution churns out the best chopped beef sandwich in Lubbock. Get there early for the brisket, it often sells out. $\overline{\$}$
Vizo's African Bar & Restaurant 3131 34th St ⓦ vizoslubbock.com. Owned and operated by two Texas Tech alums, this little gem offers a taster of West African food, drink and music. There's a bit of everything: achombo (beans and rice), egusi soup, fufu (dumpling) and eru (wild vegetable), and Cameroon-style seasoned grilled wings all grace the menu.

Amarillo and around

AMARILLO may seem cut off from the rest of Texas, up in the northern Panhandle, but it lies on one of the great American cross-country routes – I-40, once the legendary **Route 66**. The city's name comes from the Spanish word for "yellow", the colour of the soil characteristic to these parts. Sitting on ninety percent of the world's helium, Amarillo is a prosperous, laidback city with a nice mix of cowtown appeal, arty eccentricity and mouthwatering steaks.

Amarillo's small "**old town**" consists of a few tree-lined streets and some shabby homes. More interesting is the **Route 66 Historic District**, known locally as **Old San Jacinto**, a quirky stretch of restaurants, bars and stores that runs west along Sixth Street (the old Route 66) from Georgia for about a mile to Western Street.

Cadillac Ranch

10 miles west of Amarillo on I-40, exit 60 (Arnot Rd)

For a classic slice of Americana, drive ten miles west of town to **Cadillac Ranch**. An extraordinary vision in the middle of nowhere, ten battered cars, different Cadillac models introduced between 1949 and 1963, stand upended in the soil, their tail fins

1

A TEXAS-SIZED SPECTACLE

You may balk at heart-warming musical extravaganzas, but the outdoor production of **TEXAS**, about the settling of the Panhandle in the 1800s, performed within the park, has an undeniable pull in an area not exactly throbbing with nightlife. With the dramatic prairie sky as a ceiling, a 600ft-high cliff as a backdrop and genuine thunder and lightning (June–mid-Aug Tues–Sun 8.30pm, pre-show steak dinner 6pm; show tickets charge; ⓦ www.texas-show.com), it is a spectacle not soon forgotten.

---

pointing towards the heavens. Since the cars were installed in 1974, the invention of an artist-hippie collective called the Ant Farm, they have been subject to countless makeovers at the hands of graffiti artists, photographers and members of the public (and periodically 'restored' to a solid colour). All this was encouraged by one Stanley Marsh 3 (he eschewed Roman numerals): eccentric helium millionaire, bon vivant, and former owner of the land where these cars are planted (it now belongs to a trust in his name since he passed away in 2014).

ARRIVAL AND INFORMATION · AMARILLO AND AROUND

By car I-40 cuts through Amarillo, running south of downtown; the old Route 66 (6th St) runs parallel, to the north.

By bus Greyhound arrives downtown at 700 S Tyler St (ⓣ 806 374 5371).

Destinations Albuquerque, NM (3 daily; 4hr 55min); Austin (1 daily; 12hr); Dallas (3 daily; 6hr 50min); El Paso (2 daily; 9hr 20min); Houston (4 daily; 13hr).

By plane There's a small airport (ⓦ fly-ama.com) 7 miles east.

Visitor information ⓣ 800 692 1338, ⓦ visitamarillo. com.

ACCOMMODATION AND EATING

Big Texan Steak Ranch and Motel 7701 E I-40, exit 75 ⓦ bigtexan.com. Rip-roaring Wild Western fun in this famed old restaurant, which as well as serving 20oz T-bone steaks and BBQ brisket sandwiches, offers the 72oz steak challenge: if you can eat it within an hour, you get it free (losers pony up the full cost). For cowboy kitsch, you can't beat the attached motel, with its Texas-flag shower curtains, Texas-shaped pool, cow-hide bedcovers and saloon doors. Hotel $$; restaurant $$

Butterlove Biscuits 3440 S Bell St ⓦ butterlove. com. Twenty varieties of buttermilk buscuits and biscuit sandwiches (choose the turkey florentine) will leave you satisfied and happily drowsy. There's a full bar as well. $

Golden Light Café and Cantina 2906 W 6th Ave ⓦ goldenlightcafe.com. Tasty burgers and sandwiches at good value at this well-located joint. The cantina side regularly draws some of the best touring musicians in Texas. $

O.H.M.S. Cafe & Bar 619 S Tyler St ⓦ ohmscafe.com. This downtown diner serves excellent Southwestern food but is best known for its selection of tempting desserts, as well as the bar that knocks out potent martinis. $$$

Palo Duro Canyon State Park

11450 Park Road 5, Canyon · Daily 7am–9pm · Charge · ⓦ palodurocanyon.com

Palo Duro Canyon, twenty miles southeast of Amarillo, is one of Texas' best-kept secrets, which is puzzling considering it's one of the largest and most breathtaking canyons in the country. Plunging 1000ft from rim to floor, it splits the plains wide open and offers expansive vistas and a riot of colours, especially at sunset and in spring, when the whole chasm is painted with wildflowers.

The park encompasses the most scenic part of the 120-mile canyon. You can explore the depths on **horseback** (ⓣ 806 488 2180), while hikers can escape the tourist busloads by taking the Prairie Dog Town fork into more remote sections.

INFORMATION AND ACCOMMODATION · PALO DURO CANYON STATE PARK

Visitor centre 11450 Park Rd 5, Canyon (ⓣ 806 488 2227, ⓦ tpwd.texas.gov/state-parks/palo-duro-canyon).

Campgrounds and cabins ⓦ texasstateparks.reserve america.com. There are two full-service campsites and two primitive sites with no facilities. Camping in the backcountry is also permitted; check in at the visitor centre for directions to the designated area. There are also seven rustic cabins to choose from; the three more expensive options are worth it for their commanding rim views alone. Camping 𝄐, rustic cabins 𝄐, other cabins 𝄐𝄐

The Davis Mountains

The temperate climate of the verdant **Davis Mountains**, south of the junction of I-10 and I-20, makes them a popular summer destination for sweltering urban Texans. The eponymous **state park** draws the most visitors to the range, while the **McDonald Observatory** lures with the promise of world-class celestial views. South along Hwy-17, tiny **Marfa** is a windswept art community in the middle of the West Texas desert.

Fort Davis and around

Fort Davis, at the junction of Hwy-118 and Hwy-17, is a peaceful base for exploring the Davis Mountains, and you can pick up a driving map at its visitor centre; there's precious little to do in town itself, however.

McDonald Observatory
3640 Dark Sky Drive • Tues–Sat noon–5pm • Free • ⓦ mcdonaldobservatory.org

The glassy, starry nights facilitate the work of the **McDonald Observatory** about twenty miles northwest of Fort Davis on Hwy-118. Nocturnal "star parties" here provide a wonderful opportunity to look at the constellations for yourself and learn more about them (see website for times; charge). Wear warm clothing and bring food and drink. (There are daytime solar viewings and tours as well.)

Davis Mountains State Park
Open year-round • Charge • ⓦ tpwd.texas.gov/state-parks/davis-mountains

Davis Mountains State Park, four miles northwest of Fort Davis, offers good hiking and birdwatching opportunities, as well as being prime habitat for black bears and mountain lions. Departing just west of the campground on Park Road 3A, the **Skyline Drive** trail provides the fullest sense of the park's rugged environs as it winds through the mountains for 4.5 miles before emerging at the Fort Davis Historic Site. For a less taxing outing, take the **Indian Lodge** trail from the lodge's parking lot. After a somewhat steep initial stretch, the trail levels off and offers commanding views. After 1.5 miles it connects with a one-mile trail leading to a recently renovated quail-viewing platform.

ACCOMMODATION AND EATING

FORT DAVIS AND AROUND

Campgrounds Davis Mountains State Park ⓦ texasstateparks.reserveamerica.com. The state park has a variety of scenic shaded campsites, both primitive and fully serviced. 𝄐

Hotel Limpia 101 Memorial Square, Fort Davis ⓦ hotellimpia.com. Historic, characterful hotel in the heart of town with period furnishings and a small outdoor pool. Its on-site restaurant, the *Blue Mountain Bar & Grill*, serves excellent upscale dinners; choose from rich dishes such as

spanakopita or mocha-crusted pork tenderloin. 𝄐𝄐

Indian Lodge Davis Mountain State Park ⓦ texasstateparks.reserveamerica.com. The 39 rooms at the state park's romantic 1930s adobe-style *Indian Lodge* are clean and comfortable – and often booked up, so call in advance. There's a good-sized outdoor pool, and the breakfast buffet at the lodge's *Black Bear* restaurant offers a mind-boggling range of options. 𝄐𝄐

Marfa

MARFA, a small, but thriving community 21 miles south of Fort Davis on Hwy-17, is the kind of place that it's equally difficult to imagine existing where it is, and existing anywhere else. It is very much a desert oasis, with a respected **art scene** pulling artists

1

and the curious from afar in increasing numbers. It's also a decidedly offbeat town, where chic designer shops and prefab galleries are offset by historic buildings that attest to its former role as a ranching centre. It all makes for a fascinating mix. Much more ethereal, the **Marfa Lights**, a few miles east of town, consistently draw crowds, even if the lights don't always cooperate.

The Chinati and Judd foundations

Just outside town at 1 Cavalry Row is the extraordinary **Chinati Foundation** founded by minimalist Donald Judd. The avant-garde works on display across fifteen buildings here include some of the world's largest permanent art installations, set in dramatic contexts both indoors and out. Self-guided viewings are free or charged, depending on the area visited, and you can go on a full or selective guided tour (Thurs–Sun 9am–5pm; charge; ⓦchinati.org). Back in town at 104 S Highland St, the **Judd Foundation** also leads tours of its modernistic art spaces (ⓦjuddfoundation.org/marfa).

The Marfa Lights

Viewing centre at Hwy-90, 9 miles east of Marfa • Open year round

Since the 1880s, mysterious bouncing lights have been seen in the town's flat fields. Dubbed the "**Marfa Lights**", they have long attracted conspiracy theorists and alien-hunters, though their cause may be more prosaic. The town's **visitor centre** (Mon–Fri 8am–4pm, Sat 10am–4pm, Sun 10am–3pm; ☎432 729 4772, ⓦvisitmarfa.com) at the USO building at 302 S Highland Ave, can give advice on good vantage points in the area to see the ghostly illuminations; if in doubt, head for the viewing centre four hours after sunset.

ACCOMMODATION AND EATING   **MARFA**

Buns N' Roses 1613 W San Antonio St (US-90) ☎432 729 4282. Popular diner on the western edge of town, knocking out cheap and tasty breakfast plates, basic TexMex and excellent donuts and pastries. $̄

★ **Cochineal** 107 W San Antonio St ⓦcochinealmarfa. com. Understated, tucked-away spot that puts the focus squarely on a range of refined and unfussy dishes. The menu changes frequently, but can feature starters such as cucumber gazpacho with *bacalao croquettes* and mains such as seared duck breast or pheasant with blackberry compote. There's also a cosy cocktail bar. $̄$̄$̄$̄

El Cosmico 802 S Highland Ave ⓦelcosmico.com. A "magical tribe of dirt wizards" constructed this avant-garde development of painstakingly renovated Air Stream trailers and safari tents just outside town. Most of the trailers have outdoor showers only, but they are all pleasantly furnished. Camping (per person, per night) $̄, safari tent $̄$̄, trailer $̄$̄$̄, micro-home Kasita $̄$̄$̄$̄

Food Shark 222 W San Antonio St ⓦfood-shark. business.site. Beloved far and wide, the perennially popular *Food Shark* serves up Mediterranean-inspired dishes such as Marfalafel with hummus or grilled lamb kebab platter out of an old delivery truck. Arrive at noon on the dot or be prepared for a long wait. $̄

Hotel Paisano 207 N Highland Ave ⓦhotelpaisano. com. When James Dean's last film, the 1956 epic, *Giant*, was filmed in town, the cast stayed at this historic and swanky hotel. The public areas exude elegance, while the original rooms are cramped; the much larger suites have patios or balconies. Doubles $̄$̄, suites $̄$̄$̄

Thunderbird Hotel 601 W San Antonio ⓦthunderbird marfa.com. A renovated motor court turned high-end hipster hotel. Clean lines define the minimalist rooms, which feature flatscreen TVs, iHomes and designer bath products. $̄$̄

Big Bend National Park and around

Open daily 24hr • Charge • ⓦnps.gov/bibe

The **Rio Grande**, flowing through 1500ft-high canyons, makes a ninety-degree bend south of Marathon to form the southern border of **BIG BEND NATIONAL PARK** – thanks to its isolation, one of the least visited of the US national parks.

The Apache, who forced the Chisos out three hundred years ago, believed that this hauntingly beautiful wilderness was used by the Great Spirit to dump all the rocks left

HIKING, RAFTING AND HOT SPRINGS IN BIG BEND NATIONAL PARK

West of the park headquarters a spur road leads south for about six miles, up into the **Chisos Basin**, which is ringed by dramatic peaks – the one gap in the rocky wall here is called the **Window**, looking out over the Chihuahuan Desert. Several of the park's best **hikes** depart from either the road here or from the trailhead, near the store by the visitor centre.

HIKES

Lost Mine Trail An ideal morning outing in the Chisos Basin, this 4.8-mile out-and-back rises 1100ft through a series of moderate switchbacks to a ridge with breathtaking views of Juniper Canyon, the far rim and Mexico beyond.

South Rim Trail From the Chisos Basin trailhead, the 12-mile loop hike to the South Rim is one of the most popular in the park, and the views deep into the interior of Mexico are humbling. Count on a gruelling 8hr – most of which will be completely exposed – or 10hr if you elect to include the rim trails.

Marufo Vega trail For the serious (and experienced) hiker, the 13-mile loop hike to the river on the Marufo Vega trail is one of the most stunning in the entire National Park Service. It offers views of the Sierra del Carmen mountain range in Mexico and a descent into a rarely visited slick-rock canyon. Feral burros (wild donkeys) sometimes wail here at sunset, and subsistence Mexican farmers set up camps to harvest candelilla across the border. Pick up the topographical map of the trail from one of the visitor centres and check with a park ranger about the current conditions before setting out.

Rio Grande Village Trail This gentle hour-long hike from the Rio Grande Village campsite leads past a wildlife-viewing platform before ending with expansive views of the river and nearby mountains.

RAFTING

At three separate stages within the park's boundaries the river runs through gigantic canyons. The western-most, Santa Elena, is the most common rafting trip, with mostly gentle Class II–III floats; outfitters are available at Terlingua (see opposite).

HOT SPRINGS

Driving 20 miles southeast of Panther Junction brings you to the riverside Rio Grande Village – unless you choose to detour just before, to bathe in the natural hot springs that feed into the river. The hot springs can be reached via an easy 1.9-mile walk along the signposted dirt Hot Springs Rd.

over from the creation of the world; the Spanish, meanwhile, called it *terra desconocida*, "strange, unknown land". A breathtaking 800,000-acre expanse of forested mountains and ocotillo-dotted desert, Big Bend has been home to ranchers, miners and smugglers, a last frontier for the true-grit pioneers of the American West.

Today, there is camping in certain designated areas, but much of the park remains barely charted territory. Its topography results in dramatic juxtapositions of desert and mountain, plant and **animal life**: mountain lions, black bears, roadrunners and javelinas (a bristly, grey hog-like creature with a snout and tusks) all roam free. Despite the dryness, tangles of pretty wild flowers and blossoming cacti erupt into a wonderful display of colour each March and April, making it a perfect time of year to visit the area.

ARRIVAL AND INFORMATION   BIG BEND NATIONAL PARK

By car The most interesting route into Big Bend is from the west. You can't follow the river all the way from El Paso, but Hwy-170 – reached on Hwy-67 south from Marfa (see page 89) – runs through spectacular desert scenery east from Ojinaga, Mexico, which was practically wiped off the map due to floods in 2008. Before reaching the park boundary just beyond Study Butte, you pass through Big Bend Ranch State Park and the community of Terlingua.

Park headquarters In the centre of the park at Panther Junction (daily 8.30am–5pm; ☎ 432 477 2251 ⊕ nps.gov/ bibe). The entrance fee is payable here (and at all of the visitor centres listed below), there are orientation exhibits and a daytime gas station.

Visitor centres The Chisos Basin, a short drive south of Panther Junction, has a visitor centre (daily 8.30am–4pm) and a convenience store. There is also a visitor centre at the east end of Hwy-118 at Rio Grande Village (Nov–April daily 9am–4.30pm), where there's also a gas station, and at Persimmon Gap (Nov–April daily 10am–4pm), at the park's northern boundary on Hwy-385.

ACCOMMODATION AND EATING

Most camping at the park's three **developed campgrounds** (pay at a visitor centre) is first-come, first-served, though some reservations can be made for the high season (Nov–May; ⓦrecreation.gov). **Primitive sites** are scattered along the many marked hiking trails. These have no facilities, and you'll need a backcountry permit (charge) from a visitor centre. The sites at Juniper Flats are only about a 3-mile hike and are located in a nice meadow, and there are additional stunning sites in the Chisos Mountains.

Chisos Basin Campground The most popular developed campground in the park, Chisos Basin is dramatically perched at 5400ft and has the benefit of being within walking distance of numerous trails, a visitor centre and the *Chisos Mountain Lodge's* restaurant. The sixty pitches have access to running water, though there are no hookups. $\overline{\$}$

Chisos Mountains Lodge ⓦchisosmountainslodge.com. At the Chisos Basin visitor centre, the park's only roofed accommodation option offers motel-style rooms with balconies and a few stone cottages (#102 and #103 are the best). Reservations are essential. The on-site restaurant (daily 7–10am, 11am–4pm & 5–8pm) has a cheap but good all-you-can-eat salad bar. Doubles $\overline{\$\$}$, cottages $\overline{\$\$\$}$

★ **Gage Hotel** 102 NW 1st St, Hwy-90 W, Marathon ⓦgagehotel.com. Marathon, 40 miles north of the Persimmon Gap visitor centre, is best known for the luxurious *Gage Hotel*, which has exceedingly comfortable rooms outfitted with plush furnishings, and its adobe-styled *Los Portales* annexe. There's a restaurant outfitted in "upscale cowboy" decor and a bar famed for its buffalo burger. $\overline{\$\$\$}$

Terlingua

For such a small place, **TERLINGUA**, scattered across the low hills along Hwy-170, has a lot to recommend it – not least an atmospheric **ghost town**, the remnants of the Chisos Mining Company's quicksilver operation here in the early twentieth century. The whole area, which is free to roam around, includes shuttered mine shafts, the foundations of several buildings and a cemetery. Terlingua's proximity to Big Bend National Park and its rugged locale makes it one of the best spots in the state for **outdoor adventures**; several outfitters in town lead a variety of tours (see below).

ACTIVITIES

Tours Desert Sports (ⓦdesertsportstx.com), on Hwy-170 at the intersection with Hwy-118, offers a variety of rafting trips (1–12 days); allow around $450/person for a party of four for a two days guided trip along Santa Elena Canyon. It also leads group hikes, rents rafts and mountain bikes, and provides shuttles into the backcountry.

Far Flung Outdoor Center (ⓦbigbendfarflung.com), on the south side of Hwy-170 just east of the ghost town, leads a wide variety of half-day and full-day jeep tours to otherwise inaccessible corners of the national park as well as ATV tours and rafting outings.

ACCOMMODATION

★ **Big Bend Casitas** Hwy-170, between the ghost town and the Hwy-118 intersection ⓦbigbendfarflung.com. Run by Far Flung (see above), these twelve cheerful and spacious red-roofed *casitas* are each pleasantly appointed with flatscreen TVs, a/c, kitchenettes and outdoor grills. The evening starlight views from the covered porches are simply stunning, and guests receive a discount on Far Flung tours. Minimum two-night stay. $\overline{\$\$\$}$

Chisos Mining Company Motel 23280 Hwy-170 ⓦmotelsbigbend.com. On the east edge of town near the intersection with Hwy-118, this rustic compound holds

a very basic motel with spartan double rooms, as well as colourful cabins. While it's the best budget option in town, it is decidedly bereft of creature comforts and rooms can get cold at night. Doubles $\overline{\$\$}$, cabins $\overline{\$\$}$

La Posada Milagro 100 Milagro Rd ⓦlaposadamilagro.com. At the top of a hill, three luxuriously rustic rooms in a restored dry-stack stone building, along with a four-bed bunkhouse. The views are expansive and there's on-site yoga and a coffeeshop serving comfort meals for breakfast and lunch daily. Doubles or bunkhouse $\overline{\$\$}$

EATING AND DRINKING

Little Dipper Food Truck 53690 Hwy-118 ☎409 904 6498. Locals swear by this popular food truck on Hwy-118 (perched on the edge of the desert), serving up *barbacoa* or brisket breakfast burritos, juicy burgers and potent coffee. There's a good view with your breakfast too. $\overline{\$}$

★ **Starlight Theatre** 631 Ivey Rd ⓦthestarlighttheatre.com. Near Terlingua's fly-blown cemetery, this old movie house has been converted into a welcoming bar and restaurant serving crowd-pleasers including chilli and specials such as chicken-fried wild boar and tequila quail.

THE US–MEXICO BORDER

Downtown El Paso's character is shaped by the **US–Mexico border**. In times past, outlaws and exiles from either side of the border would take refuge across the river, and today's traffic remains considerable and not entirely uncontroversial. Manual labourers come north to find undocumented jobs, and US companies secretly dump their toxic waste on the south side. Drugs are a major issue, too. The border itself, the **Rio Grande**, has caused its share of disagreements: the river changed course quite often in the 1800s, and it was not until the 1960s, when it was run through a concrete channel, that it was made permanent.

An attractive 55-acre park, the **Chamizal National Memorial**, on the east side of downtown off Paisano Drive, was built to commemorate the settling of the border dispute; it has a small cultural centre (daily 10am–5pm; free; ⓦ nps.gov/cham). Elsewhere, the small but engrossing **Border Patrol Museum**, 4315 Transmountain Rd (Tues–Sat 9am–4.45pm; free; ⓦ borderpatrolmuseum.com), explains the work of the patrollers and highlights the ingenuity of smugglers.

CROSSING INTO MEXICO

On the Rio Grande, the **Cordova Bridge** – or Bridge of the Americas – heads across **into Mexico**, where there's a larger park and a number of museums. You must have a multiple-entry visa for the USA, and don't plan on travelling more than twenty or so miles south of the border. Crossing here is free; at the three other bridges – two downtown and one near the Ysleta Mission – you have to pay a small fee to walk or drive across.

Finish up with a slice of home-made chocolate bourbon pecan pie or cinnamon churros with hot fudge dipping sauce. Outside, locals linger on the porch to drink beer, gossip and marvel at the mountains. $$

El Paso

Back when Texas was still Tejas, **EL PASO**, the second-oldest settlement in the United States, was the main crossing on the Rio Grande. It still plays that role today, its 600,000 residents joining with another 1.7 million across the river in **Ciudad Juarez**, Mexico, to form the largest binational (and bilingual) megalopolis in North America. It's not an especially pretty place – massive railyards fill up much of downtown, the belching smelters of copper mills line the riverfront and the northern reaches are taken up by the giant Fort Bliss military base. Its dramatic setting, however, where the Franklin Mountains meet the Chihuahuan Desert, gives it a certain bold pioneer edge, bearing more relation to old rather than new Mexico, with little of the pastel softness of the Southwest USA. El Paso is also the home of Tony Lama, makers of top-quality **cowboy boots**, available at substantial discounts at outlets across town.

While it may be tempting to cross the border here into Mexico, remember that escalating **drug wars** have turned Juarez into one of the most dangerous cities in the world.

Ysleta Mission and the Mission Trail

Ysleta Mission 131 S Zaragoza Rd • Mon–Sat 7am–4pm • ☏ 915 859 9848 • **Mission Valley Information Center** 9065 Alameda Ave • ⓦ elpasomissions.org

Although El Paso is predominantly Hispanic, there is also a substantial population of **Tigua Indigenous peoples**, a displaced Pueblo group, based in a reservation (complete with the almost statutory casino) on Socorro Road, southeast of downtown. The reservation's arts-and-crafts centre sells pottery and textiles. Adjacent to the reservation, the simple **Ysleta Mission**, established in 1682 and the oldest mission in the United States, marks the beginning of a nine-mile **Mission Trail**, with two other missions,

1

Socorro and San Elizario – still active churches – all set among scruffy cotton, alfalfa, chilli, onion and pecan fields.

ARRIVAL AND INFORMATION

EL PASO

By plane El Paso's airport (⊛elpasointernationalairport. com) is about 5 miles east of downtown; a taxi to the centre will cost about $25, although many downtown hotels offer free van rides.

By bus Greyhound buses stop at 200 W San Antonio Ave (☎915 542 1355).

Destinations Albuquerque, NM (3 daily; 4hr 30min); Amarillo (2 daily; 9hr 15min); Austin (2 daily; 12hr 25min); Dallas (5 daily; 12hr 50min); Fort Worth (5 daily; 11hr 40min); Houston (4 daily; 18hr 5min); San Antonio (2 daily;

10hr 20min).

By train Amtrak (☎915 545 2247) pulls in at the Daniel Burnham-designed Union Station at 700 San Francisco St.

Destinations Albuquerque, NM (2 daily; 16hr 30min); Austin (1 daily; 16hr 50min); Dallas (1 daily; 22hr 45min); Fort Worth (1 daily; 21hr 25min); Houston (1 daily; 18hr 35min); San Antonio (1 daily; 12hr 15min).

Visitor centre 1 Civic Center Plaza in the convention centre complex Union Depot, 400 W San Antonio Rd (Mon–Fri 8am–5pm; ☎915 534 0600, ⊛visitpaso.com).

ACCOMMODATION AND EATING

Ardovino's Desert Crossing 1 Ardovino Drive, Sunland Park, NM ⊛ardovinos.com. Just across the state line in New Mexico and well worth the 10min drive from downtown, this enchanting restaurant serves up pasta dishes like duck cavatelli or lamb pappardelle. $\overline{\underline{\$}}\overline{\underline{\$}}$

Coffee Box 401 N Mesa St ⊛elpasocoffeebox.com. Excellent coffee served in a uber-hip converted shipping container daubed with murals and decked out with contemporary art. They also serve a huge range of teas, charcoal and coconut frappes, horchata and delicious pastries. $\overline{\underline{\$}}$

Gardner Hotel 311 E Franklin St ⊛gardnerhotel.com. Rooms in this atmospheric hotel – where John Dillinger bedded down in the 1920s – vary from singles with shared

bath to simple en-suite doubles furnished with antiques. $\overline{\underline{\$}}$

Hotel Paso del Norte 10 Sheldon Ct ⊛marriott.com. Downtown hotel in a grand old 1912 building. The romantic lobby bar *The Dome* is topped by a colourful Tiffany glass dome and surrounded by rose marble and dark banquettes, while the 357 opulent rooms and suites are all comfortably appointed with understated Southwestern accents and a large-scale map of El Paso on the headboard wall. There are also two on-site restaurants, with the more informal option serving all meals daily. $\overline{\underline{\$}}\overline{\underline{\$}}\overline{\underline{\$}}$

★ **L&J Café** 3622 E Missouri Ave ⊛ljcafe.com. A good-value joint offering up excellent Mexican food such as chicken in a mole sauce or steak tacos. $\overline{\underline{\$}}$

DRINKING AND NIGHTLIFE

The Hoppy Monk 4141 N Mesa St ⊛thehoppymonk. com/elpaso. Inviting and quirky brewpub a couple miles northwest of downtown with a stellar selection of craft ales on tap as well as better food than you might expect; try the sweet potato fries with toasted walnut aioli and the veggie monk – a black bean and pumpkin burger with provolone.

Plaza Theatre 125 Pioneer Plaza ⊛elpasolive.com/venues/plaza-theatre. If not attending a concert, you can

tour this regal and intimate downtown venue that routinely hosts top-notch rock and country acts as well as dance and orchestral performances.

Tap Bar 408 E San Antonio Ave ☎915 532 1848. A diverse local crowd hangs out at this downtown dive, which serves good, cheap Mexican-American staples, including heaped plates of nachos with shredded beef, and beers (most just a few dollars a bottle).

The Southwest

SPIDER ROCK, CANYON DE CHELLY

The Southwest

The Southwestern desert states of New Mexico, Arizona, Utah and Nevada stretch from Texas to California, across an elemental landscape ranging from towering monoliths of red sandstone to snowcapped mountains, on a high desert plateau that repeatedly splits open to reveal yawning canyons. This overwhelming scenery is complemented by the emphatic presence of Native American cultures and the palpable legacy of America's Wild West frontier.

Each state retains a distinct identity. New Mexico bears the most obvious traces of long-term settlement, with Native American pueblos coexisting alongside former Spanish colonial towns like **Santa Fe**, **Albuquerque** and **Taos**. In Arizona, it's Wild West history that's more conspicuous, in towns such as **Tombstone**, site of the OK Corral. More than a third of the state belongs to Native Americans including the Apache, Hopi and Navajo; most live in the red-rock lands of the northeast, notably amid the splendour typified by the **Canyon de Chelly** and **Monument Valley**.

The canyon country of northern Arizona – even the immense **Grand Canyon** – won't prepare you for the compelling desertscape of southern Utah, where **Zion** and **Bryce** canyons are the best known of a string of national parks and monuments. **Moab**, between majestic **Canyonlands** and surreal **Arches** in the east, is the top destination for outdoors enthusiasts. Nevada, on the other hand, is nothing short of desolate, despite the bright lights of **Las Vegas**.

You can count on warm sunshine anywhere in the Southwest for nine months of the year, with incredible sunsets most evenings. Although "snowbirds" flock to southern Arizona in winter, elsewhere summer is the peak tourist season, despite air temperatures topping 100°F, and the awesome thunderstorms that sweep through in late summer, causing flash floods and forest fires. By October, perhaps the best time to come, the crowds are gone and in the mountains and canyons the leaves turn red and gold. Winter brings snow to higher elevations, while spring sees wild flowers bloom in the desert.

The Southwest's backcountry wildernesses are ideal for **camping** and **backpacking**. Be prepared for harsh terrain: always carry water, and if you venture off the beaten track let someone know your plans.

Without your own vehicle, many of the most fascinating corners of the Southwest are utterly inaccessible. Scheduled public **transport** runs almost exclusively between the big cities – which unfortunately are not at all the destinations that make it worth coming here.

GREAT REGIONAL DRIVES

The High Road, northern NM Time-forgotten Hispanic villages in the rolling hills between Santa Fe and Taos.

Hwy-12, southern UT Stupendous desert wilderness, crossed by rivers and dotted with waterfalls.

Road between the Rims, northern AZ The 215-mile drive between the North and South rims of the Grand Canyon leads past dramatic red-rock cliffs, and across the Colorado River.

Route 66, northern NM and AZ The legendary "Mother Road" to California motors through towns like Albuquerque, Winslow and Flagstaff, and is still very much the place to get your kicks.

Self-drive route, Monument Valley, UT/AZ Teasing a reluctant rental car through the red sands of Monument Valley, passing legendary movie locations, is one of the Southwest's greatest thrills.

CIRCA RESORT & CASINO, LAS VEGAS

Highlights

❶ Santa Fe, NM Great museums, fascinating history, atmospheric hotels – New Mexico's capital is a must on any Southwest itinerary. See page 103

❷ La Posada, AZ Extraordinary restored hotel, straight from the heyday of Route 66, that's a great reason to spend a night in Winslow. See page 128

❸ The Havasupai Reservation, AZ Glorying in its turquoise waterfalls, this little-known offshoot of the Grand Canyon remains home to its original Native American inhabitants. See page 136

❹ Monument Valley, AZ/UT Though the eerie sandstone monoliths of Monument Valley

are familiar the world over, they still take every visitor's breath away. See page 138

❺ Canyon de Chelly, AZ Ancestral Puebloan "cliff dwellings" pepper every twist and turn of this stupendous sheer-walled canyon. See page 140

❻ Scenic Hwy-12, UT Crossing the heart of Utah's red-rock wilderness, Hwy-12 is perhaps the most exhilarating drive in the USA. See page 149

❼ Delicate Arch, UT This freestanding natural arch is the crowning glory of Arches National Park. See page 152

❽ Las Vegas, NV You really should see Las Vegas at least once in your lifetime, even just for a night between flying in and getting the hell out. See page 159

HIGHLIGHTS ARE MARKED ON THE MAP ON PAGE 100

THE SOUTHWEST

HIGHLIGHTS

1. Santa Fe, NM
2. La Posada, AZ
3. The Havasupai Reservation, AZ
4. Monument Valley, AZ/UT
5. Canyon de Chelly, AZ
6. Scenic Hwy-12, UT
7. Delicate Arch, UT
8. Las Vegas, NV

0 ———— 100
miles

N

OREGON

IDAHO

Bear Lake

Great Salt Lake

Salt Lake City

Park City

Utah Lake

Provo

UTAH

CAPITOL REEF N.P.

Torrey

Escalante

BRYCE CANYON N.P.

Tropic

Lake Powell

ZION N.P.

Cedar City

St George

Springdale

Kanab

Page

GRAND CANYON N.P.

North Rim

Tuba City

Havasupai Res.

South Rim

Wupatki N.M.

Grand Canyon West

Williams

Flagstaff

Walnut Canyon N.M.

Sedona

Kingman

Laughlin

Prescott

ARIZONA

Phoenix

Tucson

SAGUARO (WEST) N.P.

Nogales

Yuma

MEXICO

Winnemucca

Elko

Lovelock

Pyramid Lake

Reno

Truckee

Carson City

Lake Tahoe

NEVADA

GREAT BASIN N.P.

Tonopah

Goldfield

Beatty

Las Vegas

Lake Mead

Needles

Lake Havasu City

Colorado River

Barstow

Mojave Desert

Bakersfield

Santa Barbara

Los Angeles

San Bernardino

Palm Springs

JOSHUA TREE N.P.

Salton Sea

San Diego

Tijuana

CALIFORNIA

Mono Lake

Mammoth Lakes

Bishop

Lone Pine

Owens Lake

DEATH VALLEY N.P.

SEQUOIA N.P.

KINGS CANYON N.P.

Fresno

Mariposa

YOSEMITE N.P.

SIERRA NEVADA

Park City

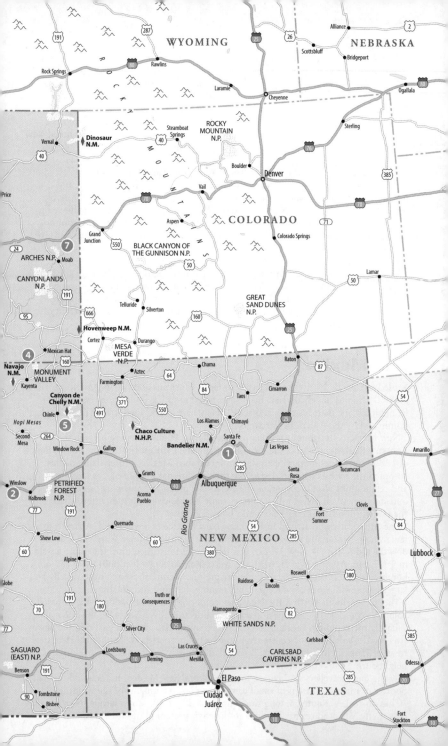

Brief history

While the **Ancestral Puebloans**, the best known of the Southwest's early inhabitants, abandoned their settlements and cliff palaces more than seven centuries ago, their descendants, the **Pueblo** peoples of New Mexico and the **Hopi** in Arizona, still lead similar lifestyles. From the fourteenth century onwards, the incoming **Navajo** and **Apache** appropriated vast territories, which they in turn were soon defending against European immigrants. The first such, in 1540, were Coronado's **Spanish** explorers, fruitlessly searching for cities of gold. Sixty years later, Hispanic colonists founded **New Mexico**, an ill-defined province that extended into modern California and Colorado. Not until 1848 was the region taken over by the **United States**. Almost immediately, outsiders began to flock through on their way to Gold Rush California.

Thereafter, violent confrontations increased between the US government and the Native Americans. The entire **Navajo** population was rounded up and forcibly removed to barren eastern New Mexico in 1864 (though they were soon allowed to return to northeastern Arizona), while the **Apache**, under Cochise and Geronimo, fought extended battles with the US cavalry. Though the nominal intention was to open up lands to newly American settlers, few succeeded in extracting a living from this harsh terrain.

One exception were the **Mormons**, whose flight from persecution brought them by the late 1840s to the alkaline basin of Utah's **Great Salt Lake**. Through sheer hard work, they established what amounted to an independent country, with outlying communities all over the Southwest, and still constitute more than sixty percent of Utah's population.

New Mexico

Settled in turn by Native Americans, Spaniards, Mexicans and Anglo-Americans, **NEW MEXICO** remains hugely diverse. Each successive group has built upon the legacy of its predecessors; their histories and achievements are intertwined, rather than simply dominated by the American latecomers.

New Mexico's Indigenous peoples – especially the **Pueblo** peoples, heirs to the **Ancestral Puebloans** – lie at the root of that cultural continuity. After the **Pueblo Revolt** of 1680 forced a temporary Spanish withdrawal into Mexico, proselytizing padres co-opted the natives without destroying their traditional ways of life, as local deities and celebrations were incorporated into Catholic practice. Somewhat bizarrely to outsiders, grand churches still dominate many Pueblo communities, often adjacent to the underground ceremonial chambers known as *kivas*.

The Americans who arrived in 1848 saw New Mexico as a wasteland. Apart from a few mining booms and range wars – such as the Lincoln County War, which brought **Billy the Kid** to fame – New Mexico was relatively undisturbed until it became a state in 1912. Since World War II, when the secret **Manhattan Project** built the first atomic bomb here, it has been home to America's premier weapons research outposts. By and large, people still work close to the land, mining, farming and ranching.

The mountainous **north** is the New Mexico of popular imagination, with its pastel colours, vivid desert landscape and adobe architecture. Even **Santa Fe**, the one real city, is hardly metropolitan in scale, and despite its world-class cultural facilities, the narrow streets of its small historic centre retain the feel of bygone days. The amiable frontier town of **Taos**, 75 miles northeast, is remarkable chiefly for the stacked dwellings of neighbouring **Taos Pueblo**.

While most travellers simply race through **central New Mexico**, it does hold isolated pockets of interest. Dozens of small towns hang on to remnants of the winding old "Chicago-to-LA" **Route 66**, long since superseded by I-40. **Albuquerque**, New Mexico's largest city, sits dead centre. The area to the **east**, stretching toward Texas, is largely

ADOBE

New Mexico's most defining feature is its **adobe architecture**, as seen on homes, churches and even shopping malls and motels. A sun-baked mixture of earth, sand, charcoal and chopped grass or straw, adobe bricks are set with a similar mortar, then plastered over with mud and straw. The soil used dictates the colour of the final building, so subtle variations are apparent everywhere. These days, most of what looks like adobe is actually painted cement or concrete, but even this looks attractive enough in its own semi-kitsch way, while hunting out such superb genuine adobes as the remote **Santuario de Chimayó** on the "**High Road**" between Taos and Santa Fe, the formidable church of **San Francisco de Asis** in Ranchos de Taos, or the multi-tiered dwellings of **Taos Pueblo**, can provide the basis of an enjoyable tour.

2

desolate, but the mountainous region **west** offers more – above all **Ácoma Pueblo**, the mesa-top "Sky City".

In wild, wide-open **southern New Mexico**, deep **Carlsbad Caverns** and the desolate dunes of **White Sands** are the main attractions, and elsewhere you can still stumble upon mining and cattle-ranching towns barely changed since the heyday of the Wild West.

Santa Fe

One of America's oldest and most beautiful cities, **SANTA FE** was founded by Spanish adventurers and missionaries in 1610, a decade before the Pilgrims reached Plymouth Rock. Spread across a high plateau at the foot of the stunning **Sangre de Cristo** mountains, New Mexico's capital still glories in the adobe houses and baroque churches of its original architects, complemented these days by superb art museums and galleries. The busiest season is **summer**, when temperatures usually reach into the eighties Fahrenheit; in winter, daytime highs average a mere 42°F, though with snow on the mountains the city looks more ravishing than ever.

With well over a million tourists every year – and twenty thousand daily commuters – descending on a town of just eighty thousand inhabitants, Santa Fe has inevitably grown somewhat overblown. It still offers a palpable, romantic continuity with the Spanish settlement of four centuries ago, however. Despite the summer crowds, the downtown area retains the peaceful ambience of a small country town, while holding an extraordinary array of cultural and historic treasures. The rigorous insistence that every building should look like a Spanish Colonial palace takes a bit of getting used to, but above all else, it's rare indeed for it to be such fun simply to stroll around a Southwestern city.

Once you've got your bearings, the best places to get a sense of local history and culture are the **Palace of the Governors** and the **New Mexico Museum of Art** downtown and the museums of **Indian Arts and Culture** and **Folk Art** a couple of miles southeast. Alternatively, set about exploring distinct neighbourhoods like the old **Barrio Analco** just southeast of downtown, home to the **San Miguel Mission**; the **Canyon Road** arts district, just beyond; and funkier **Guadalupe Street** to the west, with its lively **Railyard** development.

The plaza

The main focus of life in Santa Fe is still the central **plaza** – especially when it's filled with buyers and craftspeople during the annual **Indian Market**, on the weekend after the third Thursday in August, and during the first weekend in September for the **Fiestas de Santa Fe**. Apart from an influx of art galleries and restaurants, the surrounding web of narrow streets has changed little. When the US took over in 1848, the new settlers chose to build in wood, but many of the finer adobe houses have survived. Since the 1930s, almost every non-adobe structure in sight of the plaza has been designed or redecorated to suit the Pueblo Revival mode, with rounded, mud-coloured plaster walls supporting roof beams made of thick pine logs.

Palace of the Governors

113 Lincoln Ave • May–Oct daily 10am–5pm, Fri till 7pm; Nov–April Tues–Sun 10am–5pm • Charge • ⓦ nmhistorymuseum.org

Set behind an arcaded veranda that serves as a market for Native American crafts-sellers, the low-slung, initially unprepossessing **Palace of the Governors** fills the entire northern side of Santa Fe's plaza. Originally sod-roofed, the oldest public building in the USA was constructed in 1610 as the headquarters of Spanish colonial administration. Until 1913, it looked like a typical territorial building, with a square tower at each corner; its subsequent adobe "reconstruction" was based on pure conjecture. The interior, organized around an open-air courtyard, holds excellent historical displays and a well-stocked bookstore.

A sensitively integrated extension immediately behind holds the very visual exhibits of the **New Mexico History Museum** (same hours and ticket), including letters from Billy the Kid.

New Mexico Museum of Art

107 E Palace Ave • May–Oct daily 10am–5pm, Fri till 7pm; Nov–April Tues–Sun 10am–5pm • Charge, free first Fri of month 5–7pm May–Oct • ⓦ nmartmuseum.org

Housed in an attractive adobe on the northwest corner of the plaza, the **New Mexico Museum of Art** centres on a beautiful garden courtyard, and exhibits painting and sculpture by local artists. Selections from the permanent collection, displayed upstairs, usually include an O'Keeffe or two, while an entire room is devoted to painter and printmaker Gustave Baumann.

Georgia O'Keeffe Museum

217 Johnson St • Thurs–Mon 10am–5pm • Charge • ⓦ okeeffemuseum.org

The showpiece **Georgia O'Keeffe Museum** houses the world's largest collection of O'Keeffe's work. Highlights include the desert landscapes she painted near **Abiquiu**, forty miles northwest of Santa Fe, where she lived from 1946 until her death in 1986. Precisely what's on show varies month to month, but there's enough material to devote entire rooms to paintings of particular motifs, be it scarlet poppies or pink seashells, all characterized by O'Keeffe's trademark close focus and voluptuousness. Among the more familiar sun-bleached skulls and iconic flowers, you may be surprised to encounter such earlier canvases as her New York city scenes.

Museum of Indian Arts and Culture

Museum Hill, 2 miles southeast of downtown • May–Oct daily 10am–5pm; Nov–April Tues–Sun 10am–5pm • Charge • ⓦ miaclab.org

The excellent **Museum of Indian Arts and Culture** provides comprehensive coverage of all major Southwest groups, including the 'O'odham, Navajo, Apache, Pai, Ute and Pueblo peoples. Myth and history are explained in copious detail, while ancient artefacts ranging from pots and pipes to bells, whistles and spearthrowers are drawn from sites as far south as the Casas Grandes ruins in Mexico. Different sections describe how native peoples have thrived in such varying terrains as canyons, river basins, mesas and deserts. There's also a comprehensive array of pottery, from pristine thousand-year-old Ancestral Puebloan and Mimbres pieces up to the works of twentieth-century revivalists.

Museum of International Folk Art

Museum Hill, 2 miles southeast of downtown • May–Oct daily 10am–5pm; Nov–April Tues–Sun 10am–5pm • Charge • ⓦ internationalfolkart.org

Besides staging temporary exhibitions, the delightful **Museum of International Folk Art** is the permanent home of the huge **Girard Collection** of paintings, textiles and **clay**

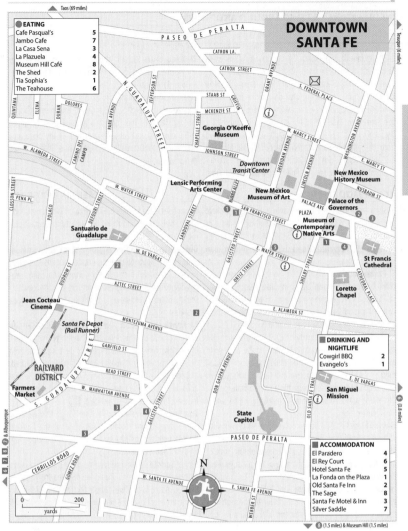

Taos (69 miles)

EATING

Cafe Pasqual's	5
Jambo Cafe	7
La Casa Sena	3
La Plazuela	4
Museum Hill Café	8
The Shed	2
Tia Sophia's	1
The Teahouse	6

DOWNTOWN SANTA FE

2

DRINKING AND NIGHTLIFE

Cowgirl BBQ	2
Evangelo's	1

ACCOMMODATION

El Paradero	4
El Rey Court	6
Hotel Santa Fe	5
La Fonda on the Plaza	1
Old Santa Fe Inn	2
The Sage	8
Santa Fe Motel & Inn	3
Silver Saddle	7

N

figurines from all over the world. These are arranged in colourful dioramas that include a Pueblo Feast Day, complete with dancing *kachinas* and camera-clicking tourists, and street scenes from countries such as Poland, Peru, Portugal and Ethiopia featuring fabulously ornate churches and cathedrals.

ARRIVAL AND DEPARTURE   SANTA FE

By plane Santa Fe's small airport (ⓦ flysantafe.com), 10 miles southwest of downtown, is only served by flights from Phoenix, Denver and Dallas/Fort Worth.

By Rail Runner From the Santa Fe Depot, half a mile southwest of downtown, the Rail Runner train line connects Santa Fe with downtown Albuquerque (1hr 40min;

ⓦ riometro.org).

By Amtrak Daily trains between Chicago and LA stop at Lamy, 17 miles southeast, where they're met by Roadrunner shuttle vans, if booked in advance (wrideroadrunner.com).

Destinations Chicago (daily; 25hr); Flagstaff (daily; 7hr 30min); Los Angeles (daily; 19hr 30min).

2

INFORMATION, GETTING AROUND AND TOURS

Visitor centres Plaza Visitor Information Center, Paso de Luz, 66 E San Francisco St (daily 9am–5.30pm; ☎ 800 777 2489, ⓦ santafe.org); Santa Fe Community Convention Center, 201 W Marcy St (Mon–Fri 8.30am–4.30pm); Water Street Kiosk, 100 E Water St (daily 10am–6pm). The New Mexico Tourism Department also operates a state visitor centre at 491 Old Santa Fe Trail (Mon–Fri 8am–5pm, Sat & Sun 8am–4pm; ☎ 505 795 0343, ⓦ newmexico.org).

By bus Free Santa Fe Pick-Up buses loop around downtown from the Rail Runner station (every 10min; Mon–Fri 6.30am–5.30pm, Sat 8.30am–5.30pm, Sun 10am–5.30pm), and out to Canyon Road and Museum Hill from the visitor centre at 491 Old Santa Fe Trail (every 30min; daily 10am–5.30pm).

Walking tours Historic Walks of Santa Fe runs regular 1hr 45min walking tours of downtown, starting from various locations (March–Dec, schedules vary; charge; ⓦ historicwalksofsantafe.com).

Bus tours The Loretto Line, based at the Loretto Chapel, 207 Old Santa Fe Trail, runs bus tours of the city, taking in Museum Hill and Canyon Rd as well as the plaza area (mid-March to Oct daily 10am, noon & 2pm; charge; ⓦ toursofsantafe.com).

ACCOMMODATION   SEE MAP PAGE 105

In summer, when every bed in town is frequently taken, you're unlikely to find a room within walking distance of downtown Santa Fe for under $150. Most of Santa Fe's **motels** are on **Cerrillos Road** (US-85), the main road in from I-25.

El Paradero 220 W Manhattan Ave ⓦ paradorsantafe. com. Converted Spanish-era farmhouse near Guadalupe St. The rooms are relatively plain and simple and furnished with folk art; thirteen are en-suite, the remaining two share a bathroom. Good breakfast and helpful hosts. $$$

★ **El Rey Court** 1862 Cerrillos Rd, at St Michael's Drive ⓦ elreycourt.com. This white-painted adobe compound offers the most character and best value of the Cerrillos Road motels, with stylish, distinctive and large Southwestern rooms adorned with Art Deco tiles, semi-private patios, some nice suites, complimentary breakfasts, a pool and a large garden. $$

Hotel Santa Fe 1501 Paseo de Peralta, at Cerrillos Rd ⓦ hotelsantafe.com. Run by Picuris Pueblo, this attractive, elegant and very comfortable adobe hotel on the edge of downtown is within walking distance of the plaza, and has its own good restaurant, *Amaya*. $$$

★ **La Fonda on the Plaza** 100 E San Francisco St ⓦ lafondasantafe.com. Gorgeous old inn on the southeast corner of the plaza, marking the end of the Santa Fe Trail, and featuring hand-painted murals and stained glass throughout. Each lavishly furnished room is different, with some lovely suites, and there's a delightful restaurant plus rooftop bar. $$$

Old Santa Fe Inn 320 Galisteo St ⓦ oldsantafeinn. com. Former Route 66 motor court, now an appealing inn; many of its tasteful, Mexican-themed rooms have their own gas fireplaces. Avoid the few rooms in the inadequately soundproofed two-storey buildings. Rates include breakfast. $$$

★ **Santa Fe Motel & Inn** 510 Cerrillos Rd ⓦ santafe motel.com. To call this delightfully stylish yet inexpensive little adobe complex a "motel" barely does it justice; even its most conventional rooms are appealingly furnished, and some have their own kitchens, while there are several gorgeous *casitas*. The rates, great for such a quiet, central location, include a cooked breakfast. $$$

The Sage 725 Cerrillos Rd, at Don Diego ⓦ thesagesf. com. Large, clean, motel, at the edge of the Railyard District, with very helpful staff and rates that include free breakfast and local shuttle. $$$

Silver Saddle 2810 Cerrillos Rd, at Siler Rd ⓦ santafe silversaddlemotel.com. Busy, down-to-earth Western-themed motel, in the finest Route 66 tradition. Each room has a little patio, some have cooking facilities, and all feature fun cowboy trappings. $$

EATING   SEE MAP PAGE 105

Cafe Pasqual's 121 Don Gaspar Ave ⓦ pasquals.com. Lovely, lively, and ever-innovative Old/New Mexican restaurant that serves top-quality organic food in an attractive tiled dining room. Dinner mains range from vegetarian, via *cochinita pibil* (slow-roasted pork), to grilled lamb chops with pomegranate molasses. Appetizers include spicy Vietnamese scallops. $$

★ **Jambo Cafe** 2010 Cerrillos Rd ⓦ jambocafe.net. Tucked away in a modern mall, this colourful café skilfully adapts African and Caribbean traditions to suit Santa Fe tastes. The menu ranges from goat, lamb or coconut lentil stews and curries to plantain crab cakes and a jerk chicken sandwich, with takeout available. $$

La Casa Sena 125 E Palace Ave ⓦ lacasasena.com. Attractive courtyard restaurant, a block from the plaza; zestful Southwestern lunches are the best deal, while typical dinner specials are a lot more. At the adjoining, cheaper *La Cantina*, staff perform Broadway show tunes during dinner. $$$

★ **La Plazuela at La Fonda** 100 E San Francisco St ⓦ lafondasantafe.com/la-plazuela. Delightful, beautifully furnished Mexican restaurant, which feels like an open-air courtyard even though it's covered by a glass ceiling. All the usual Mexican dishes are nicely prepared and sold for reasonable prices at lunchtime, and ranging, for pricier items such as sirloin steak, in the evening. $$$

Museum Hill Café 705 Camino Lejo ⓦ museumhillcafe. net. Spacious café, enjoying beautiful mountain views from a terrace between the Folk Art and Indian Arts museums. Good, inexpensive sandwiches – turkey, tuna and steak – plus tacos, *flautas*, burgers, pasta specials and salads, and a large Sunday brunch. $$

★ **The Shed** 113 E Palace Ave ⓦ sfshed.com. Casual, family-owned New Mexican restaurant in a pleasant garden compound that dates back to the 1690s, serving a steady diet of chilli enchiladas, blue-corn tortillas and even low-fat

specialities. The food itself is cheap, cheerful and tasty – try the *carne adovada* (slow-roasted pork), along with blue-corn tortillas and mocha cake. $$

Tia Sophia's 210 W San Francisco St ☎ 505 983 9880. Spicy, very inexpensive Mexican diner, a block or two west of the plaza, that's hugely popular with lunching locals. Daily breakfast and lunch specials. $

The Teahouse 821 Canyon Rd ⓦ teahousesantafe.com. Large and very welcoming café, with a peaceful garden. The star attraction is the amazing range of white, green, black, flavoured and downright bizarre teas from all over the world, but it's also a good spot to unwind over a cooked breakfast, lunchtime soup or sandwich, or pasta or *posole* main. $

DRINKING AND NIGHTLIFE

SEE MAP PAGE 105

Cowgirl BBQ 319 S Guadalupe St ⓦ cowgirlsantafe. com. Very busy country-themed restaurant and bar, with karaoke on Mondays and live music every other night, plus a billiard room.

Evangelo's 200 W San Francisco St ⓦ evangeloscocktail lounge.com. The only good bare-bones bar in easy walking range of the plaza, with a pool table and a jukebox, plus regular live music. Cash only.

ENTERTAINMENT

Jean Cocteau Cinema 418 Montezuma Ave ⓦ jean cocteaucinema.com. Much-loved repertory cinema, rescued from closure by George R.R. Martin. As well as ongoing screenings of new and classic movies, it staged free preview showings of each *Game of Thrones* series and puts on occasional gigs. It also holds a hip little cocktail bar/café, and a bookstore selling Martin's books.

Lensic Performing Arts Center 211 W San Francisco

St ⓦ lensic.org. All year round, this strikingly converted "Pueblo Deco" theatre downtown hosts musical and theatrical performances, by touring artists as well as local groups.

Santa Fe Opera 301 Opera Drive (1.4 miles northeast of US-84 exit 168) ⓦ santafeopera.org. In its much-anticipated July & August season, the Santa Fe Opera stages five separate productions in a magnificent amphitheatre 7 miles north of Santa Fe.

Bandelier National Monument

Ten miles south of Los Alamos, a total of 50 miles northwest of Santa Fe • Access to Frijoles Canyon by car mid-Oct to mid-May only; mid-May to mid-Oct free shuttle from car park at White Rock, on Hwy-4 in White Rock • Charge • ⓦ nps.gov/band

Around 1300 AD, itinerant Ancestral Puebloan groups, seeking sanctuary from drought and invasion, gathered at the edge of the forested mesas of the Pajarito Plateau to build what's now **Bandelier National Monument**, a community that amalgamated their assorted cultures.

A paved 1.5-mile trail leads through the prime site, **Frijoles Canyon**. Not far along, a side path from the circular, multi-storey village of **Tyuonyi** leads up to dozens of **cave dwellings**, their rounded chambers scooped out of the soft volcanic rock; you can scramble up to, and even enter, some to peer out across the valley. The main trail continues to the **Long House**, an 800ft series of two- and three-storey houses built against the canyon wall. Rows of petroglyphs are visible, carved above the holes that held the roof beams. Half a mile beyond, protected by a rock overhang 150ft above the canyon floor and accessible via rickety ladders and steep stairs, a reconstructed *kiva* sits in **Alcove House**.

The High Road

The quickest route between Santa Fe and Taos follows US-84 as far as the Rio Grande, then follows the river northeast on Hwy-68. US-84 passes through the heartland of the **northern pueblos**, a cluster of tiny Tewa-speaking communities, but unless your visit coincides with a feast day, there's little to see.

2

THE ANCESTRAL PUEBLOANS

Few visitors to the Southwest are prepared for the awesome scale and beauty of the desert cities and cliff palaces left by the **Ancestral Puebloans**, as seen all over the high plateaus of the "**Four Corners**" region, where Colorado, New Mexico, Arizona and Utah now meet.

Although the earliest humans reached the Southwest around 10,000 BC, the Ancestral Puebloans first appeared as the **Basketmakers**, near the San Juan River, two thousand years ago. Named for their woven sandals and bowls, they lived in pits in the earth, roofed with logs and mud. Over time, the Ancestral Puebloans adopted an increasingly settled lifestyle, becoming expert farmers and potters. Their first freestanding houses on the plains were followed by multistoreyed **pueblos**, in which hundreds of families lived in complexes of contiguous "apartments". The astonishing **cliff dwellings**, perched on precarious ledges high above remote canyons, which they began to build around 1100 AD, were the first Ancestral Puebloan settlements to show signs of defensive fortifications. Competition for resources grew fiercer during the thirteenth century, and it's thought that warfare and even cannibalism played a role in their ultimate dispersal. Moving eastward, they joined forces with other displaced groups in a coming-together that eventually produced the modern **Pueblo** peoples. Hence the currently favoured name, "Ancestral Puebloan", which has superseded "Anasazi", a Navajo word meaning "ancient enemies".

Among the most significant **Ancestral Puebloan sites** are:

Mesa Verde Magnificent cliff palaces, high in the canyons of Colorado.

Bandelier National Monument Large riverside pueblos and cave-like homes hollowed from volcanic rock; see page 107.

Chaco Canyon The largest and most sophisticated freestanding pueblos, far out in the desert; see page 116.

Canyon de Chelly Superbly dramatic cliff dwellings in a glowing sandstone canyon now owned and farmed by the Navajo; see page 140.

Hovenweep Enigmatic towers poised above a canyon; see page 155.

Wupatki Several small pueblo communities near the edge of the Painted Desert, built by assorted groups after an eleventh-century volcanic eruption.

Walnut Canyon Numerous homes set into the canyon walls above lush Walnut Creek, just east of Flagstaff.

Betatakin Canyon-side community set in a vast rocky alcove in Navajo National Monument; visible from afar, or close-up on guided hikes.

However, the circuitous "**High Road**" leaves US-68/84 a dozen miles north of Santa Fe, near Nambe Pueblo. Leading high into the wooded **Sangre de Cristo Mountains**, it passes a number of pueblos and Hispanic villages.

Santuario de Chimayó

Daily: May–Sept 9am–6pm; Oct–April 9am–5pm; Mass Mon–Sat 11am, Sun 10.30am & noon • ⓦ holychimayo.us

The quaint mountain village of **CHIMAYÓ**, 25 miles north of Santa Fe where Hwy-503 meets Hwy-76, is the site of the 1816 **Santuario de Chimayó**. Known as the "Lourdes of America" for the devotion of its many pilgrims, this round-shouldered, twin-towered adobe beauty sits behind an enclosed courtyard; a pit in a side room holds the "holy dirt" for which the site is venerated.

ACCOMMODATION AND EATING   THE HIGH ROAD

Hacienda Rancho de Chimayó Hwy-98 ⓦ ranchodechimayo.com. Immediately across from the *Rancho* restaurant, and run by the same management, this peaceful B&B inn offers seven appealing en-suite rooms, arranged around a shared courtyard; several have their own patio space. $

★ **Rancho de Chimayó** Hwy-98 ⓦ ranchodechimayo.com. The best traditional New Mexican restaurant in the state, serving superb *flautas* and a mouthwatering *sopaipilla*, stuffed with meat and chillis, on a lovely sun-drenched outdoor patio. $$

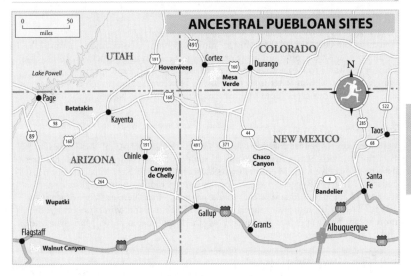

ANCESTRAL PUEBLOAN SITES

2

Taos

Still home to one of the longest-established Native American populations in the USA, though transformed by becoming first a Spanish colonial outpost and more recently a hangout for bohemian artists, Hollywood exiles and New Age dropouts, **TAOS** (which rhymes with "mouse") is famous out of all proportion to its size. Not quite six thousand people live in its three component parts: **Taos** itself, around the plaza; sprawling **Ranchos de Taos**, three miles to the south; and the indigenous community of **Taos Pueblo**, two miles north.

Beyond the usual unsightly highway sprawl, Taos is a delight to visit. Besides museums, galleries and stores, it still offers an unhurried pace and charm and the sense of a meeting place between Pueblo, Hispanic and American cultures. Its reputation as an **artists' colony** began at the end of the nineteenth century, and new generations of artists and writers have "discovered" Taos ever since. English novelist **D.H. Lawrence** visited in the 1920s, while **Georgia O'Keeffe** arrived soon afterwards.

Taos plaza

The old Spanish **plaza** at the heart of Taos is now ringed by jewellery stores, art galleries and restaurants; all conform to the predominant Pueblo motif of rounded brown adobe. Specific sights are few – a small **gallery** in the *Fonda de Taos* holds a collection of nine sexy but amateurish paintings by D.H. Lawrence (aka the "Forbidden Art" collection), and the tree-filled square itself is often animated by guitar-toting buskers – but the surrounding streets are perfect for an aimless stroll.

Governor Bent House and Museum

117 Bent St • Daily: April–Oct 9am–5pm; Nov–March 10am–4pm • Charge • ☎ 505 758 2376

Bent Street, a block north of the plaza, takes its name from the first American governor of New Mexico, Charles Bent, whose former home is now the **Governor Bent House and Museum**. The imposition of American rule was resented by Taos's Hispanic and Native American population alike, and Bent was killed here by an angry mob on January 19, 1847.

A ramshackle museum of frontier Taoseño life, his house holds Native American artefacts, antiquated rifles and even an eight-legged lamb.

Kit Carson Home and Museum

113 Kit Carson Rd • Tues–Sat 11am–4pm • Charge • Ⓦ kitcarsonhomeandmuseum.com

The dusty but evocative adobe home of "mountain man," mason, and part-time US cavalry officer **Kit Carson** stand just east of the plaza. Born in Kentucky in 1809, Carson left home to join a wagon train to Missouri in 1826, and spent the ensuing winter in Taos. He was to return repeatedly, in between escapades such as scouting for the 1840s Frémont expeditions and campaigning against the Navajo in the 1860s (see page 139).

Millicent Rogers Museum

1504 Millicent Rogers Rd, 4 miles north of the plaza • Daily 10am–5pm (closed Wed Nov–March) • Charge • Ⓦ millicentrogers.org

Focusing on both Native American and Hispanic art, and tracing how those cultures have been perceived, the **Millicent Rogers Museum** is one of New Mexico's very finest galleries. Millicent Rogers herself – a former fashion model, granddaughter of a founder of Standard Oil and "close" to Cary Grant – lived here until her death in 1953. Her collection includes superb Ancestral Puebloan and Mimbres pottery; the more recent black-on-black ceramics of San Ildefonso Pueblo potter Maria Martínez; and beautiful Navajo blankets.

San Francisco de Asis

In the small unpaved plaza of Ranchos de Taos, the mission church of **San Francisco de Asis** turns its broad shoulders, or more accurately its massive adobe buttresses, to the passing traffic on Hwy-68. Built around 1776, it's one of colonial New Mexico's most splendid architectural achievements, with subtly rounded walls and corners that disguise its underlying structural strength.

Hacienda de los Martínez

708 Hacienda Way, off Lower Ranchitos Rd, Ranchos de Taos, 2 miles west of Hwy-68 • Mon, Tues, Fri & Sat 11am–4pm, Sun noon–4pm • Charge • Ⓦ taoshistoricmuseums.org

One of the few Spanish haciendas to be preserved in something like its original state, the **Hacienda de los Martínez** was built in 1804 by Don Antonio Martínez, an early mayor of Taos. Within its thick, windowless, adobe walls – the place could be sealed like a fortress against then still-prevalent Native American raids – two dozen rooms are wrapped around two separate patios, holding animal pens and a well. Trade goods of the kind Don Antonio once carried south along the Rio Grande are displayed alongside tools, looms and simple furnishings of the era, plus a fine collection of Hispanic religious art.

Taos Pueblo

Just over 2 miles north of Taos plaza, along either of two separate approach roads off Hwy-68 • Mon & Thurs–Sun 9am–4pm, but closed mid-Feb to March, and also frequently closed for events • Charge • Ⓦ taospueblo.com

Continuously inhabited for nearly one thousand years, the two multistorey adobes at **Taos Pueblo** jointly constitute the most impressive Native American dwelling place still in use. Hlauuma, the north house, and Hlaukwima, the south house, are separated by the Rio Pueblo de Taos, which flows down from the sacred Blue Lake, inaccessible to outsiders. Pueblo residents make few concessions to the modern world, living without toilets, running water or electricity. Paying the entry fee entitles you to join guided **walking tours** led by Pueblo residents.

Although visitors are welcome throughout most of the year, only if you come on certain spectacular **feast days** and dances (when photography is forbidden) will you see anything more than the residents simply carrying on with everyday life. Most such events take place in summer; the biggest are the Corn Dances (June 13 & 24, July 25 & 26), the Taos Pueblo Pow Wow (second weekend in July), and the Feast of San Gerónimo (Sept 29 & 30).

ARRIVAL AND INFORMATION

By bus Greyhound does not serve Taos, but the RTD (ⓦncrtd.org) runs the free 305 Express bus service twice daily Saturdays and Sundays between Santa Fe and Taos, via Española, for a total journey time of 1hr 45 minutes. Buses also run Mon–Fri, for a small fee.

Visitor centre 1139 Paseo del Pueblo Sur, 2 miles south of the plaza where Hwy-68 meets Hwy-585 (daily 9am–5pm; ☎800 732 8267, ⓦtaos.org).

TOURS AND ACTIVITIES

Far Flung Adventures Full-day whitewater rafting trips through the Taos Box Canyon of the Rio Grande, which offers rapids up to Class V (April–mid-July only; ⓦfarflung. com), plus shorter half-day trips that venture into the Orilla Verde Recreation Area, from Pilar further south. The same operators also offer hiking and kayaking adventures.

ACCOMMODATION

El Pueblo Lodge 412 Paseo del Pueblo Norte ⓦelpueblo lodge.com. Southwestern-themed 1940s fake-adobe motel, half a mile north of downtown near Taos Pueblo, where the nicely furnished rooms have extra-large bathrooms and there's a decent outdoor pool and hot tub. $\overline{\underline{\$\$}}$

★**Historic Taos Inn** 125 Paseo del Pueblo Norte ⓦtaosinn.com. Gorgeous, romantic central Taos landmark, consisting of several ancient adobes welded together to create an atmospheric and very Southwestern hotel. Each room plays some variation on the Pueblo theme, with varying degrees of luxury; the cosy, convivial lobby area was once an open courtyard. $\overline{\underline{\$\$}}$

★**La Doña Luz** 114C Kit Carson Rd ⓦstayintaos. com. Delightful Hispanic-flavoured rooms of differing sizes and prices in a peaceful adobe B&B just east of the plaza. All are lovely, and have en-suite facilities; some have fully equipped kitchens and/or hot tubs. $\overline{\underline{\$\$}}$

La Fonda de Taos 108 South Plaza ⓦlafondataos.com. Vintage 1930s hotel on the plaza, modernized to hold 24 luxurious suites, with Southwestern furnishings and tiled bathrooms. The lobby even holds a gallery of D.H. Lawrence paintings. $\overline{\underline{\$\$\$}}$

THE RIO GRANDE PUEBLOS

The first Spaniards to explore what's now New Mexico encountered 100,000 so-called **Pueblo** peoples, living in a hundred villages and towns (*pueblo* is Spanish for "village"). Resenting the imposition of Catholicism and their virtual enslavement, the various groups banded together in the 1680 **Pueblo Revolt** and ousted the entire colonial regime, killing scores of priests and soldiers and sending hundreds more south to Mexico. After the Spanish returned in 1693, the Pueblos showed little further resistance and they have coexisted ever since, accepting aspects of Catholicism without giving up their traditional beliefs and practices. New Mexico is now home to around forty thousand Pueblo peoples; each of its nineteen autonomous pueblos has its own laws and system of government.

The Pueblos celebrate Saints' days, major Catholic holidays such as Easter and the Epiphany, and even the Fourth of July with a combination of Native American traditions and Catholic rituals, featuring elaborately costumed dances and massive communal feasts. The spectacle of hundreds of costumed, body-painted Pueblo people of all ages, performing elaborate dances in such timeless surroundings, is hugely impressive.

However, few pueblos are the tourist attractions they're touted to be. While the best known, **Taos** and **Ácoma**, retain their ancient defensive architecture, the rest tend to be dusty adobe hamlets scattered around a windblown plaza. Unless you arrive on a feast day or are a knowledgeable shopper in search of Pueblo crafts, visits are liable to prove disappointing. In addition, you'll be made very unwelcome if you fail to behave respectfully – don't "explore" places that are off-limits to outsiders, such as shrines, *kivas* or private homes.

Fifteen of the pueblos are concentrated along the Rio Grande north of Albuquerque, with a long-standing division between the seven **southern pueblos**, south of Santa Fe, most of which speak Keresan and the group to the north, which mostly speak Tewa (pronounced *tay-wah*). Visitors to each are required to register at a visitor centre; some charge an admission fee and those that permit such activities typically charge additional fees for still photography, for video cameras and a lot more for sketching. Many also forbid the use of mobile phones. There's no extra charge for feast days or dances, but photography is usually forbidden on special occasions.

2

Mabel Dodge Luhan House 240 Morada Lane ⓦ mabeldodgeluhan.com. This 200-year-old adobe B&B complex, not far northeast of the plaza, has impressive historic associations, with lovely guestrooms named after guests like Willa Cather and Ansel Adams. Two rooms, including the light-filled solarium, share a bathroom painted by D.H. Lawrence; the cheaper annex has more modern fittings. $$

EATING AND DRINKING

Doc Martin's Historic Taos Inn, 125 Paseo del Pueblo Norte ⓦ taosinn.com. Delicious, inventive New Mexican food in a romantic old adobe inn. Typical lunchtime burgers and burritos are good value, while dinner mains, such as buffalo short ribs or roast chicken are a bit more expensive. Unusual weekend brunch options include the Kit Carson – poached eggs on yam biscuits. $$

★ **La Cueva Cafe** 135 Paseo del Pueblo Sur ⓦ lacueva cafe.com. Tiny and very central adobe café, run by an energetic young couple and serving meticulously prepared Mexican classics, with meaty burritos and chimichangas, seafood dishes like crab and shrimp enchiladas, and lots of vegetarian options. $$

Lambert's of Taos 123 Bent St ⓦ lambertsoftaos.com. Cosy but classy historic adobe, where the cuisine is more New American than New Mexican. A local-flavoured red chilli soup is always cheap, while sumptuous mains include Moroccan spiced lamb loin. $$$

Love Apple 803 Paseo del Pueblo Norte ⓦ theloveapple. net. This beautiful former chapel, open for dinner only, holds just thirteen tables; reserve ahead to sample its locally sourced, partly foraged and mostly organic cuisine. Appetizers include succulent pates made from chicken livers or mushrooms with walnuts, while mains range from baked sweetcorn tamales in Oaxacan mole sauce to a very French beef bourguignon in puff pastry. $$$

Michael's Kitchen 304C Paseo del Pueblo Norte ⓦ michaelskitchen.com. Inexpensive Mexican and Southwestern dishes in an old adobe kitchen, plus fresh-baked pastries, cinnamon rolls and coffee in the morning. $

Albuquerque

Sprawling at the heart of New Mexico, where the east–west road and rail routes cross both the Rio Grande and the old road south to Mexico, **ALBUQUERQUE** is, with half a million people, the state's only major metropolis. The **"Duke City"** may have grown a bit fast for comfort, but the original Hispanic settlement is still discernible at its core and its diverse population gives it a rare cultural vibrancy. Even if its architecture is often uninspired, the setting is magnificent, sandwiched between the Rio Grande and the glowing **Sandia Mountains**. Specific highlights include the intact **Spanish plaza**, the neon-lit **Route 66** frontage of Central Avenue and the excellent **Indian Pueblo Cultural Centre**, while every October Albuquerque hosts the nation's largest **hot-air balloon** rally.

Although the huge international popularity of TV's *Breaking Bad* and *Better Call Saul* has certainly boosted tourism, no specific locations from the series are especially worth visiting – not that that's stopped local entrepreneurs from offering tours riding around in a replica RV from *Breaking Bad*, or indeed selling "blue meth" bath salts and sweet treats.

Old Town

Once you've cruised up and down **Central Avenue**, looking at the flashing neon and 1940s architecture of this twenty-mile stretch of Route 66, most of what's interesting about Albuquerque is concentrated in **Old Town**, the heart of the Spanish city. As the interstate billboards rightly proclaim, "it's darned old and historic". The tree-filled **main plaza** is overlooked by the twin-towered adobe facade of **San Felipe de Neri church**; it's a pleasant place to wander or have a meal, even if there's not a whole lot to do.

Albuquerque Museum

2000 Mountain Rd · Tues–Sun 9am–5pm · Charge · ⓦ cabq.gov/artsculture/albuquerque-museum

The **Albuquerque Museum**, a couple of blocks northeast of the plaza, makes a great introduction to the city's story. Besides an impressive array of the armour and weaponry carried by the Spanish conquistadors, it holds delicate religious artefacts, plus paintings and photos showing Albuquerque through the centuries.

New Mexico Museum of Natural History and Science

1801 Mountain Rd NW • Mon & Wed–Sun 9am–5pm • Charge • ⓦ nmnaturalhistory.org

With its full-scale models of dinosaurs and a replica of a Carlsbad-like snow cave, the **New Mexico Museum of Natural History and Science** is aimed primarily at kids. Its fascinating "Start Up" exhibition uses Microsoft's origins in Albuquerque in 1977 as the springboard for a history of the computer revolution. Albuquerque was where the first Altair personal computer was developed, prompting an incredibly young-looking Bill Gates and Paul Allen to move here in 1977 and establish "Micro-Soft" to write software for the first generation of home-based programmers.

2

ABQ BioPark

Aquarium & Botanic Garden 2601 Central Ave NW • Daily 9am–5pm (closed Mon Nov–Feb) • **Zoo** 903 10th St SW • Same hours • Charge both sections • ⓦ cabq.gov/artsculture/biopark

In the **ABQ BioPark**, alongside but not quite within sight of the Rio Grande, the **Albuquerque Aquarium** offers such diverse experiences as eating in a restaurant beside a glass-walled tank filled with live sharks, and walking through a tunnel surrounded on all sides by fierce-eyed moray eels. The whole place has been designed with a great eye for aesthetics. Across the park's central plaza, the **Botanic Garden** consists of two large conservatories plus a series of formal walled gardens.

A couple of miles south along the Rio Grande – buying a combined admission ticket entitles you to ride a miniature train to and fro – the **BioPark Zoo** holds everything from lions to polar bears, and posts a daily schedule of feeding times and other events.

Indian Pueblo Cultural Centre

2401 12th St NW • **Museum** Tues–Sun 9am–4pm • Charge • **Gift store** same hours • Free • ⓦ indianpueblo.org

The **Indian Pueblo Cultural Centre** is a stunning museum and crafts market, cooperatively owned and run by Pueblo peoples. As well as explaining the shared Ancestral Puebloan heritage at the root of Pueblo culture, the museum explores the impact of the Spanish conquistadors. There's also a good explanation of a topic rarely discussed with outsiders: how Indigenous religion has managed to coexist with imported Catholicism. Videos illustrate modern Pueblo life and the Indian Pueblo Store and **Shumakolowa Gallery** upstairs sells pottery and jewellery, while the good-quality Indian Pueblo Kitchen serves Pueblo specialities.

National Museum of Nuclear Science and History

601 Eubank Blvd SE • Daily 9am–5pm • Charge • ⓦ nuclearmuseum.org

ROUTE 66 IN THE SOUTHWEST

If you do ever plan to motor west, there's still one definitive highway that's the best. Ninety-plus years since it was first completed, eighty since John Steinbeck called it "the mother road, the road of flight" in *The Grapes of Wrath*, and seventy since songwriter Bobby Troup set it all down in rhyme, what better reason to visit the Southwest could there be than to get hip to this timely tip and get your kicks on **Route 66**?

The heyday of Route 66 as the nation's premier cross-country route – winding from Chicago to LA – lasted barely twenty years, from its being paved in 1937 until it began to be superseded by freeways in 1957. It was officially rendered defunct in 1984, when Williams, Arizona, became the last town to be bypassed. Nonetheless, substantial stretches of the original Route 66 survive, complete with the motels and drive-ins that became icons of vernacular American architecture. Restored 1950s roadsters and the latest Harley-Davidsons alike flock to cruise along the atmospheric, neon-lit frontages of towns such as Albuquerque and Flagstaff, or through such empty desertscapes as those between Grants and Gallup in New Mexico or Seligman and Kingman in Arizona.

Displays at the **National Museum of Nuclear Science and History**, outside Kirtland Air Force Base seven miles east of downtown, range from the early discoveries of Madame Curie to a 1953 *Life* magazine cover reading "we are in a life and death bomb race". You'll be soothed to learn how much more precise and sophisticated today's weapons are compared with the "primitive city-busting concepts" of the Cold War era, just how safe nuclear waste disposal can be and a host of other little-known facts. A gift store sells space-age novelties.

Sandia Mountains

Sandia Peak Tramway Summer daily 9am–9pm; rest of year Mon & Wed–Sun 9am–8pm, Tues 5–8pm • Charge (ski season mid-Dec to mid-March, ski area open Fri–Mon only) • ⓦ sandiapeak.com

The forested **Sandia Mountains** tower 10,500ft over Albuquerque to the east; views from the summit are especially beautiful at and after sunset, when the city lights sparkle below. In summer it's a good 25°F cooler up here than in the valley, while in winter you can go downhill or cross-country **skiing**.

The world's longest tramway, the 2.7-mile **Sandia Peak Tramway** climbs to the top from the end of Tramway Road a dozen miles northeast of town. During the uppermost 1.5 miles of its exhilarating fifteen-minute climb, not a single support tower interrupts its progress.

ARRIVAL AND DEPARTURE ALBUQUERQUE

By plane Buses connect Albuquerque's International Sunport (ⓦ abqsunport.com), 4 miles southeast of downtown, with the Rail Runner network, Mon–Sat only, while a taxi into town costs $20 and up.
By bus Long-distance Greyhound buses use the Alvarado Transportation Center, at First and Central.

Destinations Denver (2 daily; 8hr 30min); Flagstaff (3 daily; 6hr); Phoenix (3 daily; 9hr).
By train One daily Amtrak train in each direction calls at the Alvarado Transportation Center.
Destinations Chicago (1 daily; 26hr 30min); Flagstaff (1 daily; 6hr); Los Angeles (1 daily; 18hr).

GETTING AROUND AND INFORMATION

By train The Rail Runner light-rail system (ⓦ riometro. org) runs from its downtown Albuquerque station, in the Alvarado Transportation Center at First and Central, both south to Belen and north to Bernalillo, with services continuing all the way north to Santa Fe (see page 103).
By bus Downtown's Alvarado Transportation Center is also

the hub of the ABQ Ride city bus network (ⓦ cabq.gov/ transit).
Visitor centres 522 Romero St NW, in the Old Town (Mon–Sat 10am–5pm, Sun 10am–4pm; ☎ 800 284 2282, ⓦ visitalbuquerque.org), and at the airport (Mon–Fri & Sun 9.30am–8pm, Sat 9.30am–4pm).

ACCOMMODATION

The 20-mile length of **Central Avenue**, the old Route 66, is lined with the flashing neon signs of cheap **motels**. Try to have a good look in daylight, to spot which ones may turn scary at night.
Andaluz 125 2nd St NW ⓦ hotelandaluz.com. Elegant historic hotel, built in Mexican style by Conrad Hilton in 1939 and now exquisitely revamped, that's downtown's most appealing upscale option. Beautiful wood-panelled lobby, top-class restaurant and cosy bar. The hotel is also pet-friendly if you happen to want to bring your furry companion along. S̄S̄S̄
El Cuervo ABQ Guest Rooms 701 Roma Ave NW ⓦ elcuervoabq.com. This friendly guesthouse, in what was originally an 1890s private house, offers cosy private rooms, plus free parking, fresh coffee, game room and local beers served at night. LGBTQ+ owned and operated and dedicated to create a safe and relaxing environment for

everyone, adult only (21+). S̄S̄
La Quinta Inn Albuquerque Airport 2116 Yale Blvd SE ⓦ wyndhamhotels.com. Large, relatively upscale motel, served by frequent shuttles from the nearby airport, and offering accommodation that's far from memorable but safe, good-value and quiet. S̄
★ **Los Poblanos** 4803 Rio Grande Blvd NW ⓦ los poblanos.com. Set on an organic farm, 5 miles north along the river from the Old Town, this exquisite B&B offers antique-furnished rooms in two different buildings. There's also a spa with treatment rooms and wellness classes. The delicious breakfast specials change daily, while the on-site *Campo* restaurant serves dinner Wed–Sun only. S̄S̄S̄S̄
Monterey Motel 2402 Central Ave SW ⓦ themonterey motel.com. Clean, fifteen-room motel, two blocks west of Old Town, run in conjunction with the neighbouring El Vado, and equipped with a pool and laundry. S̄S̄

EATING

66 Diner 1405 Central Ave NE ⓦ66diner.com. Classic Fifties diner, with white-capped waiting staff, a soda fountain and a lively late-night clientele. Specials include Frito pie, fried catfish and enormous burgers. If you can, it's very much worth leaving space for dessert – although this might be a challenge. ⓢ

Artichoke Café 424 Central Ave SE ⓦartichokecafe.com. Simple but classy restaurant in the heart of downtown, serving a good, varied menu of California-influenced modern American cuisine. ⓢⓢⓢ

Flying Star 3416 Central Ave SE ⓦflyingstarcafe.com. Lively, crowded café serving eclectic international cuisine to a largely student clientele. Expect blue-plate specials such as Vietnamese noodles, mac cheese or pasta pomodoro. Other branches throughout the city. ⓢⓢ

Frontier 2400 Central Ave SE ⓦwww.frontier restaurant.com. Legendary diner across from the university – not quite open around the clock – where an unceasing parade of characters chow down on burgers, burritos and great vegetarian enchiladas. ⓢ

Indian Pueblo Kitchen Indian Pueblo Cultural Center, 2401 12th St NW ⓦindianpueblokitchen.org. While still serving Pueblo specialities such as Native American frybread at lunchtime, this unusual Native American restaurant is also open both for breakfast (try the blue corn pancakes or *atole* – a blue corn porridge) and for fine dining in the evening, when braised bison ribs are among its good mains. There are plenty of bakery goods for you to take home too (think home-made pies, cookies and scones and authentic Pueblo oven bread loaves). ⓢ

Java Joe's 906 Park Ave SW ⓦdowntownjavajoes.com. "Alternative" coffeeshop, on the western fringes of downtown, with wholesome breakfast specials and sandwiches and live music to go with its espresso drinks. *Breaking Bad* devotees will recognize the building as Tuco's HQ. ⓢ

DRINKING AND NIGHTLIFE

The Anodyne 409 Central Ave NW ☎505 244 1820. Downtown's most popular bar offers pool tables, pinball, a good jukebox, and an eclectic mix of customers, from beer guzzlers to martini sippers – but no food or live music.

KiMo Theater 423 Central Ave NW ⓦabqtickets.com/location/kimo-theatre. Gorgeous, city-owned "Pueblo Deco" theatre that puts on an eclectic programme of opera, dance and theatre performances, kids' movies and everything from burlesque to Beethoven, as well as live bands.

Launchpad 618 Central Ave SW ⓦlaunchpadrocks.com. Dance and live music space that showcases touring indie and world music bands; besides the fabulous space-age decor, there's also a cluster of pool tables.

Marble Brewery 111 Marble Ave NW ⓦmarblebrewery.com. Bustling brewpub, just north of downtown, where the giant vats in the brewery itself are visible behind the bar. There's no kitchen, but takeout food trucks park outside, and the (summer-only) outdoor patio makes a good place to eat.

Ácoma Pueblo

12 miles south of I-40, 50 miles west of Albuquerque • Sky City Cultural Center March–Oct daily 8am–7pm; Nov–Feb Fri–Sun 9am–5pm • Entire pueblo closed to all visitors June 24, June 29, July 9–14, July 25, first and/or second weekend in Oct, first Sat of Dec • Tours charge, plus extra for photo permit, no camcorders or video • ⓦ acomaskycity.org

The amazing **Ácoma Pueblo** encapsulates a thousand years of Native American history. Its focus is the ancient village known as "**Sky City**", perched 367ft high atop a magnificent isolated mesa. Probably occupied by Chacoan migrants between 1100 and 1200 AD, when the great pueblos of Chaco Canyon were still in use, Ácoma has adapted to repeated waves of invaders ever since. Although visitors seldom feel the awkwardness possible at other Pueblo communities, Ácoma is the real thing, and its sense of unbroken tradition can reduce even the least culturally sensitive traveller to awestruck silence.

To visit Sky City, you normally have to join one of the hour-long guided **tours** that leave regularly from the excellent Sky City Cultural Center and Haak'u Museum at the base of the mesa. The main stop is at the striking **San Esteban del Rey** mission, a thick-walled adobe church completed in 1640. Rather than follow its architectural example, the Ácomans went on constructing the multistorey stone and adobe houses around which the tour then proceeds. Note however, that in-person tours were suspended during 2020 Covid epidemic and had not restarted by early 2023 – tours will be "virtual" via the Ts'iKinuma K'aiya (Story Telling Room/Theatre) until they begin in-person again.

2

El Morro National Monument

Hwy-53, 25 miles east of Zuni Pueblo and 42 miles west of Grants • Visitor centre summer daily 9am–6pm, rest of year Thurs–Mon 9am–5pm; trail closes 1hr earlier • Free • ⓦ nps.gov/elmo

Hidden away south of the Zuni Mountains, 42 miles west of Grants, **El Morro National Monument** feels far off the beaten track. Incredibly, however, this pale-pink sandstone cliff was a regular rest stop for international travellers before the Pilgrims landed at Plymouth Rock, thanks to a perennial pool of water that collects beneath a tumbling waterfall. This spot was first recorded by Spanish explorers in 1583; in 1605, Don Juan de Oñate, the founder of New Mexico, carved the first of many messages that earned it the American name of **Inscription Rock**.

Chaco Canyon

Reached by 20-mile dirt roads from either Seven Lakes, 18 miles northeast of Crownpoint, or Nageezi, on US-550 36 miles south of Bloomfield • Loop Road daily: Nov–April 7am–5pm, May–Oct 7am–9pm; visitor centre daily 9am–5pm • Charge • ⓦ nps.gov/chcu

Few visitors brave the long, bumpy ride to **Chaco Canyon**, north of I-40 between Grants and Gallup. Although **Chaco Culture NHP** holds North America's **largest pre-Columbian city**, for beauty and drama it can't match such sites as Canyon de Chelly (see page 140) and the low-walled canyon itself is a mere scratch in the scrubby high-desert plains.

However, Chaco still holds plenty to take your breath away. Thirteen separate sites are open to visitors. Six, arrayed along the canyon's north wall, are **Great Houses** – self-contained pueblos, three or four storeys high, whose fortress-like walls concealed up to eight hundred rooms.

Both routes to Chaco Canyon entail driving twenty miles over rough but passable dirt roads, not to be attempted in poor weather. Whether you approach from south or north, you enter the park at its southeast corner, close to the **visitor centre**. The basic *Gallo* **campground** (ⓦ recreation.gov; Charge), a short way east, usually fills by 3pm.

The major stop along the canyon's eight-mile one-way **loop road** (daily dawn–dusk) is at the far end, where **Pueblo Bonito** ("beautiful town") can be explored on an easy half-mile trail. Work on this four-storey D-shaped structure started in 850 AD and continued for three hundred years; it remained the largest building in America until 1898. Entering the ruin via its lowest levels, the path reaches its central plaza, which held at least three **Great Kivas** – ceremonial chambers used by entire communities rather than individual clans or families.

Gallup

As the largest town in I-40's three-hundred-mile run between Albuquerque and Flagstaff, the famous Route 66 stop of **GALLUP**, 25 miles east of the Arizona state line, might be expected to offer a diverting break in a long day's drive. Don't get your hopes up; cheap motels make it a handy overnight pit stop, but there's nothing to hold your interest.

The Navajo and other Native Americans come together in **Red Rock State Park**, four miles east of Gallup, on the second weekend in August for the **Inter-Tribal Indian Ceremonial**, the largest such gathering anywhere (ⓦ gallupceremonial.com). Four days of dances and craft shows have as their highlight a Saturday morning parade through the town.

ACCOMMODATION AND EATING   GALLUP

★ **Hotel El Rancho** 1000 E Hwy-66 ⓦ elranchohotel gallup.com. Sumptuous Route 66 roadhouse built in 1937 by the brother of film director D.W. Griffith. From the murals in its opulent Spanish Revival lobby to the gallery of signed photos of celebrity Hollywood guests, it's bursting with atmosphere, though the guest rooms are small, and the bathrooms even smaller. Some rooms are in a less characterful two-storey motel building alongside. The decorative dining room ($$) serves burgers named after John Wayne and Humphrey Bogart, and the usual barbecue,

steaks and shrimp, while the bar stays open until 1am. $\overline{\$\$}$
Gallup Coffee Company 203 W Coal Ave ⓦgallup
coffeecompany.com. If you're passing through Gallup

and simply want a snack or an espresso, head for this lively
central coffee bar, a block off the main drag. $\overline{\$}$

Carlsbad Caverns National Park

Charged admission good for three days, under-16s free; national park passes cover up to four adults; optional tours extra

In **CARLSBAD CAVERNS NATIONAL PARK**, the Guadalupe Mountains are so riddled with
underground caves and tunnels as to be virtually hollow. Tamed in classic park-service
style with concrete trails and electric lighting, this subterranean wonderland is now a
walk-in gallery, where tourists flock to marvel at its intricate limestone tracery. Summer
crowds can get intense, but that's part of the fun – Carlsbad feels like a throwback to
the 1950s boom in mass tourism.

At three hundred miles southeast of Albuquerque, however, the park is a *long* way
from anywhere else. To reach it from the unenthralling town of Carlsbad itself, which
holds the nearest accommodation and dining, drive twenty miles southwest on US-
62/180, then seven miles west from White's City.

Carlsbad Cavern

Almost all visitors confine their attention to **Carlsbad Cavern** itself, the only cave
covered by the entrance fee. Direct elevators drop to the Cavern's centrepiece, the **Big
Room**, 750ft below the visitor centre, but you can walk down instead via the **Natural
Entrance Route** (last entry summer 3.30pm; rest of year 2pm). This steep footpath
switchbacks into the guano-encrusted maw of the cave, taking fifteen minutes to reach
the first formation and another fifteen to reach the Big Room. All visitors must ride the
elevator back out.

Measuring up to 1800ft long and 250ft high, the Big Room is festooned with
stalactites, stalagmites and countless unnameable shapes of swirling liquid rock. All
are a uniform stone grey; rare touches of colour are provided by slight red or brown
mineral-rich tinges, improved with pastel lighting. It takes an hour to complete the
level trail around the perimeter. Whatever the weather up top – summer highs exceed
100°F – the temperature down here is always a cool 56°F.

Adjoining the Big Room, the **Underground Lunchroom** is a vast formation-free side
cave, paved in the 1950s to create a diner-cum-souvenir-shop that sells a restricted
menu of small-scale snacks, plus Eisenhower-era souvenirs like giant pencils and
Viewmaster reels.

Guided tours explore beautiful side caves such as the **King's Palace**, filled with
translucent "draperies" of limestone (2–4 tours daily; charge). Additional tours can take
you along the **Left Hand Tunnel** route down from the visitor centre (charge), or on a
much more demanding descent into either **Spider Cave** or the **Hall of the White Giant**
(both charge).

INFORMATION   **CARLSBAD CAVERNS NATIONAL PARK**

Visitor centre Daily: summer 8am–7pm; rest of year
8am–5pm (ⓦnps.gov/cave). Reservations required via

ⓦrecreation.gov.

ACCOMMODATION AND EATING

Thanks to a boom in the local oil industry, accommodation
prices in Carlsbad are much higher than you might expect;
anything under $200 per night hereabouts currently counts
as a bargain. Travellers on a budget would do better to visit
the park on a day-trip from somewhere much further afield.
Blue House Bakery 609 N Canyon St, Carlsbad ❼575
628 0555. Set on a sleepy residential road, this popular

cottage café/bakery serves early-morning coffee and
pastries, then salads and sandwiches later on. $\overline{\$}$
Stevens Inn 1829 S Canal St, Carlsbad ⓦstevensinn
carlsbad.com. Large, old-fashioned roadside motel, a mile
south of central Carlsbad, that's had a thorough makeover.
The rooms are big but otherwise unremarkable, and there's
an outdoor pool. Rates include a breakfast buffet at the

2

Flume Room restaurant, open for all meals daily. $\overline{\$\$}$
★ **Trinity Hotel** 201 S Canal St, Carlsbad ⓦ thetrinity hotel.com. An unexpected find for this part of New Mexico, this former bank in downtown Carlsbad has been beautifully converted into a nine-suite boutique hotel. Most rooms have walk-in showers, and there's also an excellent restaurant, open for all meals from Monday to Saturday and brunch on Sundays. $\overline{\$\$}$

Roswell

On July 4, 1947, an alien spaceship supposedly crash-landed outside the small ranching town of **ROSWELL**, 75 miles north of Carlsbad. The commander of the local air-force base announced that they had retrieved the wreckage of a flying saucer and despite a follow-up denial the story has kept running, with TV series like *X-Files*, *Roswell* and *Taken* stoking the imaginations of UFO theorists.

Despite the wishful thinking of the truly weird visitors who drift in from the plains, the **International UFO Museum**, 114 N Main St (daily 9am–5pm; charge; ⓦ roswellufomuseum.com), inadvertently exposes the whole tawdry business as transparent nonsense. By way of contrast, the **Roswell Museum**, 1011 N Richardson Ave (daily 10am–6pm; charge; ⓦ roswell-nm.gov/1259/Roswell-Museum), boasts an excellent, multi-faceted collection, with one section celebrating pioneer rocket scientist Robert Goddard (1882–1945).

ACCOMMODATION AND EATING	**ROSWELL**
Cattle Baron 1113 N Main St ⓦ cattlebaron.com. Large, good-value steakhouse, with traditional Wild West decor, big slabs of meat, including steaks, and an extensive salad bar. $\overline{\$\$}$	**La Quinta Inn & Suites Roswell** 200 E 19th St ⓦ wyndhamhotels.com. Very dependable motel, just off the main through highway north of the centre; clean and well managed, with an indoor pool. $\overline{\$\$}$

Lincoln

Better known as **Billy the Kid**, Brooklyn-born William Bonney first came to fame as an 18-year-old in 1878, when the **Lincoln County War** erupted between rival groups of ranchers and merchants in the frontier town of **LINCOLN**, on Hwy-380 halfway between Carlsbad and Albuquerque. Since those days, no new buildings have joined the venerable false-fronted structures that line Main Street and the entire town is now the **Lincoln Historic Site** (most sites open Mon & Thurs–Sun 10am–4pm; charge; ⓦ nmhistoricsites. org/lincoln) Visitors can stroll its length at any time and visit various evocative locations. Displays in the **Anderson-Freeman Visitor Center** cover Hispanics, cowboys and Apaches, as well as the Lincoln County War. The Kid's most famous jailbreak is commemorated at the **Lincoln County Courthouse**, at the other end of the street; waiting here under sentence of death, he shot his way out and fled to Fort Sumner, where Sheriff Pat Garrett eventually caught up with him (see ⓦ billythekidmuseumfortsumner.com). On the first weekend of August the streets echo with gunfire once again, during the three-day **Old Lincoln Days** festival.

DRINKING	**LINCOLN**
Bonito Valley Brewing Co 692 Calle la Placita (US-380) ⓦ bonitovalleybrewing.com. There's nowhere to stay in Lincoln, but the one-street town does boast an	excellent craft brewer, established in 2017. The taproom inside the 18th-century Lesnet-Garcia home serves Billy the Kid Amber, 44-40 IPA and several other brews made on site.

White Sands National Park

US-70, 14 miles west of Alamogordo • Visitor centre open daily: late May to Aug 9am–7pm; mid-March to late May 9am–6pm; Sept to mid-March 9am–5pm • Charge • ⓦ nps.gov/whsa

Filling a broad valley west of Ruidoso and the Sacramento Mountains, the **White Sands** consist of 250 square miles of glistening, three-storey-high dunes, composed not of sand, but of finely ground gypsum eroded from the nearby peaks. Most of the desert valley is used as a missile range and training ground; only the southern half of the dunes is protected within **White Sands National Park** (and even that is often closed for an hour or two at a time while missile tests are under way). The **visitor centre**, just off US-70, illuminates the unique local plants and animals.

An eight-mile paved road stretches into the heart of the dunes, where you can scramble and slide in the sheer white landscape. While **hiking** is all but irresistible, the trails are not marked or even visible in the ever-shifting dunes. Be very careful not to lose your way, and above all take a gallon of **water** per person. A French couple who set off at noon in the summer of 2015, carrying a litre of water, died within hours; only their 9-year-old son survived.

Truth or Consequences

Until 1950, the small settlement in the Rio Grande Valley, 150 miles south of Albuquerque, where Apache warriors once soaked away the worries of the warpath in natural thermal springs, was appropriately known as **Hot Springs**. Then it saddled itself with the world's worst name, in honour of the radio show *Truth or Consequences* – though locals habitually abbreviate it these days to "**T or C.**"

Partly as a consequence of dam construction higher up the Rio Grande, T or C no longer any holds any natural, free-flowing hot springs. There's still plenty of thermal activity hereabouts, though, which local hotels and resorts have tapped to create spas, hot tubs and other facilities.

INFORMATION   TRUTH OR CONSEQUENCES

Visitor centre T or C's visitor centre (301 S Foch St; Sun–Thurs 10am–2pm, Fri & Sat 9am–4.30pm; ☎ 575 894 1968, ⓦ geronimotrail.com), is the base for tours to Spaceport America (ⓦ spaceportamerica.com), an ultra-remote desert strip 25 miles southeast that will supposedly be used by Virgin Galactic's commercial spaceflights (contact Final Frontier Tours for visits at ☎ 575 267 8888).

ACCOMMODATION AND EATING

Passion Pie Cafe 406 Main St ☎ 575 894 6848. Friendly, hugely popular café, serving coffee, pastries and waffles plus lunchtime sandwiches and mixed Mediterranean-style plates. ⑤
★ **Riverbend Hot Springs** 100 Austin St ⓦ riverbend hotsprings.com. As well as private and shared hot tubs, set into the banks of the Rio Grande, this lovely lodge offers comfortable suites, plus "budget doubles" that share bathrooms and can sleep up to four, and small, individually decorated "artist rooms". No under-12s. Artist rooms ⑤, budget doubles ⑤⑤, suites ⑤⑤

Silver City

Almost entirely wilderness, the semi-arid, forested, volcanic **Mogollon** and **Mimbres mountains** of southwest New Mexico soar to 10,000ft above the high desert plains and remain little altered since Apache warrior **Geronimo** was born at the headwaters of the Gila River.

Halfway up the mountains, the biggest settlement, **SILVER CITY**, lies 45 miles north of I-10. The Spanish came here in 1804, sold the Mimbreño indigenous population into slavery and opened the **Santa Rita copper mine**, just east of town below the Kneeling Nun monolith. The town was re-established in 1870 as a rough-and-tumble silver camp – **Billy the Kid** spent most of his childhood here. Ornate old buildings stand scattered along elm-lined avenues and across the hills. The **Western New Mexico University Museum**, 12th and Alabama (term-time only: Mon–Fri 9am–4.30pm, Sat & Sun 10am–4pm; free; ☎ 575 538 6386, ⓦ museum.wnmu. edu), holds the world's finest collection of beautiful **Mimbres pottery**, produced nearby around 1100 AD.

2

Comfort Inn Near Gila National Forest 1060 E US-180 Ⓦ choicehotels.com. One of the better chain motels on the outskirts of Silver City, with standard but modern rooms (with microwave and fridge), plus indoor heated pool and hot tub, and a free pass to a nearby gym. $\overline{\underline{SS}}$

Corner Kitchen 300 S Bullard St ☎ 575 590 2603. This no-frills diner in an old bakery serves up some of the tastiest breakfasts in the region, as well as big plates of pasta, Tex-Mex favourites like chilaquiles and a range of tempting pastries. $\overline{\underline{S}}$

Javelina Coffee House 117 W Market St ☎ 575 388 1350. Bright, friendly community rendezvous downtown, open daily from very early, and attracting arty types who linger over their laptops drinking coffee and eating pastries. $\overline{\underline{S}}$

★ **Murray Hotel** 200 W Broadway Ⓦ murray-hotel. com. The biggest building in downtown Silver City, this Art Deco beauty originally opened as a hotel in 1938. 53 refurbished guest rooms have a knowing retro touch – the en-suite bathrooms are particularly tasteful – and the public spaces remain impressive. $\overline{\underline{S}}$

Arizona

The tourism industry in **ARIZONA** has, literally, one colossal advantage – the **Grand Canyon** of the Colorado River, the single most awe-inspiring spectacle in a land of unforgettable geology. Several other Arizona destinations have a similarly abiding emotional impact, however, thanks to the sheer drama of human involvement in this forbidding but deeply resonant desert landscape.

Over a third of the state still belongs to **Native Americans**, who outside the cities form the majority of the population. In the so-called **Indian Country** of northeastern Arizona, the **Navajo Nation** holds the stupendous **Canyon de Chelly** and dozens of other **Ancestral Puebloan ruins**, as well as the stark rocks of **Monument Valley**. The Navajo surround the homeland of the stoutly traditional **Hopi**, who live in remote **mesa-top villages**. The third main group, the **Apache**, in the harshly beautiful southeastern mountains, were the last Native Americans to give in to the overwhelming power of the American invaders.

The **southern** half of the state holds ninety percent of its people and all its significant cities. State capital **Phoenix**, a five-hundred-square-mile morass of malls and suburbs, is larger and somewhat duller than lively **Tucson**, while there's some great frontier Americana in the southeast corner, especially in **Tombstone**.

Tucson

The former Spanish and Mexican outpost of **TUCSON** (pronounced *too-sonn*), a mere sixty miles north of Mexico, has grown into a modern metropolis of almost a million people without entirely sacrificing its historic quarters. Equal parts college town and retirement community, it suffers from a similar Sunbelt sprawl to Albuquerque and Phoenix, but has a compact centre, some enjoyable restaurants and pretty good nightlife. Some superb landscape lies within easy reach, from the forested flanks of **Mount Lemmon** to the rolling foothills of **Saguaro National Park**.

Tucson Museum of Art

140 N Main Ave • Thurs–Sun 10am–5pm • Charge • Ⓦ tucsonmuseumofart.org

The **Tucson Museum of Art**, the highlight of **downtown Tucson**, devotes its main building to changing exhibitions of modern painting and sculpture. Its huge permanent collection, displayed in various adjoining adobes and stand-alone galleries, includes Southwestern art ranging from prints by the Taos School of Artists to Native American ceramics, along with an extensive array of artworks from China, Japan and Korea, from ancient times up to the twentieth century.

Arizona State Museum

1013 E University Blvd • Tues–Sat 10am–4pm • Charge • Ⓦ statemuseum.arizona.edu

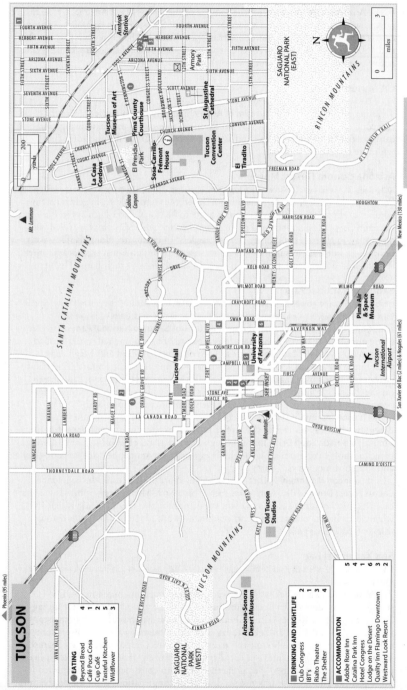

TUCSON

Phoenix (95 miles)

● EATING
Beyond Bread	4
Café Poca Cosa	1
Cup Café	2
Tasteful Kitchen	5
Wildflower	3

■ DRINKING AND NIGHTLIFE
Club Congress	2
IBT's	1
Rialto Theatre	3
The Shelter	4

■ ACCOMMODATION
Adobe Rose Inn	5
Catalina Park Inn	4
Hotel Congress	1
Lodge on the Desert	6
Quality Inn Flamingo Downtown	3
Westward Look Resort	2

San Xavier del Bac (2 miles) & Nogales (61 miles)

New Mexico (130 miles)

SAGUARO NATIONAL PARK (EAST)

RINCON MOUNTAINS

SANTA CATALINA MOUNTAINS

Mt. Lemmon

Sabino Canyon

Tucson Mall

University of Arizona

SEE INSET

A Mountain

Old Tucson Studios

TUCSON MOUNTAINS

SAGUARO NATIONAL PARK (WEST)

Arizona-Sonora Desert Museum

Pima Air & Space Museum

Tucson International Airport

Amtrak Station

Tucson Museum of Art

Pima County Courthouse

El Presidio Park

La Casa Cordova

Sosa-Carrillo-Frémont House

Armory Park

St Augustine Cathedral

Tucson Convention Center

El Tiradito

In the **Arizona State Museum**, on the campus of the **University of Arizona**, a mile east of downtown, the Pottery Project traces the history of Southwestern ceramics. A stunning case is devoted to fabulous "burden carrier" pots made by the Hohokam between 850 and 1000 AD. The large **Paths of Life** exhibition illuminates the cultures of the major native peoples of the Southwest and northern Mexico.

UA Museum of Art
1031 N Olive Rd • Tues–Sat 10am–4.30pm • Charge • ⓦ artmuseum.arizona.edu

Treasures at the eclectic **UA Museum of Art** include a morbid altarpiece from the cathedral of the Spanish city of Ciudad Rodrigo, along with prints, drawings and canvases by Rembrandt, Picasso and Warhol; a solitary O'Keeffe; and some fine Cubist sculpture by Jacques Lipchitz.

Arizona-Sonora Desert Museum
2021 N Kinney Rd, 14 miles west of downtown • Daily: June–Sept 7.30am–2pm; Oct–May 8.30am–5pm • Charge • ⓦ desertmuseum.org

Part zoo, part garden, the **Arizona-Sonora Desert Museum** makes a hugely satisfying adjunct to the nearby western section of Saguaro National Park. Displays in the museum proper explain regional geology and history, while dioramas are filled with tarantulas, rattlesnakes and other creepy crawlers. In enclosures along the loop path beyond – a hot walk in summer – bighorn sheep, mountain lions, jaguars and other seldom-seen desert denizens prowl in credible simulations of their natural habitats.

Saguaro National Park
In two sections: Tucson Mountain District is 15 miles west of downtown Tucson, Rincon Mountain District is 17 miles east of downtown •
Visitor centres at both daily 9am–5pm • Admission to either or both sections, valid for a week, charge • ⓦ nps.gov/sagu

Flanking Tucson to either side, the two sections of **Saguaro National Park** offer visitors a rare opportunity to stroll through desert "forests" of monumental, multi-limbed **saguaro** (*sa-wah-row*) cactuses. Each saguaro can grow 50ft tall and weigh eight tons, but takes around 150 years to do so. They're unique to the Sonora Desert and encountering them en masse is a real thrill. Both segments of the park can be seen on short forays from the city: in summer, it's far too hot to do more than pose for photographs, and there is no lodging or even permanent campground.

The **Tucson Mountain District** stretches north from the Desert Museum west of downtown Tucson, on the far side of the mountains. Beyond the **visitor centre**, the nine-mile **Bajada Loop Drive** loops through a wonderland of weird saguaro, offering plentiful short hiking trails. Signal Hill is especially recommended, for its petroglyphs and superb sunset views.

In the **Rincon Mountain District**, east of town, short trails lead off the eight-mile **Cactus Forest Drive** (daily: April–Oct 7am–7pm; Nov–March 7am–5pm). The saguaro cactuses thin out almost as soon as you start climbing the Tanque Verde Ridge Trail, which leads in due course to a hundred-mile network of remote footpaths through thickly forested canyons.

San Xavier del Bac
1950 W San Xavier Rd; 9 miles south of downtown Tucson, just west of I-19 • Daily: church 9am–2pm, museum see website • Donation •
ⓦ sanxaviermission.org

The **Mission San Xavier del Bac** – the best-preserved mission church in the US – stands south of downtown Tucson on the fringe of the vast arid San Xavier Indian Reservation, home to the Akimel O'odham people. It was built for the Franciscans between 1783 and 1797 and even today its white-plastered walls and towers seem like a dazzling desert mirage. No one can name the architect responsible for its Spanish Baroque, even Moorish, lines – it consists almost entirely of domes and arches, making only minimal use of timber – let alone the O'odham craftsmen who embellished its every feature. Sunday morning masses draw large congregations from the reservation.

ARRIVAL AND INFORMATION TUCSON

By plane Tucson's airport (⬭flytucson.com), 10 miles south of downtown and served mainly by regional flights, is linked to the city by the $25 shuttle vans of Tucson Stagecoach (⬭tucscoach.com). Sun Tran's bus #25 (⬭suntran.com) also runs from the airport into downtown Tucson.

By train The Amtrak station is at 400 E Toole Ave; connecting Amtrak buses run north to Phoenix.

Destinations Los Angeles (3 weekly; 10hr); New Orleans (3 weekly; 37hr).

By bus Greyhound buses stop at 801 E 12th St (☎520 792 3475).

Destinations Las Cruces (2 daily; 5hr 30min); Los Angeles (10 daily; 10hr); Phoenix (10 daily; 2hr).

Visitor centre Southern Arizona Heritage and Visitor Center at 115 N Church Ave (daily 10am–5pm; ☎800 638 8350, ⬭visittucson.org).

ACCOMMODATION SEE MAP PAGE 121

★ **Adobe Rose Inn** 940 N Olsen Ave ⬭adoberoseinn. com. Charming, great-value B&B in a peaceful residential area near the university. Six attractive en-suite rooms plus a courtyard pool and copious communal breakfasts. $$$

Downtown Clifton 485 S Stone Ave ⬭downtown tucsonhotel.com. Stylishly renovated motel from 1948, with a "Sonoran Moderne" extension and the hip Red Light Lounge on site. The comfy "bunkhouse" rooms sport a Western theme, with wood ceiling beams, handmade beds and saddle blanket bedspreads. $$

★ **Hotel Congress** 311 E Congress St ⬭hotelcongress. com. Central, bohemian "rock'n'roll" hotel, a short walk from Amtrak and Greyhound, with vintage Art Deco furnishings. Forty plain en-suite guest rooms, with loud music and dancing at night. $$

★ **Hotel McCoy** 720 W Silverlake Rd ⬭hotelmccoy. com. The most intriguing motel accommodation off I-19 just south of downtown Tucson, this 1960s retro option is enhanced with murals, free bike rentals, a heated saltwater pool, local craft beers and Arizona wines. $$

Lodge on the Desert 306 N Alvernon Way ⬭lodgeon thedesert.com. 1930s adobe resort a couple of miles east of downtown, tastefully restored to resemble a Mexican hacienda, with large, comfortable rooms and a good restaurant. $$

Westward Look Wyndham Grand Resort and Spa 245 E Ina Rd ⬭wyndhamhotels.com. Fancy resort, in attractive landscaped grounds north of the city, which retains its atmospheric 1912 core and holds almost 250 extra-large rooms and suites in private *casitas*. $$$

EATING SEE MAP PAGE 121

Beyond Bread 3026 N Campbell Ave ⬭beyondbread. com. Hugely popular cafe-bakery, with four Tucson outlets, that's great for a takeaway sandwich – most, including specials like a New Orleans-style shrimp po-boy, served as a half-portion or the whole thing – a breakfast omelette, or a hot special. $

El Charro Café 311 N Court Ave ⬭elcharrocafe. com. One of Arizona's most famous Mexican restaurants was established in 1922, featuring traditional Northern Mexico-Sonoran style food. It's also the alleged inventor of chimichanga, still one of its best dishes. $$

Cup Café Hotel Congress, 311 E Congress St ⬭hotelc ongress.com. Jazzy downtown café, straight out of the 1930s. As well as making a good morning rendezvous,

with eggy breakfasts, it offers lunchtime sandwiches and salads at similar prices, and a full dinner menu that includes fish'n'chips. $$

La Indita 722 N Stone Ave ☎520 792 0523. This no-frills spot knocks out excellent home-style Tarascan Mexican and Native American (Tohono O'Odham) food, from chimichanga and chicken mole to Native American tacos and fry bread. $

Wildflower 7037 N Oracle Rd ⬭wildflowertucson.com. Stylish mall restaurant, well north of the centre, serving fusion New American cuisine. Dine on the spacious patio, or nestle into the plush indoor seating, to enjoy appetizers like black mussels with chorizo; mains include lemongrass scallops with black rice. $$

DRINKING AND NIGHTLIFE SEE MAP PAGE 121

Club Congress Hotel Congress, 311 E Congress St ⬭hotelcongress.com. Hectic, trendy bar with live music, including some big names, three or four nights weekly, and club nights on the rest.

IBT's 616 N 4th Ave ⬭ibtstucson.com. Tucson's premier LGBTQ+ downtown dance club features contemporary DJs most nights and also puts on drag acts and revues, with a huge dancefloor indoors and another on the patio outside.

Rialto Theatre 318 E Congress St ⬭rialtotheatre.com.

1920s vaudeville theatre that's now Tucson's hottest venue for touring bands.

The Shelter 4155 E Grant Rd ☎520 326 1345. Take a trip back to groovier times in this round, windowless "go-go boot-wearing lounge"; all lava lamps, pinball machines and velvet paintings. It's barely changed since 1961, but still shakes up a mean martini and has occasional live music and DJs.

2

Tombstone

The legendary Wild West town of **TOMBSTONE** lies 22 miles south of I-10 on US-80, 67 miles southeast of Tucson. More than a century has passed since its mining heyday, but "The Town Too Tough to Die" clings to an afterlife as a tourist theme park. With its dusty streets, wooden sidewalks and swinging saloon doors, it's barely changed. The moody gunslingers who stroll the streets these days are merely rounding up customers to watch them fight, but there's genuine rivalry between groups, and some have even been known to fire live ammunition rather than blanks. The ideal time to visit is late October, for **Helldorado Days** (ⓦtombstonehelldoradodays.com), a bonanza of parades and shoot-outs, when the air is cooler and the sun less harsh.

OK Corral

Allen St, between 3rd & 4th • Daily 9am–5pm; gunfight schedule posted daily • Charge • ⓦok-corral.com

Tombstone began life as a silver boomtown in 1877, and was all but deserted again by the end of the 1880s. On October 26, 1881, however, its population stood at more than ten thousand. At 2pm that day, **Doc Holliday**, along with sheriff **Wyatt Earp** and his brothers Virgil and Morgan, confronted a band of suspected cattle rustlers, the Clantons, in the **Gunfight at the OK Corral**. Within a few minutes, three of the rustlers were dead. The Earps were accused of murder, but charges were eventually dropped.

Although the real gunfight in fact took place on Fremont Street, the **OK Corral** itself remains a big attraction. The first thing you see on entering is the hearse that took the victims away. Crude dummies in the baking-hot adobe-walled courtyards beyond show the supposed locations of the Earps and the Clantons.

ACCOMMODATION AND EATING   TOMBSTONE

Big Nose Kate's 417 E Allen St ⓦbignosekates tombstone.com. Very fancy Wild-West saloon, where the waitresses wear period costume and country musicians entertain most afternoons. The menu features good value burgers, pizzas and calzones. $$
Landmark Lookout Lodge 781 N US-80 ⓦlookout lodgeaz.com. Chain motel with classy, tasteful Western-

themed rooms and splendid mountain views, a mile north of downtown. $
★ **Larian Motel** 410 E Fremont St ⓦlarianmotel. com. Much the best of the old-style motels in the middle of old Tombstone. Clean, well-maintained rooms and exceptionally friendly and helpful owners. $$

Phoenix

Arizona's state capital and largest city, **PHOENIX**, may not be a major tourist destination, but it does hold a handful of must-see attractions, including the wonderful **Musical Instrument Museum**, the **Heard Museum** with its excellent Native American displays, and Frank Lloyd Wright's architecture studio at **Taliesin West**.

Phoenix began life in the 1860s, as a sweltering little farming town in the heart of the Salt River Valley, with a ready-made irrigation system left by ancient Native Americans (the city's name honours the fact that it rose from the ashes of a long-vanished **Hohokam** community). Within a century, however, Phoenix had acquired the money and political clout to defy the self-evident absurdity of building a huge city in a waterless desert. Now the sixth largest US city, it has filled the entire valley; more than 1.5 million people live within its boundaries, while four million people inhabit the twenty separate incorporated cities, such as **Scottsdale**, **Tempe** and **Mesa**, which make up the metropolitan area.

Above all, Phoenix is hot; summer daytime highs average over 100°F, making it the hottest city outside the Middle East. Even in winter, temperatures rarely drop below 65°F, making the Phoenix/Scottsdale area popular with snowbirds looking to warm their bones in the luxury resorts and spas, play a round of golf, or hike through the mountain and desert preserves.

Phoenix Art Museum

1625 N Central Ave • Wed 10am–9pm, Thurs–Sun 10am–5pm • Charge, pay-what-you-wish Wed 3–9pm • ⓦ phxart.org

The permanent collection at the vast and hugely rewarding **Phoenix Art Museum**, a mile north of downtown, is rooted in an extensive array of Western art. Anish Kapoor's black sculpture *Upside Down Inside Out* is another highlight, and temporary exhibitions range through all eras and styles. A top-quality gift store stocks Mexican crafts and jazzy modern ceramics.

Heard Museum

2301 N Central Ave • Daily 10am–4pm • Charge • ⓦ heard.org

Greatly enlarged while still showcasing its lovely original buildings, the **Heard Museum** provides a wonderful introduction to the **Native Americans** of the Southwest. A sumptuous pottery collection includes stunning Mimbres bowls (see page 119), clay dolls made by the Quechan and Mohave peoples as souvenirs for nineteenth-century railroad passengers, and modern Hopi ceramics. You'll also find a complete Navajo *hogan* (see page 139), some fine Havasupai baskets, Apache beadwork, painted buffalo-skin shields from New Mexico and a great collection of Hopi kachina dolls, as well as a superb store and a good café.

2

Musical Instrument Museum

4725 E Mayo Blvd, Paradise Valley, 20 miles northeast of downtown • Daily 9am–5pm • Charge • W mim.org

You could easily spend a day enjoying the enormous and utterly irresistible **Musical Instrument Museum**. It's a treasure trove of extraordinary instruments from all over the world, from an armadillo-shell lute from Peru to ornate Ashanti drums from Ghana. Successive rooms are devoted to every country and/or musical genre you could possibly think of, while local boy Alice Cooper gets his own special display. Each section also features jaw-dropping, mind-bending video clips of performances both new and historical.

Desert Botanical Garden

1201 North Galvin Pkwy • Daily: May–Sept 7am–8pm; Oct–April 8am–8pm • Charge • W dbg.org

In **Papago Park**, at the south end of Scottsdale, the fascinating **Desert Botanical Garden** is filled with an amazing array of cactuses and desert flora from around the world. Prime specimens include spineless "totem pole" cactuses from the Galápagos Islands and "living stone" plants from South Africa that at a glance you'd never suspect were alive. Separate enclaves are devoted to **butterflies** – seen at their best in August and September – and to **hummingbirds**, of which Arizona boasts fifteen indigenous species.

Western Spirit: Scottsdale's Museum of the West

3830 N Marshall Way, Scottsdale • Tues–Sat 9.30am–5pm, Sun 11am–5pm; additionally open Thurs 5–9pm, Nov–April • Charge • W scottsdalemuseumwest.org

Scottsdale's sprightly modern **Western Spirit: Museum of the West** explores the art and history of nineteen Western states. Its prime focus is on paintings, with changing exhibitions devoted to such themes as the Lewis and Clark expedition, but there's also an impressive permanent collection of bits, spurs and revolvers.

Taliesin West

114th St and Frank Lloyd Wright Blvd, 12 miles northeast of downtown Scottsdale • daily 10am–5pm, (Mon & Thurs–Sun June–Aug); see website for tour schedules • Charge • W franklloydwright.org

Frank Lloyd Wright came to Phoenix to work on the *Biltmore Hotel* in 1934, and returned to spend most winters here until his death in 1959. His studio, **Taliesin West**, is now an architecture school and design studio, with multimedia exhibits of his life and work.

Taliesin West remains a splendidly isolated spot, where Wright's trademark "organic architecture" makes perfect sense. Blending seamlessly into the desert, the complex can only be seen on guided visits. The expertise and enthusiasm of the guides makes the experience well worth the relatively high prices.

ARRIVAL AND DEPARTURE   PHOENIX

By plane Sky Harbor International Airport (W skyharbor. com), 3 miles east of downtown, is connected by free shuttles with the Metro Light Rail station at 44th and Washington (W valleymetro.org). Stagecoach Express additionally runs to other towns in Arizona (W stagecoachexpressshuttle. com).

By train Amtrak doesn't serve Phoenix, but rail passengers who arrive in either Tucson or Flagstaff can catch connecting buses to the city.

By bus Greyhound buses arrive at 2115 E Buckeye Rd (T 602 389 4200), close to the airport.

Destinations Las Vegas (5 daily; 8hr 50min); Los Angeles (9 daily; 7hr 20min); Tucson (10 daily; 2hr).

GETTING AROUND AND INFORMATION

By car Phoenix is so vast that it's much easier to drive than to use public transport – even driving, it can take hours to get across town.

By light rail The Metro Light Rail System (W valleymetro. org) follows a 26-mile route, with stations in downtown Phoenix and Tempe, but it's much more useful for commuters than visitors.

Phoenix visitor centre 400 E. Van Buren St, 6/F (Mon–Fri

10am–4pm; ☎ 877 225 5749, ⓦ visitphoenix.com).
Scottsdale visitor centre Scottsdale Fashion Square,
7014 E. Camelback Rd, Suite 582 (Wed–Sun 11am–4pm;
☎ 800 782 1117, ⓦ experiencescottsdale.com).

ACCOMMODATION
SEE MAP PAGE 125

Metropolitan Phoenix is huge, so stay near the places you want to visit. Room rates rise in **winter**, when snowbirds from all over the USA fill the upscale **resorts** of Scottsdale in particular.

PHOENIX
Arizona Biltmore Resort & Spa 2400 E Missouri Ave ⓦ arizonabiltmore.com. Extraordinarily lavish 1930s resort, retaining its Art Deco trimmings and extravagant gardens. Two golf courses, four restaurants, eight pools, plus afternoon teas, tennis and spa. $$$$
Holiday Inn Express Phoenix Airport 3401 E University Drive ⓦ ihg.com. Good-value motel whose large modern rooms make a handy stop before or after a flight from nearby Sky Harbor – connected by free shuttles. Pool and complimentary breakfast. $$
Hotel San Carlos 202 N Central Ave ⓦ sancarlosphoenix. top. To appreciate this very central 1920s hotel, you have to actively prefer an old-fashioned, frazzled and often noisy

hotel to a new, deathly quiet motel. That said, the rooms are tastefully furnished, if small, and there's a nice Mexican restaurant and rooftop swimming pool. $$$
Phoenix Hostel 1026 N 9th St above Roosevelt St ⓦ phxhostel.org. Friendly little "desert hostel" in a slightly rundown residential district, with private rooms only. No curfew, plus use of kitchen and laundry. $

SCOTTSDALE
Motel 6 Old Town Scottsdale/Fashion Square 6848 E Camelback Rd ⓦ motel6.com. Cut-price lodgings are few and far between in Scottsdale, so this totally unremarkable budget motel is well worth considering. $$
The Phoenician 6000 E Camelback Rd ⓦ thephoenician. com. Gorgeous 250-acre resort, spread out at the base of Camelback Mountain and offering every conceivable luxury, with golf course, waterfalls and lush gardens as well as lavish rooms and restaurants. $$$$

EATING
SEE MAP PAGE 125

PHOENIX
Barrio Café 2814 N 16th St ⓦ barriocafe.com. Reservations are not taken at this little local Mexican place, but it's worth the wait – bide your time sampling the huge array of tequilas, and there's live music Thurs–Sun – to enjoy authentic southern Mexican food, including succulent *cochinita pibil* (pork). $$
Fry Bread House 4545 N 7th Ave ⓦ frybreadhouseaz. com. You'll find fry bread on native American reservations throughout the Southwest; in this no-nonsense cafe, though, Tohono O'odham chef Cecelia Miller raises it to fluffy perfection. Try it with either savoury (say, chile or chorizo) or sweet (chocolate!) toppings. $
Green New American Vegetarian 2022 N 7th St ⓦ greenvegetarian.com. Simple downtown café with a delicious, totally vegan, menu. Order a "mock chicken" wrap or veggie burger at the counter, plus a craft beer or a glass of wine, then sit indoors or out on the patio. $

Pizzeria Bianco Heritage Square, 623 E Adams St ⓦ www.pizzeriabianco.com. High-quality brick-oven pizzas, in a very convenient downtown location, with ultra-fresh ingredients including home-made mozzarella. No reservations. $$

SCOTTSDALE
Arcadia Farms 7025 E 1st Ave ⓦ arcadiafarmscafe.com. Scottsdale's Old Town's most popular lunch rendezvous – salads, sandwiches and mains, including specials like crêpes and crab cakes – also serves healthy Southwestern breakfasts, and there's open-air courtyard seating. $$
The Mission 3815 N Brown Ave ⓦ themissionaz.com. This architecturally stunning "modern Latin" restaurant draws equally on Old- and New-World cuisines. Classics like made-to-order guacamole are complemented by meat and seafood dishes, prepared on either a wood-fired or flat-top grill. The tequila bar stays open until 2am. $$$

DRINKING AND NIGHTLIFE
SEE MAP PAGE 125

Bar Smith 130 E Washington St, Phoenix ⓦ barsmith phoenix.com. The best thing about this stylish downtown bar and lounge is its fabulous outdoor dancefloor, upstairs.
Bikini Lounge 1502 Grand Ave, Phoenix ☎ 602 252 0472. A gem of a dive bar since 1947, this veteran tiki bar attracts a fascinating, eclectic mix of local characters.
Four Peaks Brewing Company 1340 E 8th St, Tempe ⓦ fourpeaks.com. The best brewpub around, near the

university a mile east of Mill Ave, with good beer and pub grub, plus some outdoor seating. There's another outlet at 15745 N Hayden Rd in Scottsdale.
Last Exit Live 717 S Central Ave, Phoenix ⓦ lastexitlive. com. This rock-oriented live music venue, downtown, showcases eclectic acts ranging from country-rock to local punks.

2

Petrified Forest National Park

Straddling I-40, 108 miles east of Flagstaff • Visitor centre daily: mid-April to mid-Oct 8am–6pm; mid-Oct to mid-April 8am–5pm • Charge • ⓦ nps.gov/pefo

At **Petrified Forest National Park**, erosion continues to unearth a fossilized prehistoric forest of gigantic trees. The original cells of the wood have been replaced by multicoloured crystals of quartz, cross sections of which, cut through and polished, look stunning. On the ground, however, along the trails that set off from the park's 27-mile **Scenic Drive**, the trees are not always all that exciting. Segmented, crumbling and very dark, they can seem like a bunch of logs lying in the sand; the best viewing is when the setting sun brings out rich red and orange hues.

The park's northern section – site of the main visitor centre – is renowned for its views of the **Painted Desert**, an undulating expanse of solidified sand dunes, which at different times of day take on different colours (predominantly bluish shades of grey and reddish shades of brown).

Winslow

On I-40, 56 miles east of Flagstaff, **WINSLOW** is a Route 66 town kept alive by transcontinental truckers. It's the closest the interstate comes to the Hopi Mesas (see page 141), which jut from the desert across sixty miles of butte-studded wilderness to the north. If you only know of it thanks to the line about "standin' on the corner in Winslow, Arizona", in the Eagles' *Take It Easy*, you'll be glad there's an official **Standin' on the Corner Park** at Kinsley Avenue and Second.

ACCOMMODATION AND EATING WINSLOW

★ **La Posada** 303 E 2nd St ⓦ laposada.org. Winslow's grandest accommodation option, the last and greatest of the Southwest's railroad hotels, is totally magnificent – a worthy candidate for the best hotel in the world. The whole enormous complex oozes earthy Southwestern style. Doors from the lobby lead straight to the old railroad platform, while the guest rooms hark back to the heyday of transcontinental travel. All have en-suite baths or even whirlpool tubs, but not phones. $$$

★ **Turquoise Room** La Posada, 303 E 2nd St ⓦ the turquoiseroom.com. *La Posada*'s showcase restaurant is irresistible in terms both of its decor and contemporary Southwestern cuisine. Dinner mains range from chilli-tinged south-of-the-border specialities such as grilled chicken breast with tomatillo sauce to Colorado elk medallions with huckleberries. $$$

Flagstaff

Northern Arizona's liveliest and most attractive town, **FLAGSTAFF** occupies a dramatic location beneath the San Francisco Peaks. Poised halfway between New Mexico and California, it's much more than just a way station for tourists en route to the Grand Canyon, eighty miles northwest. Ever since it was founded, in 1876, Flagstaff has been a diverse place, with a strong black and Hispanic population and Navajo and Hopi heading in from the nearby reservations.

Downtown, where barely a building rises more than three storeys, oozes Wild West charm. Filled with cafés, bars and stores selling Route 66 souvenirs and Native American crafts, as well as outdoors outfitters, it's a fun place to stroll around, but holds no significant tourist attractions. Its main thoroughfare, Santa Fe Avenue, used to be **Route 66** and before that the pioneer trail west. The tracks of the Santa Fe Railroad still cut downtown in two, so life remains punctuated by an endless succession of passing trains.

Museum of Northern Arizona

3101 N Fort Valley Rd, 3 miles northwest of downtown Flagstaff on US-180 • Mon & Wed–Sun 10am–4pm • Charge • ⓦ musnaz.org

Flagstaff's **Museum of Northern Arizona** makes a great first stop for any visitor to the Colorado Plateau. While it covers local geology, geography, flora and fauna, its main emphasis is on documenting **Native American** life. It starts with an excellent run-through of the Ancestral Puebloan past, then turns to contemporary Navajo, Havasupai, Zuni and Hopi cultures, with rooms devoted to pots, rugs, *kachina* dolls and silver and turquoise jewellery.

ARRIVAL AND INFORMATION

FLAGSTAFF

By bus Greyhound, 880 E Butler Ave (☎ 928 774 4573). Destinations Albuquerque (3 daily; 6hr); Las Vegas (2 daily; 5hr 30min); Los Angeles (6 daily; 11hr); Phoenix (5 daily; 2hr 45min).

By train Amtrak's Southwest Chief stops in the heart of town.

Destinations Albuquerque (1 daily; 6hr); Chicago (1 daily; 20hr); Los Angeles (1 daily; 11hr 30min).

Visitor centre 1 E Route 66, in the train station (Mon–Sat 8am–5pm, Sun 9am–4pm; ☎ 928 213 2951, ⓦ flagstaff arizona.org).

2

ACCOMMODATION

★ **Bespoke Inn Flagstaff** 410 N Leroux St ⓦ bespoke innflagstaff.com. Bright 1890s Craftsman-style inn, a short walk from downtown. All nine rooms are en suite, most with fireplaces and three with whirlpool tubs; free coffee and tea. $$$

Hotel Weatherford 23 N Leroux St ⓦ weatherfordhotel. com. Restored downtown hotel with elegant wooden fittings. The finest rooms offer tasteful accommodation, with antique furnishings and clawfoot tubs plus phones and TVs; five more en-suite rooms are smaller and cheaper; and three large but basic "European-style" ones share a bathroom. $$

Monte Vista 100 N San Francisco St ⓦ hotelmontevista.

com. Attractive landmark 1920s hotel. Don't expect luxury, let alone tranquillity; with a bar downstairs, the ambience is more like a hostel than a hotel. Many of the guests are young international travellers. Shared-bath $, en-suite doubles $$

Motel DuBeau 19 W Phoenix Ave ⓦ modubeau.com. Veteran motel, just south of the tracks, which also styles itself a "travellers inn". All its appealingly converted rooms have en-suite bathrooms; the cheapest are "economy" doubles (no TV), with deluxe rooms and suites offering more space, amenities and comfort. Breakfast is free, but the common areas, complete with pool table, can get noisy at times. $

EATING AND NIGHTLIFE

Beaver Street Brewery 11 S Beaver St ⓦ beaver streetbrewery.com. Popular micro-brewery that also serves inventive and inexpensive food, including tacos and pizzas. $$

Diablo Burger 120 N Leroux St ⓦ diabloburger.com. Stylish central joint, with outdoor seating, and $12–18 burgers using beef from hormone-free cattle. Cash only. $$

Macy's European Coffee House & Bakery 14 S Beaver St ⓦ macyscoffee.net. Not merely superb coffee, but heavenly pastries to go with it, in a chaotic but friendly, student-oriented atmosphere. Sizeable mains (all vegetarian) include a Mediterranean mixed plate. $

The Museum Club 3404 E Route 66 ⓦ museumclub. net. This 1931 log-cabin taxidermy museum, popularly known as "The Zoo", somehow transmogrified into a classic Route 66 roadhouse, saloon and country music venue – live bands typically Thurs–Sat – that's a second home to hordes of dancing cowboys.

Teatro Italian Food & Wine 16 N San Francisco St ⓦ teatroitalianfoodandwine.com. Smart restaurant, serving pricey but exquisite handmade pastas, locally sourced produce, fresh Mediterranean seafood and Northern Italian inspired dishes. $$$

Sedona

There's no disputing that the New Age resort of **SEDONA**, 28 miles south of Flagstaff, enjoys a magnificent setting, amid definitive Southwestern canyon scenery. Sadly, however, the town itself is a real eyesore, consisting of mile upon mile of ugly red-brick sprawl interrupted only by hideous malls. While Europeans tend to be turned off by Sedona, many American travellers love its luxurious accommodation, fancy restaurants and almost limitless opportunities for active outdoor holidaying.

Since author Page Bryant "channelled" the information in 1981 that Sedona is "the heart *chakra* of the planet" and pinpointed her first **vortex** – a point where psychic and electromagnetic energies can supposedly be channelled for personal and planetary harmony – the town has achieved its own personal growth and blossomed as a focus

2

for **New Age** practitioners of all kinds. Whether you love it or hate it may depend on whether you share their wide-eyed awe for angels, crystals and all matters mystical – and whether you're prepared to pay over-the-odds prices for the privilege of joining them.

You can see most of the sights, albeit from a distance, from US-89A; the best parts are south along Hwy-179 within Coconino National Forest. The closest **vortex** to town is on **Airport Mesa**; turn left up Airport Road from US-89A as you head south, a mile past the downtown junction known as the "**Y**" and it's at the junction of the second and third peaks. Further up, beyond the precariously sited airport, the **Shrine of the Red Rocks** looks out across the entire valley.

INFORMATION · SEDONA

Tourism Bureau Visitor Center 331 Forest Rd (daily 8.30am–5pm; ☎ 928 282 7722, ⓦ visitsedona.com).

ACCOMMODATION AND EATING

★ **Canyon Wren Cabins** 6425 N US-89A ⓦ canyonwren cabins.com. Four large and hugely comfortable private two-person cabins, each with a kitchen and a whirlpool tub, 6 miles north of Sedona in Oak Creek Canyon; they're especially cosy in winter. No wi-fi. $$

Coffee Pot Restaurant 2050 W Hwy-89A ⓦ coffeepots edona.com. Sedona's largest, oldest diner serves a hundred kinds of omelette, and all the burgers, Mexican dishes and fried specials you could hope for. $

Elote Café 350 Jordan Rd ⓦ elotecafe.com. High-quality Mexican food in the heart of town, including delicious adobo-seasoned sea bass, buffalo ribs with mole sauce and smoked chicken enchiladas. $$$

Sedona Hilltop Inn 218 Hwy-179 ⓦ thesedona hilltopinn.com. Small, inexpensive motel, in an ideal and attractive location, with mountain views and a friendly atmosphere on its shared communal deck. $$

Williams

Although Flagstaff is generally regarded as the obvious base for visitors to the Grand Canyon's South Rim, **WILLIAMS**, 32 miles west, is in fact the closest interstate town to the national park. While it can't boast half the charm or pizzazz of its neighbour, it's a nice enough little place, filled with Route 66-era motels and diners and retaining a certain individuality despite the stream of tourists.

ARRIVAL AND INFORMATION · WILLIAMS

By train Amtrak's *Southwest Chief* stops at Williams Junction, 3 miles east of town, twice daily.
Destinations Albuquerque (1 daily; 7hr); Chicago (1 daily; 21hr); Los Angeles (1 daily; 10hr 30min).
Visitor centre 200 W Railroad Ave (daily: June–Aug

8am–6.30pm; Sept–May 8am–5pm; ☎ 928 635 4061, ⓦ experiencewilliams.com).
Grand Canyon Railway The Grand Canyon Railway (☎ 303 843 8724, ⓦ thetrain.com) departs daily from the centre of town.

ACCOMMODATION AND EATING

Canyon Motel & RV Park 1900 E Rodeo Rd ⓦ thecanyon motel.com. The word "motel" hardly does this restored Route 66 relic, east of downtown, justice. Accommodation is in individual brick cottages and converted railroad cars; two 1929 cabooses sleep five to six each, while a larger carriage holds three en-suite units, and there are fifty RV spaces. Don't expect luxury, but it's a memorable experience. RV sites $, motel rooms $, carriage rooms $$, cabooses $$$

Grand Canyon Hotel 145 W Route 66 ⓦ thegrand canyonhotel.com. Not to be confused with the larger *Railway Hotel*, this restored "boutique hotel" offers cheap single rooms with shared bathrooms, plus doubles and twins, some en-suite. Closed Dec–March. Shared-bath

doubles $, en-suite doubles $$

Grand Canyon Railway Hotel 235 N Grand Canyon Blvd ⓦ thetrain.com. The Grand Canyon Railway's remodelled flagship hotel lacks any particular flair, but the open lobby is pleasant enough, and there's an indoor pool, spa and saloon. All rooms have two queen beds. $$

★ **Pine Country Restaurant** 107 N Grand Canyon Blvd ⓦ pinecountryrestaurant.com. Traditional, very central diner with friendly staff, where you can get a full dinner, such as pork chops or chicken breast. The home-made pies, including raspberry cream cheese, are irresistible and worth saving space for. $$

The Grand Canyon

Even though almost seven million people visit **GRAND CANYON NATIONAL PARK** every year, the canyon itself remains beyond the grasp of the human imagination. No photograph, no statistics, can prepare you for such vastness. At more than one mile deep, it's an inconceivable abyss; varying between four and eighteen miles wide, it's an endless expanse of bewildering shapes and colours, glaring desert brightness and impenetrable shadow, stark promontories and soaring sandstone pinnacles. Somehow it's so impassive, so remote – you could never call it a disappointment, but at the same time many visitors are left feeling peculiarly flat. In a sense, none of the available activities can quite live up to that first stunning sight of the chasm. The **overlooks** along the rim all offer views that shift unceasingly from dawn to sunset; you can **hike** down into the depths on foot or by mule, hover above in a **helicopter** or raft through the **whitewater rapids** of the river itself; you can spend a night at **Phantom Ranch** on the canyon floor or swim in the waterfalls of the idyllic **Havasupai Reservation**. And yet that distance always remains – the Grand Canyon stands apart.

The vast majority of visitors come to the **South Rim** – it's much easier to get to, it holds far more facilities (mainly at **Grand Canyon Village**) and it's open year round. There is another lodge and campground at the **North Rim**, which by virtue of its isolation can be a lot more evocative, but at 1000ft higher it is usually closed by snow from November until mid-May. Few people visit both rims; to get from one to the other demands either a tough two-day hike down one side of the canyon and up the other or a 215-mile drive by road.

The South Rim

When someone casually mentions visiting the "Grand Canyon", they're almost certainly referring to the **South Rim**. To be more precise, it's the thirty-mile stretch of the South Rim that's served by a paved road; and most specifically of all, it's **Grand Canyon Village**, the small canyon-edge community, sandwiched between the pine forest and the rim, that holds the park's **lodges**, **restaurants** and **visitor centre**. Nine out of every ten visitors come here, however, not because it's a uniquely wonderful spot from which to see the canyon, but simply because tourist facilities just happen to have been concentrated here ever since the railroad arrived a century ago.

Exploring the South Rim

Most South Rim visits start at **Mather Point** near the visitor centre, where the canyon panorama is more comprehensive than any obtainable from Grand Canyon Village. The views to the east in particular are consistently stupendous; it's hard to imagine a more perfect position from which to watch the **sunrise** over the canyon.

Various vantage points along the rim-edge footpath nearby offer glimpses of the Colorado River. Walk west for around ten minutes – turn left along the rim from the information plaza – and you'll come to **Yavapai Point**. From here, you can see two tiny segments of the river, one of which happens to include both the suspension footbridge across the Colorado and *Phantom Ranch* (see page 135). Nearby, the **Yavapai Geology Museum** (daily: summer 8am–8pm; winter 8am–6pm; free) has illuminating displays on how the canyon may have formed.

Two separate roads extend along the South Rim for several miles in either direction from the information plaza and Grand Canyon Village, paralleled to the west in particular by the **Rim Trail** on the very lip of the canyon. Along the eight-mile **Hermit**

GRAND CANYON ADMISSION

Admission to Grand Canyon National Park is valid for seven days on either rim. All the park-service **passes** (see page 34) are sold and valid.

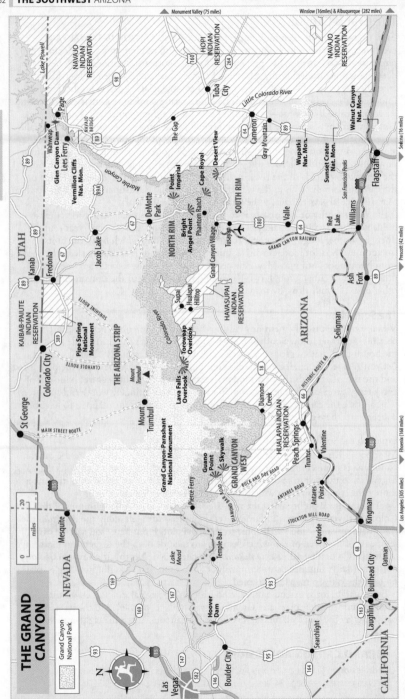

GEOLOGY AND HISTORY OF THE GRAND CANYON

Layer upon layer of different rocks, readily distinguished by colour and each with its own fossil record, recede down into the Grand Canyon and back through time. Although the strata at the riverbed are, at almost two billion years old, among the oldest exposed rocks on earth, however, the canyon itself has only formed in the last six million years. Experts cannot agree quite how that has happened, because the Colorado actually cuts through the heart of an enormous hill (known to Native Americans as the **Kaibab**, "the mountain with no peak"). The canyon's fantastic sandstone and limestone formations were not literally carved by the river, however; they're the result of erosion by wind and extreme cycles of heat and cold. These features were named – **Brahma Temple**, **Vishnu Temple** and so on – by Clarence Dutton, who wrote the first Geological Survey report on the canyon in 1881.

While it may look forbidding, the Grand Canyon is not a dead place. All sorts of desert **wildlife** survive here – sheep and rabbits, eagles and vultures, mountain lions and, of course, spiders, scorpions and snakes. **Humans** have never been present on any great scale, but signs have been found of habitation as early as 2000 BC and the **Ancestral Puebloans** were certainly here later on. A party of **Spaniards** passed through in 1540 and a Father Garcés spent some time with the Havasupai in 1776, but **John Wesley Powell**'s expeditions along the fearsome uncharted waters of the Colorado in 1869 and 1871–72 really brought the canyon to public attention. Entrepreneurs made a few abortive attempts to mine different areas, then realized that facilities for tourism were a far more lucrative investment. With the exception of the Native American reservations, the Grand Canyon is now run exclusively for the benefit of visitors, although as recently as 1963 there were proposals to dam the Colorado and flood 150 miles of the canyon, and the Glen Canyon dam has seriously affected the ecology downstream.

2

Road to the west, accessible only by shuttle bus or bike for most of the year, no single overlook can be said to be the "best", but there are far too many to stop at them all. **Sunset** is particularly magical at Hopi Point, to the west.

Driving or taking a shuttle bus along Desert View Drive to the east opens up further dramatic views. **Desert View** itself, 23 miles from the village, is, at 7500ft, the highest point on the South Rim. Visible to the east are the vast flatlands of the **Navajo Nation**; to the northeast, **Vermilion** and **Echo Cliffs** and the grey bulk of **Navajo Mountain** ninety miles away; to the west lie the gigantic peaks of **Vishnu** and **Buddha temples**, while through the plains comes the narrow gorge of the **Little Colorado**. The odd-looking construction on the very lip of the canyon is **Desert View Watchtower**, built by Mary Jane Colter in 1932 in a conglomeration of Native American styles and decorated with Hopi pictographs.

Into the canyon

Hiking any of the trails that descend **into the Grand Canyon** allows you to pass through successive different landscapes, each with its own climate, wildlife and topography. While the canyon offers a wonderful wilderness experience, however, it can be a hostile and very unforgiving environment, gruelling even for expert hikers.

That the South Rim is 7000ft above sea level is for most people fatiguing in itself. Furthermore, all hikes start with a long, steep descent and unless you camp overnight you'll have to climb all the way back up again when you're hotter and wearier.

For day-hikers, the golden rule is to keep track of how much time you spend hiking down and allow twice that much to get back up again. Average summer temperatures inside the canyon exceed 100°F; to hike for eight hours in that sort of heat, you have to drink an incredible thirty pints of water. Always carry at least a quart per person and much more if there are no water sources along your chosen trail, as well as plenty of food.

SOUTH RIM TOURS

Xanterra (contact the transport desk in any lodge, book on ⓦ grandcanyonlodges.com) runs at least two short daily **coach tours** along the **rim** to the west and east of the village, **sunrise** and **sunset** trips and **mule** rides at rim level, or down to *Phantom Ranch*, by the river.

Multiday **whitewater rafting trips** in the canyon proper – operators are listed on ⓦ nps.gov/grca/planyourvisit/river-concessioners.htm – are often booked up years in advance, while no **one-day** raft trips are available within Grand Canyon National Park. For a trip along the river at short notice, there are, however, two alternatives, at either end of the canyon. Colorado River Discovery, based in Page, Arizona, offers one-day trips that start below **Glen Canyon Dam** and take out at **Lees Ferry** (ⓦ outdoorsunlimited.com), while further west, the Hualapai River Runners arrange pricey one-day trips on the Hualapai Reservation, starting at Diamond Creek (mid-March to mid-Oct; ⓦ grandcanyonwest.com).

Aeroplane tours cost from around $170 for 40–45min up to as long as you like for as much as you've got. Operators include Grand Canyon Airlines (ⓦ grandcanyonairlines.com). **Helicopter tours**, from more like $230–290 for 40min from Grand Canyon West or Grand Canyon National Park Airport (or $500+ from Las Vegas), are offered by Maverick (ⓦ maverickhelicopter.com) and Papillon (ⓦ papillon.com).

Bright Angel Trail

The **Bright Angel Trail**, which starts from the village, switchbacks for 9.6 miles down to **Phantom Ranch**. Under no circumstances should you try to hike all the way down and back in a single day; the longest feasible day-hike is to go as far as **Plateau Point** on the edge of the arid Tonto Plateau, an overlook above the Inner Gorge from which it is not possible to descend any further. That twelve-mile round trip usually takes at least eight hours. In summer, water can be obtained along the way.

Miners laid out the first section of the trail a century ago, along an old Havasupai route. It has two short tunnels in its first mile. After another mile, the **wildlife** starts to increase (deer, rodents and ravens) and there are a few **pictographs**, all but obscured by graffiti.

At the lush **Indian Gardens** almost five miles down, site of a ranger station and campground with water, the trails split to Plateau Point or down to the river via the **Devil's Corkscrew**. The latter route leads through sand dunes scattered with cactuses and down beside **Garden Creek** to the Colorado, which you then follow for more than a mile to *Phantom Ranch* (see page 135).

ARRIVAL AND INFORMATION   THE SOUTH RIM

By car Most visitors reach the park entrance at Tusayan by driving north from I-40, either for 52 miles from Williams or 75 miles from Flagstaff.

Amtrak Amtrak trains come no closer to the South Rim than the stations at Flagstaff and Williams. Groome Transportation buses (ⓦ arizonashuttle.com) connect both stations with *Maswik Lodge* in Grand Canyon Village.

Grand Canyon Railway Restored railroad, operated by steam engines in summer, connecting a station in the heart of Williams with Grand Canyon Village (ⓦ thetrain.com).

While you don't see the canyon from the train, it's a fun way to make a short visit to the park. Services operate daily all year, typically leaving Williams at 9.30am and reaching the canyon at 11.45am, and then leaving the canyon at 3.30pm to arrive back in Williams at 5.45pm.

Grand Canyon Visitor Center The official South Rim visitor centre is immediately north of the spur road that heads west into the village from Hwy-64 (daily: March–Nov 8am–6pm, Dec–Feb 10am–4pm; ☎ 928 638 7888, ⓦ nps.gov/grca).

SHUTTLE ROUTES

Grand Canyon Village is always accessible to private vehicles, and so is the road **east** from the village to Desert View. The road west from the village to Hermit's Rest, however, is only open to cars during December, January and February. At other times, you have to use the park's free **shuttle buses**.

Village (Blue) Route Loops between Grand Canyon Village and the visitor centre, stopping at *Bright Angel*, *Maswik* and *Yavapai* lodges and *Mather Campground*.

Kaibab Rim (Orange) Route Loops between the visitor centre and Yaki Point and the South Kaibab trailhead to the east, and Mather and Yavapai points to the west.
Hikers' Express Early-morning service to Yaki Point from *Bright Angel Lodge*, via the visitor centre, for hikers using the South Kaibab Trail.

Hermit Road (Red) Route Between March and Nov, this route follows Hermit Rd 7 miles west of the village.
Tusayan (Purple) Route Regular 20min runs between Tusayan and the visitor centre, between late May and late Sept only.

ACCOMMODATION

Roughly two thousand **guest rooms** are available near the South Rim: half in and around **Grand Canyon Village** – where the few that enjoy canyon views tend to be booked to two years in advance – and a further thousand in **Tusayan**, an unattractive strip-mall 7 miles south.

LODGES AND HOTELS

Best Western Grand Canyon Squire Inn 74 Hwy-64, Tusayan ⓦ grandcanyonsquire.com. Tusayan's most lavish option bills itself as the canyon's "only resort hotel", with an outdoor pool, indoor spa and bowling alley. Most rooms are spacious and very comfortable, if unremarkable; pay extra for an enormous deluxe room with oval bath. $$$$

★ **Bright Angel Lodge** Grand Canyon Village ⓦ grandcanyonlodges.com. An imposing central lodge and a westward sprawl of rustic but delightful detached log cabins. Though reasonably sized and appealingly furnished, many lodge rooms share bathrooms and/or toilets; a few offer private showers. $$

★ **El Tovar** Grand Canyon Village ⓦ grandcanyonlodges.com. Log-construction rim-side hotel that combines rough-hewn charm with elegant sophistication. Only three suites offer canyon views; the rest of the 78 tastefully furnished rooms come in two different sizes, but are otherwise very similar. Almost all provide just one bed. $$$$

Kachina and Thunderbird Lodges Grand Canyon Village ⓦ grandcanyonlodges.com. Anonymous but perfectly adequate motel-style rooms, each with two queen-size beds and full bath, set in a low and utterly undistinguished two-storey block just yards from the rim. $$$$

Maswik Lodge Grand Canyon Village ⓦ grandcanyonlodges.com. Large complex, a few hundred yards back from the rim, with two distinct blocks of motel-style rooms. $$$

★ **Phantom Ranch** Colorado River ⓦ grandcanyonlodges.com. Located at river level, *Phantom Ranch* can only be reached on foot or mule. First call on its individual cabins goes to mule riders (see page 131), but hikers can sleep in four ten-bunk, single-sex dormitories. Reservations are essential, but even then requests are processed using an online lottery system. Note also that the Ranch was expected to be closed on and off through 2023 and into 2024 for a major renovation. Family-style meals in its restaurant are usually available for breakfast and for dinner. Dorms $, cabins $$

Seven Mile Lodge AZ-64, Tusayan ⓦ 7milelodge.com. The last remaining little roadside motel in Tusayan. Advance reservations (by phone) are only accepted up to 30 days, and walk-ins are always welcomed. Despite the slight premium charged for housing three or four guests in the same room, it's still great value for groups of (close) friends. Closed Jan. $$

Yavapai Lodge 11 Yavapai Lodge Rd, Grand Canyon Village ⓦ visitgrandcanyon.com. The largest in-park lodge, in the woods half a mile from the rim, and modernized by new concessionaires. Perfectly decent motel-style accommodation – most rooms have twin beds – in two similar sections, the newer *Yavapai East*, and *Yavapai West*. Both have a/c. $$$

CAMPING

★ **Bright Angel Campground** Phantom Ranch area, Colorado River; details on ⓦ nps.gov/grca, reserve via Permits Office, 1824 S. Thompson St, Suite 201, Flagstaff AZ, 86001. Accessible only on overnight backpacking trips, this campground, amid the cottonwoods, holds 32 sites, each with its own picnic table. Camping by backcountry permit only. $

Desert View Campground Desert View ⓦ nps.gov/grca. Simple campground, set back from the rim 25 miles east of Grand Canyon Village, open mid-April to mid-Oct only, on a first-come, first-served basis, with no RV hookups. $

Mather Campground Grand Canyon Village ⓦ recreation.gov. Year-round tent and RV camping (without hookups), south of the main road not far from Market Plaza. Sites holding up to two vehicles and six people should be reserved well in advance in summer; in winter, they're first-come, first-served. Walk-in sites for hikers and bikers year round. $

EATING AND DRINKING

Arizona Steakhouse Bright Angel Lodge ⓦ grandcanyonlodges.com. Informal, plain but good-quality restaurant, a few yards from the rim. The open kitchen serves conventional meat and seafood meals, with sandwiches, salads and simple main dishes at lunchtime, and a steak-heavy dinner menu. $$

★ **El Tovar Dining Room** El Tovar Hotel ⓦ grandcanyon lodges.com. Very grand, very classy dark-wood restaurant, with great big windows – though only the front tier of tables have actual canyon views. The food itself is rich and expensive, especially at dinner, with main dishes such as poached sea bass and steaks. Lunchtime sandwiches, tacos and so on are much cheaper. Reservations required for lunch and dinner. §§§

Fred Harvey Burger Bright Angel Lodge ⓦ grand canyonlodges.com. Straightforward, windowless diner that serves pretty much anything you might want, from snacks and salads to steaks and burgers. No reservations. §

2

The Havasupai Reservation

92 miles north of I-40 exit 123, via AZ-66 and Arrowhead Hwy-18, then 8 miles on foot, horseback or helicopter • No entry to reservation without advance lodging reservation; charge • ⓦ theofficialhavasupaitribe.com

The **Havasupai Reservation** really is another world. Things have changed a little since a 1930s anthropologist called it "the only spot in the United States where native culture has remained in anything like its pristine condition", but the sheer magic of its turquoise waterfalls and canyon scenery makes this a very special place.

Havasu Canyon is a side canyon of the Grand Canyon, 35 miles as the raven flies from Grand Canyon Village, but almost two hundred miles by road. Turn off the interstate at Seligman or Kingman, onto AZ-66, then follow Arrowhead Hwy-18 to **Hualapai Hilltop**. An eight-mile trail zigzags down a bluff from there, leading through the stunning waterless Hualapai Canyon to the village of **SUPAI**. All visitors must have advance lodging reservations; even camping, for the minimum permitted stay of three nights. Beyond Supai the trail leads to a succession of spectacular **waterfalls**, starting with two dramatic cascades, New Navajo Falls and Rock Falls, created by a flash flood in 2008. Beyond those lie Havasu Falls, great for swimming, and Mooney Falls, where a precarious chain-ladder descent leads to another glorious pool.

Note that the reservation was closed to outsiders in March 2020 because of the Covid-19 pandemic. Though it was expected to reopen sometime in February 2023, facilities were badly affected by flooding in October 2022, and recovery was hampered by a legal dispute with a former tourist operator. Check the Havasupai website for the latest.

ACCOMMODATION AND EATING   **THE HAVASUPAI RESERVATION**

Havasu Campground Havasu Canyon ⓦ havasupai reservations.com. Facilities in this creekside campground are primitive in the extreme. Tents can be pitched to either side of the creek, which is crossed by makeshift footbridges. Reservations are compulsory, all for exactly 3 nights. Rates include entry permit. §§

Havasupai Lodge Supai Village ⓦ havasupailodge. com. Set slightly apart from things on the edge of the village, this simple two-storey motel holds plain but comfortable a/c rooms, without phones or TVs. All sleep four people. Advance bookings compulsory. §§§§

Tribal Café Main Plaza, Supai Village ☎ 928 448 2981. The only place to get a meal in Supai. Fried breakfasts, and a lunch or dinner of beef stew, Native American frybread or burritos. §

The Hualapai Reservation: Grand Canyon West

Immediately west of the Havasupai reservation, and similarly inhabited by descendants of the Pai people, the **Hualapai Reservation** spreads across almost a million acres, bounded to the north by a 108-mile stretch of the Colorado River.

Fifty miles northwest of the reservation's only town, **PEACH SPRINGS**, itself 35 miles northwest of **Seligman** on Route 66, a cluster of overlooks above the Colorado river is cannily promoted as **Grand Canyon West** of the Grand Canyon. This is the closest spot to Las Vegas where it's possible to see the canyon and most of its visitors are day-trippers who fly here unaware that they're not seeing the canyon at its best. The massive Hualapai programme to attract tourists culminated in 2007 in the unveiling of the **Skywalk** (ⓦ grandcanyonwest.com), a horseshoe-shaped glass walkway which despite the hype does not extend out over the canyon itself, but above a side arm, with a vertical drop of just 1200ft immediately below. It's so extraordinarily expensive, limited in scope and time-consuming to visit – unless you pay for an air tour from Las Vegas

(Scenic Airlines, ⓦscenic.com), you have to drive a minimum of forty miles on rough remote roads from the nearest highway and pay at least $65 per person to reach and walk on the Skywalk – that it can't be recommended over a trip to the national park.

The road between the rims

The 215-mile route by road from Grand Canyon Village to the **North Rim** follows AZ-64 along the East Rim Drive to Desert View, then passes an overlook into the gorge of the Little Colorado, before joining US-89 fifty miles later at **CAMERON**.

Seventy barren miles north of Cameron, the direct route to the North Rim, now US-89A, crosses **Navajo Bridge** 500ft above the Colorado River. Until the bridge was built, a ferry service operated six miles north at **LEES FERRY**. Established in 1872 by Mormon pioneer John D. Lee, it was the only spot within hundreds of miles to offer easy access to the banks of the river on both sides. Now the sole launching point for **whitewater rafting** trips into the Grand Canyon, the ferry site stands close to the atmospheric remains of Lee's Lonely Dell ranch.

Back on US-89A, beneath the red of the **Vermilion Cliffs**, a succession of **motels** all have their own restaurants. The turning south to get to the North Rim, off US-89A onto AZ-67, comes at **JACOB LAKE**, from where it's 41 miles to the canyon itself, along a road that's closed in winter.

ACCOMMODATION AND EATING   THE ROAD BETWEEN THE RIMS

Cameron Trading Post 466 US-89, Cameron ⓦcamerontradingpost.com. Large, smart motel complex, where rooms on the upper floors have large balconies that look out across the Little Colorado. A pleasant dining room with tin ceiling and fireplace serves all meals. $\overline{\underline{\$\$}}$

Jacob Lake Campground US-89A, Jacob Lake ⓦfs. usda.gov. Lovely wooded Forest Service campground, just west of the intersection, which caters to tent campers only. Closed Oct to Apr. $\overline{\underline{\$}}$

Jacob Lake Inn Intersection of US-89A and AZ-67, Jacob Lake ⓦjacoblake.com. Sprawling complex of simple motel rooms and log cabins plus a petrol station, a general store, an old-fashioned diner counter and a restaurant serving various chicken, trout and steak mains. $\overline{\underline{\$\$}}$

Marble Canyon Lodge US-89A ⓦmarblecanyonlodge. com. More than fifty conventional motel-style rooms, with TVs but no phones, in low-slung buildings in a romantic desert-outpost setting at the foot of the cliffs, not far west of Navajo Bridge, just past the turnoff for Lees Ferry. The adequate but unexciting restaurant is open for all meals daily. $\overline{\underline{\$\$}}$

The North Rim

Higher, more exposed and far less accessible than the South Rim, the **NORTH RIM** of the Grand Canyon receives less than a tenth as many visitors. A cluster of venerable Park Service buildings stand where the main highway reaches the canyon and a handful of rim-edge roads allow drivers to take their pick from additional lookouts. Only one hiking trail sees much use, the **North Kaibab Trail**, which follows Bright Angel Creek down to *Phantom Ranch*.

The park itself remains open for day-use only after mid-October, but no food, lodging or gas is available and visitors must be prepared to leave at a moment's notice. It's shut down altogether by the first major snowfall of winter.

ARRIVAL AND INFORMATION   THE NORTH RIM

Transcanyon Shuttle The only public transport to serve the North Rim connects *Grand Canyon Lodge* with the South Rim (departs North Rim 7am & 2pm daily, South Rim 8am & 1.30pm; 4hr; ⓦtrans-canyonshuttle.com).

Visitor centre At the entrance to *Grand Canyon Lodge* (mid-May to mid-Oct daily 8am–6pm; ☏928 638 7864, ⓦnps.gov/grca).

ACCOMMODATION AND EATING

★ **Grand Canyon Lodge** ⓦgrandcanyonforever.com. Cabins and larger motel-style blocks, mostly ranged over the quiet, well-wooded hillside beside the approach road. Western Cabins have full-size bathrooms and porches and sleep up to four people; just four stand close enough to the rim to offer canyon views. Frontier Cabins accommodate three guests and have smaller bathrooms, while Pioneer Cabins have two separate bedrooms. Reservations for all are available up to thirteen months in advance, and are absolutely essential. Closed mid-Oct to mid-May. Motel rooms, Frontier Cabins, & Pioneer Cabins $\overline{\$\$}$, Western Cabins $\overline{\$\$\$}$

Lodge Dining Room Grand Canyon Lodge ⓦ grand canyonforever.com. The room itself, with its soaring timber ceiling, is elegant and impressive, and window tables enjoy awesome canyon views. Dinner mains such as blackened salmon. Reservations essential. $\overline{\$\$}$

★ **North Rim Campground** One mile north of Grand Canyon Lodge ⓦ recreation.gov. Very pleasant forest campground with 87 car-camping sites, but no RV hookups. Although all vehicle sites are often reserved in advance, additional room is always available for backpackers. Closed mid-Oct to mid-May. $\overline{\$}$

Monument Valley

Straddling the Arizona-Utah state line, 24 miles north of Kayenta and 25 miles southwest of Mexican Hat • Car park daily 24hr, visitor centre daily: May–Sept 6am–8pm; Oct–April 8am–4pm • Charge; National Park passes not accepted • ⓦ navajonationparks.org

The classic southwestern landscape of stark sandstone buttes and forbidding pinnacles of rock, poking from an endless expanse of drifting red sands, is an archetypal Wild West image. Only when you arrive at **MONUMENT VALLEY** – which straddles the Arizona–Utah state line, 24 miles north of Kayenta – do you realize how much your perception of the West has been shaped by this one spot. Such scenery does exist elsewhere, of course, but nowhere is it so perfectly distilled. While moviemakers have flocked here since the early days of Hollywood, the sheer majesty of the place still

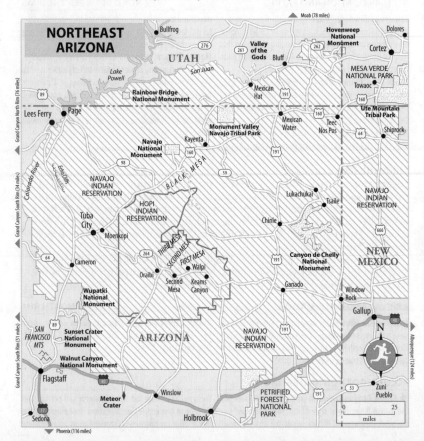

THE NAVAJO NATION

The largest Native American reservation in the US, popularly known as the **NAVAJO NATION**, covers much of northeastern Arizona and extends into both western New Mexico and Monument Valley in southernmost Utah. Everyone can speak English, but Navajo, a language so complex that it formed the basis of a secret code during World War II, is still the lingua franca. The reservation follows its own rules over Daylight Savings; in frontier-style towns like Tuba City, the time varies according to whether you're in an American or a Navajo district.

When the Americans took over this region from the Mexicans in the mid-nineteenth century, the Navajo – who call themselves *Dineh*, "The People" – almost lost everything. In 1864, Kit Carson rounded up every Navajo he could find and packed them off to Fort Sumner in desolate eastern New Mexico. A few years later, however, the Navajo were allowed to return. Most of the 300,000-plus Navajo today work as shepherds and farmers on widely scattered smallholdings, though craftspeople also sell their wares from roadside stands and tourist stops.

As you travel in this region, respect its people and places. Though the Ancestral Puebloans are no longer present, many of the relics they left behind are on land that holds spiritual significance to their modern counterparts. Similarly, it is offensive to photograph or intrude upon people's lives without permission.

On a practical note, don't expect extensive **tourist facilities**. Most towns are bureaucratic outposts that only come alive for fairs and rodeos and hold few places to eat and even fewer hotels and motels. For information online, visit ⓦdiscovernavajo.com, ⓦexplorenavajo.com; and ⓦwww.navajo-nsn.gov.

takes your breath away. Add the fact that it remains a stronghold of **Navajo** culture and Monument Valley can be the absolute highlight of a trip to the Southwest.

The biggest and most impressive pair of monoliths are **The Mittens**; one East and one West, each has a distinct thumb splintering off from its central bulk. More than a dozen other spires spread nearby, along with **rock art panels** and assorted minor **Ancestral Puebloan ruins**.

You can see the buttes for free, towering alongside US-163, but the four-mile detour to enter **Monument Valley Tribal Park** is rewarded with much closer views. A rough, unpaved road drops from behind the visitor centre and *View* hotel to run through Monument Valley itself. The seventeen-mile **self-drive route** makes a bumpy but bearable ride in an ordinary vehicle and takes something over an hour (daily: May–Sept 6am–8pm; Oct–April 8am–4pm). However, the Navajo-led **jeep** or **horseback tours** into the backcountry are very much recommended; a ninety-minute jeep trip costs from around $75 per person if arranged on the spot, with plenty of longer and potentially much more expensive alternatives. As well as stopping at such movie locations as the **Totem Pole**, most tours call in at a Navajo *hogan* (eight-sided dwelling) to watch weavers at work.

ACCOMMODATION AND EATING — MONUMENT VALLEY

Goulding's Lodge 1000 Gouldings Trading Post Rd (two miles west of US-163) ⓦgouldings.com. This former trading post, across from the park approach road, incorporates an upscale motel with long-range valley views, an indoor pool, a general store, a petrol station, a museum of movie memorabilia and a campground. Tents & RV hookups $̄$, doubles $̄$$̄$$̄$

★**The View Campground** Monument Valley Tribal Park ⓦmonumentvalleyview.com. The park campground, a short way down the road into the valley itself, has been

totally revamped. Tent pitches and RV sites share restrooms and showers, while very comfortable standalone cabins line up along the rim, each with one queen bed and two bunk beds, a full bathroom, and its own private deck. Closed Jan to mid-March. Tents & RV spaces $̄$, cabins $̄$$̄$$̄$

★**The View Hotel** Monument Valley Tribal Park ⓦmonumentvalleyview.com. All of the luxurious rooms in this stunning Navajo-owned hotel, alongside the tribal park visitor centre, have private balconies that command a magnificent panorama. $̄$$̄$$̄$

2

> **CANYON DE CHELLY JEEP TOURS**
>
> With the exception of the White House Trail (see below), the only way to get a close-up view of Canyon de Chelly's amazing Ancestral Puebloan remains is to take a **guided tour** with a Navajo guide. Typical half-day tours with operators such as **Beauty Way Jeep Tours** (ⓦbeautywayjeeptours.com) and **Canyon de Chelly Tours** (ⓦcanyondechellytours.com) will get you to and from White House Ruin; continuing beyond to see Spider Rock takes a full day.

The View Restaurant Monument Valley Tribal Park ⓦmonumentvalleyview.com. The only eating option in the tribal park enjoys a prime position overlooking the valley, with some irresistible outdoor tables. The food is good but not exceptional, with authentic Navajo dishes such as mutton stew and blue-corn frybread alongside more conventional burgers and salads. $$

Canyon de Chelly National Monument

Free 24hr access, but to rim drives only, not valley floor • ⓦnps.gov/cach

A short distance east of **Chinle**, 87 miles southeast of Monument Valley and seventy miles north of I-40, twin sandstone walls emerge abruptly from the desert floor, climbing at a phenomenal rate to become the awesome 1000ft cliffs of **CANYON DE CHELLY NATIONAL MONUMENT**. Between these sheer sides, the meandering cottonwood-fringed Chinle Wash winds through grasslands and planted fields. Here and there a Navajo *hogan* stands in a grove of fruit trees, a straggle of sheep is penned in by a crude wooden fence or ponies drink at the water's edge. And everywhere, perched on ledges in the canyon walls and dwarfed by the towering cliffs, are the long-abandoned adobe dwellings of the **Ancestral Puebloans**.

Two main canyons branch apart a few miles upstream: **Canyon de Chelly** (pronounced *de shay*) to the south and **Canyon del Muerto** to the north. Each twists and turns in all directions, scattered with vast rock monoliths, while several smaller canyons break away. The whole labyrinth threads its way northward for thirty miles into the Chuska Mountains.

Canyon de Chelly is a magnificent place, on a par with the best of the Southwest's national parks. Its relative lack of fame owes much to the continuing presence of the **Navajo**, for whom the canyon retains enormous symbolic significance even though they did not build its cliff dwellings. There's no road in, and apart from one short trail you can only enter the canyons with a Navajo guide. Visitors are therefore largely restricted to peering into the canyon from above, from the spectacular overlooks along the two **rim drives**. Each drive is a forty-mile round-trip that takes two to three hours to complete.

The South Rim

Junction Overlook, four miles along the **South Rim Drive**, stands far above the point where the two main canyons branch apart; as you scramble across the bare rocks you can see Canyon de Chelly narrowing away, with a *hogan* immediately below.

Two miles further on, by which time the canyon is 550ft deep, **White House Overlook** looks down on the highly photogenic **White House Ruins**. This is the only point from which unguided hikers can descend to the canyon floor, taking perhaps thirty to 45 minutes to get down and a good hour to get back up. The beautiful if precarious **White House Trail**, at times running along ledges chiselled into the slick rock, culminates with a close-up view of the ruins; the most dramatic dwellings, squeezed into a tiny alcove 60ft up a majestic cliff, were once reached via the rooftops of now-vanished structures. Visitors can only walk a hundred yards or so in either direction beyond the site.

Back up on the South Rim Drive, twelve miles along, the view from **Sliding House Overlook** reveals more Ancestral Puebloan ruins seemingly slipping down the canyon walls toward the fields below. Eight miles further on the road ends above the astonishing **Spider Rock**, where twin 800ft pinnacles of rock come to within 200ft of the canyon rim.

The North Rim

The **North Rim Drive** runs twenty miles up Canyon del Muerto to **Massacre Cave** – really just a pitifully exposed ledge – where a Spanish expedition of 1805 killed a hundred Navajo women, children and old men. Visible from the nearby **Mummy Cave Overlook** is the striking **House Under The Rock**, with its central tower in the Mesa Verde style. Of the two viewpoints at **Antelope House Overlook**, one is opposite Navajo Fortress, an isolated eminence atop which the Navajo were besieged by US troops for three months in 1863, while the other looks down on the twin ruined square towers of Antelope House. In the **Tomb of the Weaver** across the wash, the embalmed body of an old man was found wrapped in golden eagle feathers.

ACCOMMODATION AND EATING	CANYON DE CHELLY NATIONAL MONUMENT
Cottonwood Campground At the start of South Rim Drive ⓦnavajonationparks.org. First-come, first-served tent-only campground among the trees beside *Thunderbird Lodge*; each of the 93 sites accommodates up to four for no additional fee. No showers, no RVs. Cash only. 丂 **Holiday Inn Canyon De Chelly (Chinle)** BIA Rte-7, Garcia Trading Post, Chinle ⓦihg.com. Smart, adobe-fied motel, with a hundred comfortable, well-equipped rooms. The cosy, colourful on-site dining room is nothing	exceptional – though the roast chicken is pretty good – but it's the best you'll find in Chinle. 丂丂 **Thunderbird Lodge** At the start of South Rim Drive (BIA Rte-7) ⓦthunderbirdlodge.com. Conventional, clean if somewhat faded motel rooms surrounding a century-old trading post, which houses a large, reasonably priced self-service cafeteria that most visitors find interesting only because it's often busy with Navajo from surrounding communities. They also run daily canyon tours. 丂丂

The Hopi Mesas

Almost uniquely in the United States, the **Hopi** people have lived continuously in the same place for more than eight hundred years. Some invaders have come and gone in that time, others have stayed; but the villages on **First**, **Second** and **Third mesas** have endured, if not exactly undisturbed then at least unmoved.

To outsiders, it's not immediately obvious why the Hopi chose to live on three barren and unprepossessing fingers of rock poking from the southern flanks of **Black Mesa** in the depths of northeast Arizona. There are two simple answers. The first lies within the mesa itself: its rocks are tilted to deliver a tiny but dependable trickle of water and also hold vast reserves of coal. The second is that the Hopi used to farm and hunt across a much wider area and were only restricted to their mesa-top villages when their Navajo neighbours encroached. While the Hopi are celebrated for their skill at "**dry farming**", preserving enough precious liquid to grow corn, beans and squash on hand-tilled terraces, this precarious way of life has nonetheless been forced upon them.

By their very survival and the persistence of their ancient beliefs and ceremonies, the Hopi have long fascinated outsiders. While visitors are welcome, the Hopi have no desire to turn themselves into a tourist attraction. Although stores and galleries make it easy to buy crafts such as pottery, basketwork, silver overlay jewellery and hand-carved *kachina* dolls, tourists who hope for extensive sightseeing – let alone spiritual revelations – are likely to leave disappointed and quite possibly dismayed by what they perceive as conspicuous poverty.

The modern, mock-Pueblo **Hopi Cultural Centre** below Second Mesa holds a **museum** (July & Aug Mon–Fri 8am–5pm, Sat & Sun 9am–3pm; Sept–June Mon–Fri 8am–5pm; charge; ☎928 734 2401). Unless your visit coincides with one of the rare social events that's open to tourists, the only way to see the mesa-top villages is on a **guided tour**, which offers the opportunity to ask questions and to buy pottery, *kachina* dolls and fresh-baked *piiki*, a flatbread made with blue cornflour. These are usually available at the Moenkopi Legacy Inn & Suites outside Tuba City, but were suspended during the Covid-19 epidemic and had not resumed at the time of writing; visit ⓦexperiencehopi.com for the latest information.

ACCOMMODATION AND EATING	THE HOPI MESAS

Hopi Cultural Center Motel Second Mesa ⓦhopiculturalcenter.com. Built in a faux-Pueblo architectural style, this motel offers 34 plain but acceptable rooms that are usually booked solid in summer. The cafeteria serves good, substantial meals, including local delicacy *noqkwivi*, lamb stewed with hominy. $$

Utah

Home to the biggest and most beautiful landscapes in North America, **UTAH** holds something for everyone: from brilliantly coloured canyons, across desert plains, to thickly wooded and snow-covered mountains. Almost all of this unmatched range of terrain is public land, making Utah *the* place to come for **outdoor pursuits**, whether your tastes run to hiking, mountain biking, whitewater rafting or skiing.

In **southern Utah**, especially, the **scenery** is stupendous, a stunning geological freak show where the earth is ripped bare to expose cliffs and canyons of every imaginable hue. The region holds so many **national parks**, it has often been suggested that the entire area should become one vast park. The most accessible parks – such as **Zion** and **Bryce Canyon** – are by far the most visited, but lesser-known parks like **Arches**, **Canyonlands** and **Capitol Reef** are every bit as dramatic. Huge tracts of this empty desert, in which fascinating pre-Columbian pictographs and Ancestral Puebloan ruins lie hidden, are all but unexplored; seeing them requires self-sufficiency and considerable planning.

Although **northern Utah** holds less appeal for tourists, **Salt Lake City**, the capital, is by far the state's largest and most cosmopolitan urban centre, and makes an attractive and enjoyable stopover.

Led by Brigham Young, Utah's earliest white settlers – the **Mormons** or Latter Day Saints (LDS) – arrived in the Salt Lake area, which then lay outside the USA, in 1847 and embarked on massive irrigation projects. At first they provoked great suspicion and hostility back East. The Republican Convention of 1856 railed against slavery and polygamy in equal measure; had the Civil War not intervened, a war against the Mormons was a real possibility. Relations eased when the Mormon Church dropped polygamy in 1890 and statehood followed in 1896; to this day, over sixty percent of Utah's three-million-strong population are Mormons. The Mormon influence is responsible for the layout of Utah's towns, where residential streets are as wide as interstates, and numbered block by block according to a logical if ponderous system.

Zion National Park

Charge; valid seven days

With its soaring cliffs, riverine forests and cascading waterfalls, **ZION NATIONAL PARK** is the most conventionally beautiful of Utah's parks. It's divided into two main sections: Zion Canyon is on Hwy-9, thirty miles east of I-15 and 158 miles northeast of Las Vegas, while Kolob Canyons is just off I-15, further northeast.

The centrepiece of the park, the lush oasis of **Zion Canyon**, feels far removed from the otherworldly desolation of Canyonlands or the weirdness of Bryce. Like California's Yosemite Canyon, it's a spectacular narrow gorge, echoing with the sound of running water; also like Yosemite, it can get claustrophobic in summer, clogged with traffic and crammed with sweltering tourists.

Too many visitors see Zion Canyon as a quick half-day detour off the interstate as they race between Las Vegas and Salt Lake City. Magnificent though the canyon's

TOP DAY-HIKES IN UTAH

Calf Creek, Grand Staircase-Escalante (see page 149)	4hr
Delicate Arch Trail, Arches (see page 152)	2hr
Hickman Bridge Trail, Capitol Reef (see page 150)	2hr
Horseshoe Canyon, Canyonlands (see page 152)	5hr
Mesa Arch Trail, Canyonlands (see page 151)	1hr
Navajo Loop Trail, Bryce Canyon (see page 148)	2hr
West Rim Trail, Zion (see page 142)	1 day
White House Trail, Canyon de Chelly (see page 140)	2hr 30min

2

Scenic Drive may be, Zion deserves much more of your time than that. Even the shortest hiking trail can escape the crowds, while a day-hike will take you away from the deceptive verdure of the valley and up onto the high-desert tablelands beyond.

Summer is by far the busiest season. That's despite temperatures in excess of 100°F and violent thunderstorms concentrated especially in August. Ideally, come in spring to see the flowers bloom, or in autumn to enjoy the colours along the river.

Zion Canyon

In **Zion Canyon**, mighty walls of Navajo sandstone soar half a mile above the box elders and cottonwoods that line the loping North Fork of the **Virgin River**. The awe of the Mormon settlers who called this "Zion" is reflected in the names of the stupendous slabs of rock along the way – the **Court of the Patriarchs**, the **Great White Throne** and Angel's Landing.

Although Hwy-9 remains open to through traffic all year, the paved six-mile **Scenic Drive**, which branches north off it, is between March and late November only accessible on free **shuttle buses**. The Scenic Drive ends at the foot of the **Temple of Sinawava**, beyond which the easy but delightful **Riverside Walk** trail continues another half-mile up the canyon, to end at a sandy little beach. For eight miles upstream from here, in the stretch known as the **Zion Narrows**, the Virgin River fills the entire gorge, often less than 20ft wide and channelled between vertical cliffs almost 1000ft high. Only devotees of extreme sports should attempt to hike this ravishing "slot canyon"; specialist equipment is essential, including waterproof, super-grip footwear, neoprene socks and a walking stick, complemented in the cooler months by a drysuit, plus all the water you need to drink. You can only hike its full length downstream, a total of sixteen miles from remote Chamberlain's Ranch, twenty miles north of the park's East Entrance; Springdale-based operators provide equipment and shuttle services.

A much less demanding hike leads up to **Weeping Rock**, an easy half-hour round trip from the road to a gorgeous spring-fed garden dangling from a rocky alcove. From the same trailhead, a mile beyond *Zion Lodge*, a more strenuous and exciting route climbs up to, and into narrow **Hidden Canyon**, whose mouth turns into a waterfall after a good rain. Directly across from the lodge a short and fairly flat trail (two-mile round trip) winds up at the **Emerald Pools**, a series of three clearwater pools, the best (and furthest) of which has a small sandy beach at the foot of a gigantic cliff.

The single best half-day **hike** makes the ascent to **Angel's Landing**, a narrow ledge of whitish sandstone protruding 1750ft above the canyon floor. Starting on the Emerald Pools route, the trail switchbacks sharply up through cool **Refrigerator Canyon** before emerging on the canyon's west rim; near the end you have to cross a heart-stopping 5ft neck of rock with only a steel cable to protect you from the sheer drops to either side. That round trip takes a good four hours, but backpackers can continue another twenty miles to the gorgeous Kolob Canyons district (see page 146).

The high dry plateau above and to the **east** of Zion Canyon, reached by continuing on Hwy-9 at the Scenic Drive turnoff, stands in complete contrast to the lush Virgin

2

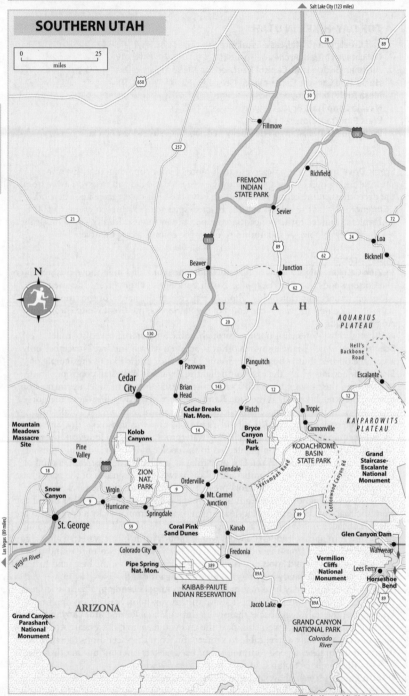

SOUTHERN UTAH

Salt Lake City (123 miles)

0 — 25
miles

28
89
650
50
Fillmore
257
Richfield
FREMONT
INDIAN
STATE PARK
Sevier
72
21
24 Loa
Bicknell
89
Beaver
Junction
62
21
62
U T A H
AQUARIUS
PLATEAU
20
Hell's
Backbone
Road
130
Panguitch
Escalante
Parowan
143
12
Cedar
City
Brian
Head
Cedar Breaks
Nat. Mon.
Hatch
Tropic
KAIPAROWITS
PLATEAU
Mountain
Meadows
Massacre
Site
14
Bryce
Canyon
Nat.
Park
Cannonville
Kolob
Canyons
Pine
Valley
Glendale
KODACHROME
BASIN
STATE PARK
Grand
Staircase-
Escalante
National
Monument
18
ZION
NAT.
PARK
Orderville
Snow
Canyon
9
Virgin
9
Mt. Carmel
Junction
Hurricane
Springdale
Kanab
89
St. George
59
Coral Pink
Sand Dunes
Glen Canyon Dam
Colorado City
Fredonia
Wahweap
Pipe Spring
Nat. Mon.
389
89A
Vermilion
Cliffs
National
Monument
Lees Ferry
Horseshoe
Bend
89
Virgin River
KAIBAB-PAIUTE
INDIAN RESERVATION
ARIZONA
Jacob Lake
89A
GRAND CANYON
NATIONAL PARK
Colorado
River
Grand Canyon-
Parashant
National
Monument
Las Vegas (89 miles)
Skutumpah Road
Cottonwood Canyon Rd

Grand Canyon North Rim (12 miles)

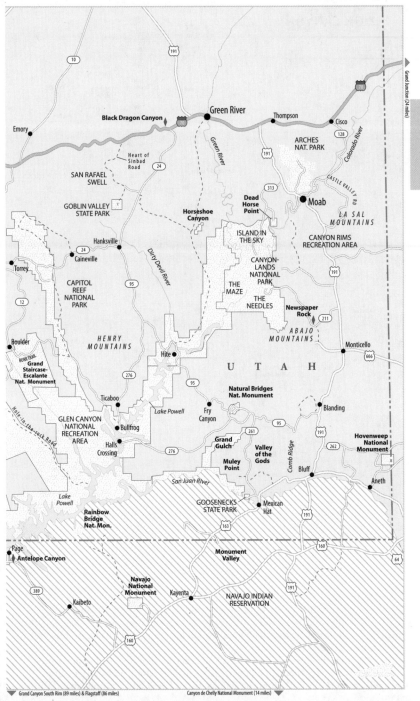

2

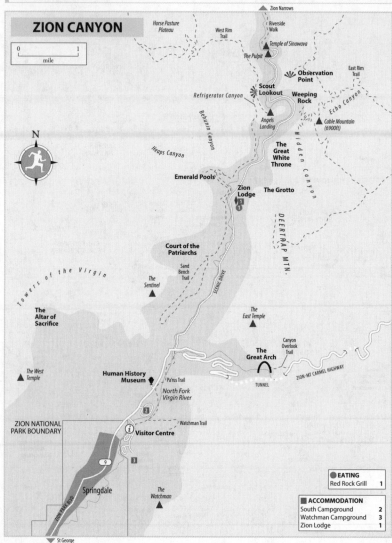

ZION CANYON

Zion Narrows

Horse Pasture Plateau

West Rim Trail

Riverside Walk

Temple of Sinawava

The Pulpit

Observation Point

East Rim Trail

Scout Lookout

Refrigerator Canyon

Weeping Rock

Echo Canyon

Angels Landing

Cable Mountain (6900ft)

Behunin Canyon

Heaps Canyon

The Great White Throne

Hidden Canyon

Emerald Pools

Zion Lodge

The Grotto

DEERTRAP MTN.

Court of the Patriarchs

Sand Bench Trail

SCENIC DRIVE

The Sentinel

The East Temple

The Altar of Sacrifice

Towers of the Virgin

The West Temple

The Great Arch

Canyon Overlook Trail

Human History Museum

Pa'rus Trail

TUNNEL

ZION-MT CARMEL HIGHWAY

Mt Carmel Junction & Bryce Canyon

North Fork Virgin River

ZION NATIONAL PARK BOUNDARY

Watchman Trail

Visitor Centre

Springdale

ZION PARK BLVD

The Watchman

St George

N

0 — 1
mile

● **EATING**
Red Rock Grill — 1

■ **ACCOMMODATION**
South Campground — 2
Watchman Campground — 3
Zion Lodge — 1

River gorge. Its most dramatic sight is the **Great Arch**, best seen from turnouts before the mile-long **tunnel** via which the highway leaves the park, en route to Bryce.

Kolob Canyons

Despite standing alongside the I-15 interstate, the immaculate **Kolob Canyons** section of Zion, 43 miles northwest of Zion Canyon, receives far fewer visitors. Here, too, the focus is on **red-rock canyons**, which in the Kolob seem somehow redder, and the trees greener, than those down below.

The view from the five-mile paved road that heads up from the small **visitor centre** is amazing, while the two main hiking trails are highly recommended. One starts two miles from the visitor centre and follows Taylor Creek on a five-mile round trip to **Double Arch Alcove**, a spectacular natural amphitheatre roofed by twin sandstone arches. The other trail sets off from the north side of the parking area at Lee Pass, four miles beyond the visitor centre, and follows a well-marked route for seven miles past La Verkin Falls to **Kolob Arch**, which at more than 300ft across rivals Landscape Arch in Arches (see page 153) as the world's longest natural rock span.

ARRIVAL AND INFORMATION ZION NATIONAL PARK

Driving to Zion Canyon Hwy-9 leaves I-15 just north of St George, and follows the Virgin River for 30 miles east to enter the park via the South Entrance, just north of Springdale.

Zion Canyon visitor centre Immediately inside the South Entrance to Zion Canyon; doubles as the base for its

two shuttle bus routes (daily: late April to late May & Sept to mid-Oct 8am–6pm; late May to Aug 8am–7pm; mid-Oct to late April 8am–5pm; ☎ 435 772 3256, ⓦ nps.gov/zion).

Kolob Canyons visitor centre Beside I-15, 20 miles south of Cedar City (daily 8am–5pm; ☎ 435 586 9548, ⓦ nps.gov/zion).

GETTING AROUND

By shuttle bus Between March and late Nov, visitors to Zion Canyon have to leave their vehicles either in Springdale or at the main park visitor centre and use free shuttle buses. The in-park Zion Canyon Shuttle runs between the visitor centre and the end of the Scenic Drive, with nine stops including

Zion Lodge. The Springdale Loop connects Springdale with the visitor centre, with nine stops en route. The shuttles tend to run on a limited basis in February and March (usually Sat & Sun only), on a normal full schedule over Christmas, but otherwise do not run at all on other days December–February.

TOURS AND ACTIVITIES

Zion Adventure Company 36 Lion Blvd, Springdale ⓦ zionadventures.com. Assorted activities just outside the park, such as tubing on the Virgin River, and guided biking, photography, climbing and canyoneering trips, plus Narrows equipment rental; and hiker shuttles, including to

Chamberlain's Ranch (charge).

Zion Rock and Mountain Guides 1458 Zion Park Blvd, Springdale ⓦ zionrockguides.com. Guided climbing, biking and canyoneering trips; Narrows equipment rental; and daily hiker shuttles, including to Chamberlain's Ranch (charge).

ACCOMMODATION

Apart from *Zion Lodge* in Zion Canyon itself, accommodation and eating facilities are concentrated in the pleasant community of Springdale, just outside the park's South Entrance.

HOTELS

★ **Desert Pearl Inn** 707 Zion Park Blvd, Springdale ⓦ desertpearl.com. Gorgeous hotel, ranged beside the Virgin River just outside the park, with superb views. Stylish rooms with high ceilings, wooden floors, huge windows and balconies, facing either riverside lawns or a lovely turquoise pool with hot tubs. $$$$

Harvest House 29 Canyon View Drive, Springdale ⓦ harvesthouse.net. Very classy B&B in a modern home, tucked beneath the sandstone cliffs. Four en-suite rooms, pleasant gardens, an outdoor hot tub, and gourmet breakfasts. $$$

Holiday Inn Express Springdale 1215 Zion Park Blvd, Springdale ⓦ ihg.com. Modern convention-style hotel at Springdale's southern end, offering spacious rooms with panoramic windows, plus a heated swimming pool. $$$

Zion Lodge Scenic Drive, Zion Canyon Advance

ⓦ zionlodge.com, see map page 146. Appealing if often overcrowded complex of low-slung wooden buildings, a couple of miles up the Scenic Drive, which offers the only food and lodging within the canyon. En-suite cabins have gas fireplaces and private porches; the motel rooms are plainer, but still have porches or balconies. $$$

CAMPING

South Campground 1 Zion Park Blvd (Zion Canyon) ⓦ nps.gov/zion, see map page 146. Arrive early for this first-come, first-served riverside campground, in a gloriously lush setting just north of the visitor centre; it tends to fill by noon. Flushing toilets and cold running water, but no showers. Open early March to early Nov. $

Watchman Campground Next to the Zion Canyon Visitor Center ⓦ recreation.gov, see map page 146. Large campground, amid the cottonwoods south of the visitor centre, with flushing toilets and cold running water, but no showers. Eighteen walk-in, tent-only sites; the rest can hold one RV or two ordinary cars. Reservations March to Oct only. $

EATING

Bit & Spur 1212 Zion Park Blvd, Springdale ⓦ bitand spur.com. Hectic dinner-only Mexican restaurant and bar,

facing the red-rock cliffs, where the food has a creative edge, and the margaritas are top-notch. Everything from chilli-rubbed steak to *chile relleno* (stuffed chilli). $\overline{\underline{\$}}$
Deep Creek Coffee 932 Zion Park Blvd, Springdale ⓦ deepcreekcoffee.com. The perfect place to greet the new day in Zion, this friendly coffeehouse buzzes from early morning onwards, serving scones, waffles and sandwiches,

and fresh smoothies to go with its powerful java. $\overline{\underline{\$}}$
Red Rock Grill Zion Lodge, Scenic Drive, Zion Canyon ⓦ zionlodge.com, see map page 146. The river views from the lodge's bright, cool, upstairs dining room will probably linger longer in your mind than its standard breakfasts and lunches. Dinners are slightly more sophisticated, with mains such as steak or trout. $\overline{\underline{\$}}\overline{\underline{\$}}$

Bryce Canyon National Park

Charge; valid 7 days

The surface of the earth can hold few weirder-looking spots than **BRYCE CANYON**, just south of US-89 86 miles northeast of Zion Canyon. Named for Mormon settler Ebenezer Bryce, who declared that it was "a helluva place to lose a cow", it is not in fact a canyon at all. Along a twenty-mile shelf on the eastern edge of the thickly forested **Paunsaugunt Plateau**, 8000ft above sea level, successive strata of dazzlingly coloured rock have slipped and slid and washed away to leave a menagerie of multihued and contorted **stone pinnacles**.

In hues of yellow, red and flaming orange, the formations here have been eroded out of the muddy sandstone by a combination of icy winters and summer rains. The top-heavy pinnacles known as "**hoodoos**" form when the harder upper layers of rock stay firm as the lower levels wear away beneath them. **Thor's Hammer**, visible from Sunset Point, is the most precarious. These hoodoos look down into technicolour ravines, all far more vivid than the Grand Canyon and much more human in scale. The whole place is at its most inspiring in winter, when the figures stand out from a blanket of snow.

The two most popular viewpoints into **Bryce Amphitheatre**, at the heart of the park, are on either side of *Bryce Canyon Lodge*: the more northerly, **Sunrise Point**, is slightly less crowded than **Sunset Point**, where most of the bus tours stop. **Hiking trails** drop abruptly from the rim down into the amphitheatre. One good three-mile trek, a great extension of the shorter **Navajo Loop Trail**, starts by switchbacking steeply from Sunset Point through the cool 200ft canyons of **Wall Street**, where a pair of 800-year-old fir trees stretch to reach daylight. It then cuts across the surreal landscape into the **Queen's Garden** basin, where the stout likeness of Queen Victoria sits in majestic condescension, before climbing back up to Sunrise Point. A dozen trails crisscross the amphitheatre, but it's surprisingly easy to get lost, so don't stray from the marked routes.

Sunrise and Sunset points notwithstanding, the best view at both sunset and dawn is from **Bryce Point**, at the southern end of the amphitheatre. From here, you can look down not only at the Bryce Canyon formations but also take in the grand sweep of the whole region, east to the **Henry Mountains** and north to the Escalante range. The park road then climbs another twenty miles south, by way of the intensely coloured **Natural Bridge**, an 85ft rock arch spanning a steep gully, en route to its dead end at **Rainbow Point**.

INFORMATION AND GETTING AROUND   BRYCE CANYON NATIONAL PARK

Visitor centre Hwy-63, immediately beyond park entrance station (daily: May–Sept 8am–8pm; April & Oct 8am–6pm; Nov–March 8am–4.30pm; ☎435 834 5322, ⓦ nps.gov/brca).
By shuttle bus Although visitors can drive to all the scenic

overlooks year-round, the park runs free shuttle buses to reduce congestion. These don't go as far south as Rainbow Point, which is normally served by two daily free bus tours, departing from six stops including *Ruby's* and the visitor centre (☎435 834 2900).

ACCOMMODATION AND EATING

INSIDE THE PARK
Lodge at Bryce Canyon 1 Lodge Way, Hwy-63 (100

yards from the rim) ⓦ brycecanyonforever.com. The only accommodation within the park itself, this 1920s lodge holds a handful of luxurious suites, a row or two of rough-hewn but comfortable cabins and seventy ordinary motel rooms. All are en suite. Lunchtime salads and sandwiches in its high-ceilinged and reasonably high-quality dining room, open for all meals; dinner mains like slow-cooked short ribs are more expensive. Closed Dec–March. $$$

North Campground Near visitor centre, Hwy-63, Bryce Canyon ⓦ recreation.gov (reservations) & ⓦ nps.gov/brca (information). Year-round campground that accepts reservations for thirteen of its 100 sites only, between mid-March and Nov only. It's usually fully occupied by early afternoon. RVs can stay, but there are no hookups or showers; sites hold up to ten people, in two vehicles. $

Sunset Campground Near Sunset Point, Bryce Canyon ⓦ recreation.gov (reservations) & ⓦ nps.gov/brca (information). Seasonal campground near Sunset Point. Only twenty of its 100 sites can be reserved in advance; all hold up to ten people, in two vehicles, and the rest are first-come, first-served, so all tend to be taken by early afternoon. RVs can stay, but there are no hookups. Open mid-April to Oct. $

NEAR THE PARK

Half a dozen accommodation options loiter just outside the park along highways 12 and 63, in what's ludicrously known as Bryce Canyon City, while there's a further cluster in tiny Tropic, 8 miles east along Hwy-12.

Best Western Plus Bryce Canyon Grand Hotel 30 N 100 East, Bryce Canyon City ⓦ bestwestern.com. Large chain motel, just off Hwy-63 a mile short of the park, with good comfortable rooms and an outdoor pool and hot tub. $$$$

Best Western Plus Ruby's Inn 26 S Main St, Bryce Canyon City ⓦ bestwestern.com. Large, modern motel complex on Hwy-63, a mile or so outside the park. Fifty of the 368 rooms feature whirlpool baths, and there's a heated indoor swimming pool plus a decent breakfast buffet. $$

Bryce Canyon Inn 21 N Main St, Tropic ⓦ brycecanyoninn.com. Standard motel rooms, plus eighteen large, newer log cabins, available March–Oct only. $$

Grand Staircase-Escalante National Monument

East of Bryce Canyon, Hwy-12 curves along the edge of the Table Cliff Plateau before dropping into the remote canyons of the **Escalante River**, the last river system discovered within the continental US and site of some wonderful **backpacking** routes. The Escalante region is the focus of the **Grand Staircase-Escalante National Monument**, the main visitor centre for which is at the west end of **ESCALANTE**, 38 miles east of Tropic. Created by a locally controversial presidential proclamation in 1996, it was cut to half its original size by another such proclamation, this time by President Trump in 2017, only to be restored again by President Biden in 2021.

The most accessible highlight is **Calf Creek**, sixteen miles east of Escalante, where a trail leads three miles upstream from a nice undeveloped **campground** to a gorgeous shaded dell replete with a 125ft waterfall (day-use charge, camping; $). More ambitious trips start from trailheads along the dusty but usually passable **Hole-in-the-Rock Road**, which turns south from Hwy-12 five miles east of Escalante. A trio of slender, storm-gouged **slot canyons**, including the delicate, graceful Peek-a-Boo Canyon and the downright intimidating Spooky Canyon, can be reached by a mile-long hike from the end of Dry Fork Road, 26 miles along. From **Hurricane Wash**, 34 miles along, you can hike five miles to reach Coyote Gulch and then a further five miles, passing sandstone bridges and arches, to the Escalante River. Under normal conditions, two-wheel-drive vehicles should go no further than **Dance Hall Rock**, 36 miles down the road, a superb natural amphitheatre sculpted out of the slickrock hills.

Thirty miles beyond Escalante, at **BOULDER**, the Burr Trail, almost all of which is paved, heads east through the southern reaches of **Capitol Reef National Park** and down to **Lake Powell**.

INFORMATION   **GRAND STAIRCASE-ESCALANTE NATIONAL MONUMENT**

Escalante information centre 755 W Main St, Escalante (Mon, Tue & Thurs–Sun 9am–4pm; closed Sat & Sun mid-Nov to mid-March; ☎ 435 826 5499, ⓦ blm.gov/utah).

Kanab information centre 745 E Hwy-89A, Kanab (Tues–Sat 9am–4pm; closed Sat mid-Nov to mid-March; ☎ 435 644 1300).

ACCOMMODATION AND EATING

Circle D Motel 475 W Main St, Escalante ⓦ escalante circledmotel.com. Old-style motel, perched at the west

2

end of town, with assorted rooms arrayed along a wooden veranda, plus a good diner serving burgers and sandwiches. §

Escalante Outfitters 310 W Main St, Escalante ⓦ escalanteoutfitters.com. Hikers' and campers' supply store with tent pitches plus seven attractive little log cabins, heated but lacking phone or TV, and sharing use of a bathhouse. There's also an espresso and snack bar. Open mid-March to Oct. §

★ **Kiva Koffeehouse** Mile 73.86, Hwy-12 ⓦ kiva koffeehouse.com. Solitary little cafe, perched on a rocky eminence. Fabulous views along the Escalante River plus simple snacks such as granola, sandwiches or enchiladas, and two very comfortable guest rooms. Open April–Oct. §§§

Capitol Reef National Park

Entry, for Scenic Drive only, charge · **Visitor centre** 52 Scenic Drive (daily: April–Oct 8am–6pm, Nov–March 9am–4.30pm; ⓦ nps.gov/care)

CAPITOL REEF might sound like something you'd find off the coast of Australia, but its towering ochre-, white- and **red-rock walls** and deep **river canyons** are of a piece with the rest of the Utah desert. The outstanding feature, a multilayered, 1000ft-high reef-like wall of uplifted sedimentary rock, looms above Hwy-24, eleven miles east of **TORREY** – home to the nearest food and lodging – and 120 miles northeast of Bryce Canyon. Stretching over a hundred miles north to south, but only a few miles across, the seemingly impenetrable barrier of the **Waterpocket Fold** was warped upward by the same process that lifted the Colorado Plateau and its sharply defined sedimentary layers display two hundred million years of geological activity. The Fold is repeatedly sliced through by deeply incised river canyons – some just 20ft wide, but hundreds of feet deep – often accessible only on foot.

Motorists who stick to the park's paved through road, Hwy-24, which follows the canyon of the **Fremont River** across the northern half of the Fold, do not incur an entrance fee. Beneath the **Castle**, an enormous rock outcrop, you'll find the park's visitor centre and campground. To the west, the **Goosenecks Overlook** gazes down 500ft into the entrenched canyons cut by Sulphur Creek. Further east, beyond Fruita's former schoolhouse, some extraordinary **Fremont petroglyphs** of bighorn sheep and stylized space-people were chipped into the varnished red rock a thousand years ago. Another four and a half miles along, a beautiful **day-hike** heads up along the gravelly riverbed through **Grand Wash** – a cool canyon where Butch Cassidy and his gang used to hide out.

If you prefer a more energetic hike, try the supremely rewarding two-mile, two-hour **Hickman Bridge Trail** that climbs out up from the main road to reach a towering, 100ft natural bridge. Alternatively, you can reach several more superb trailheads by following the paved **Scenic Drive**, which heads eight miles south from the visitor centre, passing the top of Grand Wash, to reach **Capitol Gorge**.

| **ACCOMMODATION AND EATING** | **CAPITOL REEF NATIONAL PARK** |

★ **Hunt & Gather Restaurant** 599 W Main St, Torrey ⓦ huntandgatherrestaurant.com. Inventive modern restaurant, offering slow-cooked meals from locally sourced produce, wild game, fish, organic goat cheeses and house smoked and cured meats. Reserve ahead. Open April to mid-Oct. §§§

Rim Rock Inn 2523 E Hwy-24 ⓦ therimrock.net. Modern, wood-built hotel, 3 miles east of Torrey, and

offering good-value rooms plus two recommended restaurants. §§

★ **Torrey Schoolhouse B&B Inn** 150 N Center St, Torrey ⓦ torreyschoolhouse.com. Excellent seasonal B&B, one block of Torrey's Main Street, with lovely period rooms set inside the old town school (completed 1916) and superb organic breakfasts. Open April–Oct. §§

Canyonlands National Park

Charge; valid for seven days · ⓦ nps.gov/cany

Utah's largest and most magnificent national park, **CANYONLANDS NATIONAL PARK** is as hard to define as it is to map. Where its closest equivalent, the Grand Canyon, is simply an almighty crack in a relatively flat plain, Canyonlands is a bewildering tangle of canyons, plateaus, fissures and faults, scattered with buttes and monoliths, pierced by arches and caverns and penetrated only by a paltry handful of dead-end roads.

Canyonlands focuses on the Y-shaped confluence of the **Green** and **Colorado rivers**, buried deep in the desert forty miles southwest of Moab. The only spot from which you can see the rivers meet, however, is a five-mile hike from the nearest road. With no road down to the rivers, let alone across them, the park therefore splits into three major sections. The **Needles**, east of the Colorado, is a red-rock wonderland of sandstone pinnacles and hidden meadows that's a favourite with hardy hikers and 4WD enthusiasts, while the **Maze**, west of both the Colorado and the Green, is a virtually inaccessible labyrinth of tortuous, waterless canyons. In the wedge of the "Y" between the two, the high, dry mesa of the **Island In The Sky** commands astonishing views, with several overlooks that can easily be toured by car. Getting from any one of these sections to the others involves driving at least a hundred miles.

Canyonlands does not lend itself to a short visit. With no lodging and little camping inside the park, it takes a full day to have even a cursory look at a single segment. Considering that summer temperatures regularly exceed 100°F and most trails have no water and little shade, the Island In The Sky is the most immediately rewarding option. On the other hand, for a long day-hike you'd do better to set off into the Needles.

Island In The Sky
Visitor centre Hwy-313, 22 miles southwest of US-191 • Daily: March–Oct 8am–6pm; Nov–Feb 8am–4pm • ⓦ go.nps.gov/isky

Reached by a good road that climbs steadily from US-191, 21 miles south of I-70, the **Island In The Sky** district looks out over hundreds of miles of flat-topped mesas that drop in 2000ft steps to the river. Four miles along from its **visitor centre**, the enjoyable **Mesa Arch Trail** loops for a mile around the mesa-top hillocks to the edge of the abyss, where long, shallow Mesa Arch frames an extraordinary view of the **La Sal Mountains**, 35 miles northeast. The definitive vantage point, however, is **Grand View Point Overlook**, another five miles on at the southern end of the road. An agoraphobic's nightmare, it commands an endless prospect of layer upon layer of bare sandstone, here stacked thousands of feet high, there fractured into bottomless canyons.

The Island In The Sky's only developed **campground**, the first-come, first-served and waterless *Willow Flat* ($), is just back from the **Green River Overlook**, along the right fork shortly after the Mesa Arch trailhead.

Dead Horse Point State Park
Drive 20 miles southwest of US-191 on Hwy-313, then 7 miles southeast • Daily 6am–10pm; visitor centre daily 9am–5pm • Charge, National Parks passes not valid • ⓦ stateparks.utah.gov/parks/dead-horse

A turnoff on the road towards the Island In The Sky cuts south to the smaller but equally breathtaking **Dead Horse Point**, located at the tip of a narrow mesa, which looks straight down 2000ft to the twisting Colorado River. Cowboys used the mesa as a natural corral, herding up wild horses then blocking them in behind a piñon pine fence that still marks its 90ft neck. One band of horses was left here too long and died – hence the name.

The Needles
Drive 40 miles south from Moab on US-191, then 35 miles west on Hwy-211 • **Visitor centre** Mid-Feb to mid-Dec daily 9am–4pm; closed mid-Dec to mid-Feb • ⓦ nps.gov/cany/planyourvisit/needles.htm

Taking its name from the colourful sandstone pillars, knobs and hoodoos that punctuate its many lush canyons and basins, the **Needles** district allows an intimate look at the Canyonlands environment, where you're not always gazing thousands of feet downward or scanning the distant horizon. The pretty 35-mile drive into the region from US-191 winds along Indian Creek through deep red-rock canyons lined by pines and cottonwoods.

2

A demanding eleven-mile round-trip hike from mushroom-shaped hoodoos at the road's-end **Big Spring Canyon Overlook** offers the only access to the **Confluence Overlook**, 1000ft above the point where the Green River joins the muddy waters of the Colorado, to flow together toward fearsome **Cataract Canyon**. Among the best of the shorter walks that head away from the road is **Pothole Point**, a mile earlier. A longer day-trip or a good overnight hike leaves from near the *Squaw Flat* **campground** ($) to the green meadow of **Chesler Park**, cutting through the narrow cleft of the Joint Trail.

The Maze and Horseshoe Canyon

46 miles east of Hwy-24, 66 miles south of Green River • **Hans Flat Ranger Station** Daily 8am–4.30pm • ⓦ nps.gov/cany

Filling the western third of Canyonlands, on the far side of the Colorado and Green rivers, the harsh and remote **Maze** district is noted for its many-fingered box canyons, accessible only by jeep or by long, dry hiking trails.

Tree-lined **Horseshoe Canyon**, reached halfway down a long, long dirt road that loops south from Green River itself to join Hwy-24 just south of Goblin Valley, contains some fabulous **ancient rock art**. Allowing at least an hour's driving from the highway both before and after, plus five hours for the six-mile round-trip hike into the canyon itself, you'll need to set aside a full day, but it's well worth the effort, both for the joy of the walk and for the "**Great Gallery**" at the far end. Hundreds of mysterious, haunting pictographs – mostly life-sized human figures, albeit weirdly elongated or draped in robes and adorned with strange, staring eyes – were painted onto these red-sandstone walls, probably between 500 BC and 500 AD.

It was from the Horseshoe Canyon trailhead, incidentally, that **Aron Ralston** set off on the 2003 hike to Blue John Canyon, beyond Horseshoe Canyon, which culminated in his having to cut off his right arm, as immortalized in **127 Hours**.

Arches National Park

US-191, 5 miles northwest of central Moab • Charge; valid 7 days • **Visitor centre** Daily: March & Sept–Nov 8am–4pm; April–Aug 7.30am–5pm; Dec–Feb 9am–4pm • ⓦ nps.gov/arch

The writer Edward Abbey, who spent a year as a ranger at **ARCHES NATIONAL PARK** in the 1950s, wrote that its arid landscape was as "naked, monolithic, austere and unadorned as the sculpture of the moon". Apart from the single ribbon of black asphalt that snakes through the park, there's nothing even vaguely human about it. Massive fins of red and golden sandstone stand to attention out of the bare desert plain and more than eighteen hundred natural arches of various shapes and sizes have been cut into the rock by eons of erosion. The narrow, hunching ridges are more like dinosaurs' backbones than solid rock, and under a full moon you can't help but imagine that the landscape has a life of its own.

While you could race through in a couple of hours, it takes at least a day to do Arches justice. A twenty-mile road cuts uphill sharply from US-191 and the **visitor centre**. The first possible stop is the south trailhead for **Park Avenue**, an easy trail leading one mile down a scoured, rock-bottomed wash. If you stay on the road, the **La Sal Mountains Viewpoint** provides a grandstand look at the distant 12,000ft peaks, as well as the huge red chunk of **Courthouse Towers** closer at hand.

From **Balanced Rock** beyond – a 50ft boulder atop a slender 75ft pedestal – a right turn winds two miles through the **Windows** section, where a half-mile trail loops through a dense concentration of massive arches, some more than 100ft high and 150ft across. A second trail, fifty yards beyond, leads to **Double Arch**, a staunch pair of arches that together support another.

Further on, the main road drops downhill for two miles past Panorama Point and the turnoff to **Wolfe Ranch**, where a century-old log cabin serves as the trailhead for the wonderful three-mile round-trip hike up to **Delicate Arch**. Crowds congregate each evening beside the arch, a freestanding crescent of rock perched at the brink of a deep canyon, for the superb sunset views; coming back down in the dark can be a little hair-raising, though. Three miles beyond the Wolfe Ranch turnoff, the deep, sharp-sided mini-canyons of the **Fiery Furnace** section form a labyrinth through which rangers lead regular hikes in spring, summer and autumn (charge; reserve at the visitor centre or via Ⓦ recreation.gov).

From the **Devil's Garden** trailhead at the end of the road, an easy one-mile walk leads to a view of the astonishing 306ft span of **Landscape Arch**, now too perilously slender to approach more closely. Several other arches lie along short spur trails off

2

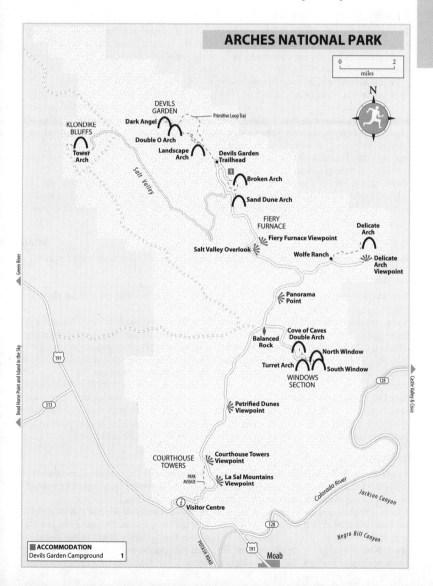

ARCHES NATIONAL PARK

0 — 2 miles

N

KLONDIKE BLUFFS

DEVILS GARDEN

Dark Angel

Primitive Loop Trail

Double O Arch

Tower Arch

Landscape Arch

Devils Garden Trailhead

1

Broken Arch

Salt Valley

Sand Dune Arch

FIERY FURNACE

Delicate Arch

Fiery Furnace Viewpoint

Salt Valley Overlook

Wolfe Ranch

Delicate Arch Viewpoint

Panorama Point

Cove of Caves Double Arch

Balanced Rock

North Window

Turret Arch

South Window

WINDOWS SECTION

128

Petrified Dunes Viewpoint

Green River

191

313

Dead Horse Point and Island in the Sky

COURTHOUSE TOWERS

Courthouse Towers Viewpoint

PARK AVENUE

La Sal Mountains Viewpoint

ⓘ Visitor Centre

128

Colorado River

Jackson Canyon

Castle Valley & Cisco

Negro Bill Canyon

POTASH ROAD

191

Moab

ACCOMMODATION
Devils Garden Campground **1**

2

the route, though one, Wall Arch, finally collapsed in 2008. Seeing them all and returning from **Double O Arch** via the longer primitive trail requires a total hike of just over seven miles.

ACCOMMODATION   **ARCHES NATIONAL PARK, SEE MAP PAGE 153**

Devil's Garden Campground Devil's Garden ⓦrecreation.gov. Arches' only campground, 18 miles north of the visitor centre, remains open all year. All fifty

sites, which hold up to ten people each, can be reserved between March and Oct; between Nov and Feb, 24 are first-come, first-served. No showers. 𝔖

Moab

Founded in the late 1800s, **MOAB** was hardly a speck until the 1950s, when prospector Charlie Steen discovered uranium nearby. When the mining boom finally waned, the town threw in its lot with tourism to become the Southwest's number one adventure-vacation destination.

Moab still isn't a large town, though – the population remains well under ten thousand – and neither is it attractive. The setting is what matters. With two national parks on its doorstep, plus millions more acres of public land, Moab is an ideal base for outdoors enthusiasts. At first, it was a haven for **mountain bikers** lured by the legendary **Slickrock Bike Trail**. Then the **jeep** drivers began to turn up and the **whitewater-rafting** companies moved in, too. These days it's almost literally bursting, all year, with legions of Lycra-clad vacationers from all over the world.

Perhaps the main reason Moab has grown so fast is that out-of-state visitors tend to find Utah's other rural communities so boring. As soon as Moab emerged from the pack, it became a beacon in the desert, attracting tourists ecstatic to find a town that stayed up after dark – even if it does amount to little more than a few miles of motels, restaurants and bars.

INFORMATION   **MOAB**

Moab Information Center 25 E Center St at Main (daily 9am–4pm; ☏435 259 8825, ⓦdiscovermoab.com).

ACCOMMODATION

Best Western Plus Greenwell Inn 105 S Main St ⓦbestwestern.com. Central, modern hotel that offers spacious good-value rooms with tasteful furnishings and fittings. 𝔖𝔖𝔖

★ **Inca Inn** 570 N Main St ⓦincainn.com. Clean budget motel where the decent-sized rooms have very comfortable beds and rather amazing disco-light showers, and there's an outdoor pool. 𝔖𝔖

Lazy Lizard International Hostel 1213 S Hwy-191 ⓦlazylizardhostel.com. This laidback independent hostel, a mile south of the centre, is really nothing special, but budget travellers appreciate its six-person dorms, private

rooms and cabins, and it also has a hot tub, kitchen, and wi-fi. 𝔖

Sand Flats Recreation Area 1924 S Roadrunner Hill ⓦsandflats.org. Minimally developed BLM campgrounds (nine in all, with 140 pitches total), intended primarily for mountain bikers, in a spectacular setting near the Slickrock Bike Trail, atop the mesa east of town. 𝔖

Sunflower Hill B&B 185 N 300 East ⓦsunflowerhill. com. Antique-furnished former farmhouse, now a twelve-room B&B, away from the bustle on a dead-end side street. All units are en suite, some are in separate cottages, and they share the gardens, pool and hot tub. 𝔖𝔖𝔖𝔖

EATING

Desert Bistro 36 S 100 West ⓦdesertbistro.com. Dinner-only restaurant, with outdoor seating. On the Mediterranean-influenced menu, there are mains such as Colorado lamb chops, gorgonzola crusted beef tenderloin and hand-made agnolotti pasta with truffles and Marsala wine. Open March–Oct. 𝔖𝔖

Moab Diner 189 S Main St ⓦmoabdiner.com. The town's most popular diner is a 1960s classic, with huge

breakfast plates, juicy burgers, steaks, strong coffee and the diner's "famous" green chili sauce. Finish off the meal with a brown butter cake sundae. 𝔖

Red Rock Bakery & Café 74 S Main St ☏435 259 5941. Small café-bakery opposite the visitor centre, with good coffee and pastries. Try the "spin", a swirl of spicy, cheesy bread that's available for breakfast with egg, bacon and avocado. 𝔖

The San Juan River

From Natural Bridges National Monument, Hwy-261 runs south for 25 miles to the edge of Cedar Mesa, high above the eerie sandstone towers of the **Valley of the Gods**. It then turns to gravel and drops more than 1000ft in little over two twisting, hairpin-turning miles down the "**Moki Dugway**". Six miles from the foot of the switchbacks, the barely marked Hwy-316 branches off to the aptly named **Goosenecks State Park** (open 24hr; charge; ⓦstateparks.utah.gov), high above the **San Juan River**. A thousand feet below, the river snakes in such convoluted twists and turns that it flows six miles in total for every one mile west.

Back on Hwy-261, sleepy **MEXICAN HAT**, just twenty miles north of Monument Valley, takes its name from a riverside **sandstone hoodoo** that looks like a south-of-the-border sombrero.

The rafts you may see emerging from the water at Mexican Hat went in at **BLUFF**, twenty miles upstream. US-163 connects the two towns, well away from the river but still an enthralling drive, while the backstreets of Bluff hold **Mormon pioneer houses**.

ACTIVITIES   THE SAN JUAN RIVER

★ **Wild Rivers Expeditions** ⓦriversandruins.com. Fabulous one-day float trips from Bluff to Mexican Hat, with visits to ancient ruins and plentiful wildlife spotting, including eagles.

ACCOMMODATION AND EATING

Comb Ridge Eat and Drink 409 S Main St, Bluff ⓦcombridgeeatanddrink.com. Dependable local diner that knocks out pricey but top-notch burgers, sandwiches and fish and chips. You can also purchase the local arts and crafts on display. Usually open February to November. $$

Desert Rose Inn 701 W Main St, Bluff ⓦdesertroseinn.com. Modern timber-built motel, holding thirty attractively designed and well-furnished rooms, plus individual cabins of similar standard. $$$

Kokopelli Inn 161 E Main St, Bluff ⓦkokoinnutah.com. Friendly, quiet roadside motel, adjoining a gas station and grocery with a deli counter. $$

★ **Mexican Hat Lodge** 100 N Main St, Mexican Hat ⓦmexicanhat.net. Former dance hall, with thirteen rooms of differing sizes. Its open-air *Swingin' Steaks* restaurant is everything you could wish for from a cowboy steakhouse, grilling meat over a fire of sweet-smelling wood. Open March–Oct. $$

Hovenweep National Monument

Hidden in the no-man's-land that straddles the Utah–Colorado border, the remote **Ancestral Puebloan ruins** at **Hovenweep National Monument** offer a haunting sense of timeless isolation. While it preserves six distinct conglomerations of ruins, all sprouting from the rims of shallow desert canyons, easy access is restricted to **Little Ruin Canyon**, behind the **visitor centre**. A mile-long loop trail offers good views of the largest ruins, including the grandly named **Hovenweep Castle**, constructed around 1200 AD. Entrance is free, but no accommodation, petrol or food is available.

ARRIVAL AND INFORMATION   HOVENWEEP NATIONAL MONUMENT

By car Drive 25 miles east on Hwy-262, which branches off US-191 halfway between Bluff and Blanding in Utah, or 35 miles west from Cortez, Colorado, along County Road G.

Visitor centre Little Ruin Canyon (May to mid-Oct daily 9am–5pm; mid-Oct to April Mon & Thurs–Sun 9am–5pm; ☎970 562 4282, ⓦnps.gov/hove).

ACCOMMODATION

Hovenweep Campground Little Ruin Canyon ⓦnps.gov/hove. First-come, first-served 31-site campground, close to the visitor centre. It has a few RV spaces, but no hookups and no showers. Potable water in summer only. $

Lake Powell and Glen Canyon Dam

The mighty rivers and canyons of southern Utah come to an abrupt and ignoble end at the Arizona border, where the **Glen Canyon Dam** stops them dead in the stagnant waters of **Lake Powell**. Ironically, the lake is named for John Wesley Powell, the first person to run the Colorado River through the Grand Canyon. The roaring torrents that he battled, along with magnificent Glen Canyon itself, are now lost beneath these placid blue waters, while the blocked-up Colorado, Green, Dirty Devil, San Juan and Escalante rivers have become a playground for houseboaters and waterskiers. The construction of the dam in the early 1960s outraged environmentalists and archeologists and created a peculiar and utterly unnatural landscape, the deep and tranquil lake a surreal contrast with the surrounding dry slickrock and sandstone buttes.

Lake Powell has 1960 miles of shoreline – more than the entire US Pacific coast – and 96 water-filled side canyons. The water level fluctuates considerably, so for much of the time the rocks to all sides are bleached for many feet above the waterline, with a dirty-bath tidemark sullying the golden sandstone. Many summer visitors bring their own boats or rent a vessel from one of the marinas that fringe the lake.

GLEN CANYON DAM itself, on US-89, two miles northwest of Page, Arizona, can be seen from the **Carl Hayden Visitor Centre** (March to mid-May & mid-Sept to Oct daily 8am–5pm; mid-May to mid-Sept daily 8am–6pm; Nov–Feb Mon & Thurs–Sun 9am–4pm; ⓦnps.gov/glca) on the west bank, which also arranges 45-minute dam tours (charge).

Salt Lake City

Disarmingly pleasant and easy-going, **SALT LAKE CITY** is well worth a stopover of a couple of days. Its setting is superb, towered over by the **Wasatch Front**, which marks the dividing line between the comparatively lush eastern and the bone-dry western halves of northern Utah. The area offers great hiking and cycling in summer and autumn and, in winter, superb **skiing**. Outsiders tend to imagine Salt Lake City as decidedly short on fun, but so long as you're willing to switch gears and slow down, its unhurried pace and the positive energy of its people can make for an enjoyable experience.

Temple Square

50 E North Temple St • Daily: April–Sept 9am–9pm; Oct, Nov & Jan–March 10am–8pm, Dec 10am–10pm • ⓦ churchofjesuschrist.org

The geographical – and spiritual – heart of Salt Lake City, **Temple Square** is the world headquarters of the **Mormon Church** (or the Church of Jesus Christ of Latter-Day Saints – LDS). Its focus, the plain granite **Temple** itself, was completed in 1893 after forty years of intensive labour. Only confirmed Mormons may enter the Temple, and only for the most sacred LDS rituals – marriage, baptisms and "sealing", the joining of a family unit for eternity.

While the Temple itself is due to be closed until 2024 for a major re-building program, almost all the surrounding structures are expected to remain open to visitors. These include two **visitor centres**, of which the northern holds a model of Jerusalem in 33 AD and dioramas of Jesus preaching in North America, and the southern concentrates on Salt Lake City's first Mormon settlers. Free 45-minute **tours** explore the odd oblong shell of the **Mormon Tabernacle**. No images of any kind adorn its interior, where a helper laconically displays its remarkable acoustic properties by tearing up a newspaper and dropping a nail. There's free admission to the Mormon Tabernacle Choir's 9.30am Sunday broadcast and its rehearsals on Thursday evenings at 8pm.

Downtown Salt Lake City

A block east of Temple Square along South Temple Boulevard, the **Beehive House** (closed for renovations until 2025) is a plain white New England-style house, with wraparound verandas and green shutters. Erected in 1854 by church leader **Brigham Young**, it's now restored as a small museum of Young's life.

The area southwest of Temple Square centres on the massive **Salt Palace** Convention Center and Vivint Arena (home of the Utah Jazz basketball team). The surrounding

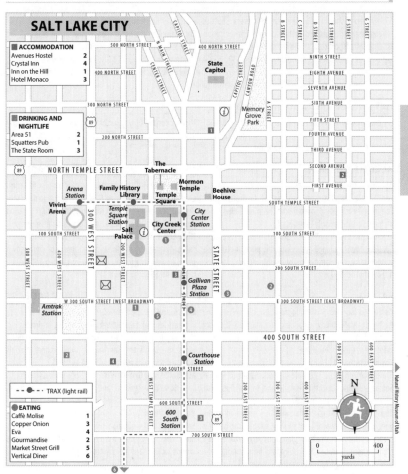

SALT LAKE CITY

ACCOMMODATION	
Avenues Hostel	2
Crystal Inn	4
Inn on the Hill	1
Hotel Monaco	3

DRINKING AND NIGHTLIFE	
Area 51	2
Squatters Pub	1
The State Room	3

EATING	
Caffè Molise	1
Copper Onion	3
Eva	4
Gourmandise	2
Market Street Grill	5
Vertical Diner	6

--- •-- TRAX (light rail)

district of brick warehouses around the Union Pacific railroad tracks is filled with designer shops and art galleries, signs that even Mormons can be yuppies.

The **Capitol Hill** neighbourhood, around the imposing, domed **Utah State Capitol** (Mon–Thurs 7am–8pm, Fri–Sun 7am–6pm; free; ⓦutahstatecapitol.utah.gov) on the gentle hill above Temple Square, holds some of Salt Lake City's grandest Victorian homes.

Natural History Museum of Utah

301 Wakara Way • Daily 10am–5pm, Wed till 9pm • Charge • ⓦ nhmu.utah.edu

Overlooking the university district on the eastern flanks of downtown, the state-of-the-art **Natural History Museum of Utah** is primarily devoted to celebrating the state's extraordinarily rich fossil heritage. Its main gallery displays a quite astonishing array of dinosaur skeletons, from fearsome tyrannosaurs to triple-horned triceratops, which includes many species that have been found nowhere else on earth.

ARRIVAL AND DEPARTURE   SALT LAKE CITY

By air Salt Lake City International Airport (ⓦslcairport. com), 4 miles west of downtown, is connected with the city centre by trams on the TRAX Green Line (ⓦrideuta. com). Alternatively, a taxi into town costs around

$25; cheaper shuttle vans are run by Xpress Shuttles (ⓦexpressshuttleutah.com), while Canyon Transportation (ⓦcanyontransport.com) serves the ski areas.

By bus Greyhound buses arrive downtown, at 300 S 600 West (ⓣ801 355 9579).

Destinations Denver (3 daily; 10hr 30min); Las Vegas (2 daily; 8hr); San Francisco (2 daily; 15hr).

By train The Amtrak station is downtown at 320 S Rio Grande Ave.

Destinations Chicago (1 daily; 34hr); Denver (1 daily; 14hr); Emeryville, CA, for San Francisco (1 daily; 16hr).

GETTING AROUND AND INFORMATION

By bus and tram Local buses and TRAX trams (trolleys) are operated by the Utah Transit Authority (ⓦrideuta.com); journeys within the downtown area are free.

Visitor centre Downtown at 90 S West Temple Blvd (daily 10am–5pm; ⓣ801 534 4900, ⓦvisitsaltlake.com).

ACCOMMODATION   SEE MAP PAGE 157

Avenues Hostel 107 F St ⓦavenueshostelsaltlakecity. top. Simple hostel a short way east of downtown, with communal kitchen and living room. Cheap but faded – not all guests are necessarily travellers. $\overline{\underline{\$}}$

Crystal Inn 230 W 500 South ⓦcrystalinnsaltlake.com. Spacious, well-equipped and reasonably priced hotel close to downtown, with large buffet breakfasts included and free airport shuttle. $\overline{\underline{\$\$\$}}$

Inn On the Hill 225 State St ⓦinn-on-the-hill.com. Central Salt Lake's best B&B is an elegant Renaissance Revival style home completed in 1906, with 11 period rooms, one mini-suite, and a two-story Carriage House. $\overline{\underline{\$\$\$}}$

Kimpton Hotel Monaco 15 W 200 South ⓦmonaco-saltlakecity.com. Stylish, very upscale downtown hotel, housed in a former bank and equipped with a fine restaurant. $\overline{\underline{\$\$\$\$}}$

EATING   SEE MAP PAGE 157

Caffè Molise 404 S West Temple ⓦcaffemolise.com. Authentic, high-quality, great-value Italian food, 2 blocks south of the convention centre downtown, with pasta mains and fancier meat dishes. $\overline{\underline{\$\$}}$

Copper Onion 111 E Broadway ⓦthecopperonion.com. Hip downtown bistro, a couple of blocks south of Temple Square, offering lunchtime salads and sandwiches, and trout, lamb or duck at dinner. $\overline{\underline{\$\$}}$

Eva 317 S Main St ⓦevaslc.com. Cosy restaurant-cum-wine bar, downtown. It's not exactly a tapas bar, but the menu consists of smallish plates, largely drawn from Mediterranean cuisines and extending from shrimp with grits and a poached egg to braised meatballs. $\overline{\underline{\$\$}}$

Gourmandise 250 S 300 East ⓦgourmandise.com. It's the pastries that draw downtown devotees in droves, but this hugely popular bakery-cum-bistro also does great lunchtime salads and sandwiches, while dinner specials feature dishes such as trout with dill butter. $\overline{\underline{\$\$}}$

Market Street Grill 48 W Market St ⓦmarketstreetgrill. com. New York–style bar and grill, serving fresh seafood, especially oysters, plus steaks in all shapes and sizes. $\overline{\underline{\$\$\$}}$

Vertical Diner 234 W 900 South ⓦverticaldiner.com. Salt Lake's finest vegetarian restaurant serves an all-organic menu that ranges from pizza to raw salads. Dinner mains include jackfruit and kimchi tacos. $\overline{\underline{\$\$}}$

DRINKING AND NIGHTLIFE   SEE MAP PAGE 157

Salt Lake City doesn't roll up the sidewalks when the sun goes down. To find out about art, music and clubland happenings, pick up the free *City Weekly* (ⓦcityweekly. net).

Area 51 451 S 400 West ⓦarea51slc.com. Named for Nevada's notorious alien zone, Salt Lake's largest club caters to young and old alike, with EBM dance music as well as 80s goth and indie in post-industrial surroundings.

Squatters Pub 147 W 300 South ⓦsaltlakebrewingco. com/squatters. This casual, friendly place is the pick of Salt Lake's brewpubs, with a dozen good beers of its own and a decent menu of burgers, salads, steaks and curries.

The State Room 638 S State St ⓦthestateroompresents. com/the-state-room. The top local live music venue, attracting big-name touring acts, and offering a dancefloor as well as auditorium seating.

Nevada

Desolate **NEVADA** consists largely of endless tracts of bleak, empty desert, its flat sagebrush plains cut intermittently by angular mountain ranges. Apart from the huge acreages given over to mining and grazing, much of the state is used by the **military** to test aircraft and weapons systems.

By far the most compelling reason to visit Nevada is to see the surreal oasis of **Las Vegas**. While its eye-popping architecture, lavish restaurants, decadent nightclubs and amazing shows offer an unforgettable sensory overload, the experience remains rooted in **gambling**. Even the smaller and more down-to-earth settlements of **Reno** and state capital **Carson City** revolve around the casino trade.

In the **Great Basin**, where the rivers and streams have no outlet to the ocean, Nevada has an eerie beauty. The main cross-state route, **I-80**, shoots from Salt Lake City to Reno, skirting bizarrely named little towns scattered with casinos, bars, brothels and motels. The other significant road, **US-50**, has a reputation as the loneliest highway in America. Older and slower, it follows much the same route as the Pony Express of the 1860s, but many towns have faded away altogether.

2

Las Vegas

A dazzling desert oasis, entirely devoted to thrilling its visitors, **LAS VEGAS** is not like other destinations. Without its tourists, Las Vegas wouldn't even exist; everything, from its spectacular architecture to its world-class restaurants and showrooms, is designed to sate their every appetite. Not only does Las Vegas hold most of the world's largest hotels, but that's pretty much all it holds; it's the hotels themselves that forty million people a year come to see. Each is a neighbourhood in its own right, crammed full of places to eat, drink, dance and play, and centring on an enormous casino, crammed with slot machines and table games.

Most visitors see no more of Las Vegas than either or both of two short, and very different, linear stretches. **Downtown**, the original core, now amounts to four brief blocks of Fremont Street, while **the Strip** starts a couple of miles south, and runs for four miles. The Strip is the real centre of the action, with each colossal mega-casino vying to out-do the next with some outlandish theme, be it an Egyptian pyramid, a Roman extravaganza, a fairytale castle or a European city.

In 1940, Las Vegas was home to just eight thousand people. It owes its extraordinary growth to its constant willingness to adapt. Far from remaining kitsch and old-fashioned, as you might imagine, it's forever re-inventing itself. Entrepreneurs race to spot the latest shift in who's got the money, and what they want to spend it on. A few years back, the casinos realized that modern gamblers were happy to pay premium prices to eat good food; top chefs now run gourmet **restaurants** in places like *Bellagio* and the *Cosmopolitan*. More recently, demand from younger visitors has prompted casinos like *Wynn Las Vegas* to open high-tech **nightclubs** to match those in Miami and LA.

The reputation Las Vegas still enjoys, of being a quasi-legal adult playground where (almost) anything goes, dates back to its early years. Most of its first generation of luxury resorts, like the *Flamingo*, the *Sands* and the *Desert Inn*, were controlled by the **Mob**, in an era when illegal profits could be easily "skimmed" off, and respectable investors steered clear of casinos. Then as now, visitors loved to think that they were rubbing shoulders with gangsters. Mob rule has however long since come to an end, and the city is now under the sway of massive **corporations**.

The Strip

In the old days, the casinos along Las Vegas's legendary **Strip** were cut-throat rivals. Each stood a long way back from the road, and was a dark, low-ceilinged labyrinth, in which it was all but impossible to find an exit. During the 1980s, however, visitors started to explore the Strip on foot. Mogul Steve Wynn cashed in by placing a flame-spouting volcano outside his new *Mirage*. As the casinos competed to entice passing pedestrians, they filled in those daunting distances from the sidewalk and between each casino and the next.

With Las Vegas booming in the 1990s, gaming corporations bought up first individual casinos, and then each other. The Strip today is dominated by just two

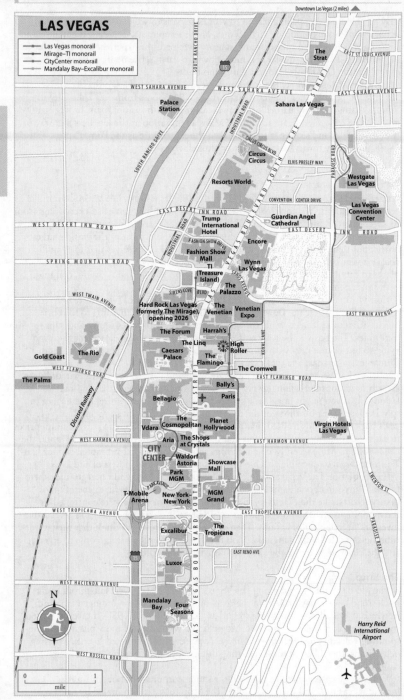

Downtown Las Vegas (2 miles)

LAS VEGAS

Las Vegas monorail
Mirage–TI monorail
CityCenter monorail
Mandalay Bay–Excalibur monorail

The Strat

EAST ST LOUIS AVENUE

SOUTH RANCHO DRIVE

WEST SAHARA AVENUE   WEST SAHARA AVENUE   EAST SAHARA AVENUE

Palace Station

Sahara Las Vegas

INDUSTRIAL ROAD

SOUTH RANCHO DRIVE

CIRCUS CIRCUS BLVD.

Circus Circus

ELVIS PRESLEY WAY

PARADISE ROAD

Resorts World

Westgate Las Vegas

CONVENTION CENTER DRIVE

Las Vegas Convention Center

EAST DESERT INN ROAD
WEST DESERT INN ROAD

Trump International Hotel

Guardian Angel Cathedral

EAST DESERT   INN   ROAD

FASHION SHOW DRIVE

Fashion Show Mall

Encore

SPRING MOUNTAIN ROAD

TI (Treasure Island)

Wynn Las Vegas

INDUSTRIAL ROAD

SIRENS COVE BLVD.

The Palazzo

SANDS AVENUE

WEST TWAIN AVENUE

Hard Rock Las Vegas (formerly The Mirage), opening 2026

The Venetian

Venetian Expo

EAST TWAIN AVENUE

ROYAL LANE

The Forum

Harrah's

Gold Coast   The Rio

The Linq

High Roller

Caesars Palace

The Flamingo

WEST FLAMINGO ROAD

The Palms

The Cromwell

EAST FLAMINGO ROAD

Disused Railway

Bally's

Bellagio

Paris

THE STRIP

The Cosmopolitan

Planet Hollywood

Virgin Hotels Las Vegas

Vdara

WEST HARMON AVENUE

Aria   The Shops at Crystals

EAST HARMON AVENUE

CITY CENTER

Waldorf Astoria

Park MGM

Showcase Mall

PARK AVENUE

SWENSON ST

T-Mobile Arena

New York–New York

MGM Grand

WEST TROPICANA AVENUE

EAST TROPICANA AVENUE

PARADISE ROAD

Excalibur

The Tropicana

EAST RENO AVE

LAS VEGAS BOULEVARD SOUTH

Luxor

WEST HACIENDA AVENUE

N

Mandalay Bay   Four Seasons

Harry Reid International Airport

WEST RUSSELL ROAD

0 ———— 1
mile

colossal conglomerates, MGM Resorts and Caesars Entertainment, each of which owns a string of neighbouring casinos. Once you own the casino next door, there's no reason to make each a virtual prison. The Strip has therefore opened out, so that much of its central portion now consists of pedestrian-friendly open-air terraces and pavilions housing bars and restaurants.

Mandalay Bay

3950 Las Vegas Blvd S • Ⓦ mandalaybay.mgmresorts.com • **Shark Reef** Daily 10am–8pm • Charge

The southernmost mega-casino, **Mandalay Bay**, consists of two golden skyscrapers towering over a huge, vaguely tropical-themed complex. Despite its notoriety as the scene of a mass shooting in September 2017, it remains busy with high-end dining and entertainment options. Set well back from the Strip, the **Shark Reef** aquarium focuses on marine predators, prowling through tanks designed to resemble an ancient temple that's sinking into the sea.

Luxor

3900 Las Vegas Blvd S • Ⓦ luxor.mgmresorts.com • **Bodies** and **Titanic** both daily: summer 11am–8pm, winter 11am–6pm • Charge • Ⓦ bodieslasvegas.com and Ⓦ titaniclasvegas.com

The huge **Luxor** pyramid, with its sloping walls of black shiny glass, was built in 1993 as the follow-up to the more fanciful *Excalibur* next door. Visitors congregate outside to take photos of the enormous Sphinx that straddles its driveway, but the interior has now lost many of its original ancient-Egyptian trappings. Upstairs, the so-called Atrium Level is home to two exhibitions – **Bodies**, a surprisingly sober and informative display of "plastinated" human corpses, and **Titanic**, displaying items salvaged from the great ship.

Excalibur

3850 Las Vegas Blvd S • Ⓦ excalibur.mgmresorts.com

Built in 1990, **Excalibur** remains the most visible reminder of the era when Las Vegas briefly re-invented itself as a vast children's playground. With its jam-packed, multicoloured turrets and ring of clunky battlements it doesn't so much look like a castle as like a child's drawing of a castle.

MGM Grand

3799 Las Vegas Blvd S • Ⓦ mgmgrand.mgmresorts.com • KÀ by Cirque du Soleil see website for dates • Charge • Ⓦ cirquedusoleil.com/ka • **Topgolf** Mon–Thurs & Sun 10am–1am, Fri & Sat 10am–2am • Charge • Ⓦ topgolf.com

The enormous **MGM Grand** casino, which opened as the largest hotel in the world in 1993, has long since lost its original Wizard of Oz theme, and rather blends into the background these days. For visitors, it's most noteworthy as home to the wildly popular shows by illusionist **David Copperfield** and KÀ by Cirque du Soleil, plus Brad Garrett's Comedy Club and **Topgolf**, a much-hyped multi-level golf attraction holding five bars and a concert arena as well as interactive golfing games.

New York–New York and around

3790 Las Vegas Blvd S • Ⓦ newyorknewyork.mgmresorts.com **Big Apple Coaster** Mon–Thurs 11am–11pm, Fri –Sun 11am–midnight • Charge

The first, and arguably the best, of Las Vegas's replica "cities", **New York–New York**, opened in 1997. Its exterior – a squeezed-up, half-sized rendition of the Manhattan skyline as it looked in the 1950s – is best admired from the tiny little yellow cabs of the **Big Apple Coaster**, which speed at 67mph around the towers.

Unveiled in 2016, the imaginatively named **The Park** is a large open space immediately north of New York–New York centring on the 20,000-capacity **T-Mobile Arena** (Ⓦ t-mobilearena.com) which hosts big-name concerts and the Vegas Golden Knights pro hockey team. The adjoining casino, previously called the Monte Carlo, was renamed **The Park MGM** in 2018 (ⓦparkmgm.mgmresorts.com), with its Dolby Live venue hosting major concerts.

Aria

3730 Las Vegas Blvd S • ⓦaria.mgmresorts.com

The focal point of the **CityCenter** "neighbourhood", an enclave of sleek skyscrapers unveiled by MGM Resorts in 2009, **Aria** looks more like a big-city corporate HQ than a casino. Its dazzling modernism is complemented by an eye-popping array of contemporary sculpture, as well as a fine crop of restaurants, but there's little reason to linger unless you're here to gamble.

The Cosmopolitan

3708 Las Vegas Blvd S • ⓦcosmopolitanlasvegas.com

Although most visitors assume that the **Cosmopolitan** is part of CityCenter's modernist jigsaw puzzle, it's a separate and independent casino-hotel, impishly squeezed onto a former parking lot that MGM never managed to buy up. A throwback to the old Las Vegas, in which it's all but impossible to find the exits, it seduces locals and tourists alike with glitzy architectural flourishes, high-profile clubs and great restaurants.

Planet Hollywood

3667 Las Vegas Blvd S • ⓦcaesars.com/planet-hollywood

The only Strip giant saddled with a brand name not otherwise known for gambling, **Planet Hollywood** has struggled to establish a strong identity. Not part of the dining chain, it opened in 2000 as a new version of the long-established *Aladdin*. The main attraction within is the large **Miracle Mile** shopping mall (actually 1.2-miles long); the actual casino is relatively small, and largely targeted at "hip" young visitors.

Paris Las Vegas

3655 Las Vegas Blvd S • ⓦcaesars.com/paris-las-vegas • **Eiffel Tower** Daily 2–10pm • Charge

Designed by the architects responsible for *New York–New York*, and opened just before the millennium, **Paris** represented the final flourish of the Las Vegas craze for building miniature cities. Its exterior remains one of the Strip's most enjoyable spectacles, and pleasing Parisian touches continue inside. Half the height of the Seine-side original, the **Eiffel Tower** that surmounts it towers 540ft tall. Its summit offers great views, with the prime time to come being the evening, to watch the *Bellagio* fountains.

Bellagio

3600 Las Vegas Blvd S • ⓦbellagio.mgmresorts.com

The must-see **Bellagio** casino surveys the Strip across the graceful dancing fountains of a broad lake. This cream-coloured vision of Italian elegance was the 1998 handiwork of entrepreneur Steve Wynn, who aimed to build the greatest hotel the world had ever seen. While Wynn himself is no longer at the helm, *Bellagio* is still going strong, now an integral component of CityCenter.

The two main attractions are the **fountains**, which erupt in regular balletic extravaganzas between early afternoon and midnight daily, and the magnificent **Conservatory**, where gardeners arrange themed displays that include bizarre whimsical props amid an extraordinary array of living plants.

Caesars Palace

3570 Las Vegas Blvd S • ⓦcaesars.com/caesars-palace

Still a Las Vegas headliner in its own right, **Caesars Palace** remains arguably the biggest name on the Strip. Cobbled together for just $24 million, it opened in 1966, complete with clerks dressed as Roman centurions and cocktail waitresses kitted out like Cleopatra. White marble Classical statues are everywhere you look, from Julius Caesar forever hailing a cab on the main driveway to the Winged Victory of Samothrace guarding a row of gently cascading pools. While the central bulk of *Caesars Palace* stands 150 yards back from the Strip, all the intervening space has been built over, most notably by the vast **Forum** mall, in which a domed false-sky ceiling cycles between "day" and "night" at hourly intervals. Major stars perform at the casino's concert venue, The Colosseum (notably Adele, Rod Stewart and Garth Brooks through 2023).

The Linq

3535 Las Vegas Blvd S · ⓦ caesars.com/linq · **High Roller** Daily 2pm–midnight · Charge

The Strip across from *Caesars Palace* holds a row of veteran casinos that include the **Flamingo** and **Harrah's**, all of which belong these days to Caesars Entertainment. What used to be the *Imperial Palace* has been transformed into **the Linq**, with a pedestrian corridor alongside known as the **Linq Promenade**. Lined with relatively interesting shops, bars and restaurants, it leads to North America's largest observation wheel, the 550ft **High Roller**, which commands superb views across the valley though not the Strip itself.

Hard Rock Las Vegas (formerly The Mirage)

3400 Las Vegas Blvd S · ⓦ hardrockhotelcasinolasvegas.com

Built as entrepreneur Steve Wynn's first Strip venture, in 1989, the **Mirage** changed the city overnight. Proving that by investing in luxury, glamour and spectacle – and adding an artificial **volcano** – casinos could bring back the crowds, it spawned such a host of imitators that now, ironically, it no longer stands out from the pack. Hard Rock International purchased the property in 2021 and is expected to begin transforming the hotel into the new Hard Rock Las Vegas in 2024, for a grand opening two years later (complete with guitar-shaped hotel tower, replacing the volcano). The Mirage's Secret Garden and Dolphin Habitat were closed in September 2022, but its popular Beatles Love (Cirque du Soleil) show is likely to continue until early 2024 (see ⓦ cirquedusoleil.com/beatles-love).

The Venetian and the Palazzo

Venetian 3355 Las Vegas Blvd S · ⓦ venetianlasvegas.com · **Palazzo** 3325 Las Vegas Blvd S · ⓦ venetianlasvegas.com/towers/the-palazzo.html · **Madame Tussauds** Mon–Thurs & Sun 10am–7pm, Fri & Sat 10am–8pm · Charge · ⓦ madametussauds.com/las-vegas

The hugely successful **Venetian** opened in 1999 as a recreation of owner Sheldon Adelson's honeymoon trip to Venice. Around a dozen of the city's landmarks squeeze side-by-side into the casino's Strip facade, while the principal echo of Venice in the opulent interior is the **Grand Canal** upstairs, where singing gondoliers take passengers on short gondola rides (charge). There's also an outlet of **Madame Tussauds** waxwork museum, where you're free to take unlimited photos of, and with, your newfound waxy friends.

Nominally a distinct entity, the adjoining **Palazzo** is effectively the same building as the *Venetian*, and has its own upscale array of boutiques, seamlessly linked by internal walkways to the *Venetian's* **Grand Canal Shoppes**. Considered on its own, on the other hand, the *Palazzo* is among the least interesting casinos in town.

Wynn and Encore

Wynn 3131 Las Vegas Blvd S · ⓦ wynnlasvegas.com · **Encore at Wynn Las Vegas** 3121 Las Vegas Blvd S

Steve Wynn, who invented modern Las Vegas by opening the *Mirage* and *Bellagio*, built his own self-named resort, **Wynn Las Vegas**, in 2005, and swiftly complemented it with **Encore** next door. Matching bronze crescents, soaring skywards, the two buildings are breathtaking. Wynn loves to fill his casinos with dazzling swathes of colour, so plush red carpets sweep through their interiors, meeting in a flower-packed central garden where trees are bedecked with fairy lights and lanterns. *Wynn's* most unusual feature is the **Lake of Dreams**, an expanse of water illuminated at night with changing projections, and peopled by mysterious mannequins. *Encore* is best known for its indoor-outdoor, day-night **Encore Beach Club**.

Circus Circus

2880 Las Vegas Blvd S • ⦿ circuscircus.com • **Adventuredome** Hours vary, see website • Charge • ⦿ circuscircus.com/the-adventuredome

The candy-striped big top of **Circus Circus** has loomed beside the Strip for half a century, but with its neighbours closing down and pedestrian traffic having dwindled to nothing, the casino these days feels all but forgotten. It does however hold Las Vegas's largest theme park, the **Adventuredome**, housed in a giant pink enclosure at the back and aimed very much at children.

The Strat

2000 Las Vegas Blvd S • ⦿ thestrat.com **Skypod & Observation decks** Daily 10am–1am • Charge, discounts for guests • **Thrill rides** X-Scream, Big Shot & Insanity charge; SkyJump charge, min age 14

The 1149ft observation tower (aka Skypod) at the **Strat (formerly the Stratosphere)** at the Strip's northern limit, is the tallest structure west of the Mississippi. The Skypod's observation decks offer fabulous views and the Top of the World revolving restaurant, while the top also serves as the launching point for several terrifying **Thrill Rides**. X-Scream is a giant boat that tips its passengers upside down; Insanity, a crane that spins riders out over the abyss; and Big Shot a glorified sofa that free falls hundreds of feet. Worst of all is the **SkyJump**, in which harnessed jumpers step off a platform to fall 855ft.

Downtown

Amounting as far as visitors are concerned to little more than three or four blocks, **downtown** is where Las Vegas started out when the railroad arrived in 1905, and also held its first casinos back in the 1930s. Although it has long been overshadowed by the Strip, many visitors nonetheless prefer downtown, feeling that by offering serious gambling, plus cheap bars, restaurants and buffets, its no-nonsense casinos represent the "real" Las Vegas. With its old-style neon signs and garish arrays of multicoloured lightbulbs, **downtown** also looks much more like the Las Vegas of popular imagination. In the artificial sky of the **Fremont Street Experience**, a canopy that covers four city blocks and lights up after dark in a dazzling light show of monsters and mayhem, it boasts a genuine must-see attraction.

Slotzilla

Fremont St • Zipline: Mon–Wed 4pm–1am, Thurs–Sun noon–2am; Zoomline: Mon–Wed noon–1am, Thurs–Sun noon–2am • Charge • ⦿ vegasexperience.com/slotzilla-zip-line

The two-tier **Slotzilla zipline** centres on what's claimed – at 120ft tall – to be the world's biggest slot machine. It ejects four riders at a time on each level, who race east–west along the full length of Fremont Street. Riders on the upper "Zoomline" level hang prone, enabling them to fly like Superman, and pass through the canopy of the Fremont Street Experience.

The Mob Museum

300 Stewart Ave • Daily 9am–9pm • Charge • ⦿ themobmuseum.org

Opened in a bid to revitalize downtown by former mayor Oscar Goodman – who as a lawyer defended many underworld figures – the **Mob Museum** offers a fascinating chronicle of both the mobsters who once controlled the city and the lawmen who eventually brought them down.

Hoover Dam

30 miles southeast of the Strip • ⦿ usbr.gov/lc/hooverdam • Daily 5am–9pm • **Parking** Daily: April–Sept 8am–6.15pm, Oct–March 8am–5.15pm • Charge • **Visitor Center** Daily 9am–5pm, last tours 3.45pm • Charge

Just under an hour's drive southeast of Las Vegas, the mighty **Hoover Dam** straddles the Colorado River. While this graceful 726ft-tall concrete marvel only supplies a modest proportion of the electricity that keeps Las Vegas running, its construction during the 1930s triggered the growth spurt, and the gambling boom, that created the modern city.

The main highway to Arizona, US-83, crosses the Colorado on a new bridge, slightly downstream from the dam. To see the dam itself, leave the highway via the spur roads at either end, park in the multi-storey garage on the Nevada side, and walk down to the Visitor Center. Displays there explain the story and inner workings of the dam, but paying a little extra entitles you to join a **Powerplant Tour**, and ride an elevator down to its base. The hour-long **Dam Tour** takes you right into its bowels, exploring dank and mysterious tunnels.

ARRIVAL AND DEPARTURE | LAS VEGAS | 2

By plane Harry Reid International Airport (ⓦharry reidairport.com) is a mile east of the southern Strip, and 4 miles from downtown. Taxi fares vary enormously; broadly speaking, expect to pay $20–27 to reach casinos on the Strip, $30 or more for downtown. Several public buses do travel between Downtown and the airport, including #108 and #109, but getting to the Strip usually involves changing

(see ⓦ rtcsnv.com for the latest).
By bus Long-distance Greyhound buses arrive at 200 S Main St downtown (ⓣ 702 384 9561).
Destinations Albuquerque (2 daily; 13hr); Flagstaff (2 daily; 5hr 30min); Los Angeles (9 daily; 5hr 15min); Phoenix (5 daily; 8hr 50min); Salt Lake City (2 daily; 8hr).

GETTING AROUND AND INFORMATION

On foot Traffic is so bad in Las Vegas that it's not worth renting a car just to explore the Strip. Be warned, though, that on summer days it's too hot to walk more than a couple of blocks.
By bus The most useful RTC bus route (ⓦ rtcsnv.com) – the Deuce (daily 24hr) – runs the full length of the Strip and connects with downtown. Buy tickets before you board.
By monorail The overpriced and less-than-convenient Las Vegas Monorail runs along the eastern side of the Strip from the *MGM Grand* to *Sahara Las Vegas* (Mon 7am–midnight, Tues–Thurs 7am–2am, Fri–Sun 7am–3am; ⓦ lvmonorail.

com), but doesn't go to the airport or downtown. Separate, free monorail systems also link *Mandalay Bay* with *Excalibur* via *Luxor*, the *Monte Carlo* with *Bellagio* via *CityCenter*, and the *Hard Rock* with *TI*.
Visitor centre 3150 Paradise Rd, east of the Strip – but not worth visiting (Mon–Fri 8am–5pm; ⓣ 877 847 4858; ⓦ visitlasvegas.com).
Websites Useful sources of information include the city's official website, ⓦ lasvegas.com, and sites such as ⓦ lasvegassun.com, ⓦ reviewjournal.com, ⓦ lasvegas weekly.com and ⓦ lvol.com.

ACCOMMODATION

The fundamental choice for Las Vegas visitors is whether to stay in a Strip mega-casino. Between them, these hold over 75,000 high-quality, and often very luxurious, rooms, but stays inevitably entail long queues to check in, a lack of personal service and endless walking to and fro. Downtown is smaller and on a more manageable scale, while finding a room elsewhere is not recommended for anyone hoping to experience all that makes Las Vegas unique. Note that every room changes in **price** every night. A room that costs $49 on Wednesday may well be $199 on Friday and Saturday; try if possible to visit during the week rather than the weekend. Almost every hotel also charges an additional "resort fee" of up to $45 per night, to cover wi-fi, phone and the like; MGM casinos charge extra for parking; and all hotel bills are also subject to an additional room tax of 13.38 percent on the Strip, and thirteen percent downtown.

THE STRIP

Aria 3730 Las Vegas Blvd S ⓦ aria.mgmresorts.com. If you're more of a modernist than a traditionalist, CityCenter's focal resort is the place for you. The rooms are classy rather than opulent, with big beds and walk-in showers as well as tubs, but check-in tends to be slow. Resort fee $45. $$

Bellagio 3600 Las Vegas Blvd S ⓦ bellagio.mgmresorts. com. *Bellagio's* opulent rooms epitomize luxury, while its location and amenities can't be beat. Premium rooms overlook the lake and its fountains, but the views from the back, over the pool are great too. Resort fee $45. $$$
Caesars Palace 3570 Las Vegas Blvd ⓦ caesars.com/ caesars-palace. Contemporary comfort wins out over kitsch at *Caesars* these days. The sheer scale can be overwhelming, but with its top-class dining and shopping, plus a fabulous pool and spa, it still has a real cachet. Resort fee $45.95. $$
Circus Circus 2880 Las Vegas Blvd S ⓦ circuscircus.com. While *Circus Circus* is showing its age, if you don't plan to linger in your room, and have a car, its rock-bottom rates may prove irresistible. Resort fee $33. $
★ **The Cosmopolitan** 3708 Las Vegas Blvd S ⓦ cosmopolitanlasvegas.com. Stylish contemporary casino where the guest rooms are classy and comfortable, with colossal beds, and all except the cheapest have Strip-view outdoor balconies. Resort fee $45. $$$
Excalibur 3850 Las Vegas Blvd S ⓦ excalibur.mgm resorts.com. Cross the drawbridge to enter the Disney-esque castle, wheel your bag through the casino full of kids, and, so long as you pay a little extra for a renovated

2

"wide-screen" room, you've found yourself a nice place to stay. Resort fee $35. $\overline{\S}$

★ **The Linq** 3535 Las Vegas Blvd S ⓦcaesars.com/linq. Although totally remodelled, the former *Imperial Palace* still represents one of the best-value casino hotels in town, with modern rooms at great prices considering the location. Resort fee $39.95. $\overline{\S}$

Luxor Las Vegas 3900 Las Vegas Blvd S ⓦluxor. mgmresorts.com. It's still a thrill to stay in one of the sizeable original rooms of this futuristic black glass pyramid, but there's a reason rooms in the newer tower next door cost a little more – they're in much better condition, and have baths and/or jacuzzis rather than showers. Resort fee $35. $\overline{\S}$

Mandalay Bay 3950 Las Vegas Blvd S ⓦmandalaybay. mgmresorts.com Effectively a self-contained resort, well south of the central Strip. If you're happy to spend long days by its extravagant pool, and while away your evenings in its fine restaurants, bars, clubs and theatres, then it's well worth considering. Rooms are exceptionally comfort-able, with both baths and walk-in showers. Resort fee $39. $\overline{\S\S\S}$

MGM Grand 3799 Las Vegas Blvd ⓦmgmgrand. mgmresorts.com. The *MGM Grand* feels a bit too big for its own good; once you've queued to check in, and walked half a mile to your room, you may not feel up to venturing out to explore. Accommodation has been largely upgraded at the expense of its former character. Resort fee $39. $\overline{\S\S}$

★ **New York–New York** 3790 Las Vegas Blvd S ⓦnewyorknewyork.mgmresorts.com. Las Vegas's own Big Apple is more appealing than most of its larger, less compact neighbours. The guest rooms are attractive and readily accessible, with some nice Art Deco touches, and the casino holds some excellent bars and restaurants. Resort fee $37. $\overline{\S\S}$

★ **Paris–Las Vegas** 3655 Las Vegas Blvd S ⓦcaesars. com/paris-las-vegas. An ideal compromise – stay in a big-name property, with excellent amenities plus "only in Vegas" features like the Eiffel Tower outside your window – without paying premium prices for opulent fittings you don't really need. Resort fee $45.95. $\overline{\S\S}$

Planet Hollywood 3667 Las Vegas Blvd S ⓦcaesars. com/planet-hollywood. "Ultra Hip" rooms – black and gold carpets and wallpaper; movie stills on the wall; and walk-in showers as well as baths – in a central location. Resort fee $45.95. $\overline{\S}$

The Strat 2000 Las Vegas Blvd S ⓦthestrat.com. Too far to walk to from either the Strip or downtown, but at least something of a destination in its own right, even if its simple but sizeable rooms aren't in the 1000ft tower. Resort fee $39.95. $\overline{\S}$

The Venetian 3355 Las Vegas Blvd S ⓦvenetian. lasvegas.com. In the very top tier of Strip hotels, in terms of the property as a whole, as well as the sheer comfort in the guest rooms. All are suites; step down from the sleeping area, with its huge bed, to reach a sunken living space closer to the panoramic windows. Resort fee $45. $\overline{\S\S\S}$

Virgin Hotels Las Vegas 4455 Paradise Rd ⓦvirgin hotels.com/las-vegas. Richard Branson's revamp of the old *Hard Rock* opened in 2021, with the casino known as Mohegan Sun Casino, the hotel managed by Hilton and the Theater at Virgin Hotels providing the entertainment. Resort fee $51. $\overline{\S\S}$

Wynn Las Vegas 3131 Las Vegas Blvd S ⓦwynnlasvegas. com. The super-large rooms in Las Vegas's most opulent property are tastefully decorated and equipped with ultra-luxurious linens, while the bathrooms feature marble tubs, walk-in showers and even TVs. Resort fee $45. $\overline{\S\S\S}$

DOWNTOWN

Bungalows Hostel 1236 S Las Vegas Blvd ⓦbungalows hostel.com. Popular with young travellers, this converted motel in the Arts District is a 10 minute walk to the Strat (and an easy Uber or bus ride to the Strip). Stylish accommodation includes 6-bed and 10-bed shared dorm rooms (mixed and female-only), which can also be booked privately (if you have a group). The management organizes tours and events, from movie nights to art therapy. $\overline{\S}$

The D 301 E Fremont St ⓦthed.com. This central downtown hotel is a real bargain. All its rooms have had a top-to-bottom makeover and the amenities downstairs are much improved. Resort fee $29.95. $\overline{\S}$

El Cortez 600 E Fremont St ⓦelcortezhotelcasino.com. Long renowned as Las Vegas's cheapest casino, a short but potentially intimidating walk from the heart of Fremont Street. The "Vintage" rooms are no better than faded motel rooms, but the "Cabana" suites, across the street, are much more appealing. Resort fee $23.99. $\overline{\S}$

Golden Nugget 129 E Fremont St ⓦgoldennugget. com. Downtown's classiest option is the only hotel hereabouts with amenities – like its amazing pool – to match the Strip giants. The actual rooms, at their freshest but loudest in the Rush Tower, are smart and comfortable, if not all that exciting. Resort fee $38. $\overline{\S\S}$

The Plaza 1 Main St ⓦplazahotelcasino.com. Since the management cleverly squeezed the unused furnishings from the never-opened *Fontainebleau* into the *Plaza's* thousand rooms, they've been looking great, and offer some of downtown's best rates. Resort fee $30. $\overline{\S}$

EATING

Las Vegas used to be a byword for bad food, with just the occasional mobster-dominated steakhouse to relieve the monotony of pile 'em-high buffets. Those days have gone. Every major Strip casino now holds half a dozen or more high-quality restaurants, run by globally renowned chefs. Prices have soared, to a typical minimum spend of $50 per head at big-name places, but so too have standards, and in casinos such as *Aria*, *Bellagio*, the *Cosmopolitan* and the *Venetian* you could eat a great meal in a different restaurant every night.

BUFFETS

Bacchanal Buffet Caesars Palace, 3570 Las Vegas Blvd S ⓦ caesars.com/caesars-palace. The finest buffet at any Caesars-owned property, and the most expensive in town, features 500 freshly made items daily, from sushi, dim sum and phô soup to fresh oysters and wood-fired pizzas, prepared by chefs at nine "show kitchens". Dinner queues tend to be long. $$$$

The Buffet at Bellagio Bellagio, 3600 Las Vegas Blvd S ⓦ bellagio.mgmresorts.com. Las Vegas's first "gourmet buffet", featuring high-quality food for all meals, sparked standards, and less happily prices, to rise all over town. Even for breakfast, besides the expected bagels, pastries and eggs, you can have salmon smoked or baked, fruit fresh or in salads, and omelettes cooked to order, with fillings such as crabmeat. Brunch $$$, dinner $$$$

★ **The Buffet at Wynn** Wynn Las Vegas, 3131 Las Vegas Blvd S ⓦ wynnlasvegas.com. *Wynn*'s plush Belle-Époque buffet remains the best in town, with dishes from lamb osso buco and smoked duck salad, to cucumber and scallop ceviche and sushi rolls. $$$

★ **Drag Brunch at Señor Frogs** Treasure Island, 3300 Las Vegas Blvd S ⓦ senorfrogs.com/las-vegas. Not your average brunch buffet; munch on chicken tinga, country potatoes and warm churros (washed down by drinks from the open bar) as you're entertained by drag queens from hit TV show RuPaul's Drag Race. $$$$

RESTAURANTS

Beijing Noodle No. 9 Caesars Palace, 3570 Las Vegas Blvd S ⓦ caesars.com/caesars-palace. Hugely enjoyable Chinese noodle restaurant, approached via aquariums that hold a thousand goldfish, and resembling a mysterious underwater cavern. Fortunately, the food matches the setting, with good dim sum buns and dumplings, and the (large) noodle dishes a little more expensive. $$

★ **Bouchon** Level 10, Venezia Tower, The Venetian, 3355 Las Vegas Blvd S ⓦ venetianlasvegas.com.

Thomas Keller's scrupulous evocation of a French bistro is a lovely, relaxed spot, with outdoor seating and food that's nothing short of *magnifique*. Brunch is the best value, with sandwiches or quiche; dinner mains like steak frites or pan-seared swordfish. Look too for the all-day *Bouchon Bakery*, outside on the Strip. $$$$

Gordon Ramsay Steak Paris Las Vegas, 3655 Las Vegas Blvd S ⓦ caesars.com/paris-las-vegas. For his first Las Vegas venture, perfectionist pottymouth Gordon Ramsay played it safe, opening a high-class steakhouse near *Paris*'s main entrance. Diners select from a trolley laden with marbled, aged slabs of prime meat; a superbly cooked veal chop, a strip steak, and even fish'n'chips. $$$$

★ **Mon Ami Gabi** Paris Las Vegas, 3655 Las Vegas Blvd S ⓦ monamigabi.com/las-vegas. Among the first Las Vegas restaurants to offer al fresco dining, right on the Strip, this exuberant evocation of a Paris pavement brasserie remains the city's premier lunchtime pick. For a real taste of France, you can't beat a croque-madame for breakfast; moules frites for lunch; or steak frites for dinner. $$$

Oscar's Steakhouse The Plaza, 1 Main St ⓦ oscarslv. com. Perched in a glass bubble, staring down Fremont Street, this shameless cash-in by former mayor Oscar Goodman is a real slice of old Las Vegas, serving top-quality filet mignon or bone-in steaks, it also has a full Italian-heavy menu of pasta, chicken and fish. $$$

Phô TI (Treasure Island), 3300 Las Vegas Blvd S ⓦ treasureisland.com. If you're looking for a simple, cheap and tasty meal that's a little out of the ordinary, there's no faulting the Strip's only Vietnamese restaurant, which occupies half of the *Coffee Shop* at TI. The speciality here is hearty bowls of *phô* soup, with chicken, beef or vegetables; rice or vermicelli noodle dishes cost much the same. $$

★ **Scarpetta** Level 3, Cosmopolitan, 3708 Las Vegas Blvd S ⓦ cosmopolitanlasvegas.com. It comes as a pleasant shock to pass through *Scarpetta*'s unassuming entrance and find yourself confronted with panoramic windows overlooking the *Bellagio* fountains. Thanks to chef Michael Vitangeli, the food is even better than the view. *Le tout* Las Vegas has flocked to enjoy appetizers such as Mediterranean octopus; pasta; and delicious main courses like veal *osso buco*. For the full works, go for the set menu. $$$$

DRINKING AND NIGHTLIFE

Every Las Vegas casino offers free drinks to gamblers. Sit at a slot machine or gaming table, and a cocktail waitress will find you and take your order; tips are expected. In addition, the casinos hold bars and lounges of all kinds; few tourists venture further afield to drink. A new generation of visitors is responsible for the city's ever-expanding **clubbing** scene. Casinos like the *Cosmopolitan* and *Wynn Las Vegas* now boast some of the world's most spectacular – and expensive – clubs and ultra-lounges.

Bar Parasol Wynn Las Vegas, 3131 Las Vegas Blvd S ⓦ wynnlasvegas.com. A quintessential example of the Wynn way with design, these twin upstairs-downstairs bars are festooned with richly coloured umbrellas. A cocktail or two, and you'll feel you're right at Las Vegas's absurd and exhilarating heart.

Chandelier Cosmopolitan, 3708 Las Vegas Blvd S ⓦ cosmopolitanlasvegas.com. Beneath the dazzling, dangling canopy of the eponymous two-million-crystal

2

2

BURNING MAN

Nevada's legendary **Burning Man** is celebrated at the end of August each year in a temporary, vehicle-free community known as **Black Rock City**, way out in the Black Rock Desert, twelve miles north of tiny Gerlach, which is itself a hundred miles north of Reno. That's a very, very hot time to be out in the Nevada desert, particularly if, like perhaps half of the fifty thousand revellers, you're completely naked.

The event, which prefers not to consider itself a "festival", takes a different theme each year, always with a strong emphasis on spontaneity and mass participation. An exhilarating range of performances, happenings and art installations culminates in the burning of a giant human effigy on the final Saturday. After that, in theory at least, Black Rock City simply disappears without trace.

For full information and the latest ticket prices, for which the standard rate is around $425 for the week, access ⓦ burningman.org. All visitors must buy tickets in advance; you can't pay at the gate. Only those who can prove total self-sufficiency are admitted; that means you have to bring all your water, food and shelter. The site holds no public showers or pools and its economy is almost entirely based on barter. No money can change hands, other than for coffee and ice.

chandelier, the *Cosmopolitan*'s centre-piece bar soars through three separate levels. On the enclosed middle floor, reached via a glass elevator, where the actions is, DJs entertain an excited, buzzy and generally young crowd.

Encore Beach Club Encore, 3121 Las Vegas Blvd S ⓦ wynnsocial.com. This luxurious multi-level complex of pools, patios, bars and private bungalows is the definitive expression of Las Vegas's craze for DJ-fuelled daytime poolside parties. Escape the crowds either on pristine white "lily pads" out in the water, or in your own cabana, but the pounding music will follow you everywhere. Expect ultra-high prices for drinks, let alone table service. Cover charge.

Hakkasan MGM Grand, 3799 Las Vegas Blvd S ⓦ tao group.com/venues/hakkasan-nightclub-las-vegas. Ranking among the world's largest nightclubs, the four-storey *Hakkasan* incorporates any number of themed lounges and high-class restaurants, as well as its huge main dancefloor, and can hold 7500 party-goers. Cover charge.

★ **Marquee** Cosmopolitan, 3708 Las Vegas Blvd S ⓦ taogroup.com/venues/marquee-las-vegas. Cutting-edge indoor-outdoor combination of a nightclub and a pool-centred "dayclub", with a 50ft-high main floor, home to regular gigs by the world's hottest DJs. Add in drinks, let alone table service, and you can expect to spend hundreds of dollars. Cover charge.

Minus5 Ice Bar Mandalay Bay, 3930 Las Vegas Blvd S ⓦ minus5experience.com. Funny, gimmicky bar that's exactly what it says it is – a bar in which every single thing is made of ice, from the walls to the glasses. Customers are loaned jackets, gloves and boots to tolerate the sub-zero temperature – yes, it's minus 5. Cover charge. See also branches in the Venetian and Linq.

ENTERTAINMENT

The Strip is once more riding high as the entertainment epicentre of the world. While Elvis may have left the building, headliners such as Britney Spears, Barry Manilow, Donny Osmond and Rod Stewart attract thousands of big-spending fans night after night (not to mention a much-delayed residency from Adele in 2023), and all the major touring acts pass through. Meanwhile the old-style feathers-and-sequins revues have been supplanted by a never-ending stream of jaw-droppingly lavish shows by the Cirque du Soleil. Tix4tonight sells **discounted show tickets** from a dozen Strip locations (☎ 877 849 4868, ⓦ tix4tonight.com).

Absinthe Cosmopolitan, 3708 Las Vegas Blvd S ⓦ spiegelworld.com/absinthe. Originally staged in a circus tent outside *Caesars Palace*, this crude and abrasive burlesque show is more of a drunken night out than a traditional show, but Las Vegas audiences have lapped it up.

Big Elvis Harrah's Piano Bar, 3475 Las Vegas Blvd S ⓦ caesars.com/harrahs-las-vegas. Las Vegas's biggest and best-loved Elvis impersonator, Pete Vallee, has a mastery of Elvis' repertoire and easy audience rapport that makes this the best free show in town.

Human Nature – Motown And More South Point, 9777 Las Vegas Blvd S ⓦ humannaturelive.com. Wholesome Australian vocal quartet, on an unlikely but surprisingly successful mission to add a Down-Under twist to the music of black America. With their fabulous voices and very likeable energy, they really are superb. Check the website for the latest dates, as locations tend to change.

★ **Love** The Mirage, 3400 Las Vegas Blvd S ⓦ cirque dusoleil.com. A genuinely triumphant collaboration in which Cirque perform superbly choreographed dancing and acrobatics to a crystal-sharp Beatles soundtrack, *Love* is much more than just another "jukebox musical". There's no story, and no attempt to depict the Beatles as actual people – though eerily we hear their voices in retrieved studio chatter – just a dazzling celebration of their music. Note that the show will likely move to another hotel in 2024, when the Mirage begins its transformation into the new Hard Rock Hotel.

★ **Mystère** TI, 3300 Las Vegas Blvd S, ⓦ cirquedusoleil. com. Approaching thirty years since it opened, Las Vegas's original Cirque du Soleil show is still arguably the best – you can see why it changed the Strip's entertainment scene forever, overnight. Pure spectacle, from the gorgeous costumes and billows of cascading silk to the jaw-dropping circus skills and phenomenal feats of strength.

★ **O** Bellagio, 3600 Las Vegas Blvd S ⓦ cirquedusoleil. com. With no disrespect to the astonishing skills of Cirque du Soleil's divers and acrobats, the real star of this phenomenal long-running show is the theatre itself, which centres on a metal-mesh stage, all or any part of which can suddenly disappear underwater, making possible a dazzling array of death-defying leaps and heart-stopping plunges.

Terry Fator New York–New York, 3790 Las Vegas Blvd S ⓦ newyorknewyork.mgmresorts.com. Even if you dread seeing a ventriloquist, make an exception for Terry Fator. Yes, this ordinary middle-American guy swaps corny jokes with soft toys, but he also has an extraordinary talent – an astonishing five-octave singing voice that delivers perfect impressions of artists from Aaron Neville to Garth Brooks, and Ozzy Osbourne to Etta James, all without moving his lips.

Great Basin National Park

Lehman Caves visitor centre Daily: summer 8am–5pm; winter 8am–4pm • 1hr tours & 1hr 30min tours charge • ⓦ nps.gov/grba

Just across the border from Utah, **Great Basin National Park** encapsulates the scenery of the Nevada desert, from angular peaks to high mountain meadows cut by fast-flowing streams. Daily all year, guided tours from the visitor centre at **Lehman Caves**, five miles west of tiny **Baker**, explore limestone caves that are densely packed with intriguing formations. Beyond the caves, a twelve-mile road climbs the east flank of the bald, usually snowcapped **Wheeler Peak**, where trails lead past alpine lakes and through a grove of gnarled, ancient bristlecone pines to the 13,063ft summit. Off-track cross-country skiing is excellent in winter.

Elko

ELKO, the self-proclaimed last real cowtown in the West, straggles alongside I-80 a hundred miles west of Utah. Amid open cattle ranges, it's a fitting home for late January's **Cowboy Poetry Gathering** (ⓦ westernfolklife.org), a get-together that celebrates folk culture and aims to keep alive the traditions of the Wild West. This area having been extensively settled by Basque shepherds, each Fourth of July weekend sees the 72-hour **National Basque Festival** (ⓦ elkobasqueclub.com), in which hulking men throw huge logs at each other amid a whole lot of carousing and downing of Basque food.

California Trail Interpretive Center

1 Interpretive Center Way (I-80 Hunter Exit 292) • Daily 9am–5pm (Oct–April Wed–Sun 9am–5pm) • Free • ⓦ californiatrailcenter.org

Eight miles west of town, the **California Trail Interpretive Center** holds excellent displays on the nineteenth-century pioneers who passed this way, lured by the prospect of making their fortunes in the West. Many came to grief; the horrendous saga of the **Donner Party**, who resorted to cannibalism after becoming stuck in the snow, is recounted in gleeful detail.

ACCOMMODATION AND EATING   **ELKO**

Cowboy Joe 376 5th St ⓦ cowboyjoecoffee.com. Friendly little coffee bar, just off the main street. $‾

Star Hotel 246 Silver St ⓦ elkostarhotel.com. Two blocks south of the main drag, this simple family restaurant, steeped in local history, serves Basque cuisine such as cod as well as American staples including grilled steaks for

somewhat more. $‾$‾

Thunderbird Motel 345 Idaho St ⓦ thunderbirdmotels. com. Traditional, old-fashioned Western motel in the heart of downtown, offering comfortable rooms plus a pool, at very reasonable rates. $‾

2

Reno

The "biggest little city in the world", **RENO**, on I-80 near the California border, is a somewhat downmarket version of Las Vegas, with miles of gleaming slot machines and poker tables, along with tacky wedding chapels and quickie divorce courts. It enjoys a superb setting, at the foot of the snowcapped **Sierra Nevada** with the Truckee River winding through the centre, but only the old downtown core is at all historic or attractive. It's still home to most of Reno's **casinos**, though newer rivals have sprung up to the south along Virginia Street, and in **Sparks** a couple of miles east.

ARRIVAL AND DEPARTURE
RENO

By plane Reno-Tahoe International Airport (⊛renoairport. com), a couple of miles southeast of downtown, is served by North Lake Tahoe Express local shuttles (⊛northlaketahoe express.com).
By bus Greyhound buses arrive at the down Amtrak station, 280 N Centre St.

Destinations Salt Lake City (1 daily; 10hr); San Francisco (4 daily; 5hr 30min).
By train Amtrak trains call at 280 N Centre St downtown.
Destinations Salt Lake City (1 daily; 10hr); San Francisco (1 daily; 9hr).

ACCOMMODATION AND EATING

Atlantis 3800 S Virginia St ⊛atlantiscasino.com. Reno's fanciest casino, this tower-block holds rooms of all degrees of luxury and a dozen restaurants including *Toucan Charlie's* buffet. $\overline{\underline{\underline{5}}}$

Silver Legacy 407 N Virginia St ⊛caesars.com/silver-legacy-reno. Venerable downtown casino, offering good-value rooms and dining and a flavour of old-style Nevada. $\overline{\underline{5}}$

Carson City

Nevada state capital **CARSON CITY** stands thirty miles south of Reno, as you follow US-395 along the jagged spires of the **High Sierra** towards **Death Valley**. Named after frontier explorer Kit Carson in 1858, it's scattered with elegant Victorian-era structures and world-weary casinos. The excellent **Nevada State Museum**, 600 N Carson St (Wed–Sun 8.30am–4.30pm; charge; ⊛carsonnvmuseum.org), covers the geology and natural history of the Great Basin.

ACCOMMODATION AND EATING
CARSON CITY

Comma Coffee 312 S Carson St ⊛commacoffeecafe. com. Lively local rendezvous, offering regular live music and community events along with breakfast eggs, lunch salads and sandwiches, and, of course, coffee. $\overline{\underline{5}}$
Hampton Inn & Suites Carson City 10 Hospitality Way ⊛hilton.com. Best of the motel accommodation

near I-580 on the edge of town, with standard but spacious rooms, flat-screen TVs and a decent breakfast included. $\overline{\underline{\underline{\underline{5}}}}$
Hardman House 917 N Carson St ⊛hardmanhouse hotel.com. A very decent budget option, with 62 bright, colourful motel rooms and friendly, helpful staff. $\overline{\underline{5}}$

PICTOGRAPHS IN HORSESHOE CANYON, UTAH

Contexts

History

The history of Texas and the Southwest is indelibly linked to the history of North America and the development of the United States. These few pages survey the peopling and political development of the regions that now form the southwestern USA.

First peoples

The true pioneers of North America, nomadic hunter-gatherers from Siberia, are thought to have reached what's now **Alaska** around seventeen thousand years ago. Thanks to the last ice age, when sea levels were 300ft lower, a "**land-bridge**" – actually a vast plain, measuring six hundred miles north to south – connected Eurasia to America.

Migration may well have been spurred by the pursuit of large mammal species, and especially **mammoth**, which had already been harried to extinction throughout almost all of Eurasia. A huge bonanza awaited the hunters when they finally encountered America's own indigenous "**megafauna**", such as mammoths, mastodons, giant ground sloths and enormous long-horned bison, all of which had evolved with no protection against human predation.

Filling the New World

Within a thousand years, ten million people were living throughout both North and South America. Although that sounds like a phenomenally rapid spread, it would only have required a band of just one hundred individuals to enter the continent, and advance a mere eight miles per year, with an annual population growth of 1.1 percent, to achieve that impact. The mass **extinction** of the American megafauna was so precisely simultaneous that humans must surely have been responsible, eliminating the giant beasts in each locality in one fell swoop, before pressing on in search of the next kill.

The elimination of large land mammals precluded future American civilizations from domesticating any of the animal species that were crucial to Old World economies. Without cattle, horses, sheep or goats, or significant equivalents, they lacked the resources to supply food and clothing to large settlements, provide draught power to haul ploughs or wheeled vehicles, or increase mobility and the potential for conquest. What's more, most of the human diseases that were later introduced from the rest of the world had originally evolved in association with domesticated animals; the first Americans developed neither immunity to such diseases, nor any indigenous diseases of their own that might have attacked the invaders.

At least three distinct waves of **migrants** arrived via Alaska, each of whom settled in, and adapted to, a more marginal environment than its predecessors. The second, five thousand years on from the first, were the "**Nadene**" or Athapascans – the ancestors of the Navajo and Apache of the Southwest.

c.60 million BC	15,000 BC	9,000 BC
Two mighty islands collide, creating North America as a single landmass, and throwing up the Rocky Mountains	First nomadic peoples from Asia reach Alaska	Humans first begin to settle in the Southwest as part of the Clovis culture

Early settlements in the Southwest

The earliest known settlement site in the modern United States, dating back 12,000 years, has been uncovered at Meadowcroft in southwest Pennsylvania. Five centuries later, the Southwest was dominated by the so-called **Clovis** culture. Nowhere did a civilization emerge to rival the wealth and sophistication of the great cities of ancient Mexico. However, the influence of those far-off cultures did filter north; the cultivation of crops such as beans, squash and maize facilitated the development of large communities, while northern religious cults, some of which performed human sacrifice, owed much to Central American beliefs.

In the deserts of the **Southwest**, the **Hohokam** settlement of Snaketown, near what's now Phoenix, grappled with the same problems of water management that plague the region today. Nearby, the **Ancestral Puebloan** "Basketmakers" developed pottery around 200 AD and began to gather into the walled villages later known as pueblos, possibly for protection against Athapascan invaders, such as the Apache, who were arriving from the north. Ancestral Puebloan "cities", such as Pueblo Bonito in New Mexico's Chaco Canyon – a centre for the turquoise trade with the mighty Aztec – and the "Cliff Palace" at Mesa Verde in Colorado, are the most impressive monuments to survive from ancient North America. Although the Ancestral Puebloans dispersed after a devastating drought in the twelfth century, many of the settlements created by their immediate descendants have remained in use ever since. Despite centuries of migration and war, the desert farmers of the **Hopi Mesas** in Arizona (see page 141), and the pueblos of **Taos** and **Ácoma** in New Mexico, have never been dispossessed of their homes. Further north, the Paiute and Shoshone inhabited the deserts of Nevada, while Utah was roamed by the Paiute, Shoshone, Navajo and Ute.

Estimates of the total Indigenous population before the arrival of the Europeans vary widely, but an acceptable median figure suggests around fifty million people in the Americas as a whole. Perhaps five million of those were in North America, speaking around four hundred different languages.

Spanish contacts

The first permanent European contacts with North America occurred on the Eastern seaboard in the early 16th century, while Spanish conquistadors began the conquest of Mexico to the south in the 1520s – indeed, it was Spanish adventurers and missionaries that would be the first to arrive in Texas and the Southwest, long before the foundation of the United States in 1776.

In 1528 the Pánfilo de Narváez expedition set out from Cuba to explore Florida but was ultimately shipwrecked off the Gulf of Mexico coast, likely Galveston Island, Texas – most of the crew died and Narváez himself was swept out to sea and was never seen again. A junior officer, **Cabeza de Vaca**, survived, and with three shipmates spent the next eight years on an extraordinary odyssey across Texas into the Southwest. At times held as enslaved people, at times revered as seers, they finally got back to Mexico in 1536, bringing tales of golden cities deep in the desert, known as the **Seven Cities of Cibola**.

One of Cabeza de Vaca's companions was an enslaved black African called **Estevanico**. Rather than re-submit to slavery, he volunteered to map the route for a new venture;

c.1500 BC	**1001–02**	**1492**
Ancestral Pueblo people begin settling in the Southwest	Ancestral Puebloan culture reaches its peak at Chaco Canyon in the Southwest	Christopher Columbus makes landfall in the Bahamas

racing alone into the interior, with two colossal greyhounds at his side, he was killed in Zuni Pueblo in 1539. The following year, **Francisco Vázquez de Coronado**'s larger expedition proved to everyone's intense dissatisfaction that the Seven Cities of Cibola did not exist. Between 1540 and 1542 Coronado reached as far as the Grand Canyon and the Colorado River, travelling through modern-day Texas, Arizona and New Mexico, and encountering the Apache, Hopi and Zuni along the way. The expedition resulted in the destruction of several pueblos and the deaths of hundreds of Native Americans – but no cities of gold.

The growth of the Spanish colonies

In 1598 the Spanish (operating out of Mexico) succeeded in subjugating the Pueblo peoples Coronado had encountered earlier, and founded **New Mexico** along the Rio Grande. More of a missionary than a military enterprise, the colony's survival was always precarious due to the vast tracts of empty desert that separated it from the rest of Spanish Mexico. Nonetheless, the construction of a new capital, **Santa Fe**, began in 1607 (see page 103). Taos was established in around 1615 following the conquest of the Taos Pueblo. Native Americans in the area soon began to resent autocratic Spanish rule. The **Pueblo Revolt** of 1680 drove the Spanish out of New Mexico altogether, though they returned in force a dozen years later, and Albuquerque was founded in 1706. Thereafter, a curious synthesis of traditional and Hispanic religion and culture evolved, and the Spanish presence was not seriously challenged.

Catholic missions (including San Xavier del Bac) were established in southern Arizona in the early 1690s, with Tucson eventually founded in 1775, though attacks by the Apaches kept Spanish development here to a minimum. Meanwhile, the first comprehensive exploration of Utah by outsiders was carried out in 1776 by two Franciscan priests, Silvestre Vélez de Escalante and Francisco Atanasio Domínguez, searching for a route between the Spanish missions of New Mexico and California. Nevada was technically part of Alta California (Upper California), but there was no effective Spanish presence here.

The Spanish began to establish Catholic missions and settlements in East Texas in 1716, with San Antonio founded two years later. The Spanish were unable to establish permanent rule in West Texas, however. From the 1750s to the 1860s, the Comanche controlled a vast area dubbed Comancheria. Their hegemony was gradually ended, beginning in the late 1840s, by waves of smallpox and cholera, in addition to violent conflict with Anglo-American settlers.

Indeed, the major killer of indigenous peoples was **smallpox**, which worked its way deep into the interior of the continent long before the Europeans. As populations were decimated, great migrations took place. The original inhabitants of the region had been sedentary farmers, who also hunted buffalo by driving them over rocky bluffs. With the arrival of **horses** on the Great Plains (probably captured from the Spanish, and known at first as "mystery dogs"), an entirely new, nomadic lifestyle emerged. Groups such as the Cheyenne and the Apache swept their rivals aside to dominate vast territories, and eagerly seized the potential offered by the later introduction of firearms. Increasing dependence on trade with Europeans created a dynamic but fundamentally unstable culture.

1528	**1610**
A Spanish expedition is ship-wrecked in Florida; Cabeza de Vaca and three survivors, including Estevanico, a black African, take eight years to walk to Mexico City	Santa Fe is founded as capital of New Mexico; horses begin to spread across the Southwest

While the Spanish maintained thinly manned outposts in the Southwest, the American frontier was pushing steadily westwards from the East Coast, as "Anglo" colonists seized Native American land, with or without the excuse of an "uprising" or "rebellion" to provoke them into bloodshed.

The American Revolution

The British-controlled American colonies prospered during the **eighteenth century** on the east coast of the continent, far from Texas and the Southwest. The British had tried to control emigration west, but this ended spectacularly after the colonies gained their freedom in the Revolutionary War (1775–1783) and settlers began to flood over the Appalachians. The war had little initial impact on Spain's Southwestern colonies. The Spanish briefly allied with the Americans to oust the British from Florida, but it was soon obvious that the newly independent United States of America – officially created in 1776 – had ambitions to expand far beyond the old borders.

The nineteenth century

During its first century, the territories and population of the new **United States of America** expanded at a phenomenal rate. The white population of North America in 1800 stood at around five million, and there were another one million enslaved Africans (of whom thirty thousand were in the North). Of that total, 86 percent lived within fifty miles of the Atlantic, but no US city could rival Mexico City, whose population approached 100,000 inhabitants (both New York and Philadelphia reached that figure within twenty years, however, and New York had passed a million fifty years later). Pressure to expand westwards was relentless.

Manifest Destiny and expansion of the USA

It took only a small step for the citizens of the young republic to move from realizing that their country might spread across the whole continent to supposing that it had a quasi-religious duty – a "**Manifest Destiny**" – to do so. At its most basic, that doctrine amounted to little more than a belief that "might must be right", but the idea that they were fulfilling the will of God inspired countless pioneers to set off across the plains in search of a new life (newspaper editor John O'Sullivan first coined the term "manifest destiny" in 1845).

In 1803 Napoleon sold France's American possessions to the United States for $15 million, in the **Louisiana Purchase**. President Thomas Jefferson swiftly sent the explorers **Lewis and Clark** to map out the new territories, which extended far beyond the boundaries of present-day Louisiana into northwest North America. The United States agreed to respect Spanish claims on Texas and the Southwest – temporarily. Mountain men, traders and settlers forged trails between the USA and the Spanish territories nonetheless, in the process exploring regions long ignored by Spanish and Mexican officials.

The Santa Fe Trail connecting Missouri with Santa Fe was established by William Becknell in 1821; Jim Bridger first spotted the Great Salt Lake in 1824; and Utah was traversed as part of the first overland journey to California by the fur trapper Jedediah

1687–1691	**1776**	**1821**
Jesuit priest Eusebio Kino established several missions in the Santa Cruz River valley of Arizona	Tucson, AZ was founded by the Spanish	Mexican independence from Spain; Southwest reverts to Mexican rule

S. Smith in 1826 (Smith died in a skirmish with the Comanche on the Santa Fe Trail in 1831).

Mexican independence and Texas

Inspired by the American Revolution and triggered by Napoleon's invasion of Spain in 1808, Spain's American colonies began to revolt. Though far from the fighting, Texas and the Southwest were decisively impacted by the Mexican War of Independence (1810–1821). The old Viceroyalty of New Spain eventually became the First Mexican Republic in 1824 under President Guadalupe Victoria – all of Texas and the Southwest reverted to Mexican rule. The changes especially affected Texas. Stephen Austin and the "Old Three Hundred", "Anglo" American citizens from Missouri, were permitted to settle along the Brazos River in 1822 – the Mexican government hoped this would reduce Comanche raids on the territory. Mexico established the port Galveston in 1825, serving thereafter as a major gateway for immigrants to Texas. By the time Mexico reversed course and prohibited immigration from the US in 1830 it was too late; the population of Texas was overwhelming Anglo-American.

The Republic of Texas

The Spanish territories of the Southwest had never flourished as colonies, and as American settlers arrived in ever-increasing numbers they began to dominate their Hispanic counterparts. The Anglos of **Texas finally** rebelled at the Convention of 1833 and under the leadership of General Sam Houston, the Texas Revolution began in 1835. Shortly after the legendary setback at the **Alamo** (see page 73) in 1836, the Texans decisively defeated the army of Mexican President Santa Anna at the Battle of San Jacinto and Texas became an independent republic. Sam Houston was president 1836–1838, with the city of Houston founded in his honour in 1837. In 1839 the city of Austin was created to be the new capital. Though Texas was annexed by the US in 1845 (a move supported by the vast majority of the Texian population) and immediately became the 28th state of the Union, this brief period of independence remains a great source of pride for Texans today.

The Mexican-American War (1846–1848)

The USA inherited Texan border disputes with Mexico, and the **Mexican-American War** was a bare-faced exercise in American aggression in which most of the future Civil War generals received their first experience fighting on the same side. The relatively easy American victory (during which the US army occupied Mexico City), resulted in acceptance of the annexation of Texas, but also of Arizona (above the Gila River), Utah, Colorado, Nevada, New Mexico and California. A token US payment of $18.25 million to Mexico was designed to match the Louisiana Purchase. The Gadsden Purchase of 1854 added more Arizona territory (including Tucson), to the south of the Gila River.

The Mormons and Utah

The development of Utah (and much of the surrounding region) is inevitably linked to the Mormons, who emigrated to the Great Salt Lake in 1847 under the leadership of Brigham Young and established Salt Lake City. The "Church of Christ" was founded

1836	1845	1847
Texas declares itself independent; Mexican general Santa Anna massacres the defenders at the Alamo four days later	Republic of Texas was annexed by the United States and immediately became a state	Mormon settlers found Salt Lake City

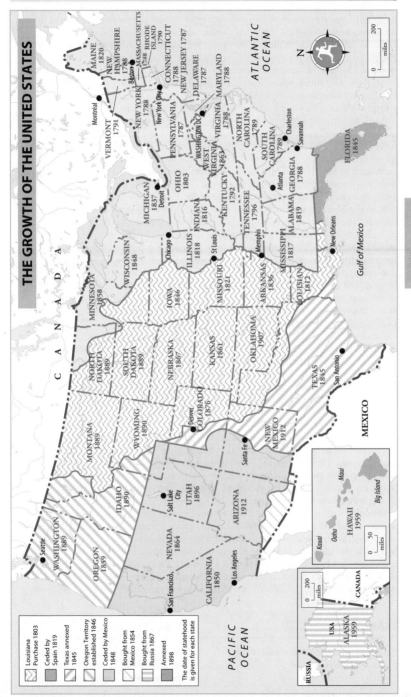

THE GROWTH OF THE UNITED STATES

Louisiana Purchase 1803
Ceded by Spain 1819
Texas annexed 1845
Oregon Territory established 1846
Ceded by Mexico 1848
Bought from Mexico 1854
Bought from Russia 1867
Annexed 1898
The date of statehood is given for each state

N
0 ___ 200 miles

ATLANTIC OCEAN

MAINE 1820
NEW HAMPSHIRE 1788
MASSACHUSETTS 1788
Boston
RHODE ISLAND 1790
CONNECTICUT 1788
NEW JERSEY 1787
DELAWARE 1787
MARYLAND 1788
VERMONT 1791
NEW YORK 1788
New York City
Montréal
PENNSYLVANIA 1787
WASHINGTON DC
VIRGINIA 1788
WEST VIRGINIA 1863
NORTH CAROLINA 1789
SOUTH CAROLINA 1789
Charleston
Savannah
GEORGIA 1788
Atlanta
FLORIDA 1845
OHIO 1803
MICHIGAN 1837
Detroit
INDIANA 1816
KENTUCKY 1792
TENNESSEE 1796
ALABAMA 1819
MISSISSIPPI 1817
Memphis
New Orleans
Gulf of Mexico
WISCONSIN 1848
ILLINOIS 1818
Chicago
St Louis
MISSOURI 1821
ARKANSAS 1836
LOUISIANA 1812
CANADA
MINNESOTA 1858
IOWA 1846
NORTH DAKOTA 1889
SOUTH DAKOTA 1889
NEBRASKA 1867
KANSAS 1861
OKLAHOMA 1907
TEXAS 1845
San Antonio
MEXICO
MONTANA 1889
WYOMING 1890
COLORADO 1876
Denver
NEW MEXICO 1912
Santa Fe
IDAHO 1890
UTAH 1896
Salt Lake City
ARIZONA 1912
WASHINGTON 1889
Seattle
OREGON 1859
NEVADA 1864
CALIFORNIA 1850
San Francisco
Los Angeles
PACIFIC OCEAN

Kauai
Oahu
Maui
Big Island
HAWAII 1959
0 ___ 50 miles

RUSSIA
USA
ALASKA 1959
CANADA
0 ___ 200 miles

in 1830 in upstate New York by a young farmer named Joseph Smith. Revered by Mormons as their original "Prophet," Smith was reputedly directed to unearthing a cache of inscribed golden plates. They provided, along with his revelations and the Holy Bible, the basis for a renewed Christian faith whose tenets he set forth in The Book of Mormon. After several migrations westwards, Smith and his followers ended up in Nauvoo, Illinois, where Joseph and his brother Hyrum were eventually murdered by an anti-Mormon mob in 1844.

Brigham Young survived a schism in Mormon ranks to emerge as Smith's successor. Though less charismatic than his predecessor, Young was a practical genius who would guide the Church's affairs ably over the next three decades. With military-like precision, he charted the great 1,200-mile (1,900-km) exodus of 1846–47 that brought the Mormon vanguard to Utah, followed by waves of others in the following years that numbered some 16,000. Once there, Brigham Young supervised the settlements that overcame harsh conditions to flourish in the Great Salt Lake Basin and beyond. By 1857 there were 96 separate communities in the Territory of Utah.

With the Mexican surrender of 1848, the vast chunk of western territory that included the Mormons' new homeland came formally under American sovereignty. A provisional State of Deseret was established in 1849, and Brigham Young and associates asked Congress for full admission within the Union, but this was rejected. Instead, Utah Territory was crafted as part of the intense jockeying between North and South that resulted in the Compromise of 1850 – the attempt to maintain a delicate balance between the admission of free states versus slave states. Mormon leaders tried to keep their distance from the searing issue – Utah was largely a neutral place during the Civil War – but this sense of apartness stirred federal suspicion about the allegiances of the LDS Church and its people.

Rumors were rife that an attitude suggesting sedition was prevalent in the territory. Worse still, in public estimation, was the practice of polygamy, affirmed in 1851 and made official Church doctrine a year later. Mormons were denounced as "a pack of outlaws" by President Zachary Taylor, who deemed them "not fit for self-government." More sympathetic was his successor, Millard Fillmore. He made Brigham Young the first governor of the Utah Territory, in 1851, and Mormon leaders reciprocated by naming the site of its first capital Fillmore (later it was returned to Salt Lake City).

Tension between Mormons and federal officials over the doctrines and lifestyle of a Church-dominated Utah Territory that hoped to be fully accepted into the Union erupted in the Utah War of 1857–58. It started when President James Buchanan, reacting to widespread public antipathy to Mormons and their "barbaric" practice of polygamy, moved to quell the perceived "rebellion" brewing there and replace Brigham Young with a non-Mormon governor.

Amid this conflict occurred one of the most heinous acts of civilian slaughter in western annals. It involved the Baker-Fancher party, a wagon train bearing Arkansas emigrants through southwestern Utah on route to California. At a place called Mountain Meadows in 1857, the emigrants were ambushed by an alliance of Mormon militiamen led by Indian agent John D. Lee, and a Paiute war band. The emigrants were deceived, then mercilessly slaughtered, women, children and men. About 120 deaths occurred, only 17 children surviving. Twenty years later, in 1877, justice was

1848	1861
Mexico cedes California and New Mexico to the USA for $18.25 million	The artillery bombardment of Fort Sumter in South Carolina marks the start of the Civil War; Texas declared its secession from the Union

finally meted out to one perpetrator – Lee was executed by firing squad at the site of the massacre. The Utah War came to an end when a deal was worked out that provided pardons for alleged Mormon offenses. Young accepted it, as well as his replacement, and a force of federal troops paraded through a nearly deserted Salt Lake City. Later, Mormons returned to their abandoned homes. In 1861, the last of Johnston's troops left Utah.

Brigham Young died at age 76 in 1877; he was succeeded as LDS leader by John Taylor. Congress made polygamy a federal crime in 1882, and many of the Mormon leaders went into hiding. They included Taylor, who was still a fugitive at the time of his death in 1887. Church sanctioning of plural marriage ended abruptly in 1890 when its new president, Wilford Woodruff, issued a manifesto urging full compliance with federal laws dealing with marriage. He attributed his action to a divine revelation. It effectively brought closure to the long-simmering "Mormon problem."

In 1893, President Benjamin Harrison granted amnesty to all who engaged in the practice of polygamy, and the following year their civil rights were restored by his successor, Grover Cleveland. Finally, on January 4, 1896, after being turned down five times between 1856 and 1887, the Territory of Utah was admitted to the Union as the nation's 45th state (a ban on Mormon polygamy had to be written into the state constitution).

The Civil War (1861–1865)

From its inception, the unity of the United States had been based on shaky foundations. Great care had gone into devising a **Constitution** that balanced the need for a strong federal government with the aspirations for autonomy of its component states. That was achieved by giving Congress two separate chambers – the **House of Representatives**, in which each state was represented in proportion to its population, and the **Senate**, in which each state, regardless of size, had two members. Thus, although in theory the Constitution remained silent on the issue of **slavery**, it allayed the fears of the less populated Southern states that Northern voters might destroy their economy by forcing them to abandon their "peculiar institution".

However, the system only worked so long as there were equal numbers of "Free" and slave-owning states. The only practicable way to keep the balance was to ensure that each time a new state was admitted to the Union, a matching state taking the opposite stance on slavery was also admitted. Thus the admission of every new state became subject to endless intrigue. The 1820 **Missouri Compromise**, under which Missouri joined as a slave-owning state and Maine as a Free one, was straightforward in comparison to the prevarication and chest-beating that surrounded the admission of Texas (which joined the Union as a slave state in 1845), while the Mexican War was widely seen in the North as a naked land grab for new slave states.

Matters came to a head in 1854, when the **Kansas-Nebraska Act** sparked guerrilla raids and mini-wars between rival settlers by allowing both prospective states self-determination on the issue. That same year, the **Republican Party** was founded to resist the further expansion of slavery. Escaped former enslaved activists such as Frederick Douglass were by now spurring Northern audiences to moral outrage, and Harriet Beecher Stowe's *Uncle Tom's Cabin* found unprecedented readership.

1862	1864	1865
President Lincoln's Emancipation Proclamation declares that all enslaved people in states or areas of states still in rebellion to be free	Nevada was admitted to the Union, becoming the 36th state	General Robert E. Lee of the Confederacy surrenders to Union General Ulysses Grant on April 9; five days later, Lincoln is assassinated

In October 1859, **John Brown** – a white-bearded, wild-eyed veteran of Kansas's bloodiest infighting – led a dramatic raid on the US Armory at Harpers Ferry, West Virginia, intending to secure arms for a slave insurrection. Swiftly captured by forces under Robert E. Lee, he was hanged within a few weeks, proclaiming that "I am now quite certain that the crimes of this guilty land will never be purged away but with blood".

The Republican presidential candidate in 1860, the little-known **Abraham Lincoln** from Kentucky, won no Southern states, but with the Democrats split into Northern and Southern factions he was elected with 39 percent of the popular vote. Within weeks, on December 20, South Carolina became the first state to secede from the Union; the **Confederacy** was declared on February 4, 1861, when it was joined by Mississippi, Florida, Alabama, Georgia, Louisiana and Texas. Its first (and only) president was **Jefferson Davis**, also from Kentucky. Lincoln eventually took the political decision to match his moral conviction by issuing his **Emancipation Proclamation** in 1862, though the **Thirteenth Amendment** outlawing slavery only took effect in 1865.

The Civil War in Texas and the Southwest

Most of the fighting in the Civil War took place thousands of miles from Texas and the Southwest. Governor and Texan hero Sam Houston actually refused to take an oath of allegiance to the Confederacy and had been replaced in 1861 – most Texans seemingly went along with the decision (made by local delegates) to join the Confederate States. Texas became an important source of soldiers (some 70,000), horses and food thereafter, though the Union successfully blockaded the port of Galveston throughout the war. There was little actual fighting in Texas; at the Second Battle of Sabine Pass in 1863, Union troops were repulsed by the local Texan garrison, but it had little impact on the outcome of the war. The now national US holiday of "Juneteenth" commemorates the emancipation of enslaved African Americans in Galveston on June 19, 1865, on the arrival of occupying Union troops after the Confederate surrender.

In 1862, the New Mexico campaign saw Confederate Brigadier General Henry Hopkins Sibley invade New Mexico Territory from Texas to gain control of the Southwest (New Mexico was nominally under Union control, though parts of what is now Arizona had voted to join the Confederacy). Sibley won the battles of Valeverde and Glorieta Pass, but was eventually forced to retreat after his supplies were destroyed. Arizona Territory was carved off New Mexico in 1863 in the wake of the failed Confederate campaign. The war left Utah mostly unaffected, though Nevada Territory was similarly carved off it in 1861 thanks to tensions between Mormons and non-Mormon settlers.

Reconstruction and Segregation

Lincoln himself was assassinated within a few days of the end of the war, a mark of the deep bitterness that would almost certainly have precluded successful **Reconstruction** even if he had lived. For a brief period, after black men were granted the vote in 1870, Southern states elected black political representatives, but without a sustained effort to enable former enslaved people to acquire land, racial relations in

1881	1896
Pat Garrett kills Billy the Kid in Fort Sumner, New Mexico; shoot-out at OK Corral, in Tombstone, Arizona	Ruling in Plessy v Ferguson, the Supreme Court creates the doctrine of "separate but equal" pro-vision for whites and blacks - Utah became the 45th state

the South swiftly deteriorated. Thanks to white supremacist organizations such as the Ku Klux Klan, nominally clandestine but brazenly public, Southern blacks were soon effectively disenfranchised once more. Anyone working to transform the South came under attack either as a "carpetbagger" (a Northern opportunist heading South for personal profit) or a treacherous "scalawag" (a Southern collaborator).

The aftermath of the Civil War can almost be said to have lasted for a hundred years. While the South condemned itself to a century as a backwater, the rest of the re-United States embarked on a period of expansionism and prosperity. Texas, and parts of New Mexico, Arizona and Nevada were segregated during this period: schools, public transport, housing, healthcare and other services were separated on racial grounds between "white" and "black", enforced by a byzantine roster of local ordinances dubbed "Jim Crow Laws".

The Indian Wars

With the completion of the transcontinental railroad in 1869, Manifest Destiny became an undeniable reality. Among the first to head west were the troops of the federal army, with Union and Confederate veterans marching under the same flag to battle the remaining Native Americans. Treaty after treaty was signed, only to be broken as soon as expedient (usually upon the discovery of gold or precious metals). When the whites overreached themselves, or when driven to desperation, the Native Americans fought back.

In 1863, as the Civil War raged between North and South, a large force of federal troops commanded by Colonel Patrick E. Connor killed over 300 Shoshone at the Bear River Massacre in southern Idaho. It put an end to hostilities involving Native Americans in northern Utah and led to creation of the Uintah Reservation for the Ute in 1864.

One more major uprising occurred in 1865 with the start of the Black Hawk War in central Utah. It was brought on when Native Americans averse to Mormons encroaching on traditional hunting grounds launched a guerrilla action under the young Ute war chief Black Hawk that cost the lives of 75 Mormon settlers, the abandonment of 25 settlements, and the loss of thousands of horses and cattle. Mormons had to rely for protection on their own Nauvoo Legion, the federal government refusing to send Army troops, and the conflict dragged on until 1872. Several hundred Native Americans were killed during the seven-year war.

In the Southwest, the Navajo were defeated in 1864 by Kit Carson, but Apache leader Geronimo, who had been resisting the United States since 1850, did not surrender until 1886. He died in 1909 at Fort Sill, Oklahoma, still a prisoner of war.

Immigration and growth

The late nineteenth century saw massive **immigration** to North America, with influxes from Europe to the East Coast paralleled by those from Asia to the West. In Texas, El Paso had been little more than a village under Spanish rule but was settled by Anglo-Americans in the 1840s and was big enough to be formally incorporated in 1873 (it was only briefly a Wild West town). Dallas was incorporated in 1856 and boomed at the end of the century as an industrial and railroad hub. With most Native Americans restricted to reservations, the Texas Panhandle began to be settled by American farmers

1912	1919	1929
New Mexico becomes the 47th state; Arizona becomes the 48th state	The 18th Amendment heralds the introduction of Prohibition; the 19th Amendment gives women the vote	The Wall Street Crash plunges the USA into economic turmoil

in the 1870s, with Amarillo established in 1887, flourishing as a cattle depot soon after; Abilene and Lubbock also emerged in the 1880s.

Phoenix was settled in 1867, and with precious metals such as gold, silver, and copper discovered nearby, mining camps in Arizona such as Tombstone were transformed into Wild West boomtowns. In 1881, the Gunfight at the OK Corral in Tombstone, and the killing of Billy the Kid by Sheriff Pat Garrett in Fort Sumner, New Mexico, seemed to herald the end of the region's lawless phase.

Spain and Mexico never established firm rule over modern-day Nevada, and it wasn't until the silver mining boom of the late 1850s that Virginia City and Carson City were founded. Nevada became a state in 1864, but development was confined to the mining areas on its western border with California; it's still the second-largest producer of silver in the US, after Alaska. Reno (founded in 1868) and Las Vegas (officially established in 1905) were small, inconsequential towns well into the twentieth century, and most of the state remained empty desert wilderness.

The twentieth century

The first years of the twentieth century witnessed the emergence of many features that came to characterize modern America. Since the discovery of oil in the early 1900s, Texas has become the nation's top oil producer, and as part of the "Sun Belt" (along with Arizona and New Mexico), it has experienced robust economic growth since the 1970s. Hurricanes took a toll on the growing state, though, especially along the Gulf Coast: a hurricane devastated Galveston in 1900, and a storm virtually destroyed Corpus Christi in 1919.

In 1912, New Mexico finally became the 47th state, and Arizona became the 48th state. Arizona remained primarily rural until the 1950s, when retirees began arriving from the northeast and the population mushroomed as part of the booming Sun Belt. Nevada legalized gambling in 1931, probably the single biggest factor in its subsequent growth: beginning in the 1940s, Reno and Las Vegas became casino boomtowns. Las Vegas is now the "gambling capital of the world" and a major metropolis of over two million people.

The Depression and the New Deal

By the middle of the 1920s, the USA was an industrial powerhouse, responsible for more than half the world's output of manufactured goods. Having led the way into a new era of prosperity, however, it suddenly dragged the rest of the world down into economic collapse. The consequences of the **Great Depression** were out of all proportion to any one specific cause. Possible factors include American over-investment in the floundering economy of postwar Europe, combined with high tariffs on imports that effectively precluded European recovery. Conservative commentators at the time chose to interpret the calamitous **Wall Street Crash** of October 1929 as a symptom of impending depression rather than a contributory cause, but the quasi-superstitious faith in the stock market that preceded it showed all the characteristics of classic speculative booms. On "Black Tuesday" alone, enough stocks were sold to produce a total loss of ten thousand million dollars – more than twice the total amount of money in circulation in the USA. Within the next three years, industrial production was cut by half, the national income dropped by 38 percent, and, above all, unemployment

1932	1941	1945
Franklin D. Roosevelt pledges "a new deal for the American people"	A surprise Japanese attack on Pearl Harbor precipitates US entry into World War II	President Truman's decision to drop atomic bombs on Hiroshima and Nagasaki marks the end of World War II

rose from 1.5 million to 13 million. The Depression hit Texas and the Southwest hard, though its effects were not immediately as obvious as in the larger US cities. Cotton farming and copper mining were especially badly hit.

Matters only began to improve in 1932, when the patrician **Franklin Delano Roosevelt** accepted the Democratic nomination for president with the words "I pledge myself to a new deal for America", and went on to win a landslide victory. At the time of his inauguration, early in 1933, the banking system had all but closed down; it took Roosevelt the now-proverbial "Hundred Days" of vigorous legislation to turn around the mood of the country.

Taking advantage of the new medium of radio, Roosevelt used "Fireside Chats" to cajole America out of crisis; among his earliest observations was that it was a good time for a beer, and that the experiment of Prohibition was therefore over. The **New Deal** took many forms, but was marked throughout by a massive growth in the power of the federal government. Among its accomplishments were the National Recovery Administration, which created two million jobs; the Social Security Act, of which Roosevelt declared "no damn politician can ever scrap my social security program"; and the Public Works Administration, which built dams and highways the length and breadth of the country. The Hoover Dam (Nevada/Arizona), Mansfield Dam and Tom Miller Dam (Texas), Austin–Bergstrom International Airport and Salt Lake City International Airport were all fruits of the PWA program.

World War II

Texas, much of the Southwest and especially Utah was transformed by America's participation in World War II (1941–1945), socially and materially. The federal government pumped millions of dollars into the local economy through new and expanded programs, especially for military training and defense. After World War II, the military-defense industry continued to grow as Utah became a missile center, with plants at Ogden, Salt Lake and Brigham City.

With the war won, Americans were in no mood to revert back to the isolationism of the 1930s. World War II had introduced vast numbers of women and members of ethnic minorities to the rewards of factory work, and shown many Americans from less prosperous regions the lifestyle attainable elsewhere in their own country. The development of a **national highway system**, and a huge increase in automobile ownership, encouraged people to pursue the American Dream wherever they chose.

In New Mexico, Georgia O'Keeffe's landscape paintings in the 1940s helped to make the area around Santa Fe a hub for artists, while the first atomic bomb was tested in Los Alamos, New Mexico in 1945, making it a hub for the US military ever since. The 1947 Roswell incident – where a flying saucer carrying little green men supposedly crash-landed in the desert – has assured that New Mexico has also been ground zero for UFO enthusiasts. Nuclear testing at the Nevada Test Site (65 miles/105km northwest from Las Vegas) began in 1951 and continued until 1962 (underground testing continued until 1992).

The civil rights years

Racial segregation of public education, which had remained the norm in Texas, Arizona and New Mexico ever since Reconstruction, was finally declared illegal in 1954

1954	1963	1964	2005
The Supreme Court declares racial segregation in schools to be unconstitutional	John F. Kennedy Assassination in Dallas, Texas	Texan Lyndon B. Johnson is elected president	Hurricane Katrina slams into the Gulf Coast, devastating New Orleans and the east Texas coast

by the Supreme Court ruling on *Brown v. Topeka Board of Education*. Just as a century before, however, the Southern states saw the issue more in terms of states' rights than of human rights, and attempting to implement the law, or even to challenge the failure to implement it, required immense courage.

After **John F. Kennedy**'s assassination in Dallas in November 1963, his successor, Texan **Lyndon B. Johnson**, pushed through legislation that enacted most of the civil rights campaigners' key demands. In 1964 the Twenty-fourth Amendment barred the poll tax in federal elections and the Civil Rights Act outlawed the Jim Crow ordinances. The federal Voting Rights Act of 1965 eliminated local restrictions to voting and required that federal marshals monitor election proceedings. Texas repealed its own separatist statutes voluntarily in 1969. Even then, violent white resistance continued, and only the long, painstaking and dangerous work of registering black voters en masse eventually forced Southern politicians to mend their ways.

In 1968, the social fabric of the USA reached the brink of collapse. Shortly after Johnson was forced by his plummeting popularity to withdraw from the year-end elections, Martin Luther King was gunned down in a Memphis motel. Next, JFK's brother **Robert Kennedy**, now redefined as spokesman for the dispossessed, was fatally shot just as he emerged as Democratic front-runner. It didn't take a conspiracy theorist to see that the spate of deaths reflected a malaise in the soul of America. The country has remained politically polarized ever since, divided into "blue" Democratic states and "red" Republican states, though the real divide is more typically between city dwellers an d rural voters; city's such as Austin, Reno and Salt Lake City tend to vote liberal and progressive despite being surrounded by solidly conservative hinterlands.

The main result of the Civil Rights era in the Southwest was to turn Texas from a blue Democrat-majority state into a conservative, red state – it's remained safely Republican (Utah and Arizona had turned Republican in the 1950s).

The 1980s and 1990s

In 1988, Texas-based **George H.W. Bush** became the first vice president in 150 years to be immediately elected to the presidency – though raised on the East Coast, Bush had moved to Texas after World War II and set up an oil company, settling in Houston. His son, **George W. Bush**, served as Republican governor of Texas from 1995 to 2000, before becoming US president. Bush had succeeded Democrat Ann Richards, who was the second female governor of Texas (following Miriam A. Ferguson, 1925–1927 and 1933–1935). Thanks primarily to oil, these were boom years for Texas, celebrated in TV shows like Dallas.

In Utah, copper production fell off following a price decline in the 1980s, but the state nonetheless leads the world in the output of beryllium today, is a major producer of coal, and it is the only state that turns out Gilsonite, an adhesive agent used in road and asphalt paving. Olene Walker (Republican) became Utah's first female governor in 2003. Democrat Rose Mofford was Arizona's first female governor (1988–1991); she was followed by Republican Fife Symington, who resigned in 1997 following convictions on charges of extortion and bank fraud (though these were later overturned). Popular war hero Republican John McCain was elected to the US Senate

2008	2010	2015	2019
Barack Obama wins election as the first black president	Huge BP oil spill in the Gulf of Mexico	Greg Abbott becomes Republican governor of Texas	Mitt Romney becomes the junior Republican US senator from Utah

for Arizona in 1986 (succeeding the conservative Barry Goldwater). He served until his death from brain cancer in 2018. Nevada is the only state in the region to never have elected a female governor.

Texas and the Southwest in the 21st-century

Though almost a third of Texans vote Democrat today, Republicans have continued to dominate the state since the late 1960s. Proud Texan and former governor **George W. Bush** went on to become US president between 2001 and 2009. Rick Perry succeeded Bush as governor, serving until 2015 when he joined the Trump administration – elected a record three times, he remains the state's longest serving executive. In line with increasing partisanship in Texas and across the USA, Perry's premiership was marked by his vocal opposition to **President Obama** (2009–2017), touting the economic strength of Texas as his most significant achievement (though it wasn't enough to get him elected US President in 2016).

Greg Abbott, Texas governor since 2015, was a vocal supporter of President Trump, and opposed implementing face mask and vaccine mandates during the Covid-19 pandemic (2020–2022), despite Texas eventually recording over 92,000 deaths and eight million reported Covid-19 cases. Nevertheless, Texas remains one of the strongest states economically, with the second highest GDP in the USA (after California), bigger than most countries – it would be the sixth largest oil producer in the world if it was an independent country and produces the most wind power in the USA. Abbott does not believe human activity is the main cause behind climate change, though Texas has been increasingly battered by giant storms and environmental disasters; Hurricane Ike (2008), the Deepwater Horizon oil spill (2010) and Hurricane Harvey (2017) all caused major damage. The Southwestern megadrought began in 2000, with many reservoirs and lakes across the region at historic lows today.

Utah is even more conservative than Texas (its governor Spencer Cox, US Senators Mitt Romney and Mike Lee, plus its three Congressional representatives, are all Republican). Utah hasn't elected a Democratic governor since 1980; a Democratic senator since 1970; or voted for a Democratic presidential candidate since 1964. The vast majority of culturally conservative Mormons vote Republican despite the LDS church officially remaining politically neutral. Salt Lake City hosted the Winter Olympics in 2002 – Mitt Romney led the organizing committee – initiating a winter tourist boom to Park City and the surrounding ski resorts that continues today. Utah's economy remains one of the nation's most dynamic, driven by cattle ranching, coal mining, salt production, and tourism, with farming and oil production also important. With its primarily rural population, Utah fared much better than urban America during the Covid-19 epidemic, but the statistics remain grim. By 2022 over 36,000 had been hospitalized and over 5,000 people had died (only around 350 people die annually in Utah from flu or pneumonia).

Arizona has been more of a battle-ground state in recent years: after the death of Republican senator John McCain in 2018, Democrat (and ex-astronaut) Mark Kelly was elected to replace him, and Democrat Katie Hobbs became Arizona's fifth female governor in 2023. This after Kelly's wife, congresswoman Gabby Giffords had been

2020

The global Covid-19 crisis hits the US hard; Texas Governor Abbott oppose face mask and vaccine mandates and blocks local governments from implementing their own; Democrat Mark Kelly is elected US Senator for Arizona after the death of John McCain

shot along with 18 others at a political gathering in Tucson in 2011 (Giffords was critically wounded but survived).

New Mexico is more firmly a Democrat state, led by Governor Michelle Lujan Grisham since 2018 – both US Senators and all three Congress reps are Democrats. Since 2008, Nevada has also become a fairly reliable Democrat stronghold in federal elections, mainly thanks to progressive voters in Reno and Las Vegas – rural Nevada remains extremely conservative. In 2018 Nevada became the first state in the United States with a female majority in its legislature, though Republican Joe Lombardo became governor in 2023.

2021	**2022**
Pro-Trump militants storm the US Capitol building in a failed attempt to stop President Biden's inauguration; Kamala Harris makes history as first female Vice-President	Over 1 million Americans have died from Covid-19. Texas records the second highest level of deaths after California

Books

Space not permitting a comprehensive overview of American literature, the following list is simply an idiosyncratic selection of books that may appeal to interested readers.

HISTORY AND SOCIETY

Leonard Arrington and Davis Bitton *The Mormon Experience: a History of the Latter-day Saints*. Still one of the best overall histories of the Mormons in North America and especially their community in Utah.

Dee Brown *Bury My Heart at Wounded Knee*. Still the best narrative of the impact of white settlement and expansion on Native Americans across the continent.

Bill Bryson *Made in America*. A compulsively readable history of the American language, packed with bizarre snippets.

Alvar Nunez Cabeza de Vaca *Chronicle of the Narvaez Expedition*. Republished by Penguin Classics, this seminal account of Native American Southwest America was penned by one of the few Spanish survivors of the doomed 1527 Narváez expedition. It's a priceless account (even given the bias of the author) of the great civilizations that existed before Europeans arrived.

Brian Fagan *Ancient North America*. Archeological history of America's native peoples, from the first hunters to cross the Bering Strait up to initial contact with Europeans.

Tim Flannery *The Eternal Frontier*. "Ecological" history of North America that reveals how the continent's physical environment has shaped the destinies of all its inhabitants, from horses to humans.

Jon Krakauer *Under the Banner of Heaven: a Story of Violent Faith*. The respected investigative journalist takes on fundamentalist Mormonism and polygamy in this tragic account of the 1984 murder of Brenda Lafferty.

Clyde A. Milner II, Carol A. O'Connor and Martha A. Sandweiss *The Oxford History of the American West*. Fascinating collection of essays on Western history, covering topics ranging from myths and movies to art and religion.

Roderick Frazier Nash *Wilderness and the American Mind*. Classic study of the American take on environmental and conservation issues over the past couple of hundred years.

T. R. Fehrenbach *Lone Star: A History of Texas and the Texans*. The most easily digested history of Texas, first published in 1968, charting the role of Spanish conquistadors and all the major trends of Texan history to the 20th century.

Stephen Plog *Ancient Peoples of the Southwest*. Much the best single-volume history of the pre-Hispanic Southwest, packed with diagrams and colour photographs.

Marc Reisner *Cadillac Desert*. Concise, engaging account of the environmental and political impact on the West of the twentieth-century mania for dam-building and huge irrigation projects.

Hampton Sides *Blood And Thunder*. Hugely readable re-telling of the exploits of Kit Carson and his role in the campaigns against the Navajo.

Wallace Stegner *Mormon Country*. A collection of 28 essays focusing on Mormon life and the wide range of non-believers who lived in Mormon country in the late 19th and early 20th centuries. There are some great tales here, and Stegner tells them superbly.

★ **Mark Twain** *Roughing It*. Mark Twain was by far the funniest and most vivid chronicler of nineteenth-century America. *Roughing It*, which covers his early wanderings across the continent, including a stint in Nevada, is absolutely compelling.

Richard White *It's Your Misfortune And None of My Own*. Dense, authoritative and all-embracing history of the American West, which debunks the notion of the rugged pioneer by stressing the role of the federal government.

Terry Tempest Williams *Red: Passion and Patience in the Desert*. This collection of essays and stories by the respected Utah author makes the case for the preservation of Utah's wild and as yet mostly unspoiled Canyon Country. See also Williams' memoir, Refuge: An Unnatural History of Family and Place.

BIOGRAPHY AND ORAL HISTORY

Donald A. Barclay, James H. Maguire and Peter Wild (eds) *Into the Wilderness Dream*. Gripping collection of Western exploration narratives written between 1500 and 1800; thanks to any number of little-known gems, the best of many such anthologies.

Charles Leerhsen *Butch Cassidy: The True Story of an American Outlaw*. The most recent biography of Cassidy, born Robert LeRoy Parker into a Mormon family in Beaver,

Utah in 1866, is one of the best, shedding light on what motivated the rustler and bank robber.

Raymond Locke *The Book of the Navajo*. An excellent introduction to the history, mythology traditions and contemporary culture of the Navajo peoples. Locke died in 2002, but his book is still one of the best.

John G. Turner *Brigham Young: Pioneer Prophet*. Essential reading for anyone interested in the origins of the Mormon state in Utah. Turner provides a fascinating portrait of the Mormon's greatest leader.

★ **Frank Waters** *Book of the Hopi*. Extraordinary insight into the traditions and beliefs of the Hopi, prepared through years of interviews and approved by tribal elders.

TRAVEL WRITING

Edward Abbey *The Journey Home*. Hilarious accounts of whitewater rafting and desert hiking trips alternate with essays by the man who inspired the radical environmentalist movement Earth First! All of Abbey's books, especially *Desert Solitaire*, a journal of time spent as a ranger in Arches National Park, make great travelling companions.

Bill Bryson *The Lost Continent*. Using his boyhood home of Des Moines in Iowa as a benchmark, the author travels the length and breadth of America to find the perfect small town. Hilarious, if at times a bit smug.

★ **Ian Frazier** *Great Plains*. This immaculately researched 1980s' travelogue holds a wealth of information on the people of the prairielands, from Native Americans to the soldiers who staffed the region's nuclear installations.

William Least Heat-Moon *Blue Highways*. Classic account of a mammoth loop tour of the USA by backroads, interviewing ordinary people in ordinary places. A remarkable overview of rural America, with lots of interesting details on Native Americans.

John Wesley Powell *Exploration of the Colorado River and Its Canyons*. Thrilling account of Powell's momentous journey down the Green and Colorado rivers in 1874, taking in much of modern-day Utah.

FICTION

Willa Cather *Death Comes for the Archbishop*. A magnificent evocation of the landscapes and cultures of nineteenth-century New Mexico.

Zane Grey *Riders of the Purple Sage*. This seminal Western novel, published in 1912, is set amongst the Mormon communities of Southern Utah in the 1870s, and follows the struggles of rich Mormon ranch owner Jane Withersteen.

Tony Hillerman *The Dark Wind*, and many others. The adventures of Jim Chee of the Navajo Tribal Police on the reservations of northern Arizona, forever dabbling in dark and mysterious forces churned up from the Ancestral Puebloan past.

Barbara Kingsolver *Pigs in Heaven*. A magnificent evocation of tensions and realities in the contemporary Southwest, by a writer who ranks among America's finest stylists.

Philipp Meyer *The Son*. One of the best novels set in Texas, anchored by three generations of the McCullough family; it begins with Eli McCullough being absorbed into the Comanche peoples after the rest of his family is killed.

James A. Michener *Texas*. Classic Michener generational novel of Texas history, beginning with the Spanish expeditions of Cabeza de Vaca, going up to the 1980s.

Cormac McCarthy No Country for Old Men. Set in Texas, along the US-Mexican border, this grim tale of a drug deal gone wrong was later made into an award-winning movie.

★ **Wallace Stegner** *The Big Rock Candy Mountain*. This harrowing historical saga of the fictional Mason family in some ways mirrors Stegner's own life, especially the sections set in Salt Lake City. Stegner is probably the most famous author associated with Utah and the West; see also the sequel Recapitulation and his autobiography Wolf Willow.

Donna Tartt *The Goldfinch*. Ranging from New York to Las Vegas, art history to terrorist tragedy, this Pulitzer-winning blockbuster puts a twenty-first-century spin on the Great American Novel.

★ **Hunter S. Thompson** *Fear and Loathing in Las Vegas*. The definitive work of "gonzo journalism" is a semi-autobiographical account of a drug-induced trip to Las Vegas by sports journalist Raoul Duke, and his attorney, Doctor Gonzo.

Maurine Whipple *The Giant Joshua*. This seminal work of Mormon fiction was published in 1941, a realistic tale of the harsh life experienced by especially female Mormon pioneers living in 19th-century southwestern Utah.

Terry Tempest Williams *Desert Quartet: An Erotic Landscape*. A thought-provoking blend of drawings and stream-of consciousness poetry as the thoughts of a woman hiking in the canyons of southern Utah.

Film

The list below focuses on key films in certain genres that have helped define the Texan and Southwestern experience – both the light and the dark. Those tagged with the ★ symbol are particularly recommended.

MUSIC/MUSICALS

The Best Little Whorehouse in Texas (Colin Higgins, 1982). Burt Reynolds and Dolly Parton star in this Broadway adaptation, set in a brothel outside a small Texas town. The brothel is shut down, but the local sheriff ends up marrying the owner, Miss Mona.

★ **Selena** (Gregory Nava, 1997). Biographical musical drama about beloved Tejano star Selena Quintanilla-Pérez, who was tragically murdered in 1995 at the age of 23. Jennifer Lopez does a superb job as Selena, despite some backlash from the Mexican American community (Lopez is of Puerto Rican descent).

WESTERNS

The Alamo (John Wayne, 1960). Wayne's portrayal of the infamous 1836 Battle of the Alamo (in San Antonio, Texas) is still the best, despite the historical inaccuracies and thinly veiled Cold War references – the 2004 remake was a box office bomb.

Geronimo: An American Legend (Walter Hill, 1993). One of the first biopics to focus on the experience of Native Americans, with Wes Studi starring as the legendary Apache war chief before his final surrender in 1886.

★ **Giant** (George Stevens, 1956). Set in 1920s Texas (much of it shot in and around Marfa), Elizabeth Taylor, Rock Hudson and James Dean star in this movie of love, jealousy and wealthy Texan cattle ranching culture.

News of the World (Paul Greengrass, 2020). Set in bleak post-Civil War Texas (but shot in New Mexico), this uplifting movie finds Tom Hanks as an itinerant newsreader befriending an orphaned German immigrant girl.

Once Upon a Time in the West (Sergio Leone, 1968). The quintessential spaghetti Western, filmed in Spain by an Italian director, but steeped in mythic Southwestern

---

ON LOCATION

Although many memorable sights are off-limits to the public or exist only on backlot tours of movie-studio theme parks, countless filmmaking locations are accessible to visitors. This list provides an overview of notable films shot in Texas and the Southwest.

2001: A Space Odyssey (Stanley Kubrick, 1968). Monument Valley, Arizona. See page 138.

Boyhood (Richard Linklater, 2014). Big Bend Ranch State Park, Texas. See page 90

Butch Cassidy and the Sundance Kid (George Roy Hill, 1969). Grafton, Zion National Park (see page 142, Snow Canyon State Park, and St. George, Utah.

Contact (Robert Zemeckis, 1997). Very Large Array (VLA) near Socorro, New Mexico.

Easy Rider (Dennis Hopper, 1969). Sunset Crater, Arizona.

Finch (Miguel Sapochnik, 2021). Albuquerque (see page 112), Santa Fe (see page 103), White Sands National Park (see page 118).

Galaxy Quest (Dean Parisot, 1999). Goblin Valley, Utah. See page 152.

Giant (George Stevens, 1956). Marfa, Texas. See page 152.

Grapes of Wrath (John Ford, 1940). Petrified Forest, Arizona. See page 128.

Natural Born Killers (Oliver Stone, 1994): Rio Grande Gorge Bridge (Taos, New Mexico).

News of the World (Paul Greengrass, 2020). Santa Fe, New Mexico. See page 103.

No Country for Old Men (Joel and Ethan Coen, 2007). Santa Fe (see page 103), Albuquerque (see page 112), Las Vegas (see page 159) and Marfa (see page 152) and Sanderson in West Texas.

Planet of the Apes (Franklin J. Schaffner, 1968). Lake Powell, Utah. See page 155.

Stagecoach (John Ford, 1939). Monument Valley, Arizona. See page 138.

The Searchers (John Ford, 1956). Monument Valley, Arizona. See page 138.

Thelma and Louise (Ridley Scott, 1991). Arches National Park, Utah. See page 152.

American themes.

Red River (Howard Hawks, 1948). Upstart Montgomery Clift battles beef-baron John Wayne on a momentous cattle drive from Texas through the Midwest. Prototypical Hawks tale of clashing tough-guy egos and no-nonsense professionals on the range.

Rio Bravo (Howard Hawks, 1959). This later work from Hawks is set on the Texas/Mexico border, with John Wayne as the righteous sheriff holding off the goons of a powerful local rancher until the cavalry arrive.

★ **The Searchers** (John Ford, 1956). Perhaps Ford's most iconic Western, with vivid cinematography and epic scale; John Wayne relentlessly hunts down the Native American chief who massacred his friends and family. Set in northwestern Texas, but filmed in Monument Valley, Arizona.

Stagecoach (John Ford, 1939). The first movie Ford shot in Monument Valley, Arizona, and the one that gave John Wayne his breakthrough. Set in the 1880s, the movie follows a group of strangers traveling by stagecoach between Arizona and New Mexico through Apache territory.

Tombstone (George P. Cosmatos, 1993). One of the best movies depicting the classic Wild West town in Arizona, with Kurt Russell and Val Kilmer starring as Wyatt Earp and Doc Holliday at the "Gunfight at the O.K. Corral". The 1957 movie "Gunfight at the O.K. Corral" starring Burt Lancaster and Kirk Douglas is another classic.

The Wild Bunch (Sam Peckinpah, 1969). A movie that says as much about the chaotic end of the 1960s as it does about the West, featuring a band of killers who hunt for women and treasure on the US/Mexican border and wind up in a bloodbath unprecedented in film history.

Young Guns (Christopher Cain, 1988). Emilio Estevez, Kiefer Sutherland and Charlie Sheen star in this depiction of Billy the Kid and New Mexico's Lincoln County War (1877–78). Young Guns II was released in 1990, and the more sympathetic TV series Billy The Kid premiered in 2022.

ROAD MOVIES

Easy Rider (Dennis Hopper, 1969). Hippies Peter Fonda and director Hopper take to the road while riding a groovy set of wheels, pick up nerdy Jack Nicholson on the way, traveling through Las Vegas, Santa Fe and Taos, and meet a futile fate. Melancholy and yearning, it's a haunting piece of cinema.

★ **Paris, Texas** (Wim Wenders, 1984). Harry Dean Stanton stars as a drifter who reconnects with his seven-year-old son and travels the Southwest in search of his missing wife, played by German actress Nastassja Kinski. Won the Palme d'Or at Cannes.

★ **Thelma and Louise** (Ridley Scott, 1991). The road movie as feminist manifesto, in which two friends (Susan Sarandon and Geena Davis) wind up on the run after one kills a would-be rapist. At last it's the girls who get to tote the guns and swig the whiskey – and Scott provides stunning images of the American Southwest.

LAS VEGAS [VEGAS BABY!/VIVA LAS VEGAS]

Casino (Martin Scorsese, 1995). This now classic depiction of mob rule in 1970s Las Vegas stars Robert De Niro, Sharon Stone and an utterly terrifying Joe Pesci (based on real people and the old Stardust Resort and Casino, demolished in 2007).

Diamonds are Forever (Guy Hamilton, 1971). Sean Connery's final James Bond movie was filmed primarily in and around Las Vegas. The Circus Circus casino is a major location (still going strong), as is Westgate Las Vegas (which was then the Las Vegas Hilton).

Fear and Loathing in Las Vegas (Terry Gilliam, 1998). Adaptation of Hunter S. Thompson's 1971 cult novel starring Johnny Depp and Benicio del Toro as the drug-addled, hallucinating "journalists" ostensibly covering the Mint 400 motorcycle race in Las Vegas.

Hangover (Todd Phillips, 2009). This comedy classic features Bradley Cooper, Ed Helms and Zach Galifianakis trying to negotiate a stag party (bachelor party) hangover from hell while avoiding drug dealers, a random baby in their hotel room, Mike Tyson, and Mike Tyson's tiger. See also Hangover Part III (2013).

Honeymoon in Vegas (Andrew Bergman, 1992). Romantic comedy starring Nicolas Cage and Sarah Jessica Parker as the honeymooners and James Caan as the Vegas pro gambler who is determined to win Cage's fiancée for himself.

Leaving Las Vegas (Mike Figgis, 1995). Cage returned to Vegas for this a very different movie, based on a semi-autobiographical novel of a depressed Hollywood screenwriter who moves to Las Vegas with the plan of drinking himself to death. Despite falling in love with a sex worker played by Elisabeth Shue, the film ends in tragedy.

Ocean's 11 (Steven Soderbergh, 2001). Perhaps the definitive Vegas movie (so far) of the 21st century, this classic heist comedy remake of the 1960 film stars George Clooney, Matt Damon, Andy García, Brad Pitt and Julia Roberts as loveable crooks, plus a kicking soundtrack arranged by David Holmes. See also Ocean's 13 (2207).

Swingers (Doug Liman, 1996). Written by Jon Favreau, this comedy features slacker Los Angeles actors and screenwriters (led by Favreau and Vince Vaughn) who take a trip to Las Vegas to help Favreau move on from his ex-girlfriend.

Viva Las Vegas (George Sidney, 1964). One of Elvis's finer movies, partly due to the effervescent presence of Ann-Margret – of all the King's co-stars only she could match him for sheer animal sexuality. The two were having an affair during the shoot, and the chemistry drips from the screen.

INDEPENDENT AND CULT MOVIES

127 Hours (Danny Boyle, 2010). James Franco stars as the real-life canyoneer Aron Ralston who gets trapped in a Utah slot canyon in 2003 and is forced to amputate his own arm to escape.

Boyhood (Richard Linklater, 2014). Set in Texas, Linklater's coming-of-age drama infamously took 12 years to complete, as he wanted to depict the same actor (Ellar Coltrane) growing up. Fabulous performances from Patricia Arquette and Ethan Hawke as his divorced parents.

Raising Arizona (Joel and Ethan Coen, 1997). Set in and around Phoenix and Scottsdale Arizona, where ex-con Nicolas Cage is in and out of jail for robbing a convenience store, this black comedy also features Holly Hunter as his wife involved in a bizarre kidnap scheme.

Reality Bites (Ben Stiller, 1994). Emblematic of 1990s grunge and Generation X, this movie follows the ups and downs of 20-somethings Winona Ryder, Ethan Hawke, Ben Stiller, Janeane Garofalo and Steve Zahn in Houston, Texas.

Slacker (Richard Linklater, 1990). Another film of Generation X ennui in the 1990s, this indie great also manages to highlight 96 characters with episodic monologues over the course of 24 hours in Austin, Texas. See also Linklater's Dazed and Confused (1993), another movie set in Austin.

Small print and index

A ROUGH GUIDE TO ROUGH GUIDES

Published in 1982, the first Rough Guide – to Greece – was a student scheme that became a publishing phenomenon. Mark Ellingham, a recent graduate in English from Bristol University, had been travelling in Greece the previous summer and couldn't find the right guidebook. With a small group of friends he wrote his own guide, combining a contemporary, journalistic style with a thoroughly practical approach to travellers' needs.

The immediate success of the book spawned a series that rapidly covered dozens of destinations. And, in addition to impecunious backpackers, Rough Guides soon acquired a much broader readership that relished the guides' wit and inquisitiveness as much as their enthusiastic, critical approach and value-for-money ethos. These days, Rough Guides include recommendations from budget to luxury and cover more than 120 destinations around the globe, from Amsterdam to Zanzibar, all regularly updated by our team of roaming writers.

Browse all our latest guides, read inspirational features and book your trip at **roughguides.com**.

Rough Guide credits

Editor: Beth Williams
Cartography: Katie Bennett
Picture editor: Tom Smyth

Layout: Katie Bennett
Head of DTP and Pre-Press: Rebeka Davies
Head of Publishing: Sarah Clark

Publishing information

First edition 2023

Distribution

UK, Ireland and Europe
Apa Publications (UK) Ltd; sales@roughguides.com
United States and Canada
Ingram Publisher Services; ips@ingramcontent.com
Australia and New Zealand
Booktopia; retailer@booktopia.com.au
Worldwide
Apa Publications (UK) Ltd; sales@roughguides.com

Special Sales, Content Licensing and CoPublishing
Rough Guides can be purchased in bulk quantities
at discounted prices. We can create special editions,
personalised jackets and corporate imprints tailored to
your needs. sales@roughguides.com.
roughguides.com

Printed in China

Help us update

We've gone to a lot of effort to ensure that this edition
of **The Rough Guide to Texas and the Southwest** is
accurate and up-to-date. However, things change – places
get "discovered", opening hours are notoriously fickle,
restaurants and rooms raise prices or lower standards. If
you feel we've got it wrong or left something out, we'd like
to know, and if you can remember the address, the price,
the hours, the phone number, so much the better.

Please send your comments with the subject line
"**Rough Guide Texas and the Southwest Update**" to
mail@uk.roughguides.com. We'll credit all contributions
and send a copy of the next edition (or any other Rough
Guide if you prefer) for the very best emails.

ABOUT THE AUTHOR

Stephen Keeling has lived in New York City since 2006 and has written several titles for
Rough Guides, including the guide to New York City, California, Puerto Rico, New England,
Florida, Canada and the US's national parks.

Photo credits
(Key: T-top; C-centre; B-bottom; L-left; R-right)

Index

Map symbols

The symbols below are used on maps throughout the book

International boundary	International airport	Spring
State/province boundary	Domestic airport/airfield	National Park
Chapter division boundary	Transport stop	Gate/park entrance
Interstate highway	Parking	State capital
US highway	Post office	Lighthouse
State highway	Information centre	Statue
Pedestrianized road	Hospital/medical centre	Bridge
Path	Cave	Battle site
Railway	Point of interest	Ski
Funicular	Viewpoint/lookout	Mountain range
Coastline	Campground	Mountain peak
Ferry route	Museum	Swamp/marshland
National Parkway	Monument/memorial	Tree
Metro/subway	Fountain/garden	Gorge
Tram/trolleybus	Waterfall	Arch

Boat
Hindu/Jain temple
Church (regional maps)
Church (town maps)
Cemetery
Building
Stadium
Park/forest
Beach
Native American reservation